Nigel Cox is the author of six novels. *Dirty Work* (1987, new edition 2006) was shortlisted for both the New Zealand Book Award and the Wattie Book of the Year, and won the Buckland Literary Award. *Tarzan Presley* (2004), *Responsibility* (2005), and *The Cowboy Dog* (2006) were runners-up in the Montana New Zealand Book Awards. In 1991 he was the Katherine Mansfield Memorial Fellow in Menton.

Nigel Cox was born in 1951 in Pahiatua and grew up in Masterton and the Hutt Valley. His early working life reads like an author trying to find his way: advertising account executive, assembly line worker at Ford, deck hand, coalman, door-to-door turkey salesman, driver. Eventually, in the UK, he found his way into the book world—he worked for many years as a bookseller, with later stints at Unity Books, Wellington and Auckland, and as a freelance writer. In 1995 he became Senior Writer on the team that developed the exhibitions for Te Papa Tongarewa, New Zealand's national museum. With fellow New Zealander Ken Gorbey he led the project team that created the Jewish Museum Berlin, housed in the famous building designed by Daniel Libeskind. After the museum opened in September 2001 he joined its staff as Head of Exhibitions and Education. He returned to New Zealand in 2005, and rejoined Te Papa as Director Experience until May 2006.

Nigel Cox died in July 2006. He is survived by his wife and their three children.

Novels by Nigel Cox

Waiting for Einstein (Benton Ross, 1984)
Dirty Work (Benton Ross, 1987; Victoria University Press, 2006)
Skylark Lounge (Victoria University Press, 2000)
Tarzan Presley (Victoria University Press, 2004)
Responsibility (Victoria University Press, 2005)
The Cowboy Dog (Victoria University Press, 2006)

Nigel Cox
Phone Home
Berlin Collected
Non-fiction

Victoria University Press

VICTORIA UNIVERSITY PRESS
Victoria University of Wellington
PO Box 600 Wellington
www.victoria.ac.nz/vup

National Library of New Zealand Cataloguing-in-Publication Data

Cox, Nigel, 1951-2006.
Phone home Berlin : collected non-fiction / Nigel Cox.
ISBN 978-0-86473-567-6
1. Cox, Nigel, 1951-2006. 2. Authors, New Zealand—
20th century—Biography. 3. Authors, New Zealand—
21st century—Biography. I. Title.
NZ823.2—dc 22

Published with the assistance of a grant from

Printed by Astra Print, Wellington

Contents

Acknowledgements

Thanks to the editors of the publications in which some of these pieces first appeared, and to all those who have helped in the preparation of this book, especially Kyleigh Hodgson, Andrew Johnston, Elizabeth Knox, Bill Manhire, Heather McKenzie and Damien Wilkins.

Susanna Andrew
Fergus Barrowman
October 2007

Foreword

In 'What I Would Have Written', which Nigel Cox wrote just two months before he died of cancer, he outlined 'quite a well-developed plan . . . to put together a book of some of my short pieces, most of them published before, that might be made together into a coherent whole'. This is that book. The previously published work is strikingly diverse, and includes essays, an interview, a keynote address, an autobiographical short story, and even two poems. Chief amongst the unpublished items is a journal of the first eighteen months of the five years Nigel and his family spent in Berlin, where he worked in a leading role at the Jewish Museum. This especially is a major addition to the canon of Cox's published work, displaying to great effect the voice he achieved in the later years of his writing life, in which he could move freely between big public issues, pure imagination, and the most private concerns.

Collectively, the pieces in this book provide a surprisingly full autobiography of Nigel Cox the writer. Early experiences and influences, and a long and determined process of self-education, are approached from different angles. A 1989 essay, for instance, shows the newly-established writer finding the sources of his first novel in the classic 'boys on islands' adventure stories he devoured in the isolated Wairarapa of his childhood. More than ten years later, the mature writer would look back on this with more reflective distance, as well as on the disturbances of a teenage year in the United States, and an infatuation with pop music which he would never 'grow out of'.

In 'Green as Editor's Ink' Nigel also takes the opportunity to put on the record the titles of the three early novels which 'shall forever remain unseen by human eyes'. If with *Waiting for Einstein* he was, like most writers, doing his growing up in public, there had also been a long period of private growing behind it.

The last 'early' essay in this book, 'When I Was a Writer', was written at the end of Nigel's term as Katherine Mansfield Memorial Fellow in Menton, France—four years after the publication of his second novel, *Dirty Work*, four years into the thirteen-year 'silence' that would finally be broken by the publication of *Skylark Lounge*. In comparison with the freedom of voice in his later writing, this essay is a revealing portrait of a writer still struggling with his motivations. The sense of willed endeavour speaks of the particular novelist's peril described by Norman Mailer in a recent interview: 'It's as if you were the general of an army of one, and this general can really drive that army into a cul-de-sac.'*

In the early years of his silence, Nigel shelved at least two completed novels—a sequel to *Dirty Work* and the Menton Book, *Atlas Walker*—that he had decided were not good enough to offer for publication. He also left bookselling,

---

* *The Paris Review* 181, Summer 2007

in which he had worked since the late 1970s, primarily at Unity Books in Wellington and Auckland, to have a go at making a living as a freelance writer. In putting this book together, we have followed the contents list Nigel drew up in February 2006, and excluded the journalism he produced during this time—mostly book reviews, author interviews and commentary pieces done for *Quote Unquote* and the *Listener* in 1993 and 1994.

The next stages in Nigel's life are recounted in the interview with Damien Wilkins—the serendipitous job as senior writer in the Te Papa project office, which launched him on what then seemed an unlikely career as a museum manager; the cancer diagnosis which reignited his desire to write fiction and led immediately to *Skylark Lounge*; the move to the Jewish Museum Berlin, which led to the five exhilarating, pressured and extraordinarily productive years recounted in 'Phone Home Berlin' and the essays which follow it here.

'Phone Home Berlin' is the biggest departure from Nigel's plan for this collection. As well as the two and a half novels he wrote 'before work' every day in Berlin, he was also writing a diary-based book that braided together the intense eighteen-month run-up to the opening of the Museum, the daily life of a Kiwi family in Berlin, and the inner life of a writer. At some stage in early 2002 he put this aside 'for later'—partly, he told me, because he hadn't quite worked out how to do it, and partly because one strand of it had broken away, turned into fiction, and become the beginning of the novel *Responsibility*.

When Nigel emailed this unfinished book to me about a week after his contents list, it turned out to be a document of 100,000 words under the title 'Love Parade'. The first half, which reached one kind of climax with the Museum's opening in September 2001, then went on to the birth of Nigel and Susanna's third child, was a series of polished vignettes. Some of these were familiar to me; he had turned them into two short essays—'On the Way to the Jewish Museum Berlin', published in 2002, and 'Phone Home Berlin', which he decided not to publish. Nigel thought that perhaps two more similar essays could be made from the 'Love Parade' vignettes, making a total of four short essays covering the first eighteen months in Berlin.

Susanna and I looked at several different attempts to make this plan work, over the months during which we slowly put this book together. In the end, we realised that Nigel's first instinct had been correct, and that braided together the different strands had much more power. 'Phone Home Berlin', as it appears in this book, is a much more substantial selection from the first half of the 'Love Parade' manuscript, retaining the dramatic arc and proportions of the original, while eliminating repetitions, unfollowed leads, and some passages that are just too personal to publish yet.

The second half of 'Love Parade', which is not represented here, is much rougher, and quite quickly turns into a raw compilation of emails about the effort to secure a major international publisher for *Tarzan Presley*. Nigel said that this process, during which each publisher's initial enthusiasm suddenly and mysteriously turned into rejection, broke his heart, but he never wrote about that. Nor did he write about what happened later, after *Tarzan Presley* was published in New Zealand.*

---

*   A British law firm representing the Edgar Rice Burroughs Corporation bought a copy from a New Zealand internet bookseller, then threatened legal action for infringement of UK copyright law, on the grounds that author and publisher had illegally imported the book into the UK. They succeeded in suppressing the book; except, of course, that the 3000 copies that were printed cannot be made not to exist.

When Nigel returned to New Zealand at the beginning of 2005, it was to the launch of his second novel in two years, and with 50,000 words of another novel already in his laptop. There were questions of adjustment, some of which he addressed in 'Before I Went Blind', and a job to be found, but as a writer Nigel was at the height of his powers and with a headful of novels burning to be written.

But Nigel discovered in late 2005 that his cancer had returned, and began intense and exhausting treatment. The limited time and strength for writing that remained he mostly devoted to completing *The Cowboy Dog*, and also to his memorable 'Hour With' at Writers and Readers Week at the 2006 International Festival of the Arts, and the long, reflective author interview. The books introduced in the heartbreakingly sad 'What I Would Have Written' are destined to remain vapour novels.

Fergus Barrowman

Our Apples

Remember, Franny had just had
her heart attack, so that's
where Mum was, which left
me, and you, one bach each

and when I wandered over
for a visit, late morning,
there were your old man's
underpants, pounded white,
wet, on the wire, wooden
pegs standing like soldiers.

Metro, March 1995

You were on the couch,
'Just having a lie-down
N.P.' and you rose
as though your bones
were a burden. I saw brown

spots on your hands—when
did they get there? You
offered me an apple,
which got us talking
about Gravenstein and Pippin and

Red Delicious—'You don't get
Cox's Orange much anymore,'
you said, 'they're dying out.'
And me, alone
in my bach,

the last of our name?
Remember, this was way back,
three pairs of glasses ago,
not like now when I'm
bouncing our baby with
my other hand as I
write: until she came
I never knew I cared.

Boys
on Islands

New Zealand is an island country, and New Zealanders are islanders; which maybe explains why, as a boy, I was especially fascinated by books about boys living on islands. Certainly I grew up to write a novel about a man who wanted to live within view of an island; who painted pictures of islands; who proposed living on an island as some kind of solution; who maybe wanted to make an island of himself.

The first of these books I remember reading was a children's novel—or maybe it was just a story in the *School Journal*. Its title has escaped, but the elements of it are still with me: a boy, in this case a Tongan or Samoan boy, has been found wanting by his family and been exiled to a small island as a punishment. There he is frightened of the dark and the loneliness. He drops the knife he has been provided with into a deep dark pond and has to overcome his fear of the

Sport 3, 1989

alien element to dive and reclaim it; the underwater world is, once entered, strangely comforting, brilliantly exotic. Then, in hunger, and almost by accident, he kills a pig. The pig is not a domesticated one, it is what is always called a 'wild pig', and in these stories it is invariably a pig with tusks, a boar—no puns allowed. The boy kills it, eats it, and, most importantly, cuts off its tusks and wears them, on a necklace woven from grass, round his neck. When his father, or the tribe, I can't recall which, comes to end his exile, there are his trophies bouncing on his chest, announcing his bravery, his independence. His manhood.*

Looking back now there are so many ways a text like that could be investigated. Tusk, for example, could be seen as a metaphor. But that wasn't how I read those stories then.

Of course I read lots of other things too: war comics, *Tarzan* comics, *The Phantom, Mandrake the Magician, Scrooge McDuck*, a series of comics that had *Moby Dick* and other Classics in it. This was New Zealand in the 1950s: there'd been a lot of educational hysteria about how comics destroyed children's ability to read properly and so in those days they were more or less forbidden in our house. But I would go round to other boys' places and sit in their bedrooms for hours, reading every comic they had. They thought I was a boring visitor. Back at home I read books, all

---

*   Elizabeth Knox suggested that this book might be *The Boy Who Was Afraid* by Armstrong Sperry, and to my delight she was right. 'There in submarine gloom a boy fought for his life with the most dreaded monster of the deep.' I have left the plot as I remembered it, but in fact there are several discrepancies. The boy in the book exiles himself, and is never comfortable in the underwater world; he has to lose two knives (to the ocean rather than a pond) before he works up the nerve to dive and retrieve one.

kinds: on puppetry, on magic, on skindiving, *Famous Fives,*
The Moonmintrolls, Tom Sawyer, Animal Farm, Brave
New World, etc. But I was always on the lookout for Boys
Stranded On Islands books. One in particular I read over and
over again: *The Coral Island*, by R.M. Ballantyne. In this
children's novel written in 1858 three boys are shipwrecked
in the South Seas. Their names are Ralph, Peterkin and Jack,
all names which will reappear here.

From *The Coral Island*:

> But now it occured to us, for the first time, that we had no
> means of making a fire.
>
> 'Ah, boys, I've got it!' exclaimed Jack, rising and cutting
> a branch from a neighbouring bush, which he stripped of
> its leaves. 'I recollect seeing this done once at home. Hand
> me the bit of whip-cord.' With the cord and branch Jack
> soon formed a bow. Then he cut a piece, about three inches
> long, off the end of a dead branch, which he pointed at
> the two ends. Round this he passed the cord of the bow,
> and placed one end against his chest, which was protected
> from its point by a chip of wood; the other point he placed
> against the bit of tinder, and then began to saw vigorously
> with the bow, just as a blacksmith does with his drill while
> boring a hole in a piece of iron. In a few seconds the tinder
> began to smoke; in less than a minute it caught fire, and in
> less than quarter of an hour we were drinking our lemonade
> and eating coconuts round a fire that would have roasted
> an entire sheep, while the smoke, flames and sparks flew up
> among the broad leaves of the overhanging palm trees, and
> cast a warm glow upon our leafy bower.

My friends and I tried this many times but it worked better
in the book.

Apart from fire-making, the coral island boys hunt and
kill pigs, make pets of the wild cats, go diving and are thrilled
by the underwater world, fight sharks, escape pirates, save a

mother and baby from cannibals and take part in a bloody battle with heathen natives, all adventures I could imagine myself enjoying.

At this age I was in no sense a serious or thoughtful reader. I just mowed through books, seeking escape. Looking back now, as I start to make the connections that link these books to my first novel, I suspect that what I really liked about the island stories, as opposed to the books set in America or England, was that they made the Wairarapa countryside seem filled with exotic possibility. I could imagine our bush as jungle, our nikau as palm trees. There were wild pigs in our hills and our family often visited Pukerua Bay where I rather timidly went skindiving. For savages, there were the local Maori; it was always Cowboys versus Indians, where it was possible to identify with whichever side you were on. But the sense I had that there were brown-skinned people who were different—it wasn't hard for me to think they were 'savage'—living in New Zealand around me fitted the sense of local excitement that reading these books gave me.

A few years ago I read Bill Pearson's *Rifled Sanctuaries: Some Views of the Pacific Islands in Western Literature to 1900*, where I learned that the Scotsman R.M. Ballantyne had never been to the Pacific and that *The Coral Island* is amongst other evils, a 'myth[s] of white supremacy in the form[s] of easy assumption of privilege or of domestication', which of course it is.

I also read and re-read *Robinson Crusoe*, which Pearson describes as 'a myth of race relations'. My interest at that time was taken up mostly with the physical details of Robinson's survival, and with the sense of the exotic, the free world, close at hand, with no rules, no work, good fishing, swimming, sunbathing and company.

The Swiss Family Robinson I didn't like so much,

probably, I suspect, because the Robinson parents survive the shipwreck.

I say that this exotic world was close at hand. But it was quite a while before I clearly understood that 'the South Seas' which is where all these stories were set was in fact the Pacific that I lived in.

I was obsessed with *Peter Pan*, whose story mostly takes place on vaguely located islands. Of course, *Peter Pan* is also a love story of sorts; in the primers my first girlfriend had been called Wendy, and for years I called myself Peter in childhood games.

I read *A High Wind in Jamaica*, *The Old Man and the Sea*, *Tarzan of the Apes*, and found some of those elements I particularly liked in all of them.

Then when I was twelve I was first given (by a friend of my parents) a copy of William Golding's *Lord of the Flies*. At first I thought it was terrific—here were those same names, Ralph and Jack, echoing, and there was to be sunshine, no work or rules, the fascinating and bountiful ocean, and the promise of a pig hunt. I remember thinking, This is just like *The Coral Island*, and other people have thought it too: when in 1983 Golding won the Nobel Prize for Literature he was accused of having plagiarised Ballantyne's book. But the two novels have entirely different intentions; as I progressed with *Lord of the Flies* its story began to be blighted by reality. Pig-hunting took on a new meaning. The scene where Simon hides under the foliage and is talked to by the pig's head of the book's title scared me. My younger cousin was called Simon; I saw him in that part all through the novel, and was worried for him, and for me: what role might I fill in a story like this?

Lord of the Flies might have put me off Boys Stranded On Islands books for a bit; I don't remember reading any more of them until fifteen years later, in 1974, when my wife and I were waiting at Paddington Station to go off on our honeymoon: I bought a copy of Ernest Hemingway's posthumously published novel *Islands in the Stream*. This, probably Hemingway's worst book, absolutely delighted me. It was set on islands in the Caribbean rather than in the Pacific, but all the familiar pleasures were in place—the seascapes, the underwater explorations, the heroic fishing sequences, the quaint natives, the characterful cats, etc. But I suspect that what I particularly liked was that the boys of my childhood books seemed to have grown up—and still there was no boring work to do. And now there were women around to be fought over, and art to argue about, and alcohol to exceed with. Even a war.

I had at this point already written what I liked to call a novel and was at work on a second. But *Islands in the Stream* sent me scurrying to my notebooks, and when my novel *Waiting for Einstein* was eventually published in 1984, it featured a painter living alone in a house by the sea, not in paid employment but keeping the dignity of work through disciplined sessions at the easel, with a cat to talk to, and a male friend to fight with over a woman, and many other elements straight out of *Islands in the Stream*. Its hero's name was Ralph, the friend was called Peter, and Ralph's alter ego, a man who is perhaps politically islanded, was named Robinson; I didn't use the name Jack, probably because it is my father's name. There's no pig hunting in the novel but many of the pig hunter's concerns were woven into *Waiting for Einstein*'s skindiving scene. The painter chose the house he lived in specifically because it had a view of an island; one of his paintings is called 'I island myself'.

These days *Waiting for Einstein* strikes me as a novel reduced by an innocence that might be called wishful thinking. It's looking for a reader who wishes that we were all still trying to make the dreams of the late 1960s real. It doesn't want to think what fiction is, or has been and might go on to be. It doesn't see the implications of its various mythologies.

I don't particularly want to knock the book; it has its strong points and has thus far sold quite a bit better than my second novel, which I think is more interesting. I introduce *Waiting for Einstein* because what catches my attention about the series of connections I've been attempting to make here is the way I was reluctant to see the New Zealand I was living in. One of the things fiction can offer is a lens to see through, a window, but as a boy I was simply not interested in reading anything written by a New Zealander or set in New Zealand. This lack of interest lasted almost until I had a novel of my own published. It wasn't that I didn't want to be here; what I suspect I wanted was for 'here' to be like the novels I felt I lived inside. It disappointed me when I realised that 'the South Seas' were the Pacific. Yet I always sought to make the escapes that I found in reading be grounded in everyday, in local reality. The insistence on connecting characters by name to members of my family, the sense that *The Coral Island* was fascinating because it might be set in the Wairarapa . . . this wasn't only reading to escape. It was also a determination to drag the exciting world I was convinced was 'over there' back here. To stay in that 'over there' world until it arrived; to not be in non-fictional 'here'.

Having that first novel published was meant to achieve all that. Surprise, surprise, it didn't. The wishful thinking meant that the novel wasn't really set anywhere that could be lived in, and at the same time it was not much of an escape, either; because it was hell-bent on making that wishful thinking 'real' it didn't have enough sense of itself as a game, as a source of pleasure. 'Well,' as Philip Larkin says, 'useful to get that learnt.'

When I look back over this strand of my reading, I sense that what I've been trying to describe is an innocence. Of course New Zealand has never been an innocent country. But I suspect we've been a country determined not to know that innocence has simply never been possible here.

These days, my reading habits have changed. I haven't re-read any of those old books for years, nor even properly remembered them until I started to work on this piece. I've never yet managed to read *Waiting for Einstein* all the way through. Not that there aren't books about boys alone on islands to read now. Michel Tournier's novel *Friday or The Other Island* is a superb reworking of *Robinson Crusoe*. Ian Wedde's *Symmes Hole* examines the same ocean of material. Albert Wendt's fictions are all set on islands in the Pacific . . .

And, like many other New Zealanders, these days I'm spending more time reading books written here, by choice, for pleasure, for entertainment. I wouldn't say I've exactly found that novel I've looked for, the one that brings the 'over there' world of fiction to the immediate 'here' of everyday New Zealand without a sense of strain, of willed arrival—but maybe that's not what I'm looking for anymore, either . . .

Homesickness

He'd always felt most at home when he was reading. Wherever the words said, that's where you were. And then in 1961 a Maori kid had come running through the school. Pete Smith, funny how you remember a name, had been out buying the lunches and had heard it on the radio: Ernest Hemingway shot his head off!

He'd read *The Old Man and the Sea* and *For Whom the Bell Tolls*. Hemingway was the first author he'd imagined. He imagined him sitting at the typewriter. Pausing, his hands held over the keys as though he was playing the piano: listening for a word. Really pleased when he heard he'd won the Nobel Prize. But why would anyone who understood enough to write a whole book kill themselves? Who was sure to be remembered?

Perhaps he wouldn't be an author after all.

Sport 6, 1991

The next year, that same Pete Smith, running through the school again, this time for Marilyn Monroe: dead in the nude. It was strange, Americans were always either getting remarried or killing themselves. Perhaps they were like the Maoris?

But in his head it was clear: death meant that you remembered where you were when you heard.

He was the only Pakeha bouncing a basketball in America. Thirteen, and two days before JFK had lost his brain in Dallas. His mother had been buying clothes pegs in a Five-and-Dime when news of the assassination had come over the radio. The proprietor turned it up. His mother said that after a moment of increasing silence everyone in the shop had put what was in their hands back on the shelves and quietly filed out. Now all of America was closed, indoors, watchful to see what would come next: the star at the end of Jack Ruby's pistol.

He had seen Ruby shoot Oswald, live. His parents had been in the kitchen; he hadn't called them. At first he wasn't sure but it was replayed again and again. He couldn't believe that they were showing that on television, slow motion reruns of a man's death; he kept waiting for his parents to tell him he couldn't watch. His parents didn't seem to know what to do. They talked in low voices, glancing at him and his sister. 'Everyone is in mourning but we aren't invited, best to lie low.' But there was only the TV, endless repeats of clips from *PT109*, LBJ's inauguration, JFK's funeral, Ruby's shot. Oswald's face collapsing inwards, sucked to a point, the sudden gasp of death looped for repetition, for detail—as though the whole nation was to look for clues. Their apartment was tiny and though they had only one small black-and-white TV set television seemed to be with them in every room: you won't want to miss any of this. His parents looked increasingly worried—for example, the shops were all shut, would they have enough food? Finally he took his basketball and went outside.

Next door was a grade school: Little League diamond, sun-burned California grass, low modular classrooms like bunkers beyond the dark rectangles of the basketball courts. The posts and baskets, the painted court markings, they looked like just what he needed. But the air was grey and full of mist. Now he noticed, in the distance, the absence of traffic. When he arrived at the asphalt its grey surface was blotched with puddles that the ball would only splash in.

He warmed up, bouncing the ball watched by no one. Then, alone on the flat of the court, he set himself at the free-throw line and shot up at the waiting basket. When the ball struck the backboard, slap, the pole shuddered, the hoop flapped wildly. A miss; the ball dropped and bounded away, miles. No one stopped it or tossed it back. Such a heavy ball, brick-coloured, its surface divided by thick black lines that seemed to be its skeleton. An American ball, bought for him by his father so that he could join in, a *Wilson*, full-size, made for big corn-fed American hands. The ball scared him, it was too bouncy, he was afraid it would smack him in the mouth. But Americans wore gloves for playing what was really just rounders, and thought that to catch a hard leather cricket ball barehanded was moronically courageous. His father made him and his sister play cricket at the school on Saturday mornings. At Mahia, on holiday, when his father stuck the wickets in the sand, all the kids on the beach had come and lined up to be picked. But here the American kids stayed at the edge of earshot and shouted, 'A game that lasts five days? No way!'

They had come to America so that his father could study

factory design. Factories were why they went everywhere, he couldn't remember all the places. But now that Kennedy was shot he knew he would remember this basketball court.

It was strange to know he was living through a time he would remember.

As he returned to the free-throw line, he glanced round quickly at the houses that backed onto the school. Curtains were drawn, dogs did not bark. He realised that he was waiting for someone to shout at him, or for another gunshot. But surely no one could tell he wasn't American unless he opened his mouth? Defiantly he kept launching the ball at the basket: New Zealanders are good at sports. He tried a lay-up; it was stupid, trying to run in jeans.

He stuck it out till he'd made three decent hook shots, then turned and, ball on hip, started to walk home. After a moment he broke into a run.

Now as he sits at his desk he remembers that that time a kid had also come running through the school, wailing the news like a siren . . .

It's dark all around him, just the light low over the white page of his notebook. For miles, everyone else is sleeping.

This time he is going to kill *all* his characters!

In the notebook he writes, *The difference between the world and a book is that the world doesn't need you to remember it.*

Back in New Zealand, sixteen, in another school, discovering that sex is also a sport and wanting to be good at it too. Finding out: this goes *here*; every action has its equal and opposite reaction. Afterwards you smoke cigarettes. In California there'd been a swimming pool attached to their complex and one morning as he'd climbed out the girl from the apartment next door had come up behind him, underwater. She was wearing a tight blue bikini; probably about thirteen too, anyway, old enough to have breasts big enough to thrust. A bit tarry, his mother had said. And she'd come across the width of the pool towards him, he'd half-glimpsed a wriggle of blue against the bottom, and then risen right behind, and as he'd pulled himself dripping up the chrome ladder she'd scratched the inside of his thighs with her fingernails.

Seven red scratches, one of them bleeding. Confused, he'd grabbed his towel and run up the stairs, followed by her laughter. Later he'd spied on her, and masturbated.

Then: sex proper as something to be begun on, something to have achieved, something to be repeated so as to be sure of having got it right. Sex as a fantastic form of stamp collection. As a reason to tell stories. Lies. Fantasies. Fantasies to make real. As something, just, natural. Good sex. Regular sex. It's-possible-to-be-bored-by sex. Sex as very good television, starring yourself. I'm-okay-you're-okay sex. Oh, okay then, sex as pleasure.

But what is this sexual need? It was disturbing that desire existed beyond *I want to score you*. Need? He'd heard the expression but now to feel it—he'd thought it was only for those without, nerds, or in prison. But this, 'I can't talk to you today!' Can't you tell that what we need is to feel the outsides of my thighs against the insides of yours? That particular arrangement, I need that. And what I need is for it not to be different, or better, or with someone else.

It's surprising . . .

I need for it to be exactly the same.

This, he decides, is the need to feel at home.

And now he is going away again. On his own. And what he discovers is that he is not going to learn their language.

He's been there before of course, has learned the greeting procedures and how to order. But he's going to forget all that. This time he's going to point in shops, and speak loudly in English. 'May I have five ounces of sliced ham please. Back home I'm a private detective. I used to be goalie for our national side, got injured out just before the World Cup.' And decline invitations, and stay in his room for hours, watching television with the sound off, drinking Steinlagers in his underpants. Turn the sound right up during the commercials. Buy sixty tins of tuna, eat nothing else, fork it straight from the tin; leave the tins, unwashed, outside his door with his empties. Say loudly to anyone who approaches, 'Our indigenous people have buried their placentas all over the country, you have to watch your step. Their oral culture is music to our ears, I'll do you a haka: taranaki, taranaki, te kuiti. Ngauruhoe ruapehu hey ranginui walker. Taumarunui taumarunui taumarunui, hey. Hey, talofa. Hey, ohakune! Vegemite pavlova! Now, could you please show me what you have by Vincent O'Sullivan. Really? And Allen Curnow? Oh, I see you've got Hugh Cook.' Take up shoplifting. No: get arrested for shoplifting. Don't wash for three weeks, wear the same shirt, but beneath your best jacket, with a nice tie. Yeah, and pinch a woman's bum.

Not write home. Change addresses and fail to notify everybody. Steal a car, kids do it all the time. I'm so sick of everything, I think I'll start smoking again.

He wonders what brand Ernest Hemingway smoked. Reading up on this, he is reminded that in fact Hemingway wrote not sitting but standing up. And that mostly, instead of a typewriter he used pencils, a special kind. His fourth wife Mary Welsh had a tower built at the Finca for him to work in, with a wonderful view of the horizon. But Hemingway preferred to write in the bedroom, on a shelf in the corner. He thinks it must have been a nuisance for Mary if she had wanted to change the sheets. But probably Ernest needed to look inward more than to look out.

Of course he doesn't read Hemingway any more, he only reads about him. These days it's increasingly clear to him that the greatest writer of the century is not Ernest Hemingway but Arthur Miller. Oh, okay then, the greatest male writer. It goes without saying that *Death of a Salesman* and *The Crucible* are very great. Yes. But what gives Arthur his true place is his marriage to Marilyn Monroe. For it was she, goddess of the century, who, having been married to the greatest hitter in sport, then chose Arthur—balding, bespectacled—and though their marriage could not last, by this choice of hers established forever that within every writer there is that virile, that modest, that big-hearted scaler of the human peak: that writers live, okay.

In a bar. Their president has just been assassinated. They are dancing in the streets, well, some of them are. The barman massages his chin, glances quickly right and left through the finger-marked windows—but surely the assassination was on television, many kilometres distant? Will it be all right if he orders another beer? He flicks his Zippo, lights his Camel. On his jacket is a sew-on sleeve patch: the Stars and Stripes. The assassins are sure to have been American.

When at last, on the way back to his room, he is thoroughly beaten up—forehead, nose rasped on the roughcast concrete— he knows he will return home a happy man.

On Top
of the World

There were years when pop music was a matter of life or death to me. I would look at a perfectly ordinary fifth-form blackboard and in my head not very much calculus was happening, unless you count trying to figure who was looking at whom in the Kinks' 'Waterloo Sunset'. Songs went with me, they were projected onto the faces of the people I was talking to. They instructed me like a bible on how to be.

However, all that was rather long a time ago. Forty years to be exact. Along the way I shifted from believer to fan to that dreaded thing, an appreciator. So among the albums (the old word) dealt to in this book there's things I've bought, played a few times, thought, 'Ah, so *that's* what the Verlaines sound like', then, then, you know, filed them away.

But I still get excited in record shops. My heart beats

Soundtrack: 118 Great New Zealand Albums,
edited by Grant Smithies, Craig Potton Publishing, 2007

faster. There's pressure. All around there's music and if I choose right I might get something that brings a tremor to the base of the spine; that I have to play to everybody. That I have to play for myself.

Back when music was more than breathing to me, you didn't actually *buy* the music. No money; anyway it was kind of disapproved of in our house. In those days (early sixties) music came out of the radio. I had a little transistor which went everywhere, and a big old bakelite valve radio (a Pioneer) that blasted holes in the walls if the olds weren't home.

I tried to like New Zealand music. Sandy Edmonds, Dinah Lee, the Chicks, Maria Dallas—you had to try pretty hard. Larry's Rebels, that was bit more like it. But actually it all sounded second-hand, like some loser trying to repeat a joke told by a stickman with more sexual experience. Try-hard, we say these days. Well, it all came from a world we didn't really believe in, didn't it. 'I Put a Spell on You'—no one I knew was putting any spells on. 'Parchman Farm'—that was, I knew, a penitentiary in the States—'I'm sitting down here on Parchman Farm'—no, you aren't, mate. And everyone knew this wasn't 'The Land of a Thousand Dances'.

Those titles all appear on the first La De Das album* and I couldn't take them seriously. This was some kind of dumb snobbery—listened to these days, they really have a good kick. Great musicianship, terrific arrangement, and most of all singers who can really put the stuff across. So what did I know?

---

*　Album title: *La De Das*. Recorded at Stebbing Studio in Auckland. Originally issued in 1966; reissued by EMI 2003. Reissue includes the original 16 tracks plus another 12, mostly from the second LP, *Find Us a Way*.

There was however one song. My mate Colin had this album and we always turned Track One way up. Nothing like as loud as I turned it up at home, Dad or no Dad. (This was on the radio, remember, you couldn't choose when you heard things—you had to seize the day.) I remember him opening the door to my bedroom, me in my school uniform (short pants) ready to head off for the day. The look on his face was part outrage: that you'd make such a disturbance. But the real thing was the sense of horror, that I'd got myself into this *state*.

'On Top of the World' was the greatest thing on the radio that week, no contest. It roared. It built and built. The guy sounded like he meant it; he could tell you about it. It got bigger and bigger. The bass thundered, it pushed the song up like a big wave coming. The chorus swung in like a wrecking ball. He was on top of the world. He *was!*

And so was I. This was the first great New Zealand single. Short pants go to hell.

Green
as Editor's Ink

It's not a widely known fact but in 1973 there were no writers in New Zealand and nothing was happening here either. So, aged twenty-three, I set off to see the world with the idea that I was going to solve both problems by becoming a novelist. So as to have a clearer idea of what might be required I was going to meet a novelist, someone to model myself on. An inspired combination, this, of the ignorant and the fatuous.

I was away nearly four years and I did write two novels: *Willowsong*, which was going to be New Zealand's first hippy novel, and *The Wall*, which would be its first international intellectual novel, along the lines of the things I liked reading in the colourful covers (bright as LP sleeves) that were then being published by Picador—books by, oh, Angela Carter, Jorge Luis Borges, Knut Hamsun. Needless to say, *The Wall* was a ploddingly naïve distillation of all of the above—Kafka

---

Metro, January 2006

reheated by, say, Ronald McDonald. This along with its predecessor and the one which followed it (*Eyelimits*) shall forever remain unseen by human eyes.

That I wrote these books at all was entirely due to a meeting I had. Looking back thirty-something years, it's tricky now to be certain of the exact sequence of events, but what I get first is my mate Brent, who had worked with me at the Charles Haines advertising agency in Wellington and then on the assembly line at Ford in the Petone suburbs—he'd flown ahead of me to the UK and, to be honest, I never expected to see him again. I was on my way to India—which is where you went in those days. But he met me at Heathrow—'Cox, ya idiot'—and persuaded me to go down to Kent with him, for a few days. He was working as a deckhand on the hovercraft which ferried between Ramsgate and Calais—long hair (which was very important then), good shoulders (he'd been in the Army), an Antipodean tan. Brent's brother Linton, who had a skipper's ticket, had lived in England for some years and was captaining one of these craft, which is how Brent got the deckhand job. Linton had met this gorgeous girl, Camilla, a blonde Englishwoman, a student, and when Camilla met Brent, big shoulders and tan trumped skipper's ticket, no worries. Once that got a bit serious, Brent decided it would be good if I met Camilla's parents, to help establish him as more than a Kiwi deckhand having an OE fling.

'Her dad's a writer,' he told me.

I also had long hair and as big a beard as I could grow, and a head full of straw to boot. But I've always made parents happy: 'A nice, clean boy; a book-lover; serious.' So along I went.

The house was a tall brick cottage, three up two down, with roses entwined about its door and flowerbeds tumbling and overgrown—this was in Kent, 'the Garden of England', in the backstreets of a little summer-holiday town called Birchington-on-Sea. I was ushered into the front room by Brent and met Jane, Camilla's mother, who was a little like the garden, tumbling and overgrown, but colourful, warm, welcoming. Plummy accent but I was learning to forgive this, as you had to then in England. She came over, shook my hand, asked if I would have tea. Yes, lovely. The room was full of light, falling from tall windows, and beyond the light I could see shelves of books and also a lifetime's collection of strange and wonderful things—an unusual clock, faded paintings, twisted jars and bottles. My kind of place: *this* was a writer's house.

And then the writer. Strangely, he was on the floor, sitting—he reached a hand up and we also shook. An older man, sixty perhaps, with a heavy, weighty body, like a wheatsack, threatening to split his dark green sweater. Christopher Charles Douglas Short, Chris to everyone who met him, Christopher Short on the spines of his books. White hands with large calluses on the knuckles and long, delicate fingers with extended, pointed nails. Muscular arms. Most important was the head. It was immense, one of the largest I have ever seen, a tall, heavy head with red veins and pale patches, like the map of some fascinating country. Long white hair hung from the sides of it and curled around his shoulders. Small mouth, a tiny nose, and in the middle of the long oval of flesh, the eyes, which were clear blue, with dark pinpoints at the centre. They looked dangerous, those eyes, as though they might flash and clear the room. He gave an impression of immense power, of kingliness, of welcoming you graciously to the centre of the world, and I was thrilled. This was the real thing, able to extend a field of command even when sat awkwardly on the floor.

Then I was out of the room. I can't think why—maybe I went upstairs to pee? Anyway, when I returned he was in a chair and the room was full of lines which converged upon him.

We drank the tea and made conversation. Brent and Camilla hung back as I proceeded to get on famously with Jane and Chris, charming them, being my best self. The plan was working. So well did it work that soon they grasped that they were no longer necessary and bunked off—maybe upstairs to Camilla's old bedroom, or maybe right off the premises, I can't recall. The only thing I am sure of is that I didn't care.

I had no girlfriend (or boyfriend—I was so lonely at that point I would have considered anything). Apart from Brent, I knew no one in the entire country—walking the streets of London I thought, 'You could drop dead here and no one would give a damn.' I was sleeping nights at this point alone in a Volkswagen van (don't ask) and by day was a deckhand on, you guessed it, the hovercraft, which was noisy and rendered conversation impossible. I started talking to Chris and Jane (by now they were sorted into that priority order) and was in no hurry to stop. This conversation was still running six months later.

There were disturbing moments. When Chris said, 'I never read any novels because I'm afraid that my style will be affected', even I, greener than editor's ink, knew that this was lunacy. Was that on that first day? I have no idea. We talked so much that the whole summer was a blur. Jane served tea and kept things going—a clever word here, cheese on toast there. I often slept over (I even slept over one Christmas Eve with Pippin, Camilla's younger sister, but this never made it into the official register of things that really happened) and was always doing errands in the VW van—Chris and

Jane had no car. That was another disturbing thing: they were poor. Weren't all writers rich? I didn't want to know—I soon learned always to bring beer and a block of cheese. And where were the crowds outside his door, fighting for his autograph?

But none of that really mattered. Here was a real writer, an example: this is what they are like! They sit around and talk big—talk in a grand manner about life and how ordinary people live. Food and drink is carried in on trays. The light falls from the tall windows. Fascinating things shine on dim shelves in the background.

Actually, what was happening was that I was talking myself into existence. Away from the constraints of home, in exalted company, I was inventing myself as I had always wanted to be. I got a grip, that year, on the person I have been for the rest of my life.

Something similar was happening to Christopher Short. The truth was, as I gradually discovered, he had been much more of a writer in the past than he was now. True, there were nine novels, there on the dim shelves, each one with his name on—I so wanted that to be me. But he hadn't published a novel for a few years. In fact, he wasn't writing right now. 'People always ask you, Nige, when you're an author, what you're doing when you're staring for hours out the window, and I say, I'm writing, but, as you will discover, no one understands.' This also sounded like lunacy. But Chris enjoyed saying things like this to me. It made him feel like an author. 'You're very good for him,' Jane would whisper. 'Please keep coming back.'

Needless to say, Camilla and Brent were nowhere to be seen.

Chris was American. He grew up in Charleston, where he

went to square dances and was, Jane told me, a very fancy dancer. This story was told over and over, sometimes by Chris, sometimes by Jane. The point was, he was a real mover, once. That's because when he was in his early twenties he got polio and had spent the rest of his life on crutches. Which was why he was sitting on the floor, why he had calluses on his knuckles, why his arms were strong-looking—he pressed down on the floor with the knuckles and swung himself.

He was determined not to be thought a cripple. Thus he almost never went out, because that meant being in a wheelchair. 'People lean down at you,' he said, 'and if you're not careful they pat your head.' Jane said, talking about his writing, 'They say, "So nice that he's got a hobby."' Thus they were poor, as they were allowed to live only on what Chris earned (plus an invalid's benefit that was also not in the register of things that really happened). There was about him something of the southern gentleman, ornately courteous, just slightly hokum—and with very clear ideas about gender roles. Jane was a lady and was never to work, was always to be kept. This was somehow heroic, I saw that even then, somehow noble—and doomed. Jane carried a burden of worry which she was only ever allowed to express after he had gone upstairs to bed (backwards, one step at a time, on his knuckles—it took about half an hour). The house was falling down. There was no money to send the beautiful daughters to university. Where, this Christmas, will the goose come from?

Not from any hugely successful book written by Chris, that was for sure. I had, rather gingerly, taken one home to read. *The Big Cat* was sub-Faulkner—very sub. *The Naked Skier* had a Giles-like cartoon of a naked skier on its cover and was as crappy as its title—I was careful not to borrow that. None of the other names have stayed with me, except for

The Black Room, which was his claim to fame. Consisting of the meditations of a homosexual archduke, it had been published by Jonathan Cape—the gold standard—and Chris had a letter from Tom Maschler, Cape's famous publisher, which declared, 'This is one of the most brilliant manuscripts ever to come across my desk.' I heard about this letter so many times that finally, sceptical, I asked to see it. And so it was produced.

That is not nothing. Maschler really was the genius publisher of his day. I dipped into *The Black Room* and decided it wasn't for me. (I am sure I took it home, pretended to read it, declared it to be brilliant. That is what you do, any writer will tell you.) A decade later I saw the book, in a Four Square paperback edition, spine-up among a pile of second-hand books in a Wellington bookshop. Chris was dead by then, Jane also, and I had long since lost contact with Brent, Camilla or Pippin. I bought it. Flicking through it, I knew I would never read it; it's unreadable. But I have it to this day.

Jane and Chris gave me a typewriter and ribbon; showed me how to set out a manuscript page; instructed me in the making of carbon copies and the need for intelligent chaptering. I set the typewriter up in my little rented room (by now I was out of the VW) on top of a large cardboard carton and set about transferring *Willowsong* from my handwritten exercise book to typescript. They asked how I was going every time I visited, which was often twice a day. Then Chris asked to read it. So I handed it over.

Before the next visit my wrists seemed to be full of jumpy nerves, I could hardly steer. They had a bottle of champagne waiting. 'It was such a relief,' said Chris. 'All this talk of you being a writer—I was worried you would turn out, like so many, not to be able to write.' Oh, that champagne! It was cheap, of course, but it had me floating. And it was so kind of them—I knew that buying it would have been Chris's grand gesture and that Jane would be fighting to find anything to put on his plate for the rest of the week.

They gave me the name of Chris's agent, Sheila Watson of Bolt & Watson, who read my book and was kind about it. She tried to find a publisher for it. She also suggested, diplomatically, that I might try reading a few people 'with a clearer idea of character and structure'. E.M. Forster, for example. I did as I was told. The rejection letters began to arrive. It was official: I was a writer.

The rejection letters kept coming steadily for the next decade, during which I moved back to New Zealand. Most of them contained things like 'however we think you can write . . . however we think you show promise . . . however we would be pleased to see your next novel, should you write one'. Writers are the Morris Minors of the careers world, able to run for years on an oily rag of hope. Then in 1984 that was all changed when my novel *Waiting for Einstein* was accepted for publication by Benton Ross. And the process that Chris and Jane started finally came to an end.

Well, sort of. It's never that simple. Jane was thrilled to hear that their faith in me had not been misplaced. (Chris was dead by then.) She couldn't wait to read the book that had finally done it—I got impatient letters. But one strand of *Waiting for Einstein* tells the story of a man very like Brent— remember him?—who marries an English girl totally unlike Camilla (but no one noticed that). They come out to New Zealand, have a baby—then the marriage goes sour and they separate. Hmm. In fact, when I first wrote that strand, Brent and Camilla were still together, but, by publication, the novel had become prophetic. Except that, by then, it didn't read that way. The silence from England was deafening.

It might be said that I was cavalier writing about my

friends like that and I wouldn't argue. Maybe I thought the book would be rejected like all the others? Maybe I thought that Brent and Camilla would never read it? Certainly I hadn't seen them for several years. Maybe I was just a bit of a jerk.

During the year that followed the wonderful summer, Chris's health began to fail. He had a series of illnesses, which weakened him. His agent couldn't get him an advance on a new novel. It was suggested that someone might make a film of *The Big Cat*—could he write a treatment? He couldn't. So I wrote one. I had no idea what a treatment might be like but I got a book out of the library, read up, and did my best. No dice. In despair, he took on a job he despised: the writing of the latest novel in *The Saint* series. 'I'm prostituting myself, Nige,' he used to say. *The Saint*'s creator, Leslie Charteris, was still alive, but couldn't be bothered writing a new book. Eventually, after a great deal of colourful grumbling, *The Saint and the Hapsburg Necklace* appeared—the cover said, 'by Leslie Charteris', and, in smaller print, 'written by Christopher Short'. There was supposed to be a second of these ghost-written titles but Chris didn't have the stomach for it.

He had trouble getting up the stairs. Jane asked me to call around at bedtime to climb with him, one tread below, in case he fell. Then the period came when I had to lift him in and out of the bath—a terrible blow to his southern pride.

When he improved, I moved to London to be with a new girlfriend (eventually we married, and then divorced—also a story told in *Waiting for Einstein*) and, as I said, moved back to New Zealand. Jane wrote often. Then I got a card, edged in black, to say that he'd died.

I had always intended I would dedicate my first book to

Chris and Jane but when the time came I didn't. I can't recall why. It's a memory that fills me with shame—writing this has brought that back.

Jane died some years later. Pippin wrote to tell me; then we lost touch. I've never seen or heard from Brent, Camilla, Pippin or Linton again. I haven't given them a thought for ages. In June 2005 I published *Responsibility*, my fifth novel.

I never did get to India.

When I
Was a Writer

The Katherine Mansfield Room is a sort of above-ground cellar beneath the terrace of the Villa Isola Bella where Katherine lived for a few months in 1920–21. A photograph in Gillian Boddy's book about her shows her on the terrace but she was very ill at that time, scarcely mobile, according to the one handed down eye-witness report I've had of her, and I suspect she never descended to this spare room, this sleep-out—so was KM ever in the KM Room? But it's a good place to work; there's a sense that work is all that's ever been done within its thick creamy walls, which keep out France, and the sound of the trains, and the heat, even when it's not hot outside.

Inside it the Fellow tries to ignore the ghosts (did Janet Frame sit facing this window or that one?) and get on with

Sport 8, 1992

justifying the grant ($36,000, to cover travel, accommodation and living—Anne, Anneli and I will make it stretch 8½ months if we're careful). This Fellow has a work chart to keep him honest; so far it's a five day week, from 8 in the morning till somewhere between 4.30 and 6pm, with on average half an hour for lunch. There's no phone calls, no visitors, no interruptions, so you get on with it (how's that, Mr McLauchlan?*). I've never really had an extended stretch of being able to write all day before; it's *tiring*.

Every morning I come across town on the train, walk under the railbridge and, avoiding the dogs', which is *everywhere*, make the short climb up the av. Katherine Mansfield to the Room. About a week ago I heard a hissing in the stone wall outside the gate to the Room's garden. A small pipe appeared to have sprung a leak within the wall; a dark trickle ran down the white of the 'ancient stones' and away along the gently sloping earth gutter. Your novelist, ever alert for a Real Story, followed the trickle ('This is your work!'), but became worried in case someone saw and thought him soft in the head.

For the next week when I turned up each morning, there was the trickle. After three days a clematis-like vine, enjoying the water, produced two bright yellow flowers. 'Voila!' I said in my excellent French. Inside the Room I pressed on with the masterwork.

Then two days ago workmen arrived, six of them, from the Menton council, to clear the ground of any weeds, overhanging branches or rubbish. Everywhere in the city you

* When Gordon McLauchlan's attack on state patronage to writers was published in the *New Zealand Herald* at least half a dozen 'friends' instantly thought of me and sent a copy. For two weeks afterwards I worked in a fury of self-justifying indignation.

can see the big clean-up in progress; August is coming and an immaculate Menton justifies the this-month-only inflation of prices. Menton (pop. 25,000) attends to presentation: the by-laws say you can paint your house any colour you like as long as it's terracotta. In my tiny garden the workmen remove all extraneous vegetable matter very efficiently, which I regret; urban France seems to be without backyards—our apartment has no 'outside'—and I rather like the little jungle at my back door. Then . . . and here's the question . . . did those workmen inform the water board there was a leak? Or is water usage in this town so carefully monitored that one of their dials told them they were losing precious drops? The latter isn't hard to imagine: this is a nation of dial-watchers, schedule-keepers and form-fillers, and France has had low rainfall for three years. The whole of Europe is short of water, I read, except (of course) England. Whatever: that afternoon the water-men arrived. I keep the gate to the Room's garden locked to deter the KM fans; I hurried out with the key. The workmen and I quickly established that we didn't have a language in common, and that I didn't know where the key to the stopcock on my end of the pipe was, and that I hadn't fiddled with it (honest!) and that, well, it was their business. This exchange had in it everything that a writer hates: failure in the language department, failure in the fixit department (okay, a male writer), a distraction from work that's not fascinating (let me rephrase that). They thrashed around in the bushes out there while I thrashed around in the bushes in here. Finally they shouted to me, 'Ay!' and the foreman asked with his hands, 'Is there a telephone in there?' 'No. Non.' He called me 'Puta!' which I didn't go for all that much (though it's Spanish, isn't it? I searched for his mantilla), but I could see him thinking, 'That effete creature is worried I'm going to get my dirty boots all over his invaluable manuscript.' I explained that there wasn't a phone—this is a writer's room—and then remembered for him that there's a cardphone at 'la gare'. He repeated the word, correcting my pronunciation, then off they went. They were back shortly with a huge spanner, which they took into the bushes—by then I was back to work and didn't watch—and departed. Later I discovered the Room's water had been cut off: no coffee, no toilet.

I waited a day, seeing if doing nothing would help, carefully recalling what had happened in minute detail. Away from home and without subtlety in the language of the country you're in, *real encounters with the locals* are rare, and these microscopic incidents loom large.

I didn't want to start going to cafés for coffee, was quite soon peeing into very yellow toilet water. At lunchtime I assembled a letter, in French, for the General Secretary of the council here, M. Kettela, who is responsible for the Room; he speaks no English. I always write any complicated messages out and pass them to people to read (this is true even when I'm in New Zealand: writers trust writing) and it was fun getting the exact words for 'outside tap' and conjugating the verbs. Then, not wanting to be a bother, I decided I should try Direct Action first and checked all the manholes and small access hatches, searching for the toby. Looking around the garden, I realised these hatches were everywhere: I found ten in as many square metres. They were slightly scary to open—I don't go much on big black spiders running up my bare arms, and I'm not sure if there's snakes around here. (At this point I remember that once, in Greece, needing a boulder to anchor a flysheet, I seized a hefty one and uncovered a nest of scorpions, one of them still on the boulder: squash!) The hatches gave access to beautifully maintained stormwater pipes, all empty. There's something eerie about pipes that you can't see up: their hollow sound, the sense that any moment something might gush from them. These were part of such a complicated network. I thought about French organisation, which can be very impressive, and their determination to have things the way they want. To my relief the pipes had no occupants to face down, though when I opened the meterbox something rattled like a rat in behind its baseboard. Then a large green lizard shot across the dials and disappeared behind the board again. I'm fond of lizards, they're always beautiful in colour, and I closed the door carefully. One day, checking the Room's mailbox (which I do obsessively about six times a day—so far it's yielded just one aerogramme), I found I'd squashed a tiny lizard, about an inch and a half long, faintly reminiscent of a tuatara, though this one, in death, was pale grey. It'd crawled in through the mail slot and then got caught in the hinge when I closed the box. These little everyday tragedies can make you feel desperate when you're away; there's no familiar for them to be absorbed into. It was another lizard that helped me feel at home here. This was a month ago, on the first really sunny day. The colours all changed and became soft, everything looked warm and sleepy in the steady light (Brian Boyd—Nabokov lived here—says, 'orange-palmy-blue Menton', which gives the feeling exactly) and as I came under the railway bridge something rattled in the stone wall. I stopped, waited, and a beautiful lizard slowly extruded itself from a hole the power board had drilled to run cable into. It came out into the sun, blackgreen, with hidden lights among the stickles on its back and the red of toadstools on the undersides of its footpads. I felt at home because after that the lizard was something I looked for every morning. Fauna that's exotic (to you) seems to tell you you're in another country. I mean, all these French people could *fly* south, settle in New Zealand and learn to eat our lumpen food, but animals, reptiles especially, don't become ubiquitous easily.

Because I can't speak the language I seem to be paying great attention in this country to the natural world. But it frustrates me; there seems no way to identify the birds whose calls I hear outside as I work—so how will I write about them?

Late that afternoon I visited the Mairie, which is the mayor's nest, the Town Hall, armed with my carefully compiled letter. In Menton the Mairie is a beautiful building, formal, modest in its dignity (terracotta, of course), with a huge, clean tricolour, and tall, highly polished wooden doors. It houses the council offices, and the local Salle de Mariage, in which you must, if you wed in France, be married. This particular Salle was designed by Jean Cocteau in 1957; it's hard to imagine anything like it being allowed in New Zealand. The chamber itself is not vast but the symbolic figures Cocteau painted on the walls and ceiling are too big for the space, so that you seem to cower beneath them: prancing outlines, pale green, ochre, faintly erotic, their stylised perfection mocking the everyday creatures who are marrying beneath them. Under your feet the carpet is royal red, spread with imitation leopard skins. A thin light rises from black, diamond-shaped shades held at head-height by metal vines which climb, writhing, from the floor . . .

I'd been to the Mairie a few times and now approached it with caution as no one there apart from the Mayor speaks any English. (Everyone everywhere else speaks some English, whatever they tell you. My French, which I always try, is so bad that as soon as they hear it they reply in English. Of course, I'm in French mode and can't switch . . .) But I had my communication all written out: 'Je suis Nigel Cox, je voudrais . . .' The counter-jumper sends me to wait by the coffee machine. Employees buy drinks from this machine every moment or two; they all talk to it. France is a highly automated country: at the station you can buy your train ticket, or something to eat or drink, or sweets, from similar machines; or reserve a sleeper for Paris, or buy an airline ticket for anywhere in Europe, or have fifty business cards printed, or make photocopies, or do your banking—all without having to deal with a person you will have to be civil to. On the motorway the toll machine sorts the coins you toss into its wire basket and instantly returns you the correct change. The machines have personality: my train ticket automaton often says to me, 'Je suis hors service.' The telephone directory comes via a little TV called a Mini-Tel, which I can't work very well, despite the English language instructions. It can deliver just about anything—horoscopes, stock-market reports, the contents of department stores, flight information—but I keep getting a list of French provinces, which one do you desire? Other people play sex games on them—a guy down the road ran up a $20,000 phone bill.

M. Kettela (still at his desk most days at 6.30) waves me into his office, reads my communication, rings Works without having to look up the number. None of this, 'It's late, they'll be closed', or, 'It's not my department', which of course it isn't. One further call, he's got the right man. 'Ah—merci bien.' Then he explains all, very fast so I haven't got a clue what he's saying. But I can guess from his face: they're checking it out, I'm to come back in twenty minutes. 'D'accord,' I say, 'd'accord. A bientôt.' See, fluent.

The 'old town' of Menton is twelfth-century and very beautiful: long cool dark streets, high-sided, like slots, wind up towards the flying campanile. Up, up, that's where you look, to the pale scrollwork and the frescoes fading back into the sand-coloured façades, but down, down, that's where

49

the drinks are, so I head down to the pedestrian precinct where you are reminded that 'café' is a French word. I have calculated that if everyone in this town wanted a restaurant seat at the same time it wouldn't be a problem. These restaurant-cafés are what the French do best. The service is casual, off-hand but deceptively attentive, and of course the offerings are so wonderfully tasty. I have a bière while many people, all better dressed and looking than I am, stroll past in what seems to me to be terrific style. I could watch the people here forever—and they wouldn't care . . .

Upon my return M. Kettela seems to have done the trick. He talks absolutely flat out and he's probably high IQ too, I can hardly catch a thing.

But I gather from his manner that he's finished with me, and I've made out 'demain', tomorrow, and he looks pleased with himself, so I go home.

Next morning when I arrive at 7.58am (still there, Mr McLauchlan?) I see everything's been dealt to. The earth is open, the vine has been ripped out and is lying like a length of old twine. Within my little kingdom, water is again flowing as it should (remember 'Clochemerle', remember Pagnol) and I am content. At 8.30 the foreman turns up, we shake hands, we peer at the earth and nod seriously, stroking our chins. Two other officials turn up to make sure that all impediments to the writing of fiction have been removed.

Which they have. It wasn't a big job, but all of it was done after hours, very swiftly, for a foreigner who doesn't speak French. I hope we could match this performance at home . . .

A bientôt, New Zealand.

Menton, late April 1991

50

That was when I was a writer. Now I'm back to being a bookseller who writes for three hours each morning—which seems another state entirely. But why? Maurice Gee, the 1992 KM Fellow, and a writer if ever there was one, tells me he only writes for three hours each morning, then he's 'finished, had it'—so is the difference in what you do for the rest of the day? In France I found the hardest thing was that, deprived of my usual distractions, I couldn't find a way to get out of my work overnight so I could come back to it fresh next morning.

So real writers stay in their writing all the time, is that it?

I did have spells of full-time writing when I was younger, patches where I was out of work or on holiday, but that was in the future-hungry days before I'd had anything published. Being the KM Fellow means that everybody you meet sees you as a writer, which is a role I find impossible to fill. In my mind writers are mythological, giants like Cocteau's Salle de Mariage figures; it's a company I aspire to.

But it was fun pretending; and I got an enormous amount of work done.

Try as I might I never felt at home in France. I did look every day for the lizard in the hole in the wall, but once I'd written this piece I never saw it again.

Auckland, January 1992

Phone
Home Berlin

Love Parade

10.15 Sunday morning—this just happened. Dadda was on the couch deep in the *London Review of Books*. Andrew-Jack, who had slept late—we went to Brandenburg yesterday, wandered looking for a hostel for three hours, had a McDonald's in despair and came home but the Love Parade meant that the trains were suddenly jammed to the luggage rails with half-naked German youth, all navel studs and pink fake-fur leggings, everything was delayed, we arrived home exhausted and thus he slept late—then appeared in the morning kitchen and his first words of the day were, 'Dadda, your toes are getting old.'

2001–2002, previously unpublished, except for extracts in *Sport* 28, 2002, under the title 'On the Way to the Jewish Museum Berlin'

He played with my toes the way kids do, your body is no longer your own, you're a climbing frame, you're a mattress. Then he said, 'I want porridge for breakfast.'

'Andrew-Jack, darling, I don't know how to make porridge, I hate the smell, I have always avoided making porridge, your mother, who is off having a swim, she's the one who makes porridge, she'll come home and make you some porridge soon.' (Which would mean I could go on reading the *London Review*.)

'No, I want some porridge now.'

'Okay, what about a lovely poached egg?'

'No, porridge.'

Dadda hires a crane, hauls himself up off the couch, goes to the food preparation area. Andrew-Jack stands by the stove and says, 'This is the stove', and turns it on. 'You get a pot,' he says.

Dadda gets the porridge down, reads the instructions but they are in a foreign language, remembers that it's only porridge and water, pours some into the pot, cheered on by Andrew-Jack. Kate appears, saying, 'I know what you're doing, you're trying to make porridge.' She looks in the pot where white stuff is sitting in a pile on the bottom and says, 'Put in some water. No, not enough. That's enough. That's too much. Oh, you'll have to put some more porridge in now.'

'I want to stir,' says Andrew-Jack. 'I'm the mamma,' he says firmly, to Kate, standing on a chair before the stove. 'I'm stirring.' Kate goes back to the TV, she is watching a 24-hour telecast of the Love Parade—thumping techno, acres of flesh, try-hard DJs shouting into the camera.

Andrew-Jack starts to stir. It looks like porridge. Dadda says, 'You stir, I'm going to go and read, you call me if you get bored, okay?'

'Okay.'

At least one second passes. 'I'm bored,' he announces.

Dadda, returning, says, 'You are a grinning dog, Jackie.'

'Yes,' says Andrew-Jack, grinning.

They stir. Andrew-Jack says, 'Isn't that a lovely picture by Kate, with a swimming pool and a slide and mushrooms and trees and a cloud and a fire, isn't that a lovely picture.' This object is pinned above the stove. Things suddenly catch his attention and he has to tell you all about them.

Kate returns to the scene. 'It looks like porridge,' she says.

They spoon it into Andrew-Jack's plate. 'Yes, porridge,' says Andrew-Jack.

Dadda goes back to the *London Review.* Kate goes back to the Love Parade, one million jiggling bodies, Susanna comes in, hair wet from swimming, says, 'My tits ache. Oooh, porridge. Is there any salt in it?' But Andrew-Jack is eating it anyway.

Why?

'Why are my jellies called jellies?' This is Kate, buckling on her transparent blue plastic shoes under a tree beside a park in Mitte, the wealthy middle of Berlin, on a Sunday afternoon. We're on our way to see the Caravaggio at the Neue Nationalgalerie. No one answers her. 'Why are bikes called bikes?' she says. Then, in quick succession: 'Why are sandwiches called sandwiches? Why are hats called hats? Why are drinks called drinks? Why are trees called trees?' She doesn't expect an answer. They get a riff and they just run it into the ground.

Reading a book to her at the moment is hell, every third

word she asks you a question. 'What does battlements mean?'

Once, in Wellington, on Sunday morning, going down in the car to get the bread, out of a silence she asked me, 'Poppa, what is light made of?'

I pulled over, stopped, tried to explain. I mean, what *is* light made of? I tried to say, particles, waves, I mentioned the sun. I tried to answer her. I did my best. It was a serious inquiry.

She used to call me Poppa in those days. It was Andrew-Jack who started in with Dadda. I guess I prefer Dadda. Poppa always sounded like something out of a feel-good American kids' book, I didn't think it described me. But whatever they say, it affects you. It is you they are referring to. They say my name every now and then but it's rare. They know what my whole name is. Kate can say the names of the books I've written. I have to say that this surprised me—and pleased me deeply. But, what they call you, it's not a thing you feel you should influence, you just have to take what you get.

For my money, Dad is the greatest three-letter word in the language.

There was also a time when she asked me what the end of the world looked like—the edge, she meant. This went on for a year or so and it kept coming up. It was on her mind: Where does this thing we are standing on end? What does the edge look like? Might we fall off? I tried to tell her. We got the map out, I said, 'The blue bits are sea.' When we were up in a plane I made sure she saw the coastline and I showed her the shape of the North Island on the map in the inflight mag. She was working on it. For a while she used to say, 'Is New Zealand in Wellington?' and so on, but then she got it figured. By the time we came to Germany she knew: we are in a different country now.

The Caravaggio was packed, instead we just cycled through the streets, finding things to look at. A show called *Vagina Monologues* (would they be in German or English?). A busker playing Barney Kessel. A man who shouted 'Einbahnstrasse!' repeatedly at us as we cycled the wrong way down a one-way street. But he was only joking.

Our Street

The name of our street is Dieffenbachstrasse, named, the little sign on the lamppost tells me, after Professor Doctor Johann Friedrich Dieffenbach, 1729 to 1847, 'Chirurg', which turns out to be 'Surgeon'.

I noted all this in my book, also the information about Graefestrasse, which crosses it—Graefe was a nineteenth-century ophthalmologist. I was practising. The thing I really wanted to note down was further along, outside number 45. I noticed it one Sunday morning, coming home with the bread. It had rained and the washed air was prompting new thoughts: for a change I walked down the other side. Dieffenbachstrasse has lots of trees, it's nice to walk in, between the high faces of the buildings—apartments, mostly. In the footpath outside number 45 I saw something I had never noticed before. I say 'it', but there were five squares of bronze, each one two inches by two inches, set in among the cobblestones. On this occasion they seemed to be shining somewhat—perhaps the rain had washed them clean. They were immediately outside the doorway, where everyone from the apartment trod on them as they went in and out. There were letters punched into the yellow-gold surface. The text of the first one read, HIER WOHNTE ROLF BRANDT JG.1924 DEPORTIERT 1942 TOD IN RIGA. I had never heard of Riga until I came to Germany. Auschwitz, Bergen-Belsen, yes. 'Tod' I knew was 'dead', or, in this case, probably, 'Died'. Jews. OSKAR KAUFMANN, ANNA KAUFMANN, ILONA SALZMANN, BELLA NISSENBAUM.

For days after that I crossed the street to read those names again. I had been living in Dieffenbachstrasse for maybe a year at that point.

Sometimes it just said RIGA, no TOD. In the case of Oskar Kaufmann, who was 63 in 1942, it said RIGA and then ERMORDET. These days, politically correct Germans don't just say 'died'. It was once 'transported', then 'killed'. These days it's 'murdered'.

With my notebook I crouched over the bronze squares and took down the wording on them. It was the middle of Sunday afternoon, a lazy time, nothing happening. Footsteps approached, someone was coming from inside 45. This is what I'd been afraid of. 'Why are you focusing on Germany's terrible past? If you think it's so bad, why are you living here? That was more than fifty years ago, why can't you just forget about it? It's our history, not yours.'

In fact she didn't say anything. It was a woman, I saw the bottom of her dress and her shoes as she brushed past. There was maybe the faintest break in her stride—this stranger, couching in your doorway, noting something down—but maybe that was my imagination.

What Kind of Life Would You Like?

I'm on a bus to Tegel, Berlin's airport—a sweaty Tuesday morning. At home, looking for something to read on the journey, I opened Adam Phillips' *On Kissing, Tickling and Being Bored*, it's been kicking about the place for ages without having been actually read. A sentence from *On Being Bored* rose out of the page: 'Being bored is the complicated desire of wishing to have a desire.'

This sentence traveled on the U-bahn with me and now sits inside me on the bus. Or maybe it's the scotch I drank last night?

It doesn't pay, I find, to go asking yourself too many questions. I don't mean, live the unconsidered life. But enough questions ask themselves, you don't have to go looking for trouble.

What kind of life would you like? This little phrase coagulates from the stuff floating in my head and it really begins to stink up the morning. Just a little bit hungover, and so sweaty. I have all the wrong clothes on and feel bloated and lumpy. Plus I hate buses, you can't read and you get bumped all the time. In fact it wasn't a real question, just a clump of words, I didn't try to think of an answer. I just let it fuck me up.

But the truth is, my life on this particular day was a reasonable prospect. I was flying away to Bonn, then a high-speed drive in a hot car would deliver me to a little place called Overath, where I was to spend all day working on a script for a flash multimedia production with flash media guys and cool computer people. There will be a big lunch, mostly in German, admittedly, but there is a forest out the window to look into if I pick the right chair, followed by a flight home with my colleague Jutta. Jutta is afraid of flying and will hold my hand. I am not dying to have my hand held by Jutta, though I like her a lot, but this kind of intensity is always an interesting proposal. The script work will only last about three hours, and it's something I'm good at and like to do—making something. Then home by 7.30 latest—this surely is an acceptable prospect for a day? But there's that question this morning, all this sweaty nausea, that question mark.

At the airport I look at women's bodies for two minutes in the dirty mags section then get a grip, buy a *New Yorker* and, splashing a bit of water on my face in the toilet, suddenly cheer up.

The woman at check-in hopes that I 'have a stress-free day'.

'Unfortunately I've made other plans,' I say.

As I pass through security I realise that I've made a cock-up by getting a boarding pass for my return flight, as Jutta will have to sit next to me.

Of course, I didn't say that cutting thing to the check-in woman, that was Joan Didion, who, according to something she wrote, said it to someone who hoped she had a nice day. You can't actually say things like that to people. I can't. I just think them. This bitter little voice, I'm sure it's harmful, but it's such good company.

Then on the plane I sit in 10A instead of 9A and fuck everything up.

This is so unlike me that I suddenly think, This might be a different kind of day, and once again I'm cheered up.

I love the *New Yorker*. Its paper is just right, stiff enough not to crease but it lets you roll the pages you're not reading under, so it's nice to hold in your hand. I know it's a middlebrow mag. I am middlebrow.

I love the puffy clouds, blinkingly white, out the little windows with the rounded-off corners. We're descending, it's always the nicest bit of a flight—the plane slides, there's less noise. The cloudscape and the blue of the horizon make me think back to being near the sea in New Zealand and I have a rare twinge of homesickness. This *is* a different day. You never see the horizon in Berlin, everything is close up.

59

I read about theatre in New York, the latest American movies, some poems, some book reviews. A prize you sometimes find in the *New Yorker* is the latest story by Alice Munro. This changes your journey—but not today. I settle for the confession of a Mafia hit man.

In Overath the studio is large, high-ceilinged, an anything space, no shape to it, equipment just plonked around. Semi-dark—screens glow, faces shine by their light. We sit round a table with a statuette of Lara Croft on it. Overhead a gigantic woman made of papier-mâché, two stories high, looms, the leftover from some promotional activity—not to put too fine a point on it, we're sitting under her crotch. A boys' outfit, this. Jutta is the only woman and everyone directs all their talk to me. Of course I've had years of training so I make sure Jutta gets heard but it's a struggle. We have little conferences so I can say what she thinks. Of course, this only makes it seem even more as though it's me who has all the ideas.

Everyone smokes. On the stage above and behind us, great images revolve slowly, pale but astonishingly convincing. The Jewish quarter of the mediaeval city of Worms can be explored by the eye and the imagination.

At lunch Jutta suggests that I have Pfifferlinge, which are a seasonal mushroom. She says, 'You mustn't eat too many, they are from the East, too close to Chernobyl.' They come in a 'noodle nest' and look like wood shavings. The taste is roughly the same, but it's a new thing.

I got the right table, I can see into the dark of the forest. They argue in German, first about copyright, then about educational politics. Every now and then someone says, 'We are arguing about politics.'

Everyone smokes.

Actually, Jutta doesn't smoke. Me either. It's a relief to get away and start the journey home, but we're both tense as we both know that the flight is ahead of us. In the lounge, Jutta uses a pipette to drop some pacifying medicine onto her tongue.

On the plane, buckled in, I start talking. I have talked to Jutta over lunch, in trains, taxis, we always have a lot to say to each other—we swap emails. But suddenly I just can't think of anything interesting. I'm scared I'm going to say something like, 'Well, I was born in a little town called Pahiatua . . .' and just make a tit of myself. But eventually I manage to find a question for her to answer.

I've pulled down the shades over the two windows near us—regretfully—I wanted to see the horizon again. But as we go through the pre-flight procedures she gets tense and there's no choice.

The take-off. She is rigid in her seat. Her hand has hold of mine so tightly that all my fingers are squeezed. She is answering my questions about her studies—Jutta is very learned, she's the one supplying the history for the Worms programme. It was her idea. Jutta is brainy and ambitious. But she's not able to front very well—she doesn't speak up in meetings. This is my role. Plus I toss in the odd idea too, and have a sense of how the script should run. We came up with the first draft in the back of a speeding van, one day when it looked like the boys might develop a script of their own. Twenty minutes, tops. It's a good script.

Even when she's talking, even with both hands clenched tightly, one on my hand, the other on the armrest, right in the middle of that she is suddenly struck by additional jolts of what I can only call pain. As though she's receiving electric currents. Jolt after jolt. Through all this she answers my questions and, halfway through the flight, settles a little.

We talk. She orders a tomato juice. Then a mild tremor passes through the plane, some routine turbulence, and she is gripped again.

'How long does it take to pass?' I ask her. 'When d'you start feeling better?'

We're on the bus now, rumbling down the K'damm. It's early evening, the footpaths are crowded, people are at tables, drinking and watching everyone else. I like the K'damm.

'It gets better when the pilot stops braking, and better when the plane come to a halt, then it gets better in stages,' she says, 'and after about an hour I'm over it.' She grins. Brainy, brave woman sitting next to me on a bus in Germany.

Then I'm on the U-bahn, alone and on the way home. I get out the *New Yorker* and don't give the day another thought.

Tyre Tracks

Every weekday morning at about 7am I go down the back stairs, quietly so as to not wake anyone, and, in the grey Berlin light of our walled-in courtyard, unlock my bike and cycle off to work.

Every day the same old way.

Outside my door the patrons of the bar called Ohne Ende (Without End—and they mean it) are laughing, red-eyed and drunk in the quiet morning. At the Turkish supermarket the Turkish man with the big droopy moustache is accepting a wet kiss from the fat-legged boy with Down's Syndrome as he sets out his trays of fruit, so brightly coloured. I love the way he is tolerant of this boy, who is not his son—not even Turkish, I'd say. In the early dawn I hear the boy bellowing like a cow that has lost its calf, a mournful old sound that takes me back to boyhood stays on farms in the misty hills of the northern Wairarapa—waking in strange beds. Where does he live? Why does he bellow?

Down to the canal, a dark water that never looks inviting. White swans glide on its dead surface and you want to say, You'll get dirty! Alongside the canal the gravel path crunches under my tyres. In winter, snow lay here thickly and tyre tracks froze into ridges that you either had to stay in or be thrown off—tricky. The snow crackled and crunched, it was the most pleasing sound, and I enjoyed the challenge of keeping my balance in that sharp, chill air. At this time the canal was iced over—the swans stood on it and you thought, Your webbed feet will be frozen solid! Then the seasons swung. In the summer heat the patients from the nearby Krankenhaus—krank is the most wonderful word for sick— all come out to sunbathe, in their underwear, one bandaged foot up in a sling, accompanied by their drips, heads capped in yards of white wrapping—leaning back, eyes shut, to cop some rays. It's a bizarre sight, but probably quite healthy. They are all smoking up large of course.

At the end of the canal path there is a little hill tunnelled in by trees and as I grind up here each day I meet a slim, long-haired jogger who, in all but the worst weather, wears skimpy shorts. She thinks she's pretty, you can tell by a certain expression, by the way she holds herself, and she thinks she's in danger of being raped. I always cycle quickly away from her. I don't want to be part of her fear. I find it hard to understand why she would wear those shorts, hold herself in that particular way, if she is so much afraid—hard to understand without a spiral of thoughts (was she raped once? Women do get raped, there are lots of dark bushes here, she has a right to wear skimpy if she wishes, but does she have to be in the same place at the same time every day? . . .) that I simply can't be bothered with, and I cycle away.

I admire her for running in all weathers.

Over the hump of bridge, there is a second canal stretch and here I look out for a man who has been spending nights for most of the summer in a sleeping bag on one of the benches. I can't imagine his life. Does he hang round the cafés all day? If it's not raining it would be a nice place to sleep—the canal flowing beside you.

Bench seats line the canal, each one separated from the next by a tree, and in the late afternoon as you cycle along here, if it's sunny, each bench is occupied by a single person. Germans. They have a thing about nature, and so they sit here, each in possession of their own bench, head slightly tilted back, eyes closed, face lifted to the sun. Being in nature. Something about this makes me groan. Nature is fine, in the same way that TV is fine, and children are fine. These things are just there, we respect them, enjoy them—when they're not driving us nuts. But this worship. What it makes you think is, Germans. They feel that as a people they are ruined, that their culture and character once led them to evil, and the only thing left that is pure is nature, nature without thought, wordless nature, that has no sin. If only they could be just natural again . . . Myself, I like a tree. I love the colour the new green leaves cast in spring. But I like a good book better. Pass the chainsaw.

Across the main road, under the U-bahn line—often the traffic is very polite here. Even in the morning rush, drivers will slow and wave you across. If you have children with you they frequently come to an actual halt, holding up other cars, so that you can safely make your way. This is the best of Germany—a warm respect.

Yes, it's a divided country, and every morning I go out

into it and ride over the same tyre tracks and meet the same things and have new divided thoughts about them. This ride is one of the few open spots in my day, when I can let my thoughts just wander, and as I go into the building where I work I am often dazed, as though I have too soon been forced to focus on the business of making a living.

Zu Lang

My German is pretty shocking, I really only know odd words. Under pressure I can construct a sentence though if you were on the receiving end I'm sure it would be like hearing some ESL beginner: 'You are having a thing of your body that is big swolled.'

A word that you have to recognise but not say, like an U-bahn station, you develop a transliteration for, and then it's hard to unlearn. For ages I talked about Knees Up Strasse because I couldn't get Gneisenaustrasse. The voice-over which tells you to mind your back, the doors are closing says 'Philip Liner Bitter,' a Radio NZ brand of beer.

But bits of language jump tracks and play in your head and these are the worst. At work I'm proofing exhibition texts, some of which are too long for the template, so the typesetter prints on the side of the proof, *Zu lang*. I kind of liked this phrase, it sounded like a good thing to me, it was like cocaine, once I had it I couldn't get enough of it, I just said it over and over. *Zu lang, zu lang, zu lang.* It took about an afternoon for me to get there, but finally I made it to the chorus. 'He's So Fine'—The Chiffons, about 1962 I would say. We have long echoey corridors here and so you can see me in them as I go now about my day, helpless, lips moving, nodding to those I pass—there goes that dopey Kiwi.

He's so fine, zu lang, zu lang, zu lang,
And you know that he's mine, zu lang, zu lang, zu lang—
what the fuck is the next verse?

But I have given directions to Germans, they stop you in the street and ask, 'Wo ist der Lindenstrasse?'

And you say, 'Das ist der Lindenstrasse.'

And you are so proud (so proud, so proud) and so you say 'Auf Wiedersehen' without the 'pet'.

Mvsevm

Inside the museum
Infinity goes up on trial.

Bob Dylan wrote that, it's from a song called 'Visions of Johanna' that came out in I think 1967. I am of that age when it's possible to recite large hunks of old pop songs without apparent effort. Any given subject, there's a lyric for it. Pop told me what love was like, what a kiss was like, a million times over, before I ever had a kiss. But this is just the way of the world for someone like me who is so much more comfortable experiencing life once removed. Reading also—I have tried, and failed, to think of an experience I have had that I haven't previously read about in a novel. Grappa—I read what it tasted like, aged eleven, in *For Whom the Bell Tolls.*

Making a museum is a little like that. The subject is always at a remove—something you've read about. Working on Te Papa, a museum that had the subtitle 'the Museum of New Zealand', I struggled as I worked each day to see that big picture of New Zealand—that accurate reflection of a whole culture that we were making. Mostly I was in meetings about whether this door would open inwards or outwards.

A museum project is so intense that you can't stand back. You're deep in the flux of it every day, pushing to meet deadlines, trying to get good work out of a colleague you think is a drongo.

You do your little tasks with a kind of historical fervour. Infinity goes up on trial.

And all the time rhetoric floats above you like the air force of an invading army—large, dark statements that you can only cower from. 'This will be New Zealand's premier cultural institution.' You read the press releases on the internal email. In the auditorium, in the company of the museum's staff, I listened to Te Papa's Chief Executive passionately say things she had said a thousand times before. 'It will touch the lives of every New Zealander.' At parties people (sceptics) said to me, 'I hear Te Papa is so PC that the Pakeha people are second-class citizens.' No—fuck off. A slogan from Marketing came through for polishing—'If you haven't seen Te Papa, you haven't seen New Zealand.' Really? Maybe. Might be true. But it paid to keep your head down.

However I mustn't pretend I was uninvolved. I wrote some of those statements.

I live in Germany at a remove. There's the language gap—I just can't understand. You tell yourself that lately you're picking up more. You say, 'Yeah, I actually understand a lot, if I concentrate. If I know what the subject is, I can follow.' And it's nearly true. I often surprise them, in meetings here, by suddenly commenting on something they thought I had missed. But this comes more from watching. I have never watched so hard in my life. How did that guy work the price-sticker machine in the vegetable section? How do you get from the U-bahn to the S-bahn? Follow everyone else. In my first month here I was asked to participate in job interviews. They were all done in German, except for one question from 'our Kiwi colleague'. I was surprised how well you could judge people just by looking hard at them. And, I have to say, my instincts about the candidates were good. Regina Wildt, I stated clearly for the record that she was drek.

The thing about language is, it's everywhere. If you can't read German you can't read the magazines, you can't read the papers, you can't follow the TV. You haven't got a clue what's going on. Maybe Kreuzberg has declared war on Mitte—I wouldn't know. It gets to you. I pass colleagues in the corridor and they're speaking German to each other. You want to say, 'Why don't you speak English? You were doing it in the meeting we just had.' On the U-bahn, one day I glanced up and they were all doing it—every single one of them was speaking German. They were doing it on purpose. None of them was struggling with the grammar. They were behaving as though it was just, you know, a natural thing to do—that anyone can do. Christ, even their bloody kids were doing it.

It really gets to you.

I have my little routes through the city, where I know the way, where I have coped before and therefore will cope again. I live inside a bubble of coping. Then one morning, biking in, I tried to accelerate away from the lights and my chain broke. I went over the handlebars and smacked headfirst into the hard black asphalt. Cars slammed on their brakes so as to not run me over. Everyone looked. (I think there is a special alarm here, when something happens. I think their history has made them anxious about events.) As I lay there, bruised, a clear thought came into my mind: 'You've broken through the bubble. Now you're really in Germany.' I saw myself trying to cope with the German medical system, explaining in sign language how my arm was broken, see, here, and could they fix it, I have insurance. It was a realisation that seemed as hard as the road my cheek was lying on. In fact the arm was only bruised. I got up and limped away.

Alles okay. Danke.

Most of the time I keep everything at a safe distance.

I didn't know a lot about the Holocaust. *Schindler's Ark*, I reviewed that when it won the Booker. I saw *Schindler's List*. Six million—this is not a number anyone thinks refers to a Lotto prize. They made them into lampshades, my dad told me that, when I was a kid growing up in dreariest Lower Hutt in the early 1960s. I remember him reading *The Rise and Fall of the Third Reich* by William L. Shirer, a great fat paperback which lay on top of his bedside tallboy for months, its bookmark sinking slowly through the pages. I'd seen the photographs of the camps taken by Lee Miller. One year I went weekly to a season of Contemporary Films From Germany at the Goethe-Institut in Wellington, and there was a theme, or the visible absence of that theme. As it happened, our immediate neighbours in Lower Hutt were Jews. I have found myself trotting this fact out to interviewers here—it's amazing how some miscellaneous bit of your past suddenly comes in handy. There were everyday references: 'He's a real little Hitler', 'You fucking Nazi', 'Belsen Was A Gas'—that was a Sex Pistols' song.

The Sex Pistols—such a great name. I love the names of things, never mind the quality. The Dead Kennedys (great name) made a record called 'Too Drunk To Fuck'—now that's language with its sleeves rolled up. *The Smoker You Drink the Player You Get* was the title of an album by Joe Walsh. 'Jesus, I Was Evil'—some New Zealand kid made a record called that before he died. It lives on. The Bob Dylan album called *Blonde on Blonde*, I still daydream about living inside that title. Pink Floyd, this is just the name of another corporation these days, but when I first heard it, I guess in 1965, I thought, that is the kind of thing that will change the world. *Third Stone from the Sun*. Captain Beefheart and the Magic Band. 'Strawberry Fields Forever'—these weren't just three words, these were things that glowed softly, like the nightlight which keeps the children from having bad dreams, like the warm red heart inside the Madonna.

Shrimp boats is a comin', their sails are in sight . . .

It's not just individual words, it's two words working together, they make your brain go round. Language, it's what I swim in, it's what is on everything, it's what holds everything, it's what makes everything sing—and here I can't understand it.

Old words play in my head all the time, carrying me far away.

Of course this is not a Holocaust museum—all our press releases stress that. The subject of the museum is, 'Two millennia of German Jewish history.' (I wrote that.) 'Jews probably entered ancient Germania with the Roman legions. The exhibitions follow the story of a people, the Jews, living among their neighbours—their way of life, their privations and their achievements. Their slow and obstacle-strewn path toward acceptance and citizenship is examined. Finally comes the decimation of the Holocaust and, in the postwar period, the slow re-growth of a small Jewish community within the German nation.' Ken Gorbey wrote that (I polished it a bit). It was Ken who brought me here from New Zealand.

Every day I work on making the museum of German Jewish history. I run meetings on how the museum will be made. I review a piece of exhibitry that I proposed, then planned, then developed, then saw through design, that right now is being built. 'Looks okay,' I say thoughtfully. I write exhibition text. 'Glikl bas Judah Leib, also known as Glückel von Hameln, was born in Hamburg in 1646 or 1647. Her Memoirs are the oldest surviving autobiography of a Jewish woman of the Early Modern period of history—from about 1500. Almost no other written record of a woman from the seventeenth century has survived.' Kiwi magic. I manage debates about whether we will call her Glikl or Glikl bas Judah Leib or Glückel von Hameln, which is how she is known popularly, but incorrectly, according to some scholars, especially one, who sits on our Academic Advisory Board and will therefore be listened to. These debates are fierce and sometimes in the corridors after my email which closes the subject there are no-speaks. The colleagues care desperately. It's inconvenient, it drags things out, but I like them for it.

But do I care? I try hard to be a good manager, to run the debate properly, to draw it to a correct conclusion. To close the subject out—we have deadlines to meet. But, apart from a general desire to be professional and give good value for money, do I care? The whole thing is very hard to see, you have your head down, you're working on just a particular bit—should we say Shabbetaj Zvi or Sabbatai Zewi? (He was a false messiah.) I think my distance is an asset. I say this over and over again to interviewers when they ask, 'So has it been a problem that you're not Jewish and not German?' I always say, 'The staff here are for very good reasons highly anxious about making a representation of this troubled history. I think they value it that Ken and I are a bit dispassionate, that we can provide objectivity—we say, "That's important, that's not", and this is valuable to them.' And I believe this, up to a point—as much as you believe anything you say to a

71

reporter who is looking at you with his pen poised over the page of his notebook.

And then I give a tour of the building and suddenly I am desperate for people to understand.

Friday Night Dinner

Gnocchi out of the packet, fresh beans, mince with some kind of tomato stuff and parmesan. Very nice. As a gesture I have kept my shirt on, it's not quite as hot as it's been. The kids and I are sitting at our places while Susanna dishes up. She's a little tired—the gynaecologist says she's still short of iron. Kate, recently turned seven, touches something on her plate, a bean, holds it and says, 'How do I know if it's hot or cold?'

This seems to be a fact question—Susanna looks at me. I say, 'What do you mean, darling? D'you mean, when you're holding it?'

'Yes.'

But I'm not sure if this is really what she meant. These questions of Kate's, you have to be careful, the pictures she has in her head seem vague to me, you have to make sure you answer what she was actually asking.

But we go with the fingers. I pick up the salt shaker and say, 'Here in your fingertip there are nerves—'

'What's nerves?'

'They're like . . . wires, inside there, right down to the tips, they go back up your arm and into your brain, and in your brain—' I draw a circle in the air beside my ear for, you know, the brain, '—and that's where you register that it's hot or cold.' Phew, not a very good explanation.

Kate is studying her inner forearm. Her arms are so skinny

72

and so white. The delicacy of children is terrifying, and yet they're as strong as hell, when you fight with them on the bed their little grip is fierce. 'Like veins?' she says.

'Yes, just like veins, only skinnier—really tiny, going right down to the tips of your fingers.'

'Skinnier than veins!' Kate I am sure has no idea how skinny a vein is, but she's enjoying this idea. She continues to stare at her arm. Then the subject seems to pass and suddenly she's eating.

Susanna is sitting down now. But we haven't made a lot of progress when Kate looks up from her plate and says, 'But who made God?'

Hmmm. This is something of a conversation-stopper, but when she asks these big questions Kate has a little shiver about her, as though she has a fever—she doesn't always need an answer to keep going. She looks into middle air—her fork loaded with broccoli—and, exploring, says, 'What I don't get is which God made God.'

'Susanna?' I say. I try to keep a note of something out of my voice. It can't be triumph. I mean, here the kid is asking about God, that He would even be on Kate's menu has to regarded as a win for the Catholic team. I suppose I am saying, Now Susanna do your stuff. But there is something. I guess I am also saying, Now you're on the spot. Now you have to explain what you believe, let's hear it.

'When there was no God,' says Kate, 'what was there?'

'He's always been there,' says Susanna.

'But who made him?'

'He's always been there.'

'Before there was the world, what was there?'

Andrew-Jack is, unusually, observing all this in silence. Andrew-Jack is five. It is hell to get him to eat anything but Kate in high inquisitorial mode has him fascinated. He even puts a forkful into his mouth. Tonight, he's next to me. Usually they're swapped over, Susanna is his favourite, he sits next to her and pretends he's going to eat if she gives him her total attention.

'That's what I don't get,' Kate says. I love her for using this phrase, it seems so adult. 'Before the world was here, where did all the people go? Before. Before it started.' She is looking towards the long window now, to the early evening light.

The subject seems to have shifted—this could be called science—and Susanna doesn't seem to want to say anything. I gather myself to launch the Discovery Channel—what? I guess I will have to have a go at the Big Bang—not my specialist field—but I have to be sure that I'm not taking over from Religious Topics before they've had a fair go. But Susanna doesn't seem to be interested in answering these questions.

Before anyone can answer her Kate says, 'I really like these beans.'

'I don't!' says Andrew-Jack.

'I do!'

'I don't!' says Andrew-Jack. 'I'm finished!' And he gets down. He roams around in the background, looking for something to be interested in. He hasn't eaten much. Susanna tells him he has to eat the broccoli if he wants to get down and I back her up. I spear a piece of broccoli on his fork and wait. Andrew-Jack is starting to run in little circles. We have the big patterned carpet spread in this kitchen room at present and he's zooming on it, making engine noises. I catch his eye, get him going on a run towards me—he will open his mouth and the broccoli will be manoeuvred in. But Susanna intervenes—mushes his food, gets a mix onto a spoon, broccoli, gnocchi, mince, and feeds him.

This kind of annoys me. I was going to do that.

But, no need to end the world over it. I drink my beer, have a moody little moment, think about what a great guy I am to put up with this in good fashion then forget about it.

Andrew-Jack returns to the table with a sheet of stickers. They're horrible things, cartoon characters off the kids' channel, probably from the Two Dollar Shop. (Strange that they don't say Two Deutschmark. But they use English in such a strange way.) 'Dadda, would you like one of my stickers?'

I try not to choose the big one in the middle, that's probably his special one, I look for a little one on the side that he won't mind me having.

'Don't you want this big one?' he says.

'You keep that one, Jackie.'

'Okay, Dadda.' But somehow he's disappointed, he wanted to give me the big one.

When I'm doing the dishes he arrives with a letter from his Post Office Manager set. I have to take off my rubber gloves, receive it properly, say, 'Thank you, Postie.' Tonight it's okay if I see him and speak to him, apparently. Off he goes.

Kate and Susanna are in the other room, putting photos into the albums. We have heaps of photos of the kids. Susanna takes them. It never occurs to me—what do you need photos for? Then if I look through them they're just wonderful. When I got home, earlier, and everyone was out, there were the albums out on the table so I got a first beer and had a look through them. The photographs capture the kids in time—which is so strange, because it's a different time, some old time, and the kids seem to live so strongly in the present. They're right there beside you, just utterly themselves, and they fill the whole of the room up. Then you look at the pictures and you see how all the time they're growing and changing.

I guess I must love my kids.

It's such a strange thing. If a reporter asked you, well, what else would you say? But I never feel I love them enough to claim it. I always feel that I'm selfish—I *am* selfish—and so wrapped up in what I'm doing that I simply can't have room in me to be adequately loving them. Susanna suggests this. She says I don't spend enough time with them. I don't want to go over that here, terrible old dialogues that make you want to cut your throat. But this is something that writing this strange diary, if that's what it is, this account, is showing me—how much I think about them, how much I do care about them. Maybe I do love them enough?

Andrew-Jack brings me more letters—hieroglyphic squiggles. 'What does this one say, Andrew-Jack?'

'This one says that you have to go and join the soldiers. The soldiers need help, they've run out of water, they've all got cups, but the rain, the rain, the rain—' he gets stuck and he just repeats the last word until he's ready, '—the rain, it isn't there and so you have to go and join them.'

Where the hell did all that come from?

'Okay, Andrew-Jack,' I say.

'Okay, Dadda.' And off he goes to write me another letter.

Iron

She's short of iron—the doctor says so. This was also true when she was carrying both Kate and Andrew-Jack, so no surprise, but it has a big effect on her. She seems tired and anaemic. The doctor has given her pills but they have to be taken an hour before eating.

As usual, I wake early. Just before I leave the house for work I tiptoe back to the bedrooms. Kate is sleeping on a mattress on our floor. At 1am she had woken with dreams and then developed a bleeding nose. Is it the heat? She's had a few, so has Andrew-Jack.

Back in the night: on this occasion Kate gets worked up, the blood is coming thickly, and when a large clot drops onto her ankle she gets hysterical. It's 1am, dark, we have the lights low, whispering, hoping to get back to sleep—it's hard to be civil if someone starts shouting when you feel sleepy, but increasingly these days Kate is quick to get shouty. Maybe it's because we're far from home? Susanna is coping, I am the gofer—toilet paper, bowls, cold facecloths. Then, standing over the sink, I remember that as a kid I had a season of bloody noses—when we lived in rural Wairarapa. I remember that feeling, the taste of blood in your throat, the sense that there is a construction of dried paper, fragile, up inside your nostrils—a bump or a change in temperature and suddenly your inner life is redly flowing out into the air. Matahiwi, or was it Kiriwhakapapa, one time someone put a key down my back; I can still remember the sharp cold of this. What help could it possibly be, really—surely it's an old wives' tale? But I have an idea that Kate will like it; I fetch the large silver key for our keller and put it down the back of her teeshirt. And, sure enough: she starts laughing.

Susanna gets her to lie down, and soon all the lights are out.

Andrew-Jack, in the kids' room, sleeps through all this. I see him in the morning, as I tiptoe past the door, blankets and pillows all kicked off, alone in the middle of the large blue rectangle of sheet, his knees drawn up. The back of his head towards me. The particular colour and texture of his hair that will never accurately be painted; that will never be anyone else's.

Kate is still there on our floor and so, going in, I tiptoe with the pill and a glass of water. Susanna is sound. She's on her side, facing away from the watery light falling from the tall windows. Her arm is exposed—it's going to be another hot day. But the skin of the arm looks pale. Should I wake her? As I come near her hand reaches out—is this a sleep movement or does she know I'm there? I offer the pill and she takes it roughly. She gropes for the water. Then she's back under again.

Phone Home Berlin

It was a desultory weekend. Susanna had the idea on Saturday that she might take the kids on a bus ride, simply to get them out of the house. I was at work, she rang me. 'You'll hate it,' she said. 'You just come home, we won't be here.'

Oooh, so tempting. I love mooning around the house by myself. A bit of reading, a bit of surfing, an investigation of the cupboards and refrigerator. I get my away-thrills at work. But I feel guilty. I'm the dad. I should join them.

'But you'll hate it.'

'Where are you going?'

'Nowhere,' she says. 'You hate that.'

'No, I won't,' I say, full of good resolution. 'I'm coming.'

I cycle madly home, leaving some work undone—this feels virtuous. I am a family man doing his duty.

Unfortunately it is in fact true that I hate buses, especially the double-decker ones where, upstairs, the ceiling is so low. On Lindenstrasse we climb to the upper floor and try to get the front seats where you have the good view but these are already taken—it's the kind of muggy, grey Saturday when all kinds of people, apparently, think a bus ride will be a good idea. (Can this be true? Really? It's unimaginable. But here is the evidence—the bus is packed.) We wind through the narrow, tall-sided streets of Kreuzberg, looking down at the dirty footpaths. People are hurrying home with their shopping in case it rains. Kreuzberg is not a glamour suburb, these are people in wretched jeans, in cheap sneakers and exhausted shoes. No one will ever make a documentary about these people, they are neither rich nor poor enough. The tall bus brushes aside the branches of trees, manoeuvres its bulk through the slot that the street makes between the apartments. What is there to look at? Kate already has her head on my knee, is lying half across me. I stroke the back of her neck, softly say nice things to her. 'My beautiful one.' She likes this. However, my feeling of virtue has evaporated. Now I am trying not to get grumpy. We shouldn't be here, it's all Susanna's fault—but I mustn't go that way. I look at the names of the shops. Such mean little frontages, with crappy signwriting. *Spiel! Spiel! Spiel!* Is there anyone in there, mid-afternoon, gambling? *Schuhmachermeister.* I figure that he's a shoe repairer. He would be a Master—that is so German. Above one doorway I see English words: *Phone Home Berlin.* That's the name of the business. They claim to have the *Cheapest Telephone Rates in the City.* There are booths inside but no one is in them. The grimness of that, ringing your distant family from a dim booth inside a hot, sweaty box of light in darkest Kreuzberg.

Andrew-Jack is working his way through everything to eat in the backpack.

Two hours of this and I am fit to be tied. But I mustn't show it. This is me trying to be a family man.

The heat of the bus is soporific and we get off to avoid

falling asleep. It's a huge relief, but now we're on a sidewalk in Mitte and what next? If we'd stayed on board we would have been home in ten minutes. We straggle down a side street, Susanna knows the way, dragging the kids. It's such a grim fact, how having children is simply the world's most extraordinary and rewarding experience and yet so much of the time you are in the company of these foot-dragging, complaining, bored, embarrassing, resisting, reluctant, dulled *little bastards*. There are no redeeming moments with them on this trip, neither of them says anything that makes me wish I had a notebook. Plus it starts now to rain.

In the Studio

Jutta and I record the voice-overs for the script we've written for the multimedia presentation of the mediaeval city of Worms. In German. Jutta's Research Assistant, Kathrin Zinkmann, is in the studio to help us—she has some experience in recording voices. Jutta has none and I have almost none.

There is a long-haired recording engineer, Thomas—all recording engineers have long black hair tied in a pony tail— and the two voices, Petra, a slim, bright theatre person, and Deiter, who brings a dog which lies on the floor and sighs, and he can't start work until he has told us what is wrong with the script and with our film and with theatre today. He is tall and has a large belly, late fifties, and wears terrible old shorts with short socks so that his long white legs are these poles you have to see. The legs have dark marks, bruises maybe, or healing sores of some sort, down around his calves and I find it completely unacceptable that he should display them to us, especially in the studio, which is tiny.

All business is in German.

I watch the dials, follow the tangled wires, watch the screens—there are six different screens, one of them with squares of dark red in which black verticals indicate the voice print. This is interesting, sort of. I try to listen to the voices. They seem fine to me, neither too colourful nor too flat. Good. But I can't follow. I am there maybe five hours. I think about what my role is.

I'm here to support Jutta. She has to be in charge, it is she who knows what Worms was like in the ninth century. Also, she has a good instinct for how to present it. What she lacks is confidence, authority. So that is my role. I am here to whisper in Jutta's ear, 'Tell them what you think.'

Kathrin also knows what she's doing, Thomas seems intelligent, the voices are good—after a while Deiter forgets that he has to be the biggest and gets on with the job. We play our film on a monitor and fit the voices to it. The voices are in a tiny booth, we see them through the window. 'They're actors,' I whisper to Jutta, 'doesn't matter how good they look, they're insecure—you have to tell them they're good very enthusiastically.' Does she need to be told this? For one second I thought so and so I offered it. But there is nothing wrong with Jutta's brain.

I find the most removed corner I can find and try not to snore too loudly.

In this way the museum gets made.

The American Way

I am also proofing the exhibition text, which arrives hourly by courier. There are many changes. Partly this is because the German typesetter has hyphenated all the English words in strange places, ho-uses, blo-oms.

But most of the changes are being made at the request of our leader, W. Michael Blumenthal, who is the chief executive of the Jewish Museum. He is an American and has insisted that in the text we change 'nappies' to 'diapers', 'aluminium' to 'aluminum', that we delete 'allotment' and say 'garden'. 'No one knows "allotment", I've never heard of an allotment,' he growls down the phone, long-distance from Palm Springs, where he lives for two-thirds of each month. For an hour I record his predilections without argument. These days, eighteen months into the contract, I have decided not to argue with Mike Blumenthal.

He's right about 'aluminum' of course. We have agreed, not without some misgivings on my part, to use American spellings in the museum. He pushed hard for this, seeing the American way as the right way, the only way. I accept that lots of American Jews will come to the museum and will feel comfortable with 'labor'—to me this just looks like a mistake, there's something inadequate about it as a word, it doesn't have the weight of the quality it is trying to describe. But the English that Germans speak has, on the whole, an American slope to it. The Americans were stationed here after the war and had a big impact. Elvis served here—the only country he ever visited. 'Have a nice day,' Germans will say to you.

And, if English is to be the world language, I can see American being the kind of English that dominates. The spellcheck on Microsoft Word tells you you can customise so that it accepts English spellings but I have never found a machine that will actually enact this command. 'Customise' still has that annoying wiggly red line under it. (It doesn't like 'wiggly' either.) Maybe this bug is a patriotic one, Bill Gates changing the world again?

Genial

I get a call from Frau Sabeck, who is Michael Blumenthal's secretary: 'Could you come and see Mr Blumenthal?'

'Now?'

'Yes, now.'

It's always now with Mike Blumenthal.

In his office, he is leaning back, relaxed. Ken is at the table, listening carefully. In my opinion Ken listens too hard when Mike Blumenthal speaks. But, just to go into a little rave here, I can't fault Ken Gorbey. He has picked up this contraption of an organisation and, in just seventeen months, made a major museum of it. He's been blocked by the power-hugging administration, by turfy staff, by German-ness (I will come to German-ness), by the museum's fucked-up history, by a shortage of budget, and etc. Through all this he has made a channel for those prepared to work on the project without reserve and, as is so often the way with these things, about ten of us have worked together and done it. It's six days to opening now, 130 hours, and we are squeezed tight—we have no room to manoeuvre, and a heap left to do. We'll need luck to make it, a few things have to go our way. The IT system, for example, is still not working. But it will. It's happening. Ken refuses to panic. He stands in the middle of an anxious gathering and makes a decision. He says, 'Storm? You call this a storm? Why, back in 1823, my, I'll tell you, we had a storm, no, this is just a bit of dodgy weather.' He pulls an extra 15,000 from a little something he has hidden under the mattress and a problem disappears. He listens to the designer tell a series of big fat whoppers with a straight face, signals that we will nod and accept the loss of a lovely design element because at this stage there is simply no point in pretending we have a choice.

I walked through the museum twice yesterday. It is really going to be wonderful—something special. Okay: sober prediction time. There will be operational problems in the Entrance area. The givens of the historic building, with an entry sequence of small, awkward spaces that can't be changed—this will cause bottlenecks. We have tried to make the best of it but basically the spaces are unworkable. Our strategy is to show this. We have a Plan B for an alternative entrance, designed and costed, but not approved—we will try and shunt this through, and open it within three months of Day One.

Also, the security will be called excessive, because it is. No exaggeration, the entrance is like a major airport at terrorist time—walk-though arches, X-ray search of all bags, pat-you-down guards. This is a fetish. Anything Jewish in Germany must be protected with fences, machine guns and bullet-proof windows against graffiti, bullets and bombs. Never mind that the last anti-Semitic bomb in Germany went off over thirty years ago. Never mind that the museum's exhibition tells you that neo-Nazis have no interest these days in Jews and instead are dedicated to beating up Muslims and people with black skin. Never mind that Ken and I smuggled a good-sized knife through the system just to show that it wouldn't actually detect all possible problems, especially plastic explosive. Never mind that it costs a bloody fortune and that despite our 'be nice' training the feedback from our visitor test day called the security staff 'aggressive' and 'gorillas'.

Just a hint there of the cultural conflicts that have been a constant feature of this project . . .

The restaurant is a disaster—the visitors will have to bring their own food or go hungry. There are not enough toilets. There aren't enough lifts and the ones we have are too slow. The museum is not very wheelchair friendly. There are not enough rest areas, or seats, or time-out spaces. There are no escape routes from the main exhibition, it's essentially a long corridor, once you've started there is no way you can leave without seeing it through to the end.

Most of these problems result from the fact that the museum's buildings were planned for a museum that would attract a fairly small number of visitors, maybe 200,000 a year, and it's obvious now that there will be a huge number. Maybe a million a year.

This week we are on the front cover of *Newsweek*.

Of course the real questions will be about the quality of the museum's presentations.

But assessing exhibitions is no simple matter. If you start with the idea that museum funding comes from taxes, and that the bulk of taxes are paid by what might loosely be called 'ordinary people'; and that most of the rest comes from gambling profits, again, mostly provided by ordinary people; and that the history the museum shows is the history made by ordinary people; and you take the universal desire of scientists, historians and politicians that ordinary people will know more about the history of their nation and think more about what their nation is and might be . . . well, it's obvious that your museum should be pitched at 'ordinary people'— right? No. Not for most critics and cultural commentators. They want to start with the idea that a museum is a quiet place, a not-very-crowded place, where people like themselves can have the aesthetic experiences which confirm their social position and educational attainments. Do I sound a little jaundiced? The reception of Te Papa amazed me. That museum made a brilliant job of achieving its goals. (Well, how should you say that? Scoring its goals?) But the critics always said, Well, those were the wrong goals. Never mind that they were set by the elected and appointed representatives. They are not my goals.

So what are your goals?

And when this question was pursued the answers were astonishingly similar. They could all be boiled down to, I don't want a crowded museum. I don't want noise. I don't want children running. (I don't want children.) I want to be spoken to in my own language, which is hieratic—that is, if I am spoken to at all—I prefer silence. No references to sport or to famous New Zealanders, please, these we are forced to endure on television. I don't care that all the things I want mean that the majority of the population won't come. That is their choice. I deserve to have the public money spent in the cultural area to be spent on culture as I define it, and if ever it isn't I must attack that occasion on every front to make sure it never happens again.

Not that Te Papa was beyond criticism or improvement, and not that it shouldn't evolve and develop. But the main thrust of the criticism seemed to me to be intent on permanently destroying all credibility for the institution, for goals that in my judgement didn't bear a lot of scrutiny, and which were frequently self-serving.

These forces will be brought to bear here. They will be expressed through the language of, 'See, this is what happens if you let foreigners make our cultural institutions.' (Blumenthal, born a German Jew, is always described as an American—which he is. Major players like architect Daniel Libeskind (Polish parents, an American, doesn't speak German), Shaike Weinberg (an Israeli, ditto), Tom Freudenheim (American, learned while he was here) are all foreigners (I said I would come to German-ness). At least those guys are all Jews. And then there's the non-Jewish, non-German, not even 'Wie gehts'-speaking Kiwis.) 'See the dumbing down. See Disneyland.' A book describing the museum's development was published nine months before opening under the title of *Jewrassic Park*. The chapter on the involvement of Ken and me was titled *Dinosaurs Roar into Life at Te Papa*. 'See the crowd, and it is the wrong crowd too.' Actually this won't be said directly, it never is. Instead it will be said through comments about the design, about the language of the labels, about the modes of presentation. But that will be the under-thrust: this type of museum attracts too many of the wrong kind of people.

However, I see that I am becoming negative, and I don't feel negative. I think critics are right to be concerned. The involvement of outsiders is always a risk. This museum will include a representation of one of civilisation's greatest failures—I think that's what Nazi Germany represents, the failure of German civilisation—and any nation would be anxious about how that is shown. The desire in this country is not that it be smoothed over. True, some people would like it forgotten. Others would like it to be 'an ice-axe to break the sea frozen inside us' (that's Kafka, writing about what a book should be). The radical strain is still strong in Germany, the desire that the Holocaust should be a wrench with which to open civilisation and force it to come out into the light. This after all is the country of Baader and Meinhof and the Red Army Faction. There is still something called The Left here.

Our research shows that the majority of Germans think they already know everything about the Holocaust and enough already. So we have tried to give a fresh approach to the Nazi years. We didn't want to glorify the Nazis. Ken commented that he's been to a few exhibitions on this period and, despite their best intentions, because of Speer's architecture, his columns and lights, because of the mass-ness of the mass rallies, because of Leni Riefenstahl's dramatic filming, because of the organisational complexity involved in successfully murdering so many people, what you come away with is a secret if grudging respect for Nazi efficiency—not a good outcome. So, instead, we concentrate on the Jewish response to the Nazi regime. Some people mutter: why did the Jews just let themselves be killed? This is a little like saying, Why didn't the blacks end apartheid by killing the white South Africans? But there was Jewish resistance and other responses and we show this. I think this will be a new angle.

But the main thing I predict is that the museum will be liked by Germans because it puts the Holocaust in context. The context is the two-thousand-year history of Jews in Germany. Some of that history isn't very nice—there were persecutions from the thirteenth century. But it is a long and complex history, full of life, success stories (Einstein, Levi Strauss), happiness, achievement and growth. This story I think will be new, a new combination of known facts, and it will make the Holocaust seem part of something that has always existed and will continue to exist, which is the Jewish presence in Germany. This will allow ordinary Germans to feel more comfortable about who they are, at the same time as it reminds them of the consequences of forgetting.

Also, the tone of the museum will be appreciated. The building that Daniel Libeskind gave us to put the museum in is full of dark emotion—constriction, confusion, anxiety. But the exhibition design has softened that and made the spaces seem what a colleague called gemütlich—comfortable, cosy. The objects are presented so that you draw close, have a personal and intimate engagement with them. The colours are warm, the shapes are pleasant. What Daniel Libeskind will think I don't know. (But I suspect he will say he's pleased, whatever. This is his first building, he will want it to have been successful in fulfilling its mission.) But visitors will thank us for giving them a trip through their history that is entertaining, challenging, informative, fresh and pleasant. They will take the museum to their hearts.

All of this is floating in the air in Michael Blumenthal's office. He has brought me here, it transpires, to formalise the offer of a contract extension. 'So how would you feel about some more money?' he says.

He thinks aloud a little. 'The main thing I'm worried about,' he says, 'is how the museum will get on without me. I won't be here forever. I have my book to write, I want to get on with the research, and, you know, I will probably drop dead at some stage—I feel pretty good at the moment. But they need someone who can guide the thing, control it. I have some people in mind.' He blows a cloud of blue smoke, looks up into it—maybe he can see the faces of his likely candidates in there.

'But I don't want to take all the credit. You, Ken, and you, Nigel—you have done very well. I'm very grateful to you. You have pulled it off. You've done exactly what I hoped. So I'm very grateful, and I want to say that to you. Also, to congratulate myself a little—some people thought I was crazy, bringing in two Kiwis who weren't Jewish and couldn't speak German. I will touch on this point in my speech. And I will mention you by name, Ken. Briefly—I don't have much time. I won't be able to mention you,' his blue eyes flick to mine, he shoots me hard, 'but you won't be there, so that won't matter. There's not time to mention everybody. But you have made a great team and I think everyone recognises that.'

Then it's over, I'm walking down the corridor. I said maybe one sentence. Tried not to nod too hard. I will, I realise, be walking down these corridors for some time to come. For a moment I'm dizzy. My world has swung—I had other plans.

During the next few hours a strange thing happens. Suddenly I find I can understand more German. People are speaking and I can follow. Not perfectly, but more than I could an hour before. Suddenly I am listening again. I am going to be staying here.

When Blumenthal's letter of agreement arrives he has raised my salary by 15,000 Deutschmarks.

Arts In Action

Saturday morning. Susanna and the kids have gone off to a lake for a couple of days so I am running the house as I like. This means radio on, TV on, internet on, while I eat my eggs and enjoy my coffee. BBC has a programme called *Arts In Action* and here as item number three I hear a description of Daniel Libeskind's extraordinary museum building, followed by a couple of errors about the date of the museum's construction and a gross exaggeration of the number of people who have already visited it. Then Ken Gorbey comes on. Ken, my lovely boss, a man keen to pour the workers a gin, the first to don a silly hat at a party, suddenly appears as a major world intellectual. I always forget this about Ken and, when I'm being interviewed in tandem with him, always get a little shock at the high level of theoretical discourse coming out of the little guy on the couch beside me. On the radio he sounds great, his thoughtful answers made distinctive by Kiwi commonsense and directness, as he deftly turns the interviewer's questions, about the way that the architectural masterpiece we have had to work with can also be used as a house, to building a museum. 'We have picked up the concept of void that Daniel handed us—his building is slashed through by empty chambers which represent the loss, if you like, to Europe of European Jewry—we have expanded that concept and, with artist Via Lewandowski, developed a "gallery of the missing", in which the notion of trauma to cultural property is explored.'

'Trauma to cultural property—can you give me an example?'

'There are many,' reports Ken confidently. 'A good one would be the Jewish Encyclopaedia, which was begun in the 1920s and worked on by Jewish scholars continuously until the Nazis seized the manuscripts and printing presses in the mid-1930s. Work was halted at the letter L—that's where they were up to—then all the scholars and their work was, where possible, shifted off-shore, and, where possible, taken up again in Israel and in America, though the encyclopaedia itself was never completed. And that knowledge, that history and culture, has never returned to Germany, which had been the centre, really, of Jewish intellectual life and thought.'

Then I am nearly at the bottom of my coffee cup when the BBC news comes on. The trailer includes the word 'New Zealand'. This word is one you simply never hear. I have never heard New Zealand mentioned on the World Service in eighteen months of living here.

There's a Norwegian ship, the *Tampa*, full of Afghani refugees, anchored off Christmas Island, north of Australia. This ship has been drifting across the news bulletins for a couple of days now. I've heard John Howard, the Australian Prime Minister, firmly rejecting all requests that the ship be allowed to land anywhere in Australia or on the Australian-controlled island, despite images of the Christmas Islanders showing signs which welcome them—one female belly features 'We want you, Afghanis' written on it in lipstick. Howard sounds like the creature he is, an ugly Australian.

And now New Zealand has shown what a great little outfit it is by agreeing, along with Nauru, to accept the refugees. I am proud. I love it when New Zealand shows its good side, which is human and welcoming. (There is another side, but I will think about that another day.)

I don't think of New Zealand often. People who live there, yes, but they are voices on the phone, they are emails. Downtown Auckland, it's not something you want to run your eye through. I think of our bach mostly, how I would like to be in an armchair there, pretending to read, watching the water and the sky.

When the All Blacks play I follow the match minute-by-minute on the web.

Walk Around

We did a walk around at two with Blumenthal. Assembled in the underground Axis of Holocaust were:
—Doreen, manager of the Opening Event
—Martina, marketing assistant
—Klaus, Head of Sponsorship
—Klaus, this is the other Klaus, who is part of the design partnership
—Cilly, who is going to be the Director when Ken leaves
—Peter, who would like to be but is in fact just head of the administration
—Ken

—me

—and himself of course. It's a bloody circus; he shows off, he asks rhetorical questions, he tries to put both Ken and me on the spot: 'Will all this be ready on time?' It's true, anyone can see, there is still tons to do, but you feel like saying to him, No, it's all going to be just like this, shit and dirt everywhere, a bloody shambles. What exactly does he think we're going to do, get in there with skilsaws and make it happen? We are in the hands of the designers now. In my judgement they're under pressure, but look likely to make it. Tired faces everywhere, and then there's rubberneckers, like us, bright-eyed, excited by what we see—but we're in the way.

We do a practice tour, a real whip through, 45 minutes, but we all agree, on the night it will take longer. The Chancellor, Gerhard Schröder, is said to be a human being. A month ago after some dumb engagement he declared loudly, 'If I don't get a beer right now I am going to resign.' This phrase was caught on tape, mixed against a funky soundtrack by some smart kid and now it's number one—and Schröder loves it. The people's politican? I couldn't say. But he will stop, ask questions and be interested. An hour and a quarter, I'd say.

But at the official opening he won't be allowed to speak. The only speakers are Johannes Rau, who is the President, and Blumenthal. The impression is, Blumenthal doesn't want anyone to steal his limelight. And this is reinforced when he suddenly spins in a corridor (for an old man he can spin very well) and barks at Doreen, 'And the President will speak for ten minutes, right?' She nods. 'And I will speak for twenty.' This is said very aggressively. 'On this one occasion I am allowed to speak for twice as long as the President of Germany. And I am going to do that.' He glares around as though one of us might stop him.

It's Over

Kate said, 'Daddy hasn't been very nice to live with for the last two weeks.' Apparently she said this to Isobel, our neighbour downstairs. So Susanna told me. But this was told during an outbreak of 'my life is worse than yours' and maybe this verdict wasn't as final as the retelling made it sound. I hope not. It isn't so good, having your kids think that clearly enough to bring it to speech.

I have been stressed. Climbing the walls, actually. Looking back now, I see that the whole project has been pressured. Seventeen months simply isn't enough time to make a major international institution of this kind, especially given the bitter divisions between the museum's various sectors, the poor state of the collection and archive, the lack of preparatory work, the shortness of budget and the difficulty of the subject. Despite that, we made it. With each week that passed the pressure mounted, and the last three months, when the task of building the design became intense, were particularly demanding. Then, with two weeks to go, that pressure rose. Big pieces were failing to fall together at precisely the time that Blumenthal was orchestrating his final push to make the opening the biggest thing on the planet. The Prime Minister of Hungary is coming! The mayor of Shanghai! There will be eight TV crews. Eleven. Fourteen. Twenty-three!

It was the last six hours which really did for me.

Then it was over. The next morning, Monday, I was dragged into a press conference in the Hebbel Theatre in Stresemannstrasse. We had a coffee first with Daniel Libeskind, who was marvellously gracious about the exhibition, then staggered in to do our stuff. It was a lovely old venue, with dark panelled wood, dim lighting—when you glanced up, there were pale faces looming from the gods. Maybe 400 journalists, from all media, not bad considering this was the B Team press conference—the A Team of 100 top journos had had their turn the day before.

We were tired. Ken looked grey. People kept telling me that soon I would able to go home and rest. In the doorway crowd, Blumenthal filed past—he paused. 'Hello, Nigel.' In the crush we shook hands, his dry old man's hand in mine. 'Congratulations,' he said, 'it looks great,' patted me on the shoulder, and moved on.

It's strange, aged fifty, to be so happy about this kind of thing; you feel you should have outgrown it.

On the stage there was a real line-up—Inka from Collections, a translator, Libeskind, Hanna to translate for Ken, Ken himself, Blumenthal, Eva from PR, Peter, Cilly, Thomas. Just names to you but I had battled with, laughed with, worked together with all these people so intensely. Here they were, in a row, under stage lighting. Cilly looked as though she had been boiled. Ken's face was sliding earthwards. Blumenthal's eyes had saddlebags. I was pleased not to be up there—too tired to feel confident of stringing a sentence together. And the questions were hard—Will this museum really make a difference? What is the museum's stance on Israel and Zionism? Why did you decide to make the museum for families; is this really a family subject? Hand grenades, all of them, and skilfully defused by Blumenthal and Ken. And then Libeskind spoke up, saying how well the exhibition design complemented his architecture, and spoke enthusiastically of the wonderful spirit of the exhibition. This more or less ended proceedings. The questions kept coming. How much do you have on Rosa Luxemburg?—this from the Communist paper. How do you summarise the relationship, in the past, in the present, and in the future, between Jews and Germans?—this in English from the Voice of America. It made the audience groan. Blumenthal rolled his eyes, declared it an impossible question, said that no one could answer such a question, not in the time available, and then proceeded to answer it. But there was no sting. There had been no controversy. Libeskind was not going to say his masterpiece had been ruined. Suddenly, everyone hurried out.

Tuesday morning, I'm at home, typing this up. Ken and I had agreed we would sleep late. Susanna has taken Kate off on the U-bahn to school, in the next room Andrew-Jack is sleeping, I will stay here until she gets back.

Then he appears, heavy with sleep, and climbs up onto my chair. Maybe he really was heavy? Whatever: the chair instantly collapses.

As we are falling—it's not far from a chair to the floor—I have the conscious thought that it is my job to get my body between his and the floorboards, and I do manage somewhat to twist his head and body away. This is a scene I have rehearsed ten thousand times. Usually Susanna is driving, a car swerves towards us and I twist myself, pour myself over into the back seat, and cover his body with mine. Kate's too, of course, while at the same time managing to get my legs across Susanna's lap so as to restrain her from going through the windscreen and leaving me alone to raise the children. Or he has fallen from the fourth-floor windowsill. I am below, locking my bike, and I glance up the sheer grey concrete wall of the apartment and imagine him falling, his body in the air, him calling, 'Dadda'; imagine how I will have to get my chest under him, he'd be hell-heavy, my arms wouldn't hold him, no, it would have to be the broadness of my chest, my body would pillow him somewhat, though my chest is hard, I would have to be falling backwards as he came so as to reduce the damage of the impact. Definitely.

We dust ourselves down. 'Dadda,' he says. That's all, it's a kind of noise made so as to restore the situation. He is wide-eyed. Then he says, 'My back was hurt,' and he pulls down the waistband of his trousers, backing towards me so that I can place my kiss in the right spot.

I tell him my back hurts too, which it does, and ask him to kiss it better too, thinking he will enjoy this. But he's reluctant, I get just a faint little peck, then he looks embarrassed. It's probably that your dad is never supposed to need kissing better.

After the press conference Ken and I taxi back to the museum. Its doors are open, but not yet to the public. This is Donors' Day—the day when those who have donated family items to the museum come to see them on display. Of course, because we had such a huge struggle to open, not all of them are in place. This will, I predict, cause some grief.

Ken and I sit in his office. Desultory conversation. The things we should be doing are way too big to be started on right now. We swap stories from the night before. There's a faint awkwardness because I was in the driver's seat during the worst period while he was riding in a limousine to hear Barenboim conduct Mahler's Seventh. But both of us know this was unavoidable. He thanks me twice.

My blood pressure is slowly coming down.

We pass through the exhibition, which is buzzing with people. I really like this exhibition, better than the exhibitions we made at Te Papa; its design is better, and the subject has more depth. Of course the Libeskind building, for all its difficulty, is something special, whereas Te Papa's building just has the difficulty. In this setting, the angles of the exhibition elements, the warm tones of the large design panels, the shafts of light serve to make a warm and engaging mix. Elsewhere I have described how the designers, Würth & Winderoll, make exhibitions with clear main highways which have what you might call roadside attractions, a sequence of personal spaces where you are invited to step off and, more or less on your own, engage intimately with an object or presentation. This again is the style they've used, and it is working. Everywhere I see people peering, looking, going close to study. They are engaged. This was always a key word for us. We wanted to make, both here and in Te Papa, exhibitions which engaged those who visited them, and in both places this is what happened.

Of course most of the donors are Jewish. I see a small man in a kippa singing what I take to be a song of welcome into a TV camera. Old Jewish faces look keenly around—have we been represented right? This pierces you. I am not Jewish, I am not close to this culture at all, and yet I have been a key player in making a representation of their cultural history.

Blood pressure goes up again.

Everywhere people stop Ken and shake his hand. He's becoming famous.

We go off to a long, slow, somewhat disjointed lunch at a classy Italian restaurant. There are curators from the Skirball, which is a Jewish museum in Los Angeles, an artist whose work is in the museum, plus an art dealer and his girlfriend, an American film-maker, and Ken's wife, Susan Foster, who I know and like, but since I know her I am not allowed to sit anywhere near her. This is my passionate desire, not to have to make conversation. I am very tired. But the wine helps.

Back at the museum we meet briefly with the designers for

a hug and a bit of back-slapping. Then everyone heads home. I have to remind myself it's Monday, I lost the weekend. It's maybe 4pm, the earliest I have ever left the museum.

Sunday was Opening Day and Ken went in early. I had stayed late the night before so I played tennis instead, got thrashed, didn't care—hurried home, hurried in, bike sliding through puddles. Drizzle, and getting heavier—it was going to rain on our parade.

Inside the building you couldn't tell what the weather was like. Here it was sweaty, close. Tired faces everywhere. These people, the installers, the designers and their workers, had been up all night, for the second night in a row. They were working. My job, apparently, was to watch. This was very hard. I don't have any installation skills, even as an erk I had nothing to offer. I had to stay out of the way.

This was very hard. I walked back and forth through the long, angled corridors of the museum. Everywhere people were drilling, skilsawing—surely construction of that order should be over? We were six hours from Blumenthal's trumpets and procession. But we were nothing like six hours from being ready—more like sixty. Some areas had almost nothing in them. People were hurrying, sure, but hurrying tiredly. Some workers were starting to hang around, to just watch.

I began making a list of priorities. In the postwar part of the narrative, at the end of the exhibition, we pose a series of questions that the visitor is invited to answer, yes or no: *Can you imagine a Jew being Chancellor of Germany in the near future? Is Germany today, September 9th, 2001, an open, multi-racial society? Do the recent attacks on synagogues and Jewish cemeteries indicate the presence of an ongoing strain in the German character?* These 'question stations' had been played up in the media and the Chancellor—the real Chancellor—was going to respond to them live on TV in six hours. But they weren't working. Apparently there was a disjunction between our network, which had been built by one company, and the software for the stations, which had been built by another. I attempted to mediate a dispute, soothed ruffled feathers, set the museum's priorities. That was my afternoon. So many tired, half-angry people to encourage. Get those labels up—those ones there! And those. From now on, all artefacts that are not in cases should be taken from the floor, we will open without them. Yes, I will take responsibility for that. I am sorry, that guy is an unpleasant person, please ignore what he said to you. You're doing a great job. That concrete—get a broom, sweep up the loose bits, cut round the edge of the black plastic, that will do. That area is finished, we need cleaners. That is my decision. I'm really sorry that you had to do that, please, carry on, you're doing a great job, keep going, you'll make it. Klaus, we *must* have that theatre open.

All the time asking, What should you be doing? What could you do?

At 1.30 Ken shook my hand and I realised he was leaving. 'You're doing a great job,' he said to me, 'keep going, you'll make it.'

Half an hour later I was in a huddle with Petra Schramm—our Petra—Klaus Würth and the other Petra, Petra Winderoll, who were the designers, Würth & Winderoll. We planning a council of war at 3pm, when there was suddenly an exchange in German. Flashing eyes, and no one's meeting mine. The meeting broke up. As we walked away, our Petra told me that Klaus and their Petra would not be able to make the council of war as they were also going to hear Barenboim.

Klaus must have heard me shout, 'No!' Our Petra said to

me, 'Leave them for a minute.' We hurried away and went on with telling people what a great job they were doing. Then, half an hour later, when Klaus went past he said to me, 'We will stay.'

At 3.30 we had no show and I was figuring how I would communicate to Ken and the official party that half the lower floor could not be visited. There were bare wires hanging, paintings leaning in corners, little abandoned stacks of labels, cleaners cleaning things that were dirtied again within minutes. Glass doors of cases swung open but nothing was being put in them. Every face was tired, defeated.

And the goddamn police were everywhere. I tripped over a sniffer-dog that was sniffing an area for the third time in ten minutes. Security guys with walkie-talkies, standing around, watching sceptically—their antennae were so long they drooped like fishing rods. Rubber-neckers were arriving, people starting to go, 'Oh, that's nice!'—but who the fuck were they? The sense that a huge climax had been announced and there was only going to be a whimper.

Blood-pressure in the red now. Headache. Feet sore from covering so many miles of concrete floors. Face sore from grinning. Pushing, pushing, pushing.

At 4.30, without warning, I saw that we were getting somewhere (guys were swimming, guys were sailing). Everywhere I looked I saw . . . it doesn't look so bad. All of a sudden the pace quickened. People could sense we were going to make it. Some staff were leaving—one shook my hand, a little sadly, and said, 'We tried.' But in fact we were winning.

Klaus and I agreed he would eat humble pie and ask the network developer (name withheld in advance of litigation) to make a final attempt to get the Yes-No stations working for us. 'There is hope,' he said, wearily. 'I don't promise it.'

Petra—our Petra—and I made our final patrols. We gave last orders. I picked up bits of dirt and put them in my pocket, when no one was looking I attached labels.

When at 6.45pm Blumenthal led the Chancellor through the door it was to an exhibition that was looking distinctly presentable. In the entrance Schröder happily wrote his name on a cardboard pomegranate and hung it in our pomegranate tree. (That tree is a beauty, it looks like something growing out of the exhibition floor. It's a Jewish symbol of life.) Looking very like a royal procession, the official party advanced, were guided and led. It was strange, I think, for so many powerful people not to know where to go—they seemed to want to be in control of themselves. They hardly glanced around, the tour was going hot-foot. Soon they were out of sight.

I had managed to slip Ken a note covering the four no-go items, so that he could steer them away from trouble.

Then people in very expensive black clothes began to arrive. I was tired, and I don't speak German—I took myself off to the background and lurked significantly (significant lurking is a specialty of mine).

Kissinger arrived with his own guide and began to stare at a big multimedia screen which asked, How did the Jews come to Germany? He looked just like his pictures, short, wide, rather squat. Extraordinary spine, S-shaped, and a voice pitched lower than your knees. I had to intervene and say, 'The museum is in great shape, and that piece will be, too, if we have just about six more hours to work on it—meanwhile, why don't you just shuffle along.' Well, something to that effect.

In they streamed. I was dismayed to find that I knew a few people and was required to open my mouth. Michal Brenner from our Academic Committee, the director of the Jewish

Museum Frankfurt, an art dealer who had remembered me from some arty shindig. I muttered incoherently, waited for them to go away. But everyone was so smiley and nice, it was not okay to be buggered. Then Daniel and Nina Libeskind came and congratulated me and this I cared about.

At 11.30 someone said that those of us who were not official Hosts could maybe be dispensed with and I was gone before the words hit the ground.

At 6.15pm, in Ken's office, changing from my sweaty exhibition-boss gear to my own best black, I had suddenly grasped that it was over, that I didn't have to keep pushing to get the exhibition finished. Nothing would get the not-working elements going now. A great weight fell from me.

And right then I didn't care about the opening, or Blumenthal's big-wig guests, or the celebration. It was over. I wanted to go home.

A strange moment. This was, I realised, the end of seventeen months of pushing.

But I got a second wind. At home Susanna said, 'Well, how was it?' and as I started to explain the tiredness lifted. I poured a fat whisky, went to the TV, began to surf. We were on three different channels simultaneously, plus a four-minute item on BBC World. One feature was four hours long. Blumenthal's speech, which was broadcast live in its full twenty-minute splendour, referred to Ken as 'Berlin's—and my—favourite Kiwi' and was gracious and generous about him, which really pleased me.

The museum looked simply wonderful.

Terrible Things

My colleague Gelia, who has been managing text files for me, came into our office and said, 'Terrible things, Nigel.'

At first it just sounded like a plane crash, or that two planes had crashed together, into public buildings in America. I didn't get it.

As it happened Susanna and the kids were with me, at the museum, when this news was communicated. They had come in for a visit. They loved it. So the kids were hearing this as we did and I didn't want that. Thomas, the head of the research workers, drew me into a doorway and said, hysterically, 'Thousands are dead, thousands.' He was shaking. There was hysteria in the air. The Germans feel any moral outrage very intensely—they are highly sensitised to that. In the lobby of the building where I work the staff were gathered, sitting on the floor, watching a grainy picture on a TV. Open-mouthed. I wanted the kids out of there, and we went home quickly.

Two days of watching reality TV. A grey, ashy feeling.

Closed Due to Tragedy

The museum found a flag and flew it at half mast. Then it was decided that we had to close. So the public opening, which was at 7pm on the Tuesday (two days after the big-wigs' do—weird) was cancelled. And we were shut the next day.

More Terrible Things

1. Kate painted a picture at school—all the kids did. Hers showed a plane flying into a building and underneath she had written, *I am pleased that Mummy and Daddy and Andrew-Jack weren't kaled.*

2. I got an email re a book that refused to arrive from Amazon.com and the woman who wrote it ended by wishing that I would 'have a safe day'.

3. Sunday morning. In the course of a conversation with my parents, long-distance from New Zealand, Susanna heard my mother say—I had it on speaker-phone—that she had okayed the tenant in our house to saw off some branches of the pohutukawa that were brushing against the windows. This occurred at an awkward moment, I had just announced that Susanna would now come on the line and she was mouthing angrily at me that no one was to cut any branches off that tree.

'They're cut already,' I mouthed.

Susanna made her I-hate-stinking-you face.

I held the phone out—my mother dangled from 18,000km away. But Susanna was furious and wouldn't speak. I rounded up Kate, stuck her on and then, in the background—modern phones have good microphones—Susanna and I had an argument. It was about the tree, about the day, which, out the windows, was dull, about the weekend which was drifting to nowhere. It got a little energised, a little ugly, meanwhile Kate was talking happily about her new school, and then Susanna capped it by saying tersely, 'I think I will go home' (and leave you alone here in Germany to see how you like it).

We were due to go to a circus and when the call ended off we went. But it was a disaster. The U-bahn ride was endless, we arrived late and had to run—Susanna is huge and shouldn't be running, I didn't want her to, but whatever I want is what she doesn't want so I had to shut up. Then it cost 56 DM to get in. Susanna had done some price research and assured me that family tickets cost 10 DM but I know a bit about circuses, I once wrote a novel with a circus quotient, and I had warned darkly that no circus worth seeing could be that cheap. And of course I was right. So we emptied our pockets, scraped up the necessary—all the while I was casting my circus-expert's eye over the assembled tents and trailers and I could see this was seriously flea-bag. And so it proved. The sound system had a terrible hum, or wasn't working, one of the hands was in a rage and threw the props about, our seats were crappy, we had to look through a jumble of poles. The first juggler dropped a ball—and she was only juggling three. The costumes were so revealingly cut that you weren't sure just what kind of a show it was supposed to be. And then the animals—horses, ponies, geese (who ever saw geese in a circus?), oxen, Jack Russells—were all mangy and smelly and it was just too grim. Susanna decided it was making her feel sick and went to sit outside, leaving me to have a kid on each knee, trying to convince them this was a good time.

I had, earlier that morning, read a piece by the English writer Ian McEwan, on the *Guardian* site. McEwan is not one of my favourites, his last four books or so have been inflated, plodding, empty. I used to like him, especially the early stories, I used to read those and think, How could I write like that? This item was called *Only Love and Then Oblivion*—not a promising title. But he described how those in the World Trade Centre and those in the planes had used their cellphones to ring last messages home. I love you, said the messages, over and over again. I love you. He made you put yourself in the burning buildings, in the brushed steel toilets of the planes, and asked you what you would say. 'Now we know,' he said.

Quiet

People are leaving. Koray-Ali Günay, who has been working for me as a translator and copy-editor, finished his contract on Friday. Joshua Derman, who developed my computer interactives, has flown back to the States. Big Stephanie finished last week. Gelia, my Text Manager, finishes next Friday. The place is empty and suddenly rather quiet—this afternoon in particular, as everyone's gone to a Barenboim concert.

I didn't bloody know it was on. I guess there was a mail in German, which I was too busy to translate. Bugger.

Last week, on Monday night, Susanna and I went to hear the Berlin Philharmonic under Kent Nagano play Verdi's *Ave Maria* and Schönberg's *Jacob's Ladder*. The Verdi was nice.

The concert was associated with the JMB's opening— *Jacob's Ladder* is said to be embodied in the concept for the Libeskindbau's Stair of Continuity. It's a ladder where angels go up and down to Heaven, I think. Must look that up on Britannica.com. All the JMB staff who had worked on the Opening Day Sunday and thus missed Mahler's Seventh have been given free tickets.

This is in the Berlin Philharmonic Concert Hall—as, when I went to the web to check the venue, I was informed by an article on Kent Nagano, in German, read via the 'automatic translation' offered by the Google search engine.

An automatic translation, made 'with no human involvement' said the FAQ listing—this is completely wonderful. I read the piece, grinning—'. . . for the best opera accommodation of the yearly 2000 impressive one acknowledged.' It's a new kind of English, but one I can understand. The future, now. I love it.

It is so pleasant to be in this hall, with its slabs of panelled wood. Our seats seem hung in the air. We look down on the orchestra—and also down on the rows of seats where I can see the faces of all the colleagues I have worked with over the last seventeen months. So many of them I won't see again—for Stephanie Kluth, today was her last day. Susanna is beside me—along from her is Helmuth Braun, who heads the Temporary Exhibition programme—he's Permanent. Down there is Henriette who worked so hard we just had to find a way to keep her. (Stephanie too, but she didn't want to stay.) I see Christine Zahn, who I know is a Schönberg fan—tomorrow I will ask her about the music.

The sound is perfect—especially the silence before the music begins. So many people in one place and every one of them stifling all coughs, all movement. Human silence. I feel it deeply. I have had so little time to enjoy the culture of Berlin. I resolve that from now on I will get out more. And so it is with this pleasing prospect in mind that the first sounds of the choir come to me and I am happy as I go under.

'that place where those buildings fell down'

This phrase is passed to us by Isobel, who lives downstairs. She said her cleaner, Ejangeline, said it. Sorry, I am sure I don't have her name spelled correctly—I asked twice and that's what I got—sometimes, here, it takes you ten goes to get a person's name properly right. Ejangeline is from Brazil, nineteen, and seems very worldly, says Susanna—she was also our cleaner for a while. Ejangeline and Isobel speak Spanish to each other and so it was in Spanish that Ejangeline said this thing: 'that place where those buildings fell down.'

It's Saturday morning, Isobel's daughter Aida has come up to play with our kids and Isobel, Susanna and I are sitting in a room strewn as only kids can strew a room with toys, string, board games, crockery, bits of food—if the Welfare came we would all cease to be parents.

'She can read and write,' says Isobel. 'That's something. But, see, she don't even know what America is. Most of the world don't know. In Afghanistan there is no TV, the Taliban outlawed it. Those people living on the ground, what do they know about America?' We all listen carefully when Isobel talks about this. Her doctorate was in Islamic art, she knows stuff we don't know. We have a discussion about how it is managed that a man can have two wives, the rules of Islam.

On BBC World, it's wall-to-wall, everyone is on a crash-course—what does it really mean, Islam?

Later, I hear Alistair Cooke talking about a letter from Einstein to Roosevelt, sent in maybe 1937, warning of the destructive possibilities of splitting the plutonium atom.

His last words are a quote, I think from one of the saints: 'This is a new world, we must all get used to it.'

Further Apart

They're getting further apart, these recordings. I wonder if they're going to dry up. I haven't felt the need to write anything down for days. Now that the museum is open, a slackness has descended. I send emails to people all over the world, I take my time over routine replies to my colleagues. I stop in the corridor to chew the fat.

I brought a CD player in today, *Kind of Blue* is floating in the background.

There aren't so many colleagues. It's now twenty-two days since opening and already the numbers are down. I guess forty people have left in the last six weeks.

You feel like a survivor, like someone who made it. There are people who didn't and are angry about it. People who think they deserve a permanent contract, who manoeuvred and promoted themselves, who are shocked to find that it didn't work. I am not sympathetic. The worst case is a guy whose work was poor—who couldn't budget, couldn't manage, who ignored decisions to the contrary and went on doing what he had planned. This guy has got two more weeks and then he's gone. He thuds down the corridor, he glowers in the doorway. His shoulders are slumped. His head is held forward, as though he is trying to hang his jaw out where it will be noticed. I am totally unsympathetic. I want him gone. That is what this is, a time of waiting for those who are going to go, so that the new order can emerge.

I'm bored stiff and I have a headache.

Jaunty

There are all kinds of communications which arrive from New Zealand. Emails of course, every day at work I get a couple of those. Parcels from rellies. Parcels of books from Unity Books whose place in Heaven is secure. Envelopes which contain clippings from New Zealand newspapers about the museum.

And every now and then something goes back—in terms

of actual post, I mean. Post is now a drag, that haul to the actual post office, I get there once every three months, max.

Which is why, I insist, I have taken so long to send a present to my godson. He is Lawrence Something McColl, known as Billy, born about six months ago now, and this weekend I finally managed to send off to him a little something, as a goddad is supposed to do.

It was a zinc statuette of a little man in a hat striding out. It was accompanied by a teeshirt with the same little man on it in green, and a poem, and a letter. Here's the poem.

Jaunty
for Billy

When East and West reunite
West is where the sunrise lies
the future leaves the East behind
Who wants those dreary buildings
those great stone faces? In the name
of the masses
tear Socialism down

But a spirit lingers, a laughter
in deserted railway stations
painted eggs, a wedding where
a fiddler makes everyone dance

And this little man
who when the light changes
strides out
jaunty
history under his hat

Well, I don't write many poems. I like the idea that I'm going to write one but they're hell to get right. I can write great doggerel, for when a staff member leaves and so forth, charms the pants off everyone who's never read a real poem.

More Germans

As I cycled in this morning I saw a car with its hood up, underneath a street light—it's getting darker—and three men gathered round, peering into the engine, stroking their chins. Another car was parked nearby with its lights on and had obviously stopped to help.

One Saturday morning when Thomas and I were off to play tennis, his battery was flat. He produced some jumper leads and, when a car went past, held them up like evidence. The car didn't slow. But at the end of the street it U-turned and came back. The first car.

'Oh, they will always stop to help you,' said Thomas. 'They should do that—why not?'

It's autumn right now, high autumn, and the footpaths are patterned with stiff, dry, leaves, orange-brown and crisp, they make a lovely crackling sound when you walk on them—it reminds me of walking on fresh snow. The German word for this season is Herbst, which has just the nicest flavours in it, and is full of interesting smells and a broken light. Berlin is a city of trees; they were mostly planted after the war, and they have a stronger presence here than any city I've been in. It's as though their task is to prove that nature will still function here. That life can regenerate.

The leaves come down so thickly. One leaf in the air is one thing, it floats, wafts, utterly charming, but all the leaves from all the trees, this is a serious matter. There were uncountable numbers of leaves. Of course the Germans are ready. There is a special blower, like an elephant's trunk, with which you chase leaves into a pile. The piles are eaten by little sit-upon machines, which carry them to dumps, where they are rained on and become soggy and dark. I have seen the dumps in the park near us, vast mounds of mulching leaves, sinking back into the ground.

You can tell when snow is about to come. Little sit-upons, different ones, appear and go busily round the footpaths spreading grit. How do they know so surely that it will snow? But they are never wrong. There's a sense of people having lived here for thousands of years, that the patterns have been observed, and responses developed. Lives pass through, but the patterns go on. In New Zealand we are more certain that our span is the span that is the measure.

Every day has its own pace. The seasons bring this out, I feel—you're always asking, So where are we up to? This morning it went well with Kate, without trying we were out the door five minutes early. It was really dark, down in the courtyard I had to tilt my keyring to the sky to find the bike key.

As we ride, Kate says, 'Where are we going?'

'To Sadie's.'

'Am I going to go to school with her?'

'Yes.

'Does Mamma know?'

'Yes.'

'Did she say it was okay?'

'Yes.'

'Okay,' she says.

We ride on through the dark. Yellow light from the windows of shops, people wrapped against the cold in thick coats. The first cars, their dark bulk behind the bright

113

headlights. I drop her in the lobby of Sadie's building, see her up the stairs. We blow kisses.

Then I cycle off, slowly. I'm early, no need to rush. I can already tell, it's going to be an early, no worries, easy day.

Herbst

I have to say something about the leaves. They are all coming down now. Looking out the window, along the street you can see every shade from a translucent pale lemony yellow to a baked orange brown—every tree seems to have arrived at a personal and distinctive colour. The bare trunks are just coming through, dark, so stark and scary—winter is scary here. But it isn't scary yet, there are enough leaves holding to provide that memory of warmth. And then as you ride along the streets the layer of leaves is *so* thick. It's like riding over layers of parchment, each leaf is thick in itself. It really is as though something like a library is underfoot, you walk over the pages of books. And they're huge—when you see them up in the trees you don't realise that they're the size of dinner plates. They're heavy. They have real presence. And then you ride across them, you have to, there's nowhere else to go, they're everywhere and everyone walks on them and they are broken into little pieces, and then it rains, and they darken and mush up. Then the busy little machines come, already they are, and make piles, and there's a deep compost smell, a smell of mould. Of decay. All of this is something made visible that is not usually, in our country, so visible. As a metaphor it's the ultimate cliché. But as a process it strikes you deep every time you see it.

Nothing for Ages

I have written nothing into this account for ages. There are many reasons for this—Christmas, shifting apartments, etc. But I think the main one is that my imaginative energy has been devoted to my new novel.

It's a very complicated subject, that imaginative energy. I don't mean that I have been thinking about the novel. I do a bit of that, true. But I think mostly about it as I am writing. I go inside the book, descend into it, like a man going down into his home workshop, to work on his mad invention. And while I am making the words of it, I have a steady flow of ideas about its shape.

The rest of the time, what I think about is its reception.

Sometimes I imagine it being rejected. This is invariably pleasurable. There is the warm satisfaction of rejection itself—not of course that *real* rejection is warm. My last novel, *Skylark Lounge*, was rejected—that's what I feel. The damned thing sold less than my two previous books, and was not even shortlisted for our Fiction of the Year award. However, this was the best kind of real rejection, in that the book was very well reviewed ('art of a high order', 'Cox writes brilliantly', 'one of the year's very best', etc) as well as—this is what really made me happy—being very well liked by all the writers and serious readers that I care about. So I enjoyed an excellent sense of rejection here, one that was in fact not a real rejection at all; more a sense that I had been wronged, and that all right-thinking people thought so.

But I have had very enjoyable fantasies of rejection of the new novel. These are delicious, mainly because, in my heart of hearts, I do not believe the book will be rejected. So I am free to variously imagine it being rejected in New

Zealand but not in New York, rejected by the critics but not by the mass audience, rejected by literary readers but adored by Elvis enthusiasts (the novel features Elvis Presley). These fantasies, if it has been a bad enough day, can be extreme. I see myself running away from my wife and children (any excuse), rejecting my publisher, living in a secluded rural valley with only sheep for company, in a shepherd's hut, where I eke a living from the land (catching fish from the stream which runs past my door) and become bronzed and fit and somehow *weathered* while attending to my main business, which is of course the production of a universal masterpiece which will triumph in *every* sphere.

But in the main the fantasies are of success. I hugely believe in the new book and so I enjoy composing acceptance speeches for major prizes, or seeing myself in hotel rooms, amid a 52-state promotional tour, or producing, to silence the odd uppity author of my acquaintance, a letter from my agent (unfortunately I have no agent) along the lines of, Dear Nigel, this is to confirm our telephone conversation—you said you wanted the good news in writing and so here it is: not counting film rights money (though Mr Spielberg continues to leave answerphone messages) the global package for the two main English language territories comes to ... I am embarrassed to end the sentence.

I enjoy these fantasies. But I am utterly serious about them. I know this because when I visit a website which gives the numbers achieved by various major sellers in various major book markets last year, I am always chastened: they aren't high enough! If my book is going to do the numbers that I have in mind it will be the biggest seller since *Lord of the Rings*.

But now I am finished—or, at least I thought I was. Let me explain.

116

I wrote the first draft of this new novel in a fever. This was the biggest experience of my writing life. The novel poured out of me. I woke earlier and earlier, spent more time in the evening preparing—ironing my shirt, laying out my breakfast—so that all possible morning hours would be devoted to the book. I wrote in near darkness, with only the light of the screen and an extremely dim light to see the keys by. I wrote with my glasses off. Since I am very short-sighted, this meant I couldn't see. Somehow it seemed to mean that I got further inside my imagination. The words poured out of me.

I began to be convinced that this was something special. But I managed to keep a hold on my dreams until, in the middle of last year, my publisher, Fergus Barrowman, came to stay with us. He knew about the novel. Well, I'd sent him the odd email cunningly designed to capture his maximum interest and then he'd asked for a synopsis to take to the London Book Fair. The synopsis excited him. Then, during his stay, he stayed home one day, sick. From our house, he mailed me at work: 'Okay, so I'm here and there's nothing to read. Where's your manuscript?' I had anticipated this and had decided that *as long as he asked for it* he could have it. So I mailed him back: 'In the wooden box under the computer.'

He read the first third of it and told me that it was good. We were walking to a pizza place for lunch and I said, 'Yes, I think it's good too.'

Everyone being very cool.

Then, over lunch he upgraded that to 'very good'. He is experienced at measuring out comments to authors. And I am experienced at receiving them—I sensed that there was a further upgrade lurking there. He is a large, fleshy man, Fergus, with a very large head, covered in tight dark curls.

I could sense a faint quiver about him. Soon he was talking about how this book could be the big breakthrough for me.

When he got home to New Zealand, he emailed me: 'You do know that that is a very BIG book you are writing there, don't you—and that it could be very BIG.' These words, from someone as measured as Fergus, this made a growth area of my fantasy department.

With them etched on my brain I plunged into a second draft. He and I both agreed that there were some problems with the novel's beginning, but that these weren't serious. I began to revise. And, within about nine months, I had completed a second draft, which was much better. I approved of having his encouraging words in the front of my mind. I approved of the overtime being put in by the fantasy department. Plenty of time for coming down to earth when the novel is nearing publication. What I was trying to do now was to make myself ambitious—to make sure that I wrote a BIG novel.

The numbers!

Stay With Us

We went to the hospital early. Everyone said, 'Oh, third baby, it'll just fall out.' Susanna had convinced herself that this was going to be so and was in a hurry. It was Friday night, that end-of-the-week feeling, I wanted to find a couch and drown in Scotch but I could feel the adrenaline rising. We managed to dispatch the kids, one each to old hippie families—thank god for hippie helpfulness—and were alone in our bed, timing the contractions. They were irregular. Susanna, a huge mound under the blankets, was in pain. But she kept saying, 'It's going to be tonight, no question.' I felt strangely calm. Well, I had badgered her until finally we had a bag packed, CDs chosen, children and keys distributed. At nine o'clock she couldn't stand it any more and called for an ambulance. But the contractions were, at their closest, five minutes apart, her waters hadn't broken, so I called instead for a taxi. First worry came to nothing: I got an English-speaking taxi dispatcher who understood that I needed a taxi, now.

At the Krankenhaus she struggled her painful way in through the Emergency exit. I was a little ahead, opening doors, trying to alert reception. But the receptionists were polishing their fingernails. Anyone could see, this was a woman in need, but they just kept on talking, took not a flicker of me. Then an orderly saw us, one look and said, 'Wheelchair?'

He told us dumb jokes as he got us up to the delivery suite—'German efficiency will make sure the baby comes on time.' But he was lovely, distracting us from our fears as he efficiently manoeuvred us down miles of empty green corridors. The lino squeaked.

The delivery staff on duty spoke English—phew. They gave her an ultrasound and checked her progress: two centimetres. I knew what they were going to say and they said it: 'Too early, go away.' Susanna was mad and so they said, 'Go out for a walk, for an hour.'

So off we went—out into the night. It was mild, the end of winter, but still cold, so I gave her my gloves, scarf and hat. She squeezed my arm hard and walked in granny steps. Actually it was a beautiful night, the air smelled sweet, a warm moon, and Dieffenbachstrasse looked very romantic in the moonlight. I was delighted to be out in it, but I knew better than to tell her this. Since we only lived half a mile away, we went home. There, in the dim light of our front room, with Schubert playing just at the bottom of the sound scale and all the lights muffled, she relaxed, and the contractions began to come faster. She has been tense for two weeks now and every time she tenses, the contractions stop and she goes off the boil. She knows this and I know it, and now at last, with the kids in a good place, and the hospital and midwife waiting, now at last the baby can come.

Suddenly she decides she wants to have a home birth.

After I have talked her out of that we set off again. We've been away an hour and a half. The walk back nearly kills her, she is in real pain. I encourage her—'You're doing great!' I feel like a real bastard—a manager. I'm all right, Jack. Well, what should I have done, taken a pain injection? But I feel I'm having an easy ride.

In the delivery suite they talk her into having an enema. This is unpleasant and she gets madder—she's pretty mad all through the birth, you have to watch what you say. It makes me laugh, but, you know, to myself. But they are right—the enema speeds the process.

She gets into the big bath, naked, and lies there, sweating. She is the centre of all attention, in pain—in labour—there in the bath in front of us. It is just irrelevant that she's naked in front of the three of us. This is something Susanna would never allow, but right now no one even registers it.

Except me. I can't help registering everything. This is, I know, going to be my last child. I am never going to be here again. I am trying very hard to see everything—to notice, to understand. It's as though I saw some of Kate's birth, and most of Andrew-Jack's and now I am going to see all of this one. I see the pale 'nowhere room' nature of the birth chamber. No one lives here. It's like a motel, people check in and out. And yet it's so much more than that. You know because of the screaming. Down the hall two women in other such chambers are yelling at the top of their lungs. This is no yell of release, nothing to help them get through. This is straight pain. It's humbling, this sound, to a man—to know that you will never know it.

The midwife tells Susanna that it's time, she should get out of the bath, but she says no. She's having contractions steadily now—leans into me, clenches me. Sweat is running from her forehead. I talk to her in an undertone, trying to be a help, trying not to be an irritant. By now I am the message deliverer, Susanna is too far gone inside herself to be trying to understand the German-English that the midwife and doctor are using. The midwife says, worried, 'Are you going to have the baby in the bath?' 'No,' I say firmly, and I make eye contact with the midwife, Claudia, who has been very sympathetic and responsive. I cajole Susanna, who is pretty cranky by now, up the steps of the bath, get her across the floor of the room and lift her up onto the bed. 'My waters haven't broken,' she gasps. The doctor, an older woman, tough, firm, says she is going to do it. 'No!' says Susanna. Again, I catch an eye, nod yes—I can see that this birth is about to happen.

And suddenly it is, suddenly the midwife is saying, 'The head is clear! Little pushes, little pushes now.' I have my arms around her shoulders. There really is nothing like this happens in life, it's a thing alone. A huge thing, happening to the person right there in your arms, and you have only the limits of your imagination to understand what it might be like. My fabulous imagination seems utterly inadequate.

Susanna says, urgent: 'I need pain relief!' Again, I shake my head and there is none. We had discussed this, she didn't want any, and there is no time, the baby is coming—but when I tell her this the next day, she gives me a very old-fashioned look.

But immediately it's out, there it is, out on the sheet, the baby has come. It's tiny, curled in like a bean, livid in colour, with white matter and blood and my first glance at it, anxious, is to tell me that it seems okay—that it seems normal and okay. 'A boy,' the midwife says, wondering how this information will be received. She lifts him clear—I wish we had his name ready for him—and asks, 'Does someone want to cut the cord of this baby?' That's me, I abandon Susanna's head and go down to the business end, and, taking the proffered scissors, cut the pale, gristly cord. Then they lift him clear and place him, mucky boy, on Susanna's chest. She's grinning.

A couple of hours later I staggered home. It was 5.30, taxis were in the streets, people were about. The sweetness had gone from the night. I was tired, so tired, all I wanted was to quit on the nearest park bench. But I got myself home, rang her mother in New Zealand, then my mother. 'Made it.' Into bed. I thought I would never sleep, my head was too full, I was too tired for sleep.

Then, from ten thousand feet under, I heard the phone ringing. The clock said it was 6.30—which day? I staggered through the house. It was Susanna, she said, 'Come and get me! You've got to get me out of here.'

Back into my clothes, back up the street. I found her, in a ward, pale, in pain, angry. She wasn't staying there. I didn't want to know why. We collected the baby, got her down to the front door—granny steps again, in pain, she had given birth three hours before, but no wheelchairs could be found—grabbed a taxi and headed home.

And there he was in his cot for the first time. I sat up, drinking coffee—there was no point in trying to sleep.

He's been there ever since. It's twelve days now. We are back to doing our normal lives now—scrapping with the kids, getting the meals, getting the dishes done. But now he's with us. Now he'll always be with us.

I worry about this—that he'll live. Not that he's in any way endangered. But life seems so much more open to me these days, so much more changeable and temporary, so full of the unforeseen and the random and the various. I have a little prayer I utter—not to anyone, you understand. But I just offer it. To life, maybe, to the random forces—a prayer against the power of the random forces. I look at him, or I see him in my mind's eye, and I say, 'Stay with us.' How he will turn out, who he will turn out to be: no one can know this. But I have to stick to my bottom line. Full of fear, I say it, hands clenched and meaning it. 'Stay with us, little one. And you other kids, you little buggers. Stay with us.'

Eva from
the Tyre Factory

Since the Wall came down, it's all one Germany now. That's the theory. And in fact it is all one Germany—West Germany. The country that used to be the East is in the process of, like the sun, sinking into the West. That is because everything in the East was so terrible—coffee, cars, buildings, all crappy, plus they had the Stasi, the secret police, who were mean, low and dirty. No, best to forget all that.

However, forgetting is not the German way. When at the Jewish Museum where I work we interview a candidate for a job, afterwards my colleagues will inevitably say, 'Ah, but he is from the former East.' What they mean is, his second language is more likely to be Russian than English, his education will be of a poor standard, and he will be rather inflexible. There are over four million registered unemployed in Germany and the vast majority of these are from the former East.

Sport 29, 2002

The museum is dedicated to exploring how minorities fare in contact with dominant cultures, with the Jews of course as the prime example. However, as I have written elsewhere, the Jewish question is now largely an historical one here in Germany. If the museum is going to stay relevant it must explore the ways that that thread from the past runs through into the present and future. How, for example, do the Turkish minority fare here? How will Indians, who will be coming in increasing numbers to service the country's dopey IT systems, get on?

Thus on a Tuesday morning I find myself in a hired Citroën people-mover—a *Picasso*, according to his signature imprinted on the steely grey wheel-arch—travelling with four colleagues towards Beeskow, one hour away, east and south of Berlin, and with every mile, the DDR that was rises with increasing vigour—though maybe vigour is not exactly the right word; perhaps exhaustion. Yes, with increasing exhaustion and pallor and dilapidatedness and overgrown sprouting-ness, I won't go on—the East subsides outside the windows.

I have of course been in the East before. It's folksier than the West, you see the occasional horse and cart, and houses that would make good postcards, everything sags, rooflines and washing lines and jowls, and the shops are full of kitsch. 'Horrible coffee,' mutters my colleague Inka Bertz from the navigator's seat. A red light brings us to a halt outside a florist's that advertises 'Blumen mit pfiff', and we try to figure how this might translate. Flowers with a whistle? Flowers with puff? They mean special.

A forest of slim trees, open-spaced so that the eye traces paths between them, makes Kiwi Ken Gorbey in the back seat say that 'this is nearly as nice as New Zealand'.

We pull into an industrial complex where large, low buildings and glowering machines are offset by mounds of stones graded by size. One of the purposeful buildings apparently houses the office of the local department for cultural affairs. Here? Yes, up a grim set of stairs, in a lino-floored corridor that has travelled untouched from the 1950s, is a set of bad oil paintings which indicate a cultural emphasis. We are redirected to another building and also told that we have parked in the wrong place. (It's easy to get such things wrong in Germany; not a lot of she'll-be-right in this country.)

And now here to meet us is the day's first human from the former DDR. Her name is Frau Giesler. Standing diffidently in the grey light of the carpark, she's about thirty, rather thin, has clumpy shoes, any old jeans, a black teeshirt with CLOTHING DISTRICT in white letters, lank hair, a complexion that has unfortunately suffered land mines, and a limp handshake with averted eyes—this is not how your typical Berlin artnik presents. To combat the mines she has applied a white preparation to the lower half of her face, which makes her look particularly ghostly. Everything about her seems typical of the East—everything is faded here, less present. I know I shouldn't be staring at her (I used to have terrible acne myself) but this is what happens; the colleagues speak in German and I hang in the background and stare.

Frau Giesler is the registrar of a body of artworks that we have come to see. Her boss, Herr Doktor de Bruyn, is unfortunately away at a conference, which is why she is dealing with us.

The artworks, Inka explains to me as we crunch across the gravel courtyard behind Frau Giesler, are from offices of officers of the former administration, from the halls of former youth associations, from former official clubrooms, from offices of the Party. This then is official art, approved art. Now the regime which approved of it no longer exists, and the offices and halls and clubs have other functions or, more likely, are boarded up. But the art still belongs . . . to whom exactly? Someone. The new local administration, apparently. What are they doing with it? 'Well, they are owning it,' Inka says.

We arrive outside a large building that looks to me like a barn, only taller. No windows to speak of. Paint flakes from the wood. Apparently it once housed the machinery that raised and lowered a lock gate. I can't see any water.

Inside, the lobby is constricted, it's hard to find a place to stand, but here are the first artworks: a waist-high bust of Marx, in bronze, accompanied by two little bronze Marxes and a plaster Lenin.

The first room Frau Giesler leads us into has a ceiling so low that I have to keep my neck bent. At one end a wall has been constructed by hanging a curtain of bubble-wrap, through which an office of second-hand furniture can be seen. In fact the whole place resembles a second-hand shop very precisely—overcrowded, everything precariously arranged, no apparent order. What it's crowded with is art. Against every wall lean stacks of paintings, twenty, thirty deep. 'They might even have bothered to put a slat of wood between,' growls Inka, confident that Frau Giesler speaks no English. It's true that I have never seen art treated as roughly as this, or so randomly framed.

Inka Bertz, our Head of Collections, is an art historian and her clothes are much more carefully chosen than Frau Giesler's. They are also much more carefully chosen than mine, but nearly everyone's clothes are more carefully chosen than mine. Today, a day when I publicly represent the museum, I have the Gap from head to toe, the result of a recently enforced Friday-night session with my wife, and now I look . . . how do I look? I look new. My shoes let me down a little but, old Docs, they were all I could find in the dark this morning. Okay, enough about me. But my new clothes meant I was part of the Berlin art crowd—I could see that—as far as Frau Giesler was concerned. She was answering questions from Inka and also from our director, Cilly Kugelmann, with caution and great reserve. Yes, these paintings belonged to the Labour Union, the Society for Russian-German Friendship, and to the Party, Cilly explains, translating for the New Zealanders. Now they belong to the Lands of Brandenburg, Berlin and Mecklenburg.

The paintings themselves—let's get this over with—are pretty terrible. Every art movement of the twentieth century is represented here. But each movement has somehow been reduced to the bach-art level. Here is a huge bach-art version of a Léger. A bach-Cézanne, a bach-Chagall, a bach-Lowry—and Lowry was kind of bachy to begin with.

The lighting is weird. It consists of a line of fluorescents at waist-level. I guess this is a concession to the low stud, but it under-lights our faces and casts disturbing Expressionist shadows on the ceiling. Around the walls, narrow-drawered cabinets of veneered wood obviously hold works-on-paper, but I am not encouraged to look.

We move through to another part of the room, where the light is dimmer, but with spotlights. Here each stack of paintings has had the top painting turned so that, in the oval of light, you see the images. It's a display of sorts. A large holiday-colours picture of people splashing in the seaside shallows is explained carefully by Frau Giesler and interpreted for us by Cilly. Cilly is careful to get the date of the painting right. It matters at which stage the politics had arrived. 'This is the late 1970s. You can see that there are different types of people, Slavs and Northerners, and also the black man, so the theme here is the brotherhood of all human mankind. But nobody is looking at anybody else. They are not even looking at us. Officially all people were part of the human mankind family but in fact the law said it was illegal to fraternise with foreigners and everyone kept to themselves. The black man is even further apart from the others and he has his hands out, waiting to have the ball tossed to him—this is possibly symbolic. There are mild protest elements here.' Well, I had more or less figured most of that, but I wouldn't have had the confidence that what I was seeing was purposeful. Cilly is supremely confident. This political and cultural confidence is impressive, and daunting. She is a Jew of Polish extraction— siblings murdered in the Holocaust, obsessively political, disillusioned, brilliantly well-informed, but not cynical; smokes seventy a day; loves literature and life, interested in everything. Sorry for the cultural cringe, but talking to Cilly Kugelmann makes me think I should stick to potty-training pop culture subjects like UFOs, Tarzan and Elvis.

Down an alley between paintings we find, leaning against a shadowed wall, two portraits of Russian soldiers. This is different. Each man is sitting in space on a red plank, against a red background, with tightly crossed legs. The uniforms are dark green, the faces are meat-coloured. There is something of Bacon about these paintings, which are by Thomas Ziegler—humans trapped by nothing more substantial than an atmosphere. They make us realise that there really is some art here.

Now we find, several paintings down a stack, a picture featuring Joseph Stalin. The email from Inka which confirmed the travel arrangements for this outing was titled 'Heading Towards Stalin', but it turns out that this is the only image we see of Uncle Joe all day. 'The collection is mostly from the early 1960s and onwards,' Inka says. 'When Stalin died in 1953, his image was removed. That's why you don't find it here.' This one picture isn't great art, it's too literal for that. But it is interesting. Stalin in the foreground, large, dark, surrounded by dark banks of his Party officials, all of them with large red haloes. Deep in the banks, some of the officials have no faces. Further beyond them are skulls. (Maybe this should have been the cover for Martin Amis's new book, *Koba the Dread*—but we don't care about Martin Amis any more, do we.) There's a hammer and sickle on a red field, an image of happy workers. This was probably a brave painting at one time—it seems to be from the late 1970s—but you wouldn't want to own it.

Happy workers after a harvest. Two well-fed pigs in a sty. Buildings and progress. I know, I know, it's a strain reading about paintings. Just one more. This one was found by Frau Giesler—in a somewhat offhand manner she placed it where a good light might fall on it. It was tall, two-thirds the size of a door, in colours from the khaki sector of the palette—a realistic, naturalistic picture of a young woman in a locker room, probably at the end of her working day. Her large eyes, filled with feeling, had something of the appeal that you find in paintings of kittens. 'Kaufhaus kunst,' said Cilly Kugelman, 'department-store art', and immediately I saw how it would look in Kirkcaldie's in Wellington, among art-to-go versions of bridges, haywains and waterlilies. However, without wanting to seem enthusiastic, Frau Giesler was trying to get us to look harder at this painting. Inka turned it over and translated the title: *Eva from the Tyre Factory*. Frau Giesler says that many East German women would have understood this painting. 'There was a great deal of pressure on women, who had to work all day in the factory and then work in the home.' Cilly and the others wander away but Inka and I linger. Every time you try to take it seriously, the painting lets you down—just that faint hint of appeal or explanation. Eva's hands are in the foreground, clasping her knees. The hands are practical, strong, but there is still something feminine about their long fingers. Her upper arms, bare, are strong-looking, muscled, but still manage to suggest that if she held you you would be the lucky guy. She is framed by lockers with their doors open; inside them is dark nothing—is this symbolic? That's the problem with everything in this room, the sense that it should all be over-read is overpowering. Eva's eyes, you are supposed to read these deeply, to be read by them, this is all but written on the locker door.

However, the painting is successful in making me think hard about the lives of those in the former DDR. With a khaki shudder.

Other rooms, other voices, all saying the same thing: we are a soulful people living a hard life that is better than other lives being lived anywhere in the world. Four tightly-packed floors—my guess is, fifty thousand pieces of art. Tapestries, collages, mosaics, string-works, mud-works, sawdust-works, glue-works, it's all here. A small room, with only a narrow walkway, where sculptural busts are so tightly shelved that you're careful with your elbows when you turn around. Bronze, plaster, wood, amber, glass—heroic, abstract, naturalistic, bach, every style is represented. Marx and Engels have a much greater purchase on the past than Lenin, but that pointed beard does poke through their bushy ones from time to time. There's too much, you can't really see anything.

As we move between floors I quietly ask Cilly Kugelmann, what does Frau Giesler think of this? 'I think she's proud,' says Cilly. 'She was very reserved at first, until she was sure of what we thought. When she sees that we ask serious questions and are well-informed, then she starts to show that she has a regard. Not for all of it.' Now Ken asks if we can go back to a room we had visited earlier. Frau Giesler turns to oblige and I realise that she does understand English. Quickly, I think back over what I might have said.

We buy postcards of the artworks in the shop of the museum which is associated with the warehouse, shake hands once more with the still limp fingers of Frau Giesler (no one ever gets to hear her first name). She speaks directly to Cilly and Inka but with the foreigners her eyes continue to be averted.

The *Picasso* people-mover moves us quickly through a lunch beside a pond, a baroque church within a still-functioning monastery, then on through a succession of treescapes and crappy little towns. I shouldn't brush over things like that, everything was major, especially the church, in Neuzelle; I have never seen so much vaulted, writhing decoration—'religion as theatre,' says Inka—and the bones in the little reliquary were high-gruesome, resting in their glass house like something in a Cornell box. At lunch, the cucumber soup was to die for. But we were late and these things had to be rushed through, especially when there was so much museum gossip to catch up on.

Our next appointment was at 3pm, in the steelworks of a former DDR town called Eisenhüttenstadt.

The steelworks had once been a major DDR industrial site and was a proud example of how the former East had adapted to its changed circumstances. Our guide, Herr Kumich, told us that he had trained as an engineer and had been devoted to the plant for most of his life. Now he was a guide. We could tell there was something sad about this and gradually it became clear that Kumich was a steel nut. He described chairs made of steel, buildings, cars, houses—he told us that in the town we should look out for steel artworks. His enthusiasm for steel made his arms flail about. He was about fifty-five, maybe four years older than me, but a different being entirely—another human, sure, but an utterly different thing. We both have mild paunches and wear glasses. His hair is greyer. His face and stature remind me vaguely of my dad—same skin tone. But my glasses have frames by Calvin Klein and his are steel. No, I made that up, actually they were sort of clear plastic, but you know what I mean. Generic.

The steelworks—Ekostahl—is immense, ten square acres, he tells us. He squeezes into the *Picasso* with us and guides us through a quick drive-around. The shapes of the place loom overhead—great chimneys, dark against the sky, stoop-necked like giant birds; miles of fat pipes, intestinal, accompany us, bend over us, stretch away into the distance; trains without drivers haul wagon-loads of coal and ore. But lots of the site seems dead and it transpires that only one of the former big smelters plus one smaller new one are now working. Herr Kumich explains that eleven thousand people used to work here, now it's two thousand. There used to be a coffee bar, a restaurant, a crèche, a bank, a gymnasium—he produces a list of things that used to be here so long that Cilly rolls her eyes instead of translating. Herr Kumich is maybe a little nutty. I guess that's how we think of that kind of over-identification with your workplace.

He was once a research engineer and his task was to see how best-quality steel might be produced without burning so much coal. Then, when the works was sold—again Cilly's eyes are rolling, his history of its ownership since the fall of the DDR would take ten pages—they didn't need him to be a researcher any more and he stayed on in the gatehouse and eventually became a guide. 'He was one of the lucky ones,' says Cilly.

I have never been in a steelworks before and have this idea that I'm going to see molten steel being poured. It is gently explained to me that it's a sealed process, you can't see inside, from go to whoa it takes place inside the big furnace complex without human observation. 'Because you would get burned to cinder.' Oh. However, we do get to see steel being milled.

This is preceded by a fifteen-minute lecture from Herr Kumich on the milling process. He has his telescoping pointer out from his vest pocket and taps on the multicoloured wall diagram to make sure we are following. Cilly translates what she can but her eyes are rolling right out of her head. Also it's getting very hot.

When finally we go inside the mill we can see why. Before they can mill the steel they have to heat it. There's the oven, a series of square, squat shapes fifty metres below the catwalk where we, up near the ceiling, are sweating—beyond it, the interior of the great building stretches away into darkness. Through a gap in the oven's plates we can see a burning spot of yellow light, like the eye from *Lord of the Rings*. Then the oven opens and huge forks go in to extract the slab of steel. It's longer than a cricket pitch, maybe a yard wide and a foot thick. It rides on the forks towards us, glowing fiercely, the colour of the inside of the sun. My face feels as though it's being cooked by its heat. That slab is 1250 degrees Celsius. Everything in the entire mill seems to recoil from it. Burning there on the arms of the forklift, it is one of the most wonderful, terrible sights I have ever seen.

Steel rollers spin, shooting the burning slab along to the mill where, amid great shudderings and gouts of steam, it is rolled back and forth and pressed out until it is quite thin and maybe a hundred metres long. Your eyes, streaming from heat and chemicals, can hardly believe what they're seeing. The end of the slab is now rounded, so that it looks like a tongue—like a long, burning devil's tongue. Then suddenly the elongated strip is shot into a coiling machine, where it is tightly rolled. It's still burning hot. I have to say that somehow I was afraid watching this process. It was as though this was too big a thing to really be happening, or if it was happening then I shouldn't be seeing it.

I staggered outside and told Herr Kumich that his mill was better than all the special effects of every science fiction movie I'd ever seen rolled into one.

Next stop on this explore-the-living-past trip was the museum of 'Culture of Everyday Life in East Germany'.

The museum, like the steel mill, was in Eisenhüttenstadt. Eisenhüttenstadt was a model town, built to show what the future of socialism was going to deliver. Its clean, wide streets (a steel artwork on every corner) were lined with formations of workers' housing. Balconies hung in the air, footpaths were tree-lined. All very fine, but these days it's hard to see anything particularly special. Well, there was no graffiti. Traffic moved smoothly. The general air was of a retirement village; the purpose had gone out of the place. But there is still pride. Everything is fresh-painted. The steel art is polished, with trimmed footings. Once, Soviet leaders and workers' tour groups were brought here to glimpse how the rest of the world would be some day.

The museum's glass cubes held fifties kitsch. A blender made of clear plastic—suspended in time. Balls of wool, portable typewriters, bicycles. Filing cabinets, transistor radios, instant coffee: you know, they had everything in the former East. Enclosed within the cases were the things that make an everyday life. I was told that citizens of the former

East come here and are delighted to be reunited with the things they once used. This is complicated. Cilly tells me: 'When the Wall fell, all the people who lived in these towns threw out everything in their houses. The footpaths were piled big with their household effects. They went to Ikea and refurnished. This lasted for two years. Then they became disillusioned with the life the West was offering them. They became nostalgic for their old products. An industry came into being, presenting updated products in old packaging. Now people come to museums like this and get in touch once again with the things they lost.'

That night we ate dinner outdoors, beside a river. Poland was on the far bank. Under large umbrellas, at solid wooden tables, we drank dark beer infused with herbs and ate horse meat—fabulously exotic. The chef, a former navy man, had been to New Zealand; he could pronounce a recognisable version of 'Wellington'. I'd never eaten horse before, it was delicious. No khaki here, now. As we ate we talked about how people ate horse in hard times, it was considered a hardship food. Horse was for dogs, it usually came in cans. But people eat dogs, too. It all depends. That's what we said, with the broad river flowing steadily past and Polish grass over there and Polish trees and Cilly smoking number 68 for the day, the smoke curling up into the night, and the chef bringing us a complimentary glass of schnapps, which hung gleaming and tasty in the bottom of a tall, slim glass—again, something never tasted before. Definitely. It all depends.

The Ball
is Round

The Jewish Museum Berlin is a history museum and, although you can argue that sport is part of history, my first two years working here have been more or less sport-free. Like many New Zealanders, I'm a sports fan, used to chewing over the weekend results with my colleagues. But not at the Jewish Museum. Sport is part of what drives intellectuals to intellectual pursuits, and museums are made by intellectuals, especially in Germany. Plus, mourning the defeat of Man United seems a trivial indulgence beside the Holocaust.

But the soccer World Cup changed all that. In June 2002 Germany had the kind of dream run at the tournament that even the museum's concept staff could not ignore.

It wasn't that Germany had a great team. Their biggest star was their goalie and they appeared to have no attacking players at all—among their strikers was Carsten Jancker, so

Listener, 12 October 2002

lumbering that an English commentator said his inclusion proved that Germans have a sense of humour. But somehow this seemed to mean that the ordinary German citizenry could enjoy their team's participation. Nothing was expected, Germany had nothing to lose. Germany would simply be a nation among nations. Which, after all, is what it's been seeking to be ever since the end of World War II.

The cup was hard to ignore. 'Weltmeisterschaft!' thundered every newspaper headline. The museum's security guards carried the commentary from the matches in the early rounds live on their headsets. In the middle of a meeting about whether the museum should remove its Christmas tree from an exhibit about assimilation, fireworks exploded outside the window—'Germany has scored,' remarked a colleague dryly.

Then an email from the Museum's *Geschäftsführer* (I was surprised that anyone at a Jewish museum would accept a title with the word *'führer'* in it, but apparently this is an everyday word) informed us that because Germany had made the quarter-finals of the cup, all staff would be allowed to stop work and watch the next game live in the museum's auditorium.

You don't get too many perks at a German institution and this was something for nothing—maybe that's why the auditorium was so full? Whatever, when I stuck my head round the door, there were already thirty people staring expectantly at the big screen. Most of them were folk I don't have much to do with, the museum's *Hausmeisters* and clerks—not because I'm a snob, never, but because we don't have a language in common. *Hausmeisters* and the like don't receive enough education to speak English, most of them can't even manage 'hello', and my pathetic inability to learn other languages means that in this country I am always an outsider. But today these people embrace me as a brother. They are comforted that one of the museum's senior staff would arrive to legitimise this occasion.

The game is to be shown on a huge screen, garishly bright at one end of the darkened hall. The commentary is in German, of course, and maybe a little droll—there's lots of nervous laughter at the commentator's jokes, but I don't understand and have to concentrate on the football. Germany's opponents are the US, who in footballing terms are bunnies. Which makes everyone nervous: it would be okay for Germany to lose to, say, Brazil, but if the Americans beat them, this will be a humiliation.

Another humiliation. Is it too much to suggest that every German since the Holocaust feels they were humiliated before they were born? Living among these people, that is what you sense, painful knowledge of original sin. The scorn about things German—especially the German character—can be vicious. Not because they're Jewish. No more than 5 per cent of the museum's staff are Jewish. There are only about 80,000 Jews in Germany today, and 70 per cent of those are Russian immigrants who have in the last decade discovered their Jewishness—since the war, all Jews wanting to live in Germany have ease of entry. 'He is a typical German,' one colleague says of a contractor and this is not a compliment. 'That is so German,' I am told, never with pride. Yet they are all just people, funny and sad in the normal human proportions.

On the big screen the camera crawls past the faces of the German team, stonefaced as the national anthem is played. Over them the TV producers have imposed a hovering, ghostly image of a man's features. Martina on my left informs me that this is Fritz Walter, a famous German player, who died today, 81 years old. He was 'the *Ehrenspielführer*, the leader of the team by honour'. Back when we had honour—but she doesn't say that. The team all wear black armbands.

Finally, the game starts. Well, in hindsight, what can you say about a game of football? Some guys kicked the ball and then other guys kicked the ball—it was the feeling in the room that mattered. Quickly I realise that I am in a patriotic crowd, a first for me in Germany. I'd been among soccer fans, Hertha-Berlin guys jamming up the U-bahn, drunk and rowdy, but they were exhibiting a purely local fervour. National pride is a strangled emotion in this country. When, last year, a conservative German politician announced in the Bundestag that he was 'proud to be a German', it made headlines and he was denounced. This is a country that wants to be proud, but isn't sure it is allowed.

One by one, somewhat sheepishly, the museum's concept staff slip in and find seats. The auditorium is now full. In the half-dark, in the crowd, people are abandoning their reticence and cheering openly for Germany. I realise that I am rooting for the Americans. I hadn't known I would feel like this and it gives me a little shock. For two years I have been careful never to show any anti-German feeling. Now I am having to make sure I don't shout when the Americans look like scoring. It's strange how your emotions can capture you. I tell myself that I'm not homesick, but then when I hear English spoken I get a rush of feeling. To be an outsider, it's uncomfortable. To always be adapting yourself to the ways of others.

At half-time, with the score at nil-nil, the lights go up and everyone hurries out for a nerve-calming cigarette. In this country, they all smoke like crazy. Is this some post-Holocaust self-destructiveness? No. It's simply European.

But I'm no smoker, plus I'm feeling maybe a little strange.

So I stay in the lobby and examine a display entitled 'Juden im Deutschen Fussball—Jews and German Soccer'. In three vitrines there are kippot with soccer-ball patterns, pennants from Makkabi, a Jewish soccer club. These seem like minor objects, it's as though something is being insisted upon. Clippings, old newspaper photographs, faded old guys kicking a faded old ball—what Don DeLillo has called 'the graininess of history'. The introduction tells me that 'the Jews in Germany actively took part in this sport'. Interestingly, the whole of the text uses the past tense, as though there are no Jews in Germany today, no Jewish life. This is not far from the truth. Where the Jews of Germany are concerned, it's no contest, the past will always outweigh the present.

> In the more than 100-year history of German soccer only two Jewish players were members of the national team: Gottfried Fuchs, who played six internationals between 1911 and 1913, and Julius Hirsch, who appeared in seven games during the same period. Fuchs scored 10 goals in a 16-0 victory over Russia during the 1912 Olympics, a world record that stands to this day. Both men served as soldiers in World War I and received the Iron Cross. Fuchs emigrated to Canada in 1937. Hirsch, who divorced his Christian wife in 1939 to protect her and their children from the Nazis, was deported on March 1 1943 to Auschwitz and murdered.

The second half of the match is very much like the first, but only a dreamer would fail to notice that during the break the German analysts have cracked the American game. All American attacks are snuffed out with what can only be called Teutonic thoroughness. But can the Germans be creative enough to actually score a goal? The crowd is worried. The tension in the hall is as palpable as a heartbeat. Yet another German attack ends with a whimper—around me, breath is released in a sigh of disgust. I feel a little twisted. I want to stand up and shout it out, to come clean: 'I am for the Jews!' Sorry, I got that wrong, of course I mean the Americans. This is such a country to be an outsider in.

This country did put itself through some hell.

But not for nothing has it won the World Cup on two previous occasions. Eventually, inexperience in the US defence allows an overlap on the left and German striker Michael Ballack calmly boots the ball home. The hall erupts. People make fists, one even raises a little flag. There is relief—and maybe defiance.

Soon after, it's finished. One-nil over America, this is not really a result to celebrate, especially since the German team looked so clubfooted. The mood quickly evaporates, particularly when the camera lifts to show the German fans. Live from Korea, their paint-smeared faces are filling screens all over the world. Wearing plastic wigs in the German colours, they jump up and down like excited kids, brandishing their beer cans. Lots of them are fat, white inches of bulging German underbelly are exposed and wobbling. Inside the auditorium the crowd hisses—no one wants to be associated with those guys. Quickly, someone snaps the lights on and everyone leaves. 'A win for German efficiency,' remarks a colleague with heavy irony.

'Before the game is after the game.' As a little knot of us make our way back to our office Martina tells me that this is the most famous saying in German soccer. I like this, it gives you more to think about than 'a game of two halves'. Out of kindness to me, everyone is speaking English. Now Martina says that, 'The other famous saying is "the ball is round".' Well, yes, I think we can all go along with that. As we walk, there is no excitement about the win, only analysis. It's as though the boring inevitable has happened.

Four days later we are all in the auditorium again to see Germany beat Korea and thus progress to the big showdown. This time people are excited. 'We made the final!' With this team!—but no one says that. In the final they will meet the Brazilians and even the biggest dreamer in the hall knows they will not beat Brazil, not with this team, not playing football like that. But honour is satisfied. Against all odds, German honour is satisfied.

And so it goes. The ball is round and so it rolls as it should: in the final Brazil duly beat Germany 2-0 and are the big winners. This match took place on the weekend and I watched it at home, without my colleagues. I didn't really care who won. Maybe I hoped for Germany, so I could see the effect a win might have.

But even losing had an effect. It drew something out. This happened live on television, when the German team were welcomed home, by a huge crowd, in Frankfurt. I saw bits of it, the usual images of the team waving down from open-topped buses to the pressing hordes. A landscape of painted faces, flags waving—there was something mediaeval in this—everyone in striped German shirts, chanting, 'Deutschland! Deutschland! Deutschland!' It was all very familiar. The soccer tribe doesn't feel it has to come up with anything new—quite the opposite. Ritual is the thing. But it was the voice-over that was interesting. It was in German, I didn't understand and changed channels. Then on the Monday, a colleague told me. 'What the sportscasters said, talking over the pictures of the cheering crowd, was "Today we must be allowed to do this." To wave the flag, to chant the name of our team, our country, to thump our hearts and visibly swell with pride. We must be allowed to do this. What harm can it do?'

I Give You
My Money

Berlin is a city with roughly the same number of inhabitants
as New Zealand, in an area the size of Wellington. What
that means is, living here, you have more encounters with
people per minute and more of those encounters are with
people you don't know and will never know. This affects
your idea of yourself as a thing worth a second glance—my
wife asked a friend, 'Do you think I can wear this?' and was
told, 'In Berlin? Wear what you like.' Some people respond by
becoming extroverts. Not many, punks mostly, pretending it's
still 1977 (tartan miniskirts are back this year). A few put in
a big push and become Somebody, and that is the last we need
concern ourselves with them. The rest of us are reduced to a
kind of stoic anonymity. Okay, let's get racist for a moment:
this is Germany and so no one was that demonstrative to
begin with. Flair is on a long lunch hour here. As a German

colleague dryly remarked when Deutschland ground out a win at the World Cup of soccer, 'Another victory for German efficiency.' After a while what descends is something like the grey weather of the soul.

This then is about one New Zealander out in that weather.

On my way to work, there's this guy I give money to, pretty well every day. He is an item I tick off, along with checking to see how many cranes are currently swinging over Potsdamer Platz and whether there are any crows in this one big field. But now I see that he's actually on my train, with the other passengers. Then he gets off at my station, Hallesches Tor. I guess this isn't so surprising, because it's at Hallesches Tor that I usually see him, sitting down with his back against the base of one of the big concrete pillars that hold up the train line.

In Berlin there's your selection of people to give money to. Over four million unemployed in Germany, plus immigrants who aren't even on the radar, and rising. I usually give something to the Turkish women—I think they're Turkish—who sit on the footpath, which strikes me as a chilling thing to do, with a paper cup held out, their heads wrapped by scarves, which is their custom but also, under these circumstances, a hood within which they can retreat. They don't look up, these women, they're just a huddle, down there to your left, against the wall, attached to a cup that hangs in the air. Sometimes they have kids with them and this looks terrible. The kids always look stilled by the cold, half-dead.

So how much do you give? I see people give their 'klein geld', their little money, copper coins and shiny cents. I usually give a Euro—I want to make them think, 'That was a good hit!' I want to see them pleased, to see them cheer up.

Well, I don't think I have to grind through the emotions here, they're highly familiar.

I usually give to the guys who come onto the trains selling *Motz*, which I've never looked at, since it's in German, but as far as I can see no one ever does look at it. They never take a copy, they just pass over a Euro or so and the guys go *Danky shern*, or, when they realise that I speak English, Dank you. Dank you. Lots of nodding and smiling. *Motz* is, I presume, one of those newspapers like *The Big Issue* which, I have read, unemployed people sell in London. For some reason it's an easier transaction to give to the *Motz* sellers. I guess it's like they're working.

It's easier if everybody's working.

There's a guy who stands just along from Hermes in the Friedrichstrasse who looks a lot like George Burns—a little guy in a cardigan, with hair slicked flat across an oval head and glasses with large round black frames. But George never looked as downbeaten as this guy, who is red-faced and always has a frosting of white stubble. He has semi-decent shoes and corduroy trousers with turned-up cuffs. You can see he had a good job once. He holds a ragged cardboard sign. He always stands—standing is work—and holds his sign in front of his chest like a guy in an American police photo. I can't read it—it would be uncouth to stop and study the words—but I know what it says: 'They fired me for being boring, my wife left me for a younger man, then my daughter kicked me out, whatever you give will be employed only for the purposes of flagellation.' At first I used to give this guy the go-by, he annoyed me, but I only ever see him when I'm on my way to Dussmann's to buy as many CDs as I think I can sneak into the house, and I started to feel bad.

My technique is, I go past them, decide, step into a doorway so that I can go through the coins in my wallet unobserved, and go back. I can't imagine deciding in front of them—'Oh, no, not the twenty-Euro note, why should I? No, ten cents will do for you.'

Once, in Wellington, this was years ago, I saw a guy with a sign and a bowl and I gave him a few coins. I was shocked—in New Zealand! Then a few days later I decided to give him a hit and I dropped a five-dollar note into his bowl. His eyes popped. But he didn't look at me—of course I had walked on but I contrived to see him. He stared at the note. Then he looked up and down the street, canny, picked up his sign and the bowl, and made off. I was chuffed. A few days later I saw his picture in the local paper. There was an interview with him but it was incoherent. The accompanying text was sombre—'Begging In Wellington.' But a friend said to me, 'Oh, that guy, he's a bit of a character. I see him noshing at that fancy bistro place in Upper Willis Street, he doesn't need to beg.'

What was it Johnny Rotten used to snarl at the end of Sex Pistols gigs? 'Ever feel you've been cheated?'

Sorry, this is turning into a short history of. But suddenly all kinds of memories come to me. In Los Angeles, this was in 1991, I was approached, early evening, as I came out of a bookstore, by a tattered-looking guy with a Stars and Stripes sewn onto his denim jacket. 'I'm a vet,' he said. He had his hand out. There was something pathetic and needy in this, and also something aggressive. He knew I guess that I was the right age—that I had marched against the war. (That's the Vietnam War for you younger readers—my war. Iraq is your war—did you do anything about it? Me, I marched. I took my daughter. This was in Berlin, where we did the right thing, over a million of us, or even two million, depending on who's telling. The music they played was from my war—see, I was right. Sixties music is best.) I hurried away. My justification was his aggression and also I had a kind of fear-of-America which was telling me, Don't get into uncontrolled encounters with the natives. But I have never managed to forget this guy. He had a droopy moustache like one of the *Doonesbury* characters, but dirty, a loser. I guess I owed him.

Well, they just drink it all don't they.

And in Spain the women maim their kids and then show you the stumpy limbs to tear at your heart. Is that true? I have no idea, but I have been told it twenty times. My heart was utterly ripped apart, in Madrid and also in Ventimiglia on the Italian border. Exhausted women sitting in the dust holding children in extremis, while you decide whether 900 francs is too much for a leather jacket.

Yet somehow it survived and later that year I used it to fall in love, again. My heart, I mean.

There are gangs, you know, it's all organised, a good beggar can make a heap of money—haven't you ever read *The Threepenny Opera*?

And the gypsies hassle you and curse you if you don't cross their palm. I have seen them, in Greece and in Spain. They ganged up on a woman I know, a little team of them got her flustered and stole every cent in her purse. That really happened.

Anyway, the guy I give to is on my train and I guess I found this disturbing.

He's respectable.

I started giving to him about ten months ago. I can remember the first time. I had just had a piece of good news and it looked like I was suddenly going to bring in a pile of cash. Okay, I confess: I'm a writer and after years of trying it looked as though I had finally produced a book that might actually make some money. Real money—the big time. Well, as we used to say in the playground: dreams are free. And I did dream. Going up the Friedrichstrasse, next item after George Burns is a car dealership and in the window they have an immense Bentley on a turntable, dark red, as though the fires of Hell have been sublimated and polished, and I would walk past and think, Why not? Why would you deny yourself that? Of course, it would be a bugger to park—you'd have to find somewhere where people can't get at it. They scratch the paintwork, you know, with coins, out of envy.

On cloud nine.

And it was around this time that I really started giving money away. I think the idea was to propitiate the gods. To make Fate think that I was a good guy to whom big money could be entrusted. Oh, maybe I'm being too hard. Maybe it was just that I was feeling good. Whatever: my wallet opened.

And there was this guy, at Hallesches Tor.

He kept, I discovered, business hours, more or less. And when I observed him I saw that his clothes weren't too bad—faded jeans, denim jacket, sneakers. All fairly clean and every now and then looking like they had been ironed. White hair, combed back, and a white beard. Maybe he looked a little like John Huston? It's always best, I find, to use people from the media for these IDs. On bright days he had a real cool pair of sunglasses that he would wear. He'd take his sneakers off and sit there toasting his toes, bum on a square of newspaper to keep the cold from rising. Out front he had a paper plate which I recognised as coming from the nearby döner place—he would get a fresh one every day and set it out, and then sit beside it in exemplary fashion, looking around interestedly, waiting for some money to arrive.

I gave him a bit of change, and then a bit more; then the day came when he'd just sat down and I placed maybe four Euro in his dish, a minor cascade of coins. That made him stare. Then he looked up at me and said, animated, 'Danke schön.' And there was something else, too, but I shook my head and said, 'Sorry, I only speak English.' So he mimed, eagerly, that he was going to go and eat—his hand came up to his mouth and he rubbed his tummy. This made me feel terrific. I was feeding this guy.

As it happened, I was early that day and didn't have a lot on, so instead of going to work I wandered off and sort of hid on the far side of the bridge which is just at hand there and watched the river flow. From that distance I kept an eye on what he did. Immediately he went across to the kiosk, bought cigarettes, came back, sat down and smoked one.

This pissed me off.

At the same time . . . I have to say, I really liked the way that he enjoyed that cigarette. It was obviously the first of the day. I have never been a smoker and its pleasures fascinate me. Lighting one up in bed—the flare of the match in the darkness. The way that smoke would curl from your fingers. My guy bent over this cigarette—he was squatting now like an Indian—and concentrated on it. I saw that it sent him off into a zone.

I continued to give to him. He developed an intense, emphatic way of delivering thank-yous. But he never said hello. He never looked at me. What he looked at was the plate, to see how much he'd got.

Some days I'm not in the mood.

And sometimes he sleeps. His plate is still there, waiting, with a copper or two as your starter. But he's sleeping on the job! It's like he's a fisherman who has his pole in the river and when the bite comes there's no one home. It's like he expects the plate to do the work.

I wonder about his life. Is he sleeping out? No, his clothes are too clean. Some days he wears white shirts, two buttons undone, and in this he looks like some rogue from a noir movie. How does he manage to keep a white shirt clean? I never can. Does he have a wife? Maybe she thinks he's got a job—every morning, a peck and out the door. The papers he reads are always uncrumpled—does he buy his own fucking papers?

If it's hot he sometimes has a beer. The can, it's always Beck's, none of your cheap beers, sits beside him on the ground. He takes a sip. How come he doesn't look like a drunk? There are drunks for miles round here, they claim all the public benches and have bench parties, shouting, disputing, laughing as though they're having the best of it. If they catch you looking they laugh at you—as though you're the latest thing that the television of the world has served up for their entertainment.

But I am always looking.

What's there to see in Berlin? It's not a pretty place, nor is it grand. The façades of the buildings are scarred—and that is the strongest impression, that this is a place where things have happened, where history was made. The faces of the buildings are lined, deep grooves running from the nose to the corners of the mouth. Mouth set hard to ensure there are no infractions. Rheumy old eyes. You can never surprise this city. But partly that's because it's beyond surprise, or even interest. That's it: nothing new will happen here.

And then I'm standing at a crossing, watching for the light to change. It's early winter. A truck approaching from my left sees that the woman beside me has started to cross and slams on its brakes. The driver had cleared the frost from his windscreen with a scraper. But he hadn't looked on his roof. When he stops a flat sheet of ice, two metres square, slides forward, down the bonnet, and slaps onto the road, where, right at my feet, it explodes into a thousand shining pieces. Driver, woman and I all grin at each other.

Swans walk on the frozen surface of the canal, slap-footed.

A squirrel, thirty metres up, gets from one tree to the next by flying.

There is a jackhammer inside the woodpecker's head.

It surprises me, all this nature in the city. Every street is thick with trees and they are always telling you the time—spring time, summer time, autumn and time for all the leaves to fall. Every tree is numbered—well, this is Germany—and is managed so that it thrives. The streets are kept scrupulously clean, as long you live in one of the better suburbs. There are squads of people to manage the snow, and the leaves, and the railway lines—recently, when there was a fender-bender outside my house on Saturday morning, a team of eight orange-suited guys arrived to bounce the cars to the curb. That was in addition to four cops and twenty rubber-neckers. For a dent.

Yes, everything runs like clockwork. But what's it all for?

I'm lifting an espresso to my pointed lips at Einstein's (who are they kidding?) when I see that he's sitting, four tables away, in the sun, cool shades on, legs crossed and thinking of nothing. My guy—where does he get the money for luxury coffee?

I follow chicks (one day I'll use that word without shying) through the streets. Well, not really, but you're trucking it up to Dussmann's and she passes you and even from behind the gap between her short top and her hipsters is somewhere that your eyes can warm themselves. The back is underrated, in my opinion. The spine. That rich latte colour—oh, groan. I would hate for anyone to think I'm a stalker, I always fade away before I do any harm—though maybe girls can sense you back there? But, curves like that, it's enough to make you feel young again.

I'm sure he hasn't got a wife. Somewhere he has a small room, where his selection of books is utterly rigorous. Five CDs, Monk, Bird or Coltrane. At night he stands outside clubs, in the cold, ear to a grating, eyes half closed, inside the saxophone, the bassman's thwack. People offer cigarettes. On the first Sunday of every month the museums are free and this is a big day for him.

Do these guys pay to ride the U-bahn?

Finally we get a sitter and my wife and I can go out with friends. They know somewhere special, in Prenzlauer Berg, a little restaurant with character and a bit of history, called Offenbach Stuben—very German. Very expensive. We ride through the night on the bumping train. The carriage is crowded and we are separated. It's a huge crush of no one that I know. Faces an inch from mine, bodies almost pressed.

Prenzlauer Berg is where they took Bill Clinton for a stylish coffee.

Box of Light

With blood fresh on his chin
The young man pushed through the carriage
Explaining that he was starving
His hand open before him
'Bitte, Bitte, Bitte.'

A skinny boy saved us all
Produced a gold coin
Helped wipe the blood away
They shook on it
Then his skinny hand drifted down
To tangle the fingers of the quiet girl
With the diamond in her navel
As the train rocked
I spied on their secret caresses
Later we ate expensively
In a restaurant famous
For entertaining the apparatchiks
Of the former GDR.
When we'd paid, the proprietor
Also produced a coin
From yesteryear, worn thin

Which, dropped into a slot,
Made stiff little dolls dance
To the music of a scratchy violin
Inside a wooden box of light.

Sinai Holiday

We flew from Berlin to Sharm El Sheikh at the bottom of the Sinai peninsula. I knew that's where Sharm El Sheikh was because I'd looked it up—I wouldn't have been able to place it within a thousand miles. Don DeLillo says that Americans learn geography by fighting wars with other countries. For me it's tourism. I have to have a map and know where I am. As I'm sure you know, the Sinai is the triangle-shaped piece of desert that lies between Africa and Asia. The Red Sea lies vertically and, at its top, two arms, like the horns of a snail, reach upwards. The left arm is the Gulf of Suez and the right the Gulf of Aqaba. Sharm El Sheikh is at the bottom tip of the triangle and that's where we flew to, Air Berlin, a flight carrying mainly Germans and Arabs, big-time smokers both, which may be why the voice-over suddenly announced that those in rows twenty to thirty-five could now light up. I think it must be two decades since I was in a smoking plane.

2004, previously unpublished

On arrival we had to buy visas from an Arab guy who could, without a word of any language other than Arabic, take whatever currency you had, indicate what to do with the visa stamps, and still make a reasonable profit on the deal. The Egyptian pounds he gave me for change were so limp they looked like all possible value had long been wrung from them.

It was pretty hot. I had been wondering just how hot it would be—this was like an Auckland thermometer-topper. I presented my passport with the immigration card cunningly placed so that the guy opened directly to the page with the new visa stamps. I didn't want him thumbing through and seeing that I had been in Israel recently. It worked—and one item was crossed off my worry list.

There were a few others. I did ask our Embassy if we were wise to travel there but they found this inquiry insufficiently urgent to warrant a reply. Our Berlin neighbour is a worry wart, the day before we left he said, 'Make sure we have all your passport numbers and travel details and health insurance and where you're staying and take your mobile phone and all of our contact numbers.' Okay, thanks for that.

On the plane I had been reading the *Lonely Planet*, which said that so much as opening a door for you was regarded by Egyptians as the justification for baksheesh and so it proved (I love it when experience follows the guide book, it gives confidence). The baggage carousel was manned by Egyptians who took every bag off before you had a chance and then said, 'Three children, three children', insistently, and then in German also in case that would do the trick. 'I've got three too,' I said and claimed my bag. Well, I didn't have any change, except the limp pounds, and I hadn't had a good enough chance to study them yet. Oh dear. It's terrible how mean you get when the holiday is incredibly cheap, as though your sole aim is to make it cheaper still.

Everywhere you turned people were offering to do things for you but I carried our bags and kept my head down. The touting wasn't nasty—completely not. It was friendly, warm. That was my experience of all the Arabs we met.

Out into the hot blue afternoon of the taxi depot and within seconds our friends spotted our driver and the unstructured part of our holiday was over. From exiting the plane it had lasted maybe five minutes.

We had travelled from Berlin with our friends Isabel and Thomas and their two kids and Thomas's medical colleague Holger, and were headed for something called an 'eco-resort', named Basata, where Isabel and Thomas have been coming for fifteen years. I had of course checked out the website and stared anxiously at pictures of the sleeping cabins, communal area, kitchen and the 'Bedouin Room'. Isabel and Thomas said it was a place where eco-values where strongly observed—that you slept in semi-enclosed shanties on the beach, that there was no electricity or shop, no town, no hot water, just nature—oh, and camels that walked past your door. I have suddenly remembered that they promised these camels, I promised them to our kids. But these camels were not delivered on.

We travelled from Sharm El Sheikh in a communal taxi, a white mini-van, about twelve of us, our bags tied to the roof and everyone all eyes. I was excited. I admit it. I love a new country. Also I knew that the first hours are the most amazing, that's when everything thrills you. I positioned myself at the very back of the van, where no one wanted to sit, and drank the windows.

Sand.

The road was thick, black, fresh tarseal, with no markings, and it lay on the sand as though someone had been determined to draw a line. On either side sudden walls of rock rose to stand in the air, jagged and dramatic, as apparently two-dimensional as movie flats in the vivid blue air. Between the road and the rocks was the sand, drifts of it, panels of sand divided by sand ridges and sand ripples and sand peaks. Nothing growing. There was something exciting about the sand, something alive—as though it was the active element here, the defining substance. There was sand everywhere you looked, sand all the way to horizon and, you know, plenty more where that came from.

The road signs were in squiggly Arabic writing! I loved this. That writing is so beautiful and so indecipherable. That is the thrill of a new place, that even the 'No Parking' signs can increase your heartbeat.

Actually, there was almost nothing to see, but this absence was amazing.

The kids were restless so Isabel said, 'Who will be first to see a camel?' I competed fiercely. But there would, I knew, be no camels here, nor any people. This wasn't a land where anyone could live. It's like Antarctica, which I visited a few years ago, in that you know in your heart that humans are not intended to be here. The sand, bound to be burning, and then the peaks of rock, raw, jagged like stegosaurus spines, and the glassy air—no, nothing could live here. Immediately Isabel said, 'Camel', and there you could see him, a mile away, standing, that distinctive outline, like an image on a postage stamp. It was completely astonishing to see a camel outside a zoo. 'Two camels,' said Isabel (well, she's been here before) and this time they were closer, tethered in the sand by lines connecting their noses to pet rocks. They were nothing like zoo camels—skinny, hard, stripped-down creatures, sand-blasted and dry like beach wood.

Suddenly there were camels everywhere, camels walking, camels being ridden, camels sitting with their legs tucked up, cat-like. Now I could see that those things I had thought were square-shaped clumps of rock, or maybe piles of road-working gear, were in fact dwellings, made of breeze-blocks, with flapping awnings of plastic. People in robes were walking into what seemed to be a stiff breeze, their heads covered, or sitting in the shade. Frankly, these houses seemed like slum dwellings. 'The Bedouin,' said Thomas. Now, to the right, between looming rocks, suddenly there were many camels, all sitting, and as the road curved I saw more and more of them, fifty camels, a hundred, hunkered down in the sand. And between them, groups of people in robes, sitting in circles. 'It's Friday,' said Thomas, 'their day of rest. They get together and socialise.'

Out there in the landscape? You think they could find a nicer place.

But there is no nicer place, everywhere you look it's the same, hard sand and terrible rocks and nothing else. This is where they live and you just can't get over the amazingness of the human will to make a home of every circumstance that the planet can offer.

Overhead, a falcon floats, its wings curved back so that it makes a crescent shape, like a flying crossbow. That's right, I'd forgotten, falconry started here.

On the rocks, spray-painted words—in Arabic script! This amazes. Road signs are one thing, obviously there are official experts who know how to inscribe this gorgeous writing. But to use it for graffiti, that is just written by anyone—this seems like the casual possession of amazing knowledge.

I trust I'm not coming off as too much of a honky here.

Other gatherings, more camels—I collect them as though they have been arranged for my education. Long stretches of nothing, just sand and those violent rocks. Then, standing in flat vista of utter inhospitality, a sign with the gorgeous script and, below it, the words, 'NO TRESPASSING.' But who would go there? Maybe they have a lot of trouble with petanque players.

The trip north from Sharm El Sheikh takes, I know from the guide book, two and a quarter hours. I am waiting to glimpse the sea but so far it's just been sand, anyone? Occasionally now there are single trees, slim, in-drawn things which look as though the moisture is being sucked out of them from below. In their meagre shade the odd goat can be seen.

Now the road takes us towards a roadblock. Metal barrels painted bright blue have been placed so as to make a winding path that the van has to slow to negotiate. There are soldiers with dark-gleaming guns, and, low, a block house. 'Passports,' says Isabel. The soldiers come and scrunitise our documents very carefully. They open the side door of the van and, one by one, identify us. It's impersonal, and therefore a little threatening. But there are no problems, and they wave us on. No smiles. Nothing nasty either, but it reminds you that you are in the Middle East.

Behind the block house, on the broad curve of the bald brown hilltop, someone has made huge letters with lines of white stones: LOVE SINAI. There is something old about this, like the Nazca lines or the chalk horses of England.

We press on. There continues to be absolutely nothing to see—sand, rocks, road signs—and I continue to be thrilled by it. Genuinely, I feel wild-eyed, hungry. It's as though the very barrenness is an empty space that your imagination fills with teeming significance. The driver, Ali, drives very fast and is quite happy overtaking on blind corners. But he seems utterly competent and I accept the risk-taking as a professional doing his expert work. Up an endless hill, a twenty-minute climb. In fact there are very few cars on the road. A local camaraderie is at work—Ali honks, waves, often at things that I can't see. Then we are running down to the coast and everyone in the van cheers.

'There's the sea, kiddies!' Nothing like stating the obvious to make everyone completely, utterly happy.

The land on our right, half a mile between us and the water, is suddenly thick with seaside resorts. 'Blue Wave', 'Dolphin Bay', 'Red Rocks', now all the language is English. 'Freedom Beach—visit The Freedome!' But nobody is. Hundreds of little cabins are arranged in rows, in artistic shapes, against the blue of the Red Sea. Many of these places feature roadside art—a giant plaster teapot and teacups, bright yellow and reminiscent of the Mad Hatter, somehow imported and wilfully nutty. Ethnic shapes to the window frames, eccentric structures. Mud huts. Grass huts. White plaster huts. But no people.

Thomas explains. 'They built all these places, thinking there would be a tourist boom—this is the Egyptian Riviera. But it wasn't what people wanted, they have all failed. And that was even before September eleven.' Now I see that many of the buildings have been abandoned mid-completion. But others have been kept up and are fresh-painted and eager-looking. It makes no difference. There is clearly not a single customer in the twenty miles of continuous resorts that we pass. It's eerie.

Then suddenly a hoarding says, BASATA—A PIECE OF NATURE, and we're slowing.

Basata is one of those places where you know instantly upon arrival that here there is nothing, absolutely nothing whatsoever, to do. Immediately you begin to walk more slowly. The heat hangs heavy in the air. Beneath your feet, now shoeless, the sand is soft and dry. The waters of the Gulf of Aqaba are blue and clear. Across the water, ten miles, the hills of Saudi Arabia rise to make faint pencil tracings against the sky. As the night comes in you can see, to the north, the glow of Aqaba itself, a city of legend, and, along the Saudi shore, a string of lights above the water—very reminiscent of the view from Wellington towards the Orongorongos. Nothing moves. There are no seagulls, not even sparrows. However, after two days, even baby Frank knows how to say 'bloody flies' in a suitably exasperated tone.

We settle ourselves in the hut we have been allocated, in the third row back from the beach, much to Susanna's chagrin. If we didn't have such a very good marriage she might have said some very cross words to me about allowing this hut to fall to us. Obviously the ones right by the water were better but, darling, we didn't get one of those.

The huts are made of bamboo, with large bamboo poles at the corners and as rafters and bundles of thin bamboo stakes sewn together to make the walls. There are lots of gaps where, now that it's dusk, we can see the first stars. The wind whispers through. But that's good, it's hot.

There is a bamboo sleeping platform with two thin mattresses, a bamboo shelf, a bamboo stool and two more mattresses on the floor, which is sand, covered by striped rugs woven from rag. We have a little bamboo veranda and, when we glance outside, a Mercedes Benz made of bamboo is driving the length of the foreshore. No, I made that up.

We amble along to the evening meal. You have to sit, Arab-style, at low tables, on large cushions. Seventy-year-old Germans in kaftans and Birkenstocks can do it, kids can do it effortlessly, but I cannot do it and for the entire time we are there I kneel upright so that I loom over the table, or, if I can get away with it, lie full length, my mouth at table level—hugely elegant. The Basata team appears from the kitchen bearing trays and with some ceremony the food is placed about. Piles of spiced rice, stuffed peppers, avocado whip, red beans with corn, spicy red sauce, creamy slaw, shredded carrot, baked potatoes with potato chips that were not shaken from a packet, a bowl of baba ganoush. It all looks wonderful, brightly coloured on the hospital white of chipped enamel plates and, on the first night, tastes delicious. But over the next few days, despite changes in colour and texture, the taste doesn't vary much and you start to wonder if maybe the cook leaves out strong spices in deference to European palates. Then, on the fourth day, baby Frank says it to the whole table, loud into a silence: 'Want meat!' But there is no meat in Basata.

Mostly the eating is done in a silence heavy with appreciation. This meal, in a place where there is nothing to do, is the focal point of the day, when the senses are lifted. At the same time there is a particular quality to the meals, which is that this is just simple food—the food of the people. It takes me a day or two to figure. Basata is a resort. Normally we would have waiters bringing plates with, oh, caviar and Gorgonzola, and you would exercise your discrimination. Here there is a 'this is it, take it or leave it' quality. And of course we take it; it's what we're here for. We take the hand-made shanties that we sleep in. We take the water restrictions, the lack of electricity, the sand floors. Some of us, the virtuous, come back from walks on the beach with handfuls of plastic bags and other rubbish. This is an eco-resort and we are here, I realise, to suffer privation, and to pay for the privilege. Meanwhile those who serve us live in normal houses, up on the ridge at the back, and have mains power.

During the day people read—I was tempted to open a bookshop. There's something wonderful to a booky person to walk along the beach and see in every shanty a body in togs and sunglasses with its face in a volume. The sea is great for swimming, very clear, and there are coral reefs to snorkel over, thick with fish. The fish are amazing, brightly-coloured and in every shape from the boxy to the steam-rollered. I saw a scorpionfish, with its corolla of poison barbs, and what looked like a John Dory, listing, and nameless fish that glowed as though they were lit from inside, and melancholy fish which drifted alone above gently waving pastures of green. Angelfish—one aggressive little bugger nipped me on the ankle, twice. A coral-covered rock which had brain coral and branch coral and no doubt Thousand Island coral also.

To tell the truth, I am quickly bored by skindiving.

So we ambled about—went for long walks on the beach with the kids. South of the resort beach there were rock pools thick with starfish—long feathery arms, like the limbs of gibbons, curling from beneath every stone. Squirting anemones. Little octopi, the size of potatoes, which jetted ahead in the shallows, in that surge-then-fade pattern which keeps them just out of reach. Little fish—how children do scream for little fish. Crabs. The crabs were also potato-sized and, when you approached, broke from the water to run up the sand slope. They could really motor! We chased them all but they had holes dug in advance into which they bolted. Pretty shells, plastic buckets full of shells, and fragments of coral, which, because we were good, we threw back. The Arab fishermen, in long pale green robes with matching turbans, broke from cleaning their net to give us the thumbs-up for this, and big grins. Approval from the natives, this is warming to the eco-heart.

Up behind the central complex (bamboo) where meals and the fridge were to be found (it's not true about the electricity, that's only in the shanties; there was a big diesel generator) was the stone office complex and, beyond, the industrial production area. I came to know it intimately as, back here, there was a stone-walled enclosure with, working upwards, doves, chickens, sheep, goats, donkeys, and, wait for it, a camel. This camel had to be visited by Frank in the company of his father at least four times a day. Since the animal complex was Fly Central, and since the camel never did so much as flick us an eyelid, these were trying times. But Frank can be very persuasive.

Beyond the camel was a piece of open ground where ten thousand mud bricks were drying. I loved them—loved every hand-slapped one of them. It looked like mud-pie heaven. Every brick was hedgehogged with bits of straw. Covering my actions with my back, I gave one a good whack. It broke in half. But they were building houses with these things; I went to look at one under construction. The exposed piece of wall had the bricks piled higgledy-piggledy inside, gappy, but two feet along, the plaster covered all. The walls were fifteen inches thick. There was something marvellous about the use of these bricks, it was as though they were timeless pieces of simple ingenuity.

I stared at the guys who were the workers—faces ranging from the merely tan to sparkling coal-black.

I stared at the Bedouin woman who came, face enscarfed, to spread her beadwork and crochet on the rugs of the dining room—how she lifted the underside of her facial wrap to slide the cigarette up underneath. Her chocolate-coloured bare feet.

I struggled my way through *The Cross and the Crescent: The dramatic story of the earliest encounters between Christians and Muslims*, 150 large-type pages in six slow days. I looked and looked, I wanted to know what I was seeing. I wanted the exotic. Edward Said was growling in my ear but he's dead now, I didn't care. But this was a resort.

Lovely breakfasts, though. Abu, the baker, he of the sparkling black skin, a Nubian, would make hot rolls and cheese breads and feta turnovers which you just helped yourself to, marking what you took on a kind of score sheet. The big fridge, too, ran on an honesty system and there was something sweet about just helping yourself to whatever you wanted and never fumbling for change.

Hours spent in the communal area, flicking away flies, talking to strangers, sighing.

So this is eco-tourism, you thought, and had another can of cold Coke.

On my return a friend said, 'Eco-tourism? You blew that by flying there.' True, only too true, but I am a bastard son of capitalism and don't you forget it. In the bamboo shelves of the communal area I found a recent *Scientific American* which questioned the eco-holidays craze, and a piece in the *Cairo Times* ditto. Nevertheless Basata is pretty much fully booked, a total contrast to the empty non-eco places up and down the coast.

There were day trips and, feeling that lazing on the beach was finally not quite sufficient, we took one. Thomas and two of his kids, me and our two oldest, plus Holger and, oh, at the last minute an immensely fat German social worker called Stephan, he really was a walking tent, with his charge, fifteen-year-old Martin, a druggie in rehab. We took the Day Safari to the White Canyon.

I won't drag you through the hours of anxious preparation—enough sunblock? Enough water? But what will she wear on her feet?—that preceded departure. At 9am on the appointed day we sped off in Ali's white mini-van, an hour to the south and then inland, to the Katherine Tourist Facility—I saw this name inscribed on the face of a rock. The rock was the bookend of a range of hills and beneath the rock was sand. Sand for miles. But where was the office?

A couple of miles later Ali swung off the blacktop and we saw, to one side, some crappy buildings beneath a huge overhang, and, tethered in the sand, a few stringy camels. A group of Bedouin appeared. They were all men, about eight of them, rather small in stature, dark-faced, with turbans and frocks and jackets. The general appearance was rather battered and slummy but then the usual thing happened, a cellphone rang and from beneath his robes one of these primitives produced the very latest model.

As further camels were produced, the kids began to speculate: which camel would be unlucky enough to get Stephan? But I couldn't enjoy this. I was a worried dad, wanting to be sure that his kids would be safe (parenthood has amplified the worrier in me). I coached Kate as best I could: 'When he stands up he will tilt you way back, so hang on very tight. Then he'll tip you forward. Then back again. Just hang on—okay?' Anxious smile. Between the tufty humps of her camel was a wooden saddle with two pommels, fore and aft, rising high like stunted flagpoles. The Bedouin lifted her on, went 'Hutt' to the camel (remember that sound from *Lawrence of Arabia*?) so that it lurched to its feet—and there she was, miles above me, triumphantly grinning. Then it was my turn. Since I was the Dad I had to show no fear.

Actually, I don't like riding on animals. Horses ... all horses with me on their backs turn into grazing animals that have no sense of destination. As my camel tilted I clenched the pommel. There was danger of whiplash and, to my chagrin, no stirrups. So what do you do with your legs? They just hang, and flap.

Then I saw that, to my delight, there were no reins. We were going to be led.

And so off we went, across the road, a little caravanserai, each Bedouin leading two camels, the kids shouting and waving, everyone looking proud—oh, and just a little humiliated. I mean, it was such a zoo ride. The Bedouins were walking! We were being led! But that theme song from *Lawrence* is such a nice piece of music, why shouldn't it play in my head?

On the sand the camels stepped slowly. They aren't like horses in that there's no sense of distraction. They have to keep stepping on towards the water. Their feet are huge, like plates, and leave pools in the sand. The head is articulated out in front of you and seems to move independently of the body, carrying the nose up here, now down there, while the legs keep stepping forward. A slight wind in the face. Sand everywhere you look, and then the creviced, sand-blasted rocks. The sun, high.

An hour of that. It was a wonderful, slow, rocking swaying hour, with the quiet shushing of the feet and no other sounds. I tried to ignore the tyre tracks which indicated that we were merely doing by camel what everyone else did in four-wheel drives, and to forget my legs, which were I knew receiving no blood whatsoever, and just gazed around at the sand, and the rocks.

I feel I have failed to rave sufficiently about the rocks. Maybe it's the light? But every rock I saw in Egypt had presence, drama. I saw the Sphinx a million times—eyeless faces that look undaunted out over the sands. We rode beneath like heroes.

Then we were dismounting. 'Mind your balls!' shouted Thomas, who had got off first, and I seized my pommel just in time as my camel went down, throwing me forward. My, it was good to stand. We stretched, thoroughly impressed with ourselves. One of the Bedouin explained to Thomas that we were to go on alone now. The canyon appeared, off to one side—it was just an opening in the sand, like the stairs down to a basement, with white walls of rock. 'Is difficult?' asked Thomas, peering down. 'No. Not difficult.' I was having a closer look and thought it seemed alarmingly steep. At my glance, Thomas asked again, 'Is very difficult for children?' 'Yes, for children.' 'Is very difficult for children.' 'Is difficult. No. Yes. No. You okay. Go.' And with that the Bedouin went back to the camels.

And it was a bit difficult. The canyon was of limestone and anywhere else in the world you'd say it had been gouged by water. There were twisty bits, narrow bits to wriggle through—the kids looked measuringly at Stephan—climbs where you just weren't sure you would make it. But we had managed the camels and everyone was in a terrific mood. On the steep places we passed the children hand to hand. Later my son Jackie objected to this—'Mum, every time there was somewhere dangerous they just lifted us up!'—but we Dads were going to bring home the bacon.

Meanwhile, the canyon, which was like a set from *Raiders of the Lost Ark*, so high-walled and white, making a narrow world in which there was no sound, no escape. The floor was soft, golden sand. Nothing growing. We laughed as we walked.

There's an echo, we declared, and everyone shouted.

Thomas's son cowered. 'Dad,' he asked, 'is the echo danger-ous?'

Stephan and I had a highly civilised conversation about social work. His job is to solo this troubled kid, Martin, for three years, to give him experiences which will open his eyes. 'The choice was Florida or here and I thought he might find it harder to find people to go wrong with here. We'll do Cairo and Giza and a few other places.' All courtesy the groaning German taxpayer—and Holger later informed me, 'There is no research of the efficiency of this controversial treatment.'

But Martin proved brilliant at backpacking the kids when they were tired.

An hour and a half of that and suddenly, ahead, in the frame of the end of the canyon: the tops of palm trees. Hundreds of them, in the dry of the desert. An oasis! I have walked through the desert to an oasis—dear diary, today I lived!

In the oasis there was kind of band rotunda, with rugs to lie on and palm leaves for a roof. Here we took off our shoes, lay down and congratulated ourselves. The local Bedouin made us sweet black tea served in shot glasses, and chopped the vegetables we had brought into a salad which was eaten inside folds of the flat, damper-like bread they had baked on the lid of a metal barrel. There was a bit of a dispute. Thomas argued. But I didn't care. I knew they'd taken half our bottles of water and half our bananas and all of the apples. It didn't matter. We had enough. When you walked around their settlement if was hard to know what to feel. Shame? The dwellings were of the most terrible kind, sewn together from plastic sacks and rags, held up by forked sticks and flapping in the breeze. Everything dirty. It was only a kind of camp, but I knew that all that they had were other camps, all of them more or less like these. But then those contradictions—suddenly there were five slabs of Coke cans and they were holding the most famous brand of the West out to us. When Stephan took one the Bedouin said, 'Expensive!' So Stephan gave it back.

Water was abundant, there were wells everywhere and big holding tanks, and, in the dirt, dark-soaked channels where water had been guided through a tour of the palm trees. Then I saw an orange tree, burdened by oranges. Isn't it great when your eye falls on a cliché.

We hung around and hung around. This part of the day went on too long. Off to one side there was a kind of large concrete bus shelter and under its shade several of our Bedouin were sleeping. They had actually got under blankets, heads and all, against the flies I guess, and were just gone from us. What to do? We hung around some more. Finally we had drunk so much of our water that we thought we had to leave. Thomas did a bit of shouting and, sleepily, everyone roused themselves.

It was a strange relationship with the Bedouin. They weren't sulky, or even difficult. They just didn't take us very seriously.

Back on the camels. By now my legs were stiff and my back was sore. The ride back wasn't much fun, I could have happily done it in a four-wheel drive. The wooden pommel ground into my stomach, a week later I am still raw there, and my mouth was dry. Oh and suddenly the camels seemed slow, incredibly slow. We crawled through the landscape.

But the kids were still excited. Kate waved at her Bedouin, he saw her shadow waving and turned, and she conveyed to him that she wanted to take the lead rope. He glanced at me, I nodded, and he passed it up. Nearly everyone else had earlier taken control of their own camels and it seemed to be okay. So Kate took command. I was behind her. But even from there I could see she was beaming.

Back at Basata, we had a quiet drink. One of my resentments against that place is that you can't have a cold beer. At the end of a hot day! How do the Muslims do it? They let you bring what you like but it has to be managed discreetly. But vodka was better than nothing.

One last night in the shanty, squashed together on the sleeping platform, each of us under our mosquito nets (in the mornings Frank is bundled like a netted fish and has to be rescued). One last swim, one last shower in the dribble of cold water.

Then suddenly I was leaving. I shared the taxi with two German women, one obviously of Arab descent. They laughed as I waved madly at my children, on and on, as the taxi carried me into the distance. 'You have to wave,' I explained, 'otherwise they think you don't love them.' But it's quite okay to leave them.

The conversation in the taxi mainly consisted of the Arab-descent woman conversing animatedly with the driver, Achmed, and then translating for us. Okay, fine. Then, casually, she asked me where I worked in Berlin. Deep breath. I had come to Egypt without my business cards. I had hidden the Israeli visa stamp in my passport. But I was leaving now. I said, 'At the Jewish Museum Berlin.'

This produced five minutes of absolute, shocked silence.

After a while the conversation, in Arabic, started up again. Finally she turned back to me, gave me a hard eyeball. 'We hate the Jews,' she said.

Okay, fine.

And we got on with the ride. Later, she relented and bought me an ice-cream. She found out my name and she and her friend sang what they declared was my theme song, 'Making Plans for Nigel'. They were a little horrified when I told them this had come out in 1979, they had thought they were younger. At the airport, they made sure I got through the check-in okay. Thank you.

But it's always there, you see, that thing that you worried about, that thing that your brain tells you must exist, even if you can't see it. You look and you look, you read around and try to use your imagination. And then when it appears, it's like the recognition of a cliché, deeply satisfying.

On the flight home I was seated in the smoking section. The plane was wall-to-wall Germans, all deeply tanned, all sporting various tourist purchases, beads and headscarves— smoking their stinking heads off. I finished my book and, bored, read the in-flight magazine, even though it was in German. Amazingly, it had pictures of Basata. They looked as promising as the real thing.

NZ Return

My boss at the museum smokes a big cigar and casts a long
shadow. He was at one time the Secretary of the Treasury of
the United States—I have a one-dollar bill with his signature
printed on it; a cover of *Time* magazine (January 30, 1978)
featuring his mid-seventies face. His name is W. Michael
Blumenthal; Google him and be impressed. He says to me,
'Nigel, whaddya want to go back to Noo Zealan for? You'll
have a great time for a month, seeing your friends, telling all
your stories. Then you'll look around and say, "What am I
doing here, miles from anywhere?" And you'll wanna come
back.'

He wants me to stay on at the museum (that's the Jewish
Museum Berlin, where I have been since Christmas 1999).
Well, it's nice to be wanted. But we're leaving. My wife and
our three kids are homesick—me too. When six months ago

2004, previously unpublished

I was offered a permanent position, we thought we should, being wise, accept it—a fine salary, an interesting job in one of the world's great cities: bingo! But the day after I agreed, it felt as though we were now locked into living here forever and we got sad. One day I said to my wife, 'Let's go back to the old contract.' She threw her arms round my neck and wept.

So we're coming home.

But home to what? Okay, family and friends—of course. But we've outgrown our old house in Strathmore, so a new house. I have no job, so a new job—and therefore maybe a new city. A new car, a new computer, finding someone sensible to cut my hair, finally having to deliver on promises like, 'You can have a dog when we're back in New Zealand.' A new figure—I've put on weight here ('Fat!' says my wife) and, as a friend remarked recently, New Zealand is a fitness boot camp. Groan.

On the other hand I have a big new novel to ride into town on: *Tarzan Presley*, coming your way in a blizzard of publicity. And I'm greying at the temples, quite distinguished-looking, I say to my morning mirror. Oh and that certain something that, if we've been overseas, we New Zealanders like to trade on: 'When I was speaking at the Kultur-Werkstatt . . .' Yes, definitely, there'll be a period when I strut around with my chest out. Give me room (a wide berth).

Okay. But what I don't want is a new New Zealand. While you're away you kind of want your country to hold still, so that you don't get horrible surprises, so that it still feels like home. The same old same old is fine, thanks. And I wonder if that's what I will get? What's all this about Don Brash going up in the polls by playing the race card? That was on the *Guardian* site; at work my colleagues questioned me. Germans have an extremely positive view of New Zealand

and that kind of thing is bad for tourism (not to mention the national health). Plus I hear disturbing reports of how every inch of coastline is being bought up, and that Israeli spies want to ramp up the scrutiny New Zealand passports will get at check-in counters. I guess we won't mention the All Blacks.

And I'll have to leave my bike in Berlin—last time I tried to ride to work in Wellington, the head-wind meant I was constantly being driven towards cars that were already hunting me with their bumpers. Berlin is laced by bicycle lanes and when you do have to venture onto the road the fine for hitting a cyclist is so serious that people actually *drive around you*. A radical idea, no? Maybe we could try it. In fact German drivers are amazingly courteous and safety-conscious. And, in Berlin, a city of over four million, there's not really a rush-hour. That's because of the brilliant public transport system. We've lived here for over four years without a car, no problem. Hello, Auckland?

Oh and the trees. Coming here from the home of green, I had no idea that Berlin would be so verdant, but in spring you feel all the positive forces on the planet have been saving themselves and are now making leafy explosions just above your head. Every street seems to be tree-lined and the air is so sweet. It softens the acres of tar and cement. Spring itself— why don't we have a proper spring in New Zealand? The way the seasons are articulated in Europe—the brightness, the withering, the renewal—is such an education to the soul.

I could go on. The opera (four full-time companies in Berlin alone), the galleries, the concerts, the media attention given to culture. The importance of high culture—we could also give that a whirl. The bio-fresh food! The breads! The sense of personal safety—the absence of murders and rapes on the news. You can walk anywhere here, without bravado.

Women sunbathing alone in parks and no one bothering them. The parks themselves—everywhere. The architecture! The sense of history!

Ah yes, the sense of history. Let's for once not mention the war.

But recently I was asked—actually, this was at the Kultur-Werkstatt—what I thought of Berlin. You're always being asked this: how do you find Germany? Makes me feel right at home. Germans have the same sense of wanting the perspective of outsiders that is such a cliché in New Zealand. But for a different reason.

I said I wouldn't mention it, and okay. But there is, as I said to that Werkstatt audience, a sense that this is a city that has seen too much. And everyone nodded. There's a sense that the hope of the city—the idea that something new might happen—has been used up. This is especially true in the parts that once were West Berlin. They are wealthy, clean, decent—but sterile. In the former East, especially in the district of Prenzlauer Berg, there is among the young people who have taken over the area a real air of living for the moment. Kids in love with their art, or their clothes, or their cigarettes—some very stylish smokers up there. But no sense of there being anywhere to go.

That's what I find oppressive here, the sense that history has been made and now we have to live with it.

Whereas in New Zealand . . .

What a bunch of optimists we are! I love it. Every time I return to New Zealand I feel as though I will be challenged, over every cup of coffee, every casual beer, by people who are so casually enthusiastic, so vigorously getting on with things, that I feel I will struggle to keep up. I have often been visited at the Jewish Museum by New Zealanders who have come to see the architecture of Daniel Libeskind, and every time

I am floored by their worldliness, their informed alertness. The way they're interested in everything. Yes, under the towelling hats, beneath the any-old-shirts, New Zealanders keep brains which are so accustomed to problem-solving, hearts that history has not broken, that the thing I instantly think upon meeting them is, *Hire these guys!*

But I wonder, when you're actually home in New Zealand, if this sense of appreciation is the dominant one? Isn't there a little bit of a knocking culture? People trying to be worldly by being smarter-than, more up-with-the-big-apple? Sneering at the local as though this will make them big-time—I see that in the New Zealand media. On the other hand, last time I was back for a visit I also heard rather a lot of people saying, 'New Zealand is the world leader in this field.' Try standing on a sidewalk in New York and saying that, see if you stop the traffic.

I guess it comes from being a small country far away. You're always caught between saying, 'We know we're tiny', and, 'See how big we are!' The little-country syndrome—always gotta be wearing those elevator heels. It's the confident path between these two poles that's so hard to find, isn't it. And yet increasingly I sense that the straight way has been found. Last time, I also encountered so many people who were taking great strides and were also genuinely modest about it. Writers, mostly—that's who I tend to hang out with—people like Jenny Bornholdt and Damien Wilkins, to name a couple, but it's a long list, of people doing remarkable things and making nothing special of it. Fills me with hope.

And pride. I'm proud of New Zealand. When I hear Helen Clark on the radio I think, *That's the voice of reason.* (When she was in Berlin, so many Germans said to me, 'Your prime minister is a woman!' They were impressed.) I'm proud of the way we can be counted on. I stand behind our efforts to face up to our past and, as long as they don't falter, I will continue to tell people with pride that ours is a nation with a conscience. But it's a strange quality, national pride. It's strangled in Germany, and the nation is the worse for it. But, in Americans, we fear it. It's tedious when expressed through sport. But we need it.

It's funny, coming back. You ask yourself: will I be readmitted? Too fat, maybe? Okay, I'm not *that* fat. But it's those elevator shoes. You want to have grown by being overseas, but not to have got too big for your boots.

I'm sure I'll be told.

We've Seen It in the Movies, Now Let's See if It's True

When I was twelve, my father won a Fulbright Exchange Teaching Fellowship and we moved for a year to California. This was definitely the key event of my growing up—if I can be said to be grown up—and its effects have never left me.

At the time I was in Form Two at Masterton Intermediate in the Wairarapa, wearing short pants, taking Marmite sandwiches every day in a brown leather satchel, the usual stuff. My friends were Dougie, Rex, and Keith. On Saturday afternoons we went, like everybody, to what we really did call 'the flicks' and sat through Elvis movies and Pathé newsreels without rioting. We stood for the Queen.

When I tell these stories—I'm a writer, everything is a story—I usually say 'in darkest Masterton'. This was in 1963, before television. It was before the Beatles. The world reached us via the *Listener*, large-format in those days, but

2004, previously unpublished

I don't recall that I ever read it. The Wairarapa is ringed by hills; 'outside' meant where we played. When I read this over I stare at 'played'. I was twelve. I guess it was sports mostly. I thought I was going to play hockey for New Zealand, which was something that would make me world-famous. We lived at the edge of town (more darkness) and, after school, after the movies, my friends and I would take off into the bush, looking for something interesting to do.

When at school they found out I was going not just to America but actually to California—home of Hollywood!— well, this did something for my status (something needed to). Another friend, whose initials were M.M., like Marilyn Monroe, except that he was a boy—that was special, to have matched initials, I was jealous. To have something distinctive, that was important. To have some way of standing out. Anyway, this kid, who when I strain back, seems to have been called Murray McCully but surely not?—took me aside and said, grimly, 'You'll have to watch out over there, you know. The kids carry switchblades, you might get stabbed.'

Maybe he'd seen *West Side Story*? We had the soundtrack LP with the original Broadway cast, I knew the songs. 'Okay by me in Am-er-i-ca . . .'

Actually, I knew lots of songs. I thought I could sing and as well as being a famous hockey player I thought I might also be a famous pop star. That year I liked 'Oh, Pretty Woman' and 'Surfin' USA'. If I am brutal I will admit that I also liked 'Lucky Lips' which unfortunately is by Cliff Richard. I'd seen his movie, *Summer Holiday*, but even a small-town believer like me could tell it was a snore. But I did like his songs. 'We've seen it in the movies, now let's see if it's true.'

There was a local radio station and on Thursday evenings at seven o'clock a Masterton appliance store called Steele and Bull sponsored *The Hit Parade*. When I asked my parents if

I could listen to it, I firmly expected to be told, No. At that time pop music (no one talked about rock'n'roll any more and this was before 'rock') was pretty tame but in my mind there was something risky and maybe even dirty in it. I needed some dirt. I knew that. I was the cleanest boy on the planet. My parents were liberals. Not hip—no one in Masterton was hip—but not wowsers; they said, Why not? I couldn't have told them.

At school in California everyone was bigger—taller, filled out, and that was just the boys. The girls wore lipstick and beehives with lots of hairspray; in my class we had a Cindy, a Darlene and a Sherry. Hardly any other Nigels. This was in eighth grade, at Hill Junior High, in Novato, a small town twenty minutes north of San Francisco. For forty years I have searched for an association for Novato—every American town is famous for something. Recently I discovered that the Grateful Dead were formed in Novato. How cool is that? It must have been around the time we were there, but all I saw were crew-cuts and tans. Story of my life.

First day at school, Cindy Garten said to the history teacher (that's *American* history), 'Make him say hello to me.' I said, 'Hello.' 'Huh, he speaks English.' Within the next few hours kids asked me didn't we have to fight the natives every day and have I ever killed a lion? Plus it was hot wearing jeans in the classroom and I could tell I had absolutely the wrong kind of sneakers—Keds were for kids. By home-time I was feeling seriously weirded-out—this phrase didn't come in for a few years but for once I was ahead of the curve—and the next day I refused, for the first time in my life, to go to school; ditto my sister.

My parents took pity and so we went into 'town'—on an eight-lane highway, with huge, green-and-white highway

182

signs and billboards and long, low American cars. The Golden Gate! The San Francisco–Oakland Bay Bridge, which is the longest in the world!

We ate American and gawped. To be honest, I can't actually remember anything specific about that day, except this: eventually we finished up at a junk emporium called the Jolly Frog. Everything was five dollars or less and my parents said we could buy ourselves a treat. My sister bought some Mexican jumping beans. I thought she'd done the best— twitching on your palm, those beans were really spooky. But I had found a book.

It was unlike any book I'd ever seen. It seemed to have been dipped in ink of a thick, bright chemical green, with an utterly stiff cardboard cover, where a bronzed, muscle-bound figure swung in on a vine. There was a bronze bracelet round his bicep, a necklace of teeth and wild jungle foliage. Also swinging in was the lettering of the title: *Tarzan of the Apes*. It was the trashiest thing I had ever owned.

In Masterton, we'd seen plenty of Tarzan movies. When Rex, Keith and Dougie were in the bush with me, we would compete to untonsil the best Tarzan yell: *Ah-ooooooooooooooo-gh!* And there were Tarzan comics and Tarzan underwear with a leopard-skin pattern—I actually knew a kid, Ricky, who had a pair. But it had never occurred to me that there would be a book.

School continued to be more difficult than can be imagined. No switchblades, but first thing every day you had to put your hand on your heart and pledge allegiance to the flag, except that, as an alien, I wasn't allowed. Then the teacher took a scratchy 45 and played 'The Star-Spangled Banner' on a little record player. It was more solemn than standing for the Queen, no one 'goofed off'. Plus they'd never heard of hockey, and cricket—'You mean this game goes on for five days and then at the end maybe there's no result?' When the reporter from the school mag interviewed me I said my favourite pop stars were Helen Shapiro and, um, Cliff. She hadn't heard of either. This was California, why didn't I say the Beach Boys? So dumb. Oh, and when I look at the school yearbook, such a bad haircut.

So, at nights: *Tarzan*. Under the covers. Every scene pored over, every paragraph read three times. I *flogged* that book (read this any way you want).

The first time round, I missed Elvis Presley. Well, I was only four years old. And then the Twist, followed by the assassination of JFK, followed by the Beatles' first ever American appearance, on *Ed Sullivan*, which, historically, I witnessed.

We returned to Masterton. Kids said I spoke with a yankee twang—I hoped so. At Wairarapa College, one guy settled a dispute with another on the asphalt of the tennis courts, banging his head until his teeth broke. The headmaster, Tommy Holmes, put all the strength of his one arm into caning boys—if you were caught watching you got one too. Gee but it's great to be back home.

Years passed. I turned the flogging into fiction, sort of grew up, became a writer of sorts. In the 1980s, seeking a different kind of book to write, I went back to Tarzan. My 1987 novel *Dirty Work* features a writer who for two sentences imagines *Tarzan of the Apes* set in New Zealand: *Tarzan pushed aside the manuka branch. Down in the clearing he could see the Natives dancing a fierce haka . . .* I nursed this idea for years. When I re-read the Edgar Rice Burroughs original (published 1912; 40 million copies sold, or 400 million, depending) I saw it was much more coy about what happened between Tarzan and Jane than I had remembered—well, I was the guy to fix *that*—and that the story didn't really close. This was because Burroughs suddenly realised he wanted to write a sequel, so he fudged the ending. So, if I was going to rewrite it I would have to come up with an interesting second part to Tarzan's life . . .

I have never stopped being thrilled by pop music—did I mention that I haven't really grown up?—so when Peter Guralnick's biography of Elvis appeared to great reviews, I didn't hold back. In that (great!) book the most lovingly described scene is when Elvis, guitarist Scotty Moore and bass-player Bill Black stumble onto what became 'That's All Right (Mama)', which, I realised, was the birth of pop culture—live! I read that chapter over and over. I wanted to be in that scene!

That's it, I think: all my life I have used day-dreaming and music and movies and books—oh, and the occasional flog—to lift myself out of the world which surrounds me. To escape, which is really what I write about. And years have passed. Amazingly, I have a job, a picturesque wife, three often-lovely children. I have lived in a variety of countries, even some where they don't speak English very well! I have stayed out of jail and debt and cults and car crashes. Pinch me.

But, as every escapist comes to know, there is in fact no escape. You just go deeper. When I put Elvis and Tarzan on the same page, wow—there was a glow that lit up everything for miles. I started to work properly on the novel in Germany, while fellow New Zealander Ken Gorbey and I were leading the development of a major museum. While I was coping with being an alien, while my wife and I were having a baby—a crazy, crazy time. In the early morning I would pound the keyboard in a kind of frenzy, then at 7am leap up, throw on my clothes, and cycle madly through Berlin with the steam-heated words streaming behind me like the tail of a comet—Memphis, Graceland, Las Vegas.

But the setting I chose for Tarzan was the bush-covered hills of my boyhood, in the Wairarapa. When Tarzan goes to America to turn into Elvis, well, it transpires that he lives in Petaluma, just up the road from Novato.

Tarzan Presley is the most adventurous novel I have written, and the least autobiographical. But, when I hold it in my hands, I can see that I have never left the small town that I came from. I just went in deeper.

To Fictionland
and Back

In July 2000 I was on an aeroplane flying to Munich and needed a pencil. The woman next to me had one which I borrowed. She glanced at what I was reading, Saul Bellow's *Seize the Day*, and said, 'A real book.' She was a professor of literature. I had after thirteen years published a novel, so we got talking. Eventually I had to say something about my book. I explained it was called *Skylark Lounge* and described an encounter between a man having family difficulties and some aliens from another planet. She asked, 'What do the aliens stand for?'

'Nothing. They're just aliens.'

She laughed. 'Writers always say that.'

'And professors of literature never believe them.'

After a while she said, 'Do you believe in aliens?'

'Of course not.'

Sunday Star Times, 16 May 2004

'But you have them in your book.'

'The man in the book thinks he believes in them.'

'Ah,' she said. We talked about Saul Bellow. No aliens in his books. But my novel had just been published and I wasn't able to shut up about it.

'However, the book is careful to explain,' I said, 'that it's more or less impossible for aliens to have visited this planet. It says that for any aliens to be here now, travelling at a million miles an hour from the nearest place they might live, they would have to have left home in the time of Moses.'

'Does the man in the book know that?'

'It's he who tells us.'

'So he tells us aliens couldn't exist but he believes in them?'

'Exactly.'

'Ah,' she said again.

Deranged. Preposterous, implausible, kitschy. It's hard these days to come up with a fictional reality that does justice to the world we live in.

Irony doesn't cut it—detachment is for the terminally privileged. 'We're all beautiful creatures living on the most astonishing planet,' is for astral travellers. Revolution has been tried, also faction, novels about novels, and language, and writers using language to write novels about writing novels made of language. And who wants more domestic realism? However, I'm backing myself into a corner. If I keep going this way I am going to have to declare I think I've found a new way to write novels. What I'm trying to do is make an argument, for myself as much as anyone, about the nature of the place where my recent fiction seems to be set. *Skylark Lounge* has aliens, and I don't believe in aliens. My latest novel *Tarzan Presley* has an angel, and that's probably the least of its weirdnesses—wetas as big as cows, gorillas in the uninhabited jungles of the Wairarapa.

Poet Bill Manhire, when asked to comment on the manuscript of *Tarzan Presley*, wrote: 'Once you've finished reading it, it's hard to tell if the book is being told by a deranged person or is simply taking place in some kind of parallel universe.' For a second I was insulted. True, the story the narrator tells is preposterous. But we know that, because of the title. While we're reading we have one eye on the story and one on 'the real world' which is where, we know, some version of this must be taking place. Better than 'deranged', what I warm to is Bill's 'taking place in some kind of parallel universe'. The more I think about it the more I like this description. It suggests the place where I think fiction is set. All fiction. I call it Fictionland.

It doesn't bother me overmuch where Fictionland is. It might be inside a can of corned beef gathering dust at the corner dairy. I'm not well-read enough to know the history of its existence. Maybe it was there in *The Book of Genji*, which people say is the first novel. But *Don Quixote* is set in Fictionland. Others might say it's a parable, or uses metaphors, or is symbolic, but to me those systems of description seem to squeeze the book into a box. The relationship between the events in the book and the occurrences in what we call the real world is to me one of the deepest pleasures of reading.

It is of course possible to tilt at a windmill. Simply get a horse and a lance and tilt your heart out. There's a passage about this in *Skylark Lounge*. It says: 'Right, you're a lawyer, you live in Wadestown, one morning you look out the window and a lion is savaging your dachshund. You say, "Impossible!" But it's not impossible. It's unlikely.' That is true of so much that happens in novels. Willing suspension of disbelief gets us through hailstorms of flying bullets, gymnastic love scenes, miraculous escapes. But I am talking about more than unlikely. Kafka, writing *The Metamorphosis*, didn't believe Gregor Samsa was turned into a cockroach, and I, reading, didn't worry about this transformation. I knew what was going on. We—Kafka, Gregor and I—were in Fictionland.

What is Fictionland like? Well, for a start, princes and princesses live there. No problem; princes and princesses exist. But what about giants? Giants could be just 'very big men'. So what about fairies, or hobbits? Or love affairs between men and angels, a river of blood that runs from beneath the murder victim's door to the house of the murderer?

I spoke earlier against 'domestic realism', but the domestic is where most of us live. Most of us want to escape it. So is the journey to Fictionland an escape? Not if the fiction's good. The fantastic for its own sake is only of interest to those who smoke a lot of herb. No, what gets me going about, say, angels is that the image of an angel carries a human desire. A human idea. This is also true of God, or monsters—we look at George W. Bush and see the outline of a man. But we know that really what we should be seeing is a blood-slavering beast; a grinning creature of death out of Hieronymus Bosch. Those images are what we need to describe what Bush has loosed into the world, what he bears.

When fiction goes inside such people, when it goes inside the play of the world, then we turn to the embodiment of ideas in images—humans who suck the blood of others, heroes who are immortal, an arrow of love which pierces the heart (of course, that should be 'the heart'). These are the images human culture has developed to explain what it feels, what it knows is there, but what does not show up on television.

There are people who say: 'Why read novels? It's all made up.' Do they have an inner life of Excel spreadsheets? Since I learned to read I cannot remember having a single experience

190

in life I hadn't first read about in a novel. We bring images to our every experience. The world and the Excel version of it: to negotiate between Fictionland and 'the facts' we use the skills we have developed through listening to the politicians and squaring what they say with what we know.

The professor finally asked me, on that aeroplane: 'So do your aliens exist?' I said: 'Of course they do—they're in the book! Isn't that a real existence?'

Before
I Went Blind

So where do you start: Winston Peters? I don't think so—but, coming back, your eyes fall on such things and you think: You, still alive! I want him gone by lunchtime. The inner groan when you see that Judy Bailey is still reading the news. And such news! That's the news? Surely New Zealand is at its worst in the run-up to an election.

But you're pleased to be back. That's what you keep telling yourself—you've thrown the dice, there's no turning back, so, of course you're pleased to be back. But in fact you are. For the first couple of weeks I walked around with a big dopey grin on my face, loving everything. Fish 'n' chips in the rain under a Norfolk Pine at Mission Bay: magic. The wine! The food! For five years we had the pick of European food and wine, and what we have here, I'll take it any time. And so

---

Going West keynote address, 9 September 2005;
Sport 33, 2005

cheap! And so good! Of course, for the first few weeks back after five years, wine with fancy food in the company of old friends is what takes up most of your day. Not *too* much wrong with that [*pats fat stomach*]. And all the no-brainer stuff: the All Blacks with a decent scrum. Everyone speaking English! It's like a return to real life.

And that's the problem. You can feel real life settling in, real thoughts, and, although you don't want to, you can't help noticing a few things. Where to start?

In Germany, maybe. As I said, I was there for five years, with my wife and our two kids—in fact we came home with three—working on the Jewish Museum Berlin. Now that museum is a whole other topic and I don't propose to go there tonight, but what it meant was that, unlike other countries I have spent time in, that job meant I really did go *in* to German society; or at least some way in. I look at myself now with a Kiwi eye and I think, So are you more serious? Are you less flexible? Or is that just age? Are you taking yourself more seriously? Or is that just hubris? The casualness of New Zealand, this is not a big feature of everyday life in Germany.

It's one of the big things which strike you here, this casualness. I want to start now on a long slow circle into the middle of what I have to say tonight and out at the edge as I start what I get is the greeting from the heavyweight Maori guy who inspects my passport at Immigration: 'Great to have you back, fella. Welcome home.' After cops with machine guns, you've gotta love that. The bloke getting you into lines for Customs clearance: 'Look everybody, we're a bit overloaded here, everyone just go over into those two outbound lanes, would you—just ignore the markings on the floor.' *Ignoring markings!*—never in Germany, Bruce.

Then you step outside, and everything is so open—the

skies, for one. In Berlin there's always a building rising right in front of your face, there's no horizon, no distance. I can't tell you how lucky we are to be able to escape, so quickly, from the enclosingness of cities. And the freshness of the air! After a year in Berlin my nose was like a chimney that needed a sweep, and it stayed like that for the next four years. I'd been back a week when I noticed that it was getting better. It's all the exhaust emissions etc in the air, and in fact there's no wind in Berlin to blow it away—well, nothing that we'd call a wind. It did blow a bit one day and all the dead branches came down off the trees, killing seven people and closing the roads for days.

Okay, quickly now on the weather: it's too soon for me to be missing the way the seasons are articulated in Europe but I know I will. It's not so much the snow—though I did love the way that white blanket smoothed everything back to elemental shapes. It's the changes—the way you can so strongly sense the world turning, and your life going through its seasons. Makes you more reflective. Somehow instead of seasons, what we have here is weather.

And what's that weather like? Well, we don't really notice. In New Zealand we are increasingly of the idea that the weather should be constantly warm and permissive of outdoor leisure activities, and any weather that's not is somehow an aberration, an insult to our idea of our lives. Accordingly we wear warm-weather gear no matter what. To see people in Courtenay Place Wellington during a southerly in a teeshirt or shorts is to remember what Jock Phillips said, in this case about New Zealand men: that the culture of not giving expression to pain has become a culture of not giving expression full stop.

Just to do a little truck-stop here on clothes: the unbelievable casualness of the clothes New Zealanders wear is one of those things that poke your eye out, right up there with the popcorn quality of the TV news—TV in general, actually—and the obsession with violence (more on this later). Peter Jackson on set reminds me of Les Murray's poem, 'The Dream of Wearing Shorts Forever'. Guys wearing to work the jersey they used to wipe the dipstick. Jandals at the dinner party, the lawn-mowing trousers . . . At the same time, New Zealanders have become a lot more conscious of style. Travel back with me if you will to my boyhood in the Masterton of the 1950s (please, let's not stay there too long): what I can see walking down Queen Street is the daggy, the saggy, the raggy and the self-rolled tobaccy. Not too much of that about these days, outside of Speights commercials. Lots of people seem to have one eye out for that TV camera that might just suddenly put a frame around them and make their day. So the style is, be casual, but with streets of cool.

When you pause and look around at the skies here, one of the things you see everywhere is wires. Black lines cutting the open into pieces—telephone wires, power lines, looping, sagging, making cobwebs. Doesn't anyone care what things look like? The Germans have been getting rid of power lines for years. And signs. Our cities are thickets of signs. The whole country has gone berserk on marketing itself. Every little Lotto outlet and heel bar has a brand and a tagline and they just have to get it poked right into your eye. Doesn't anyone want the cities to breathe a little? Oh, that's right: our cities are for commerce, not for people. And all that marketing competes with another category of signs, you know the ones, which read, 'In case your eye catches this sign instead of the thing right in front of you, these are stairs, which means you have to lift up your feet or else you'll have a nasty accident.' Doh. If we didn't have so many of these signs maybe we'd see the stairs better?

The wires-in-the-sky thing extends to pylons—so we're really going to have pylons marching across all our paddocks? Is there no money in this country for beauty?

Or do we think we have so much of it down south that up here, where most of us live, we don't have to care? And wind turbines. In fact I think wind turbines are relatively interesting-looking, and I'm all for eco-friendly sources of power. But has anyone looked at what's happening in Germany? There, they've had serious investment in wind power for over twenty years—thanks to significant government subsidies, many farmers erected big propellers on their land and sold the power to the national grid. You see them, stately forests of them, seeming to cartwheel across the horizon, when you take a train journey. They're intrusive, yes, but not ugly. Nevertheless . . . Just recently the Germans have concluded that the propellers are not an economic source of power, and are going to abandon them—just as we are about to invest heavily in this area. And Germany is a country with an infinitely greater commitment to ecological sustainability than us—is anyone paying attention?

Of course the eco-commitment of the Germans can get tedious. To get rid of your rubbish you need to sort it into at least five types, each of which must go into precisely the right bin down in the courtyard. These bins are used communally and when you move into a new apartment block you are given comprehensive instruction on how to divide and deposit your stuff—it's detailed in your lease, and woe betide if you get it wrong—phalanxes will arrive to set you straight. Colour-code your empties into the correct white, brown or green bin or face a good dressing down. When you move out of your apartment, take it back to the bare white walls you started out with—the exact shade of white, naturally, which is also specified in your lease. No question that any improvements you might have made would be worth keeping—everything must go. Is that smart? When we left Berlin I spent four days unbolting and throwing away a massive mezzanine floor that was so big and solid you could have landed the space shuttle on it—and the next tenants were only going to have to put it up again. Remove the light fittings, fill the screw-holes, and leave only bare wires. Remove the sink bench, leave only the outflow pipe. Now, what do you do with the sink bench, which was custom-built and won't fit anywhere else. Well, there's no market for it—actually, there's more or less no market for any second-hand stuff. I guess it's because for the last hundred years or so Germany has been so incredibly wealthy. Maybe that's about to change—unemployment is way up and rising steadily; economic growth is non-existent. But, for now, what you do is get your friend with a van to come round and take it to an urban recycling centre. It's what Berlin has instead of a dump. My first visit to one of these amazed me. For a start, it's so clean you could hold a picnic in the middle of it. No smell, none whatsoever. It is simply another urban facility standing cheek-by-jowl with crowded apartment blocks and shops. Men in bright, clean overalls direct you where to put everything. (They are all men. It's men in charge in Germany. When Helen Clark visited the Jewish Museum, all my colleagues said, '*Your prime minister is a woman?*' Angela Merkel, who very likely will be Germany's next Chancellor, faces hatred from the men in her party who resent being told what to do by a woman. Never happen here, would it.) Back to the recycling centre: everything is divided into shipping containers, which, when full, are shipped off for use as raw materials. Neat, clean, self-serviced. But it does feel a bit counter-intuitive. You want to get rid of your perfectly good old desk, so you break it down at the recycling centre, using the crowbars they provide, into splinters, for wood pulp—is that necessarily a good idea? Your old chair, which isn't good for recycling, is dragged away somewhere and crushed. Unless it's an antique, hardly anything is ever used again. All the old fridges, washing machines, dryers, in a container for scrap metal. It does make you wonder.

But there's no question: German ecological practice makes this country look like a cowboy outfit where anything goes. We met a German eco-freak who, terrified during Ronald Reagan's 'star wars' era that Europe would get caught up in a nuclear war, emigrated to New Zealand because it was, he figured, the cleanest, greenest, furthest-away place he could think of. And he was shocked by what he found here. He stayed as long as he could bear it, but the state of the rivers, the way we think about land use, the dumping of fertilisers, the way we build things: it was just too hideous, and he faced his fears and went back. In fact many Germans spoke to me about this: New Zealand does not care enough for itself. For a country that says it's clean and green, that sells those qualities, we're not trying hard enough. After living in Germany, it's difficult not to think: the only reason New Zealand is as clean and green as it is is because we have a small population.

Look: this is where we live. We're so lucky—we don't have acid rain dropping in from the primitive economies across the border. We don't have a thousand years of manufacturing as an inheritance. So what are we thinking about?

I suppose that's where, circling, circling, I start to bear down on what is at the centre of what, after five years, I find in this country.

I mean, I love it here. I can't tell you how I maundered on about New Zealand to my poor colleagues at the Jewish Museum. I explained our recent history, the Treaty, Roger Douglas—despite which, they offered me a permanent contract. So, you see, we could have stayed in Germany. We chose to come home.

And it's as though, having done that, somehow you end up holding your own country to account. 'I committed myself,' you say, 'so you better deliver.' It's unfair, really. What part, tell me, of the modern world really measures up? The problem is, when it doesn't, then you feel: Okay, then I don't have to either.

After a few weeks, as I've said, various things started to come to the surface. The visual clutter; the casualness—which, in the main, I see as a huge positive; the obsession with superficial style; the indifference to beauty.

All done too with great confidence. Confidence, now there's a thing. The magazines—*Metro, Next, Pavement*, various magazines I found on coffee tables—had pictures of us, the New Zealanders, shot from below, gazing confidently into the middle distance. A gas station attendant with a good tan—what a hero. A king of business—look at the guy. Look at those haircuts powering their way along Lambton Quay. Yep, there's real confidence here these days. It's as though we've come through. Come through what? I guess that would be Rogernomics—we took the pain and suddenly here we are, out on the other side, and thriving. And why not? It's good to be confident, it's good to love your country.

But, magazines—whatever happened to *New Outlook*? *The Republican*? *Quote Unquote*? They're gone. Okay, magazines do come and go, that's their nature—but what's replaced them? Style bibles, full of heroic portraits, full of flattery. Where's the *Listener* as it used to be? *Metro* as it used to be? Does no one want that kind of serious consideration of the country any more?

Within a few weeks of being back I heard three times in various media broadcasts people saying, 'You're not trying to get into that old "national identity" crap are you?' . . . 'All that navel gazing about national identity' . . . 'the national identity discussion is so old hat.' I found this hard to believe. Okay, the literal phrase 'national identity' has probably done its dash. But all over the world people are debating the idea of their nation—in France, in Germany, in the States. The whole world has, since September 11, had some hugely fundamental questions thrown at it: can we live with one another? Can we keep living like this? Surely the discussion about who we are, about what the essential, it-must-not-be-lost quality of this country is—that's a discussion which, one way or another, has to go on forever. But, coming back, I pick up a great reluctance to talk seriously about these things, to consider who we are, where we're going. The only question everyone seems happy to address is, Is it good for business?

Where are we, Switzerland?

Because that's what I'm getting. That this is a nation obsessed all over again with material satisfaction; that anyone who wants to discuss things in any context except, 'What will it do to the sharemarket?' is just causing trouble—'Come on, wanker, get your boat shoes on, get down to the Loaded Hog.' You know, it's like a return to the 1950s. We're all right. We're satisfied. We got what we wanted. Everything's okay. Don't frighten the horses.

Of course there are things that people mention. The violence. It's hard to get good figures for comparison but it seems that Germany has about as many murders, per capita, as New Zealand. But you'd never know that from the news. The same is true of violent crime. There's an obsession about these subjects in this country—but no commitment to discussing why that might be. A friend remarked recently that this was 'a country full of rage'. Is it true? Why? Sure, the media kick things around—but always in the context of who's the winner and who's the loser—the big concern is, who lost face. Politics in particular. Never focusing on, Where is this taking us? What are we becoming?

The public transport systems: the clear message they give you here is, 'If you can't travel by car you're just shit and that's how you'll be treated.' On the bus to work each day, I can't sit down properly because I'm too long from hip to thigh for the moulded plastic seats. But I'm not *that* tall. Who says our buses should be so squashy, so noisy, so jerky, so ill-lit? Is it because public transport isn't the stylish way to go, so it's okay to default to like-it-or-lump-it? (Margaret Thatcher said, 'If you're catching the bus to work at 30, you're a loser.' So is that our attitude?) German buses, compared, are like limousine luxury. Everybody hates our public transport but does anybody have anything to say except, 'That's what the market dictates'? I don't mean, just moan. I don't mean, find out who is to blame. I mean, ask ourselves: Is this who we are?

The media: everyone bellyaches about it, but then we tune in just the same. The news: there's Judy saying, 'Today the fig leaf of political respectability was torn from the bleeding body of Rodney Hide, who was exposed as having sold his principles down the drain when he dot dot dot.' Isn't she trying to say, 'Today the Act party changed one of its policies'? After five years of listening to the BBC World Service, the language of the news here is just astonishing to me—as though it's being tabloid-ised for a tabloid nation.

On the cultural scene, there's a powerful sense that there's a rich cultural life, that terrific work is being produced, and lots of it, some amazing stuff—the 'Small World, Big Town' show, for instance, at the City Gallery in Wellington is full of art that is at least as exciting as anything I saw in Berlin galleries—but does anyone care? Somehow, it's work in which there's nothing essential at stake. The nation has found a way to consume culture without being affected by it. And the practitioners feel that, and turn their faces towards each other, each looking in towards the 'higher ground' of aestheticism, towards 'those who know'. The cultural scene is segmented: the literary arts cut off from the visual, architecture cut off from theatre—and all of it cut off from 'real life'.

Isn't this is what people used to say about New Zealand way back? Aren't these the clichés I grew up with in the 1950s? But maybe they're coming back to bite us.

Or was it that they never went away and we just forgot about them? It's only a few weeks since his death, but the passing of David Lange really gave me pause. I can't help remember that time, that first year when he came to power and, even though our economy was on its knees, we found ourselves. Remember the excitement of us going nuclear-free. Of having a prime minister who could make us laugh. New Zealanders laughing—that was a real breakthrough. New Zealanders who could really talk—Kim Hill, Derek Fox, Bill Manhire—suddenly that's what New Zealanders were, interesting talkers. That same year Keri Hulme won the Booker and soon after Lauris Edmond and Dinah Hawken won Commonwealth Writers' Prizes for poetry—we all read those books and everyone was talking about them. *An Angel at My Table*—first the books and then the wonderful movie. The Treaty settlement process was launched. The rugby tour to South Africa had been stopped. There was a sense that we were going somewhere. The *Rainbow Warrior* went down— suddenly we were worth attacking—and we had a heightened sense of who we were. In 1990 I had lunch in Paris with Judith Trotter, who at that point had been our ambassador for four years; she said, 'This nuclear-free nonsense, New Zealanders have no idea of what it's costing us.' And I got on my high horse. 'I think you've been away too long,' I said. 'I think New Zealanders know the price and they've decided they're prepared to pay.'

That's the thing I ask myself, now: is there any price we are prepared to pay, for anything? What are we prepared to forgo, in the interests of 'something better'? Tax cuts?

Interesting when you turn to Germany. That is a nation defined, even today, by the terrible things done in its name sixty years ago. It's true that, fifteen years ago, the fall of the Wall did provide a new focus. But then the problems of reunification gradually swelled, most visibly in the unemployment numbers, at the same time as economic growth subsided, so that today the country is at a loss: unable to afford the strong social provisions it has regarded as eternal, but not yet ready to give them up in favour of a market-driven society. Good on them, I say. Hang in there, Germany.

Of course, in many ways there's no real comparison possible between the two countries. Totally different histories, languages, geographies, climates, social make-up. Levels of discussion: in Germany they really know how to give an issue the complete three-sixty—by judgement day, you've heard all the angles. Is that true of us? My impression is, New Zealand is made up of what I call 'agreement groups'. People only associate with people they agree with. Are we afraid everything will fall over if we say boo? Our books: after twenty years in the book trade here what I think people want from a new novel is: one, to be flattered; two, to be comforted; and, three, that the book be decorative. Doesn't exactly sound like Günter Grass, does it?

And yet Germans are ready to feel a great affection for New Zealand, an affinity—they see us as who they'd like to be, if only. There's a shared sense that it's the human that matters.

And they're right. The human side of New Zealand is amazing. I know I've been having a good old moan, and everyone hates a moaner, me especially—so throw your bananas now. But it's the people here. You know, Ken Gorbey and I didn't get that museum open when no one else could because we were such great museum makers, because of our brilliant skills at synthesising cultural history. It was because we are Kiwis. Sorry if that sounds a bit trite, but you can't overstate, I don't think, the way that New Zealanders know how to solve a problem, how to cut through the crap, how to focus on what really matters. This is the upside of the casualness: we have a terrific sense of how far to go, of the unnecessary. Jandals at the dinner party: it's not going to break any bones. When you say of Germans, 'They didn't know when to stop', a real shiver goes down the spine. 'They didn't know when to pull back.' But do we?

As everyone knows, I'm quite keen on pop music. So I've been catching up. Trinity Roots, Fat Freddy's Drop, these are CDs you might pick over music from anywhere in the world. While I'm sitting there listening, I like to look at photographs—at the moment, two books in particular: Marti Friedlander's Godwit collection and Ans Westra's *Handboek*. Mostly, what you've got there is pictures of the 1960s and 70s. Wonderful pictures, so expressive—but not timeless. On the contrary, they're very much of their time. It's the faces—our 60s and 70s faces—that amaze me. I stare at them. Those people are astonished to be here; and at the same time they're not sure of where they are.

You couldn't say that these days. Those heroic photographs I saw in *Metro* and the other magazines—New Zealanders are so self-possessed now, so expert, so competent. So aware of their competence. We know where we are. We know who we are. We're in the middle of our lives in the middle of our world here in the middle of the Pacific.

But what are we doing with this knowledge, that has been so hard-won? Have we arrived—at the end of our history? Is this it? Is this [*waves hand around*] what we had in mind? Or are we bored with the idea of issues, or are there no issues left, or is it that the media reduces everything to porridge; or are we just too busy with our own struggles to care what kind of society we're making?

Have we arrived, New Zealand, at the place we were going to?

Thank you.

PS: Three weeks later, some of the dust stirred up by the election has settled. The first thing I note—with pride—is that we seem not to have been bought off by the promise of tax cuts. Sure, lots of people voted National, but this was, I gather, more because of an anxiety about where Labour was taking the country. So I have to be happy with that.

And, along with everyone else, I am delighted that the Maori Party has four seats. That's one of the most interesting things to happen in years. Roll on the stoushes.

Still, the sense of a near miss is very strong. A close call. We—I don't just mean Labour sympathisers—very nearly went under.

But suddenly party politics seems rather reduced in significance. Oh the relief. So now what happens? We let them get on with it and return to blow-by-blow coverage of backpacker murders, or who fronts the TV news. Otherwise it's default to dedicated study of the market. Gives the phrase 'business as usual' a certain quality, doesn't it?

Interview
with Damien Wilkins

Nigel has been a friend for almost twenty years. He is also married to my favourite cousin. Their daughter and our elder daughter have grown up together. Naturally this all suggests immense good taste—in friends, cousins, daughters. In books too. I first met Nigel behind the counter of Unity Books, where his verdicts carried the necessary balance of sense and mischief. Who can forget that portrait of Alan Preston, his boss at Unity, with his 'trouser-coloured trousers'? We're so used to the winding, casual speech of Nigel's prose that we sometimes overlook the compressed poetry of certain phrases, and the craft. The indelible opening of Tarzan Presley *should be taught in rhetoric classes. It's one of the prettiest pieces of persuasion in our literature:*

Sport 34, 2006

He's human, he's born, so we have to agree that somewhere back in there he had a mother. Tarzan always wanted to have a mother, it was a big thing with him. Somewhere back there he was fed by a mother. Breast-fed. I can see him, and I think the picture is a reasonable one, lying along his mother's arm, with her nipple in his mouth. Now that is a very intimate moment of contact and I think every human likes to think they had it, once, even if no one can remember it. Whenever I've seen babies at the breast they always look extraordinarily contented, gazing up at the elements of colour and light above them, immense shapes, a great statue's face seen from below—but the statue is warm, it breathes. The rising cliff of brow, and the cloud of hair which frames the face, with the blue sky behind, and real clouds going past. The face of an angel against the sky. I suspect that Tarzan's mother may have had black hair.

I always laugh when I read that 'reasonable'. And I'm always surprised at how this paragraph swells and ripens in front of us, just as—well, yes—just as the breast grows from the nipple to the warm, breathing statue of the body to which it belongs and out to the sky and the clouds. Wonderfully, the reader's eye is drawn up at the same rate as the baby's until we're looking at this angel above us too. Whatever's kitschy and hammy—Tarzan's mother?—is not forgotten in this lifting but rather accepted and given a curiously affecting life. This is talk raised to the level of art.

The talk that comes from Nigel's mouth is similarly addictive, generous and surprising.

This interview, perhaps more than most, is a sort of pretend occasion. I mean friends don't normally arrange their conversations into such a pattern: 'Tell me about your childhood.' However, I'm very glad we did pretend since Nigel's replies suggested areas of experience that our friendship hadn't traversed—and might never have but for this formal setting. I learned a lot of stuff. I should add that at no point did Nigel 'submit' to the process. He was keen to do it. He was ready to talk. He has little of the writer's wariness at being prodded and poked. At a certain point in his life he decided to say 'yes'—a big yes, I think. Yes to this interview. Yes to the requests to be a public person. But also a more private yes. Yes to a set of desires that at first blush seemed a bit risky, which appeared even antithetical to the idea of the Important New Zealand Writer. Yes to aliens, to Elvis, to thrillers and westerns, to fable and fantasy. Yes to cowboys. Of course. This has become Nigel Cox territory. His imagination now throws a long lasso. And there's never any special pleading on behalf of neglected forms, nothing of the cultural theorist's remote interest or the satirist's queasy attention. His work is whole-hearted and meant and it lives in these places because he lives there. The fictions come with naturalness, the fan's infectious relish, but also—because this writer knows his Saul Bellow as well as his Charles Willeford—with canniness and calculation and a palpable pleasure in their own making. The books that have flowed from such a vivid embrace are singular and essential works in our writing.

On the night of the interview in late January, I arrived at the Cox household—a rented beachfront cottage in Seatoun—at the agreed time. Nigel wasn't home. He arrived shortly after, wearing slippers and pyjamas—he'd been down the road at his GP's. More consultation, more drugs. He changed into clothes for our session, mainly because I'd bought along a digital camera to record proceedings. There's a DVD copy of the interview, where the evening light fades as we talk. The film is the truest account of our ninety-minute conversation. One day copies might float up somewhere.

In the face of Nigel's pitiless illness, this was an amazing *performance. Barbara Anderson said to me recently that she got furious when people suggested there was no such thing as heroism. Yes.*

The text published here has been fiddled with a little, to eliminate repetition and re-gather the occasional lost thought. Nigel has declared himself happy enough with it, though he wonders whether anyone will be particularly interested in the level of detail. He said to me, 'Won't they go, "Who is this guy?"' I think they will say that, since Nigel's work, despite recent success, remains a little invisible. It's Nigel's argument—a rare moment of despair—that books don't matter in our culture any more. My feeling is that anyone reading what follows will be prompted to prove him wrong. After all, Nigel's own resilience, courage and imaginative daring are themselves the strongest arguments in favour of preserving what he loves most and what, with good reason, he fears we don't love enough.

DAMIEN WILKINS

Let's start with the writer's idyllic childhood in Lower Hutt. Do you have a theory about Lower Hutt, and particularly Hutt Valley High, producing writers? We know the list: you, Lloyd Jones, Jenny Bornholdt, me. In the original Author's Note to *Dirty Work* you seem to be making a point about this—seeking revenge maybe? It says 'not educated' at Hutt Valley High.

NIGEL COX

That's true, but it was meant to be a bit of a joke. However, in the way Bob Ross, the publisher, wrote it up it came out as a flat joke. I wanted him just to say Nigel Cox was born here, and lived here and was not educated at Hutt Valley High School and he turned it into 'He claims he was not educated', but I didn't see that until the book came out. I didn't have a happy time at Hutt High. At that time the school was very, very authoritarian and wrapped up in rugby and those sorts of things. For example, the rugby team got beaten every week which was a shame to the whole school and nation and the headmaster would sternly read out the results, but I was in the hockey team and we won every week but this would not get read out in assembly because it was a poofter's game and so there was that, and there was a general atmosphere of anti-intellectualism, not that I think I am a great intellectual, but there was a lack of interest in the arts generally and anything like that. It was a sort of sausage factory school.

DAMIEN WILKINS

So you think at that stage you were heading towards the arts, even then?

NIGEL COX

I was completely interested in all that. The only idea I ever had to do with myself was to be a writer. It wasn't an idea that was very intelligently held. I didn't know how to be a writer and I didn't set about learning how to be a writer either.

DAMIEN WILKINS

Where do you think that idea came from? In your 'Boys on Islands' essay you talk of getting obsessed with adventure stories—*The Coral Island*, *Peter Pan*. Were you connecting with those books purely in terms of story and escape or as a kind of appealing literary life? Were you the boy in the story or the writer of the story?

There are two things. It was story and escape and adventure and I've always been interested in escapism. I think if there's a theme in all my books it's escapism and the problematic side of that is that it has to be a serious escape or a real escape and I keep causing problems for the escape but I do think that if there's a theme in the books that's what they are about—escapism. You could argue that that is all about wanting to get away from rural New Zealand, or wanting to get away from my family, or wanting to get away from the Hutt Valley or something, but that's there. I also had an idea of the glamorous writer's life, and the first writer I really knew about was Hemingway. My parents had a very good library, as a lot of parents did, of school prize books. They are little books, perhaps six inches tall, and we had those. I read them all. *Moby Dick*, *Two Years Before the Mast*, *20,000 Leagues under the Sea*, *Black Beauty*, *Treasure Island* and so forth—all of what I would call the light classics. I read all of those as a kid but there was nothing about an author in there. Then Dad gave me, when I was about eleven, *The Old Man and the Sea* in that classic edition with the woodcuts in it and I read that, and then he gave me, not long after, *For Whom the Bell Tolls*. That was a real book. The first real modern adult book I read was *Lord of the Flies*—but the Hemingway book, I could see there was a kind of myth in there and it attracted me. Even though I was only a kid I felt there was a connection between Robert Jordan who is the hero of the novel and Hemingway who is the writer of the novel. You were supposed to get that. I knew that then and he was a figure I thought it would be good to be. This guy who is wealthy and famous and is out there living on the edge. Secondly I suppose I thought I could do it, be a writer. I had this idea I could do it.

DAMIEN WILKINS

Were you writing at this stage? Were you more attached to language than other kids?

NIGEL COX

I guess. For example I was much more interested in the words of pop songs than other kids I knew. We all liked pop songs but I was interested in the words. Also I had, when I was younger, seven or eight or nine, told people I was going to be a writer. I don't exactly know why I had told them. I had this in my mind's eye and it wasn't until a bit later on that I started figuring out what that might mean, but it was an idea.

DAMIEN WILKINS

That connection you saw between the author Hemingway and the character—which suggests the book is somehow always about the writer—is quite a sophisticated take for a young reader. But I was wondering how that works with your theme of escapism? You're suggesting the book is a means or a tool for getting out of your life, but that it's also a tool for reflecting on your life?

NIGEL COX

That's the problem I was talking about. I think that as a young guy growing up I had a very, very negative self-image, like many others, and I never ever thought I was going to do anything. The whole thing of being a writer was at one remove. It was an escape, it was a fantasy, it was something that would happen to another person, or another version of me, and when I actually sat down—I think I was about sixteen—and started to write a novel I was shocked that I was doing it.

DAMIEN WILKINS

Was it a dirty secret or was it an open secret? Did you tell your mother?

NIGEL COX

The family knew because it was a loud old typewriter, with a ding at the end of the line. But I didn't tell kids at school and that is partly because I had a couple of experiences that warned me off it. One was much later, but one was earlier on. We had a very good teacher when I was in Standard Three and Four, Mr Parkin, English, and he really tried to teach us and I can remember a lot of specific things he taught us but at one point he did this strange exercise. He said, 'You know boys and girls you are all going to grow up one day and so you should be thinking about what you are going to be. And he started in the far corner of the class and everyone said what they were going to be.' One boy was going to be a jockey, one girl was going to be an actress, and all that sort of stuff and he gave a little smirk every now and then when some who were not such bright stars decided they were going to be something great. I was quite near the end of the class and I was quite self-conscious about this moment coming up but I knew exactly what I was going to say, and I was proud of it too. He came round to me and he said 'Cox', and I said, 'I'm going to be an author', and it was the only negative reaction—an actual 'No'—that he gave in the whole class. He said, 'Don't be silly Cox, people can't be authors, you have to be something proper.' These words are carved in my mind and I said, 'All right I'll be a teacher then', because my father was a teacher and I had vaguely thought about that but it seemed potentially boring. There was another incident when I was about twenty and I was playing for the Northern United Hockey Club and we had played a game.

In the changing rooms afterwards the captain, who was a bit of a jerk, suddenly said, 'Hey you guys, did you know Nigel Cox writes books!', and to this day I don't know how he could have found out. I must have told someone who told someone—this was long before I had written a book that anyone might have published—but there was that around and I was aware that it wasn't something you walked around with a banner saying, 'I'm a writer', the way people might today.

DAMIEN WILKINS
You mention the hockey, which you played through college and beyond to representative level, and there is that suspicion that *good with words* is sometimes a synonym for *bad at sports*, that the two things—athleticism and bookishness—are separate forever, but this wasn't the case with you. You weren't with the rugby crowd but you were this good hockey player, you played tennis, you were a physical guy. Tall and athletic . . .

NIGEL COX
Up to a point. Skinny. It's true, I was sporty, absolutely . . .

DAMIEN WILKINS
So you weren't the kind of nerdy weed who—

NIGEL COX
Oh, I was nerdy. I was very nerdy. I was a sort of bedroom obsessive, and what I was obsessed about were things like writing, and pop music especially. I was very wrapped up in the magic of the world of pop music. It was like magic, it was the right season for it—we're talking about 1967 when pop music really believed it was something—but I was like that

and I had arty aspirations, except that I didn't know how to have an arty aspiration.

DAMIEN WILKINS
Did you have friends who were into the same things?

NIGEL COX
I had friends but I didn't have friends who were obsessed with the inner life of pop music. I didn't know anybody who was really interested in that although I had a girlfriend and she was interested in that and we used to talk about it a lot but there were a couple of interesting people at Hutt High: Cathy Wylie, who was dux, and Malcolm McAlister, and they edited a magazine called something like *Puke*, something quite offensive and they were only allowed to publish two editions and the school stopped them, and then they wrote a play together called *Drop*. Later I realised it was about dropping acid—whether they had actually dropped acid I wouldn't know but that was put on as the school play one year. I used to talk to them a bit but there wasn't really an arty crowd at Hutt High at that time and if there was I don't know if I would have been part of it.

DAMIEN WILKINS
When I was growing up in the Hutt in the seventies, there wasn't a lot going on. You caught the train into town, into Wellington, and suddenly the world just opened out. I imagine it would be the same for you?

NIGEL COX
No, it wasn't actually the same because there was a whole lot of pop activity in the Hutt. The Lower Hutt Town Hall ran dances called Dancelands and people from Wellington would

come out to see the Lost Souls and Bari and the Breakaways and a whole lot of early pop groups and I would go along. And it was so strange on a Sunday afternoon because it was dark in the hall and you'd go in from the light and there would be girls dancing round their handbags on the floor, and wallflowers like me standing watching the band. Then there was a nightclub called The Kryptos which was under a church in Lower Hutt and they had quite good people there and my band played there once. There was a little scene in the Hutt. There were a couple of good groups based in the Hutt, one called the Soul Sect and also the Roadrunners which had a guitar player called Chaz Burke-Kennedy who went to Hutt High and he was later in the Underdogs and was a real musician. It was only when I got to be eighteen or nineteen that I started coming into town to go to the psychedelic places because in the Hutt it had always been pop music, pure-as pop, whereas the next thing was people with long hair and the druggie culture.

DAMIEN WILKINS
What was the story with your band? You've jumped from this kid in his bedroom listening to pop music by himself to being in a band.

NIGEL COX
That was very strange. There was a series of events in my life when I kind of went, 'Pinch me, I'm doing this.' That was one of them. The guy who ran the school band approached me. It was a trumpet-playing band, a Herb Alpert sort of band, and he was a musician, Mark Hornibrook, and later on he played in Blerta and then with Rodger Fox and he approached me and said would I like to sing some songs. So I got up, amazed to find myself there because I was a super

out-of-tune singer, and sang 'Bonnie and Clyde' and a few things like that. I don't know why he approached me but one of the things that happened within the Herb Alpert band, there was a good guitar player, a guy called Mark Te One, and he and I decided to form a sort of pop group, a splinter group to the school band, and we became for a while the Hutt Valley High School band and played at school dances. We played Yardbirds songs and Rolling Stones songs. I was the singer, a terrible singer. Then we played a couple of little gigs at other places. We practised in my garage and it was one of those events when I found out I had crossed over from dreaming about it, to doing it, even though I knew I wasn't doing it well.

DAMIEN WILKINS
Did your life change? Did you pull chicks and all that sort of stuff?

NIGEL COX
Unfortunately not. That was the plan of course! Actually at that point I did have a girlfriend. I was also a singer who sang and I didn't know how to be a pop person who danced, who had a style. The other pop people who sang were culture stars.

DAMIEN WILKINS
Were you writing your own material?

NIGEL COX
I wrote some songs. We never played them but I did write some songs. There was a guy called Clinton Brown who was in a little band called Society which was a big Hutt Valley group and then went on to be in Rockinghorse and then the

Warratahs, and I went round to his place a couple of times with my little songs and he played the guitar and suddenly it all sounded good.

DAMIEN WILKINS
Your father was working in the Education Department at this stage, the Head of the Curriculum Development Unit, and from what I know of him he was very much a person who believed in advancement through education. He'd taken you off to the States to further his own education. Now that wasn't the path you chose. For someone who is interested in language, interested in books, arts, etc—you would think the obvious place to go would be to university, especially in that period?

NIGEL COX
What happened was I spent three years in the sixth form. I was a reasonably intelligent sort of student, and I did okay in School C, but by the time I got through that I was so fantastically distracted from trying to do any work at school because of the music and the sport and everything else. I was a rather obsessive teenager and still am but at that time I was completely obsessed about trying to be a really good hockey player and trying to become a pop musician, just starting to work at trying to be a writer, and all the things that interested me, reading and so forth, and school just didn't interest me. I was completely disconnected, and so I spent three years in the sixth form, which was a humiliation and a school record (probably a world record). People who had been a year below me were now a year ahead of me. Finally they gave me UE to get me out of the school, I think.

DAMIEN WILKINS

What did your father make of this?

NIGEL COX

He had pushed me very hard and I know he felt regretful about this afterwards. He had pushed me very hard into the subjects he was interested in so I finished up in the first year in the sixth form doing mathematics and a whole lot of technical subjects which were absolutely not my forte so what happened was, I was near top of the class in English and bottom of the class in everything else. Then he said, 'All right, that was a failure', so the next year he said, 'You have done it once so you must get it right this year', so I did it all again and failed again. That caused a revolution in our house. He had to face it that this just wasn't working and so for the final year I did a completely new set of subjects and the teacher adviser said to me, 'Don't you think you should stick to the subjects you have done for two years now, you must have learned something?' But I did history and art and other things and finally I did pass. I had had enough of failure at school and I didn't want to go to university in case it all happened again, which was a childish thought. I was very suggestible at that time and, just off-hand, the person who was head of the art department asked me what I was going to do and said he thought I would be good in advertising—and that was it! Advertising, which at that time seemed glamorous and pop, and I suddenly thought fantastic, wonderful, I'm going to go into advertising! And I did. That put the whole university thing right out of the picture, which was a massive mistake. Then I was taking home $29 a week, working full-time. I started out as a junior and that was really dogsbody work, but they picked up that I was interested in writing so I did a bit of copywriting, and I was also what's called a junior executive and I worked a bit in the production side too. I assisted in the making of some TV commercials. It wasn't clear in the agency where I was headed and I didn't know either but it was obvious that I probably was headed somewhere and that was good because after all this failure I was succeeding at something.

DAMIEN WILKINS
I feel a moral crisis approaching.

NIGEL COX
Pretty much. The truth was, I was a fish out of water in advertising—a Values voter surrounded by card-carrying National Party stalwarts. So I decided OE was the next thing for me—I quit and got a job putting vinyl roofs (remember them?) on Cortinas and Falcons on the assembly line at Ford, out in Seaview. Off to England—then you get that string of jobs listed on the back of my books: deckhand, coalman, driver, door-to-door turkey salesman, bookshop assistant . . . I was briefly married to an English woman, Harriet Hudson. We came back to New Zealand but it didn't last. And suddenly there I was, home again. I had of course planned to return as the conquering author—dreams are free. But I had actually finished two novels: *Willowsong*, which was a sort of hippy romance, terrible stuff, and *The Wall*, which was dime-store Kafka. Amazingly an English agent had actually taken them seriously enough to submit them to a few publishers. Who were kind and encouraging. Which was all I needed. Ever since the time in the States—maybe even earlier—all I'd *really* wanted to do was be a novelist, and somehow I'd got started.

DAMIEN WILKINS

Can we backtrack a bit to the period you had in the States as a boy? Your father took the family to California on a Fulbright Exchange Teaching Fellowship.

NIGEL COX

Right, that was early sixties. We were there when the Beatles first came to America and we were there when Kennedy was shot. That was a remarkable thing because in New Zealand before that year I had never seen television. I don't think we even had television in New Zealand, and Masterton, where we were living, was a very small and isolated town, probably 20,000 people, and we went to the movies on Saturday afternoon and saw things like *Kissing Cousins* with Elvis in it. So to go to the place where that culture all came from was extraordinary. I remember being immensely excited, not just about America but California, and it was the most immense cultural shock. I met my sixth-form English teacher quite some years afterwards and she said, 'You were still in shock four years later', and I thought that too. It was overwhelming.

DAMIEN WILKINS

Was it overwhelming being there or when you came back to New Zealand and thought about what you had seen?

NIGEL COX

Both. It was like living on the set of *Grease*. I'd been in short pants at school and here were these kids with duck's arses and guys who really did have a comb in their pocket and spent the whole day stroking their hair and girls with Beehives and a whole sort of teen culture that was articulated in a way I had only ever seen in the movies. And yet it was nothing like the movies. It was much more real and of course also the whole unbelievable alienation of it all. You know people really did say things like—well I remember going into the history class and a girl called Cindy Garten said to the teacher, 'Make him say hello to me', so I just said hello, and they said to me things like, 'So have you killed a lot of lions?', and you thought, 'Lions, you must know they are Asia and Africa. What's with you people?'

DAMIEN WILKINS

You've said about your novel *Tarzan Presley* that it picks up on a lot of those reactions. So that the Tarzan figure, when he goes to America, is a bit like Nigel in America?

NIGEL COX

No question. In fact people have always accused me of writing autobiographical books and of course we all know that's a lie but *Tarzan Presley,* I think, is the most autobiographical book I've written. It is actually set, apart from the piece in Graceland where I never got to, it's all set in places where I have been. Every single one of them. The scene where Tarzan first appears in public in the bowling hall—some of the dialogue there is drawn from that first day at school: 'Make him say hello to me.'

DAMIEN WILKINS

There's a gap of more than thirty years between the experience in America and using it in your fiction. Had that material been bothering you? Had you tried to use it before?

NIGEL COX

I had. When I was a Katherine Mansfield fellow I made a special and very complicated and expensive detour to go back to Novato, where I had lived, because I felt there was some material there. And I did. There was a thirteen-year period when I didn't publish a novel. One of the things I tried to write was a memoir of being in America. It didn't work. Someone said to me, 'Aren't you a bit young to be writing your memoirs?', etc, but I did try to write down what happened there but I couldn't get an angle on it. I knew that it was a big thing and I was aware I was going to have to try to get something out of it somehow.

DAMIEN WILKINS

When you were working on *Tarzan Presley*—we're leaping ahead again—was that part of the strategy? Did you think— 'Tarzan . . . and he's going to become Elvis and he's going to go to America, which fits with my life.' Was it all calculated in that way?

NIGEL COX

No. It was a survival strategy. The whole of *Tarzan Presley* was a massive effort to cope with the concept of the book. The book was too big for me really, and I still think there are things wrong with the novel because it I struggled to cope with it. I relied hugely on places I had been to and experiences I have really had to ground the book because I was terrified the whole time of it turning either into a satire, which is what I didn't want, or else collapsing. It felt much more grounded to put it in those places, and I also thought—when I was in the States it was 1962/63 and what we call the sixties hadn't really started and Elvis was in America in 55/56 so that is not such a terribly long stretch, probably the mood in America wasn't so hugely different and so I drew on that and that gave me a bit of confidence so that I could write about it.

DAMIEN WILKINS

Don't you think though that novel writing is a survival strategy all along? Is that how you feel? The books start off with a great idea or even a daft idea and then you keep going and you get it up and running and then you're just hanging on?

NIGEL COX

Absolutely. In fact, on the other hand I think that is one of the things that make writing exciting for me, but it is absolutely, at every minute, you are desperately trying to find things that are authentic and real for this ghastly trouble you have got yourself into.

DAMIEN WILKINS

There's that great thing Annie Dillard says that every book has an impossibility at its heart. An obstacle which is just impossible. The writing of the book is the going around the obstacle or in some way disguising that obstacle from the reader. The books you write you know where the obstacles are. Is this true for you? Do you know where the problems are?

NIGEL COX

No question. Look at *Skylark Lounge*. The idiocy of trying to write a serious book about aliens. It was standing there a dumb fact in the middle of the room. I knew that from the first minute I started work on that book, the whole problem of dealing with the nitwit alien culture that's around on the one hand and on the other actually sort of thinking, 'Yeah but you are at some point going to have to write a real encounter with some real aliens if this book is going to work.' That was hugely in my mind. It was making me sweat every minute of the day. *Tarzan Presley* was the same. At every moment of that book I was thinking, 'How are you going to deal with this, how are you going to do it? How?'

DAMIEN WILKINS

So that terror, that's what keeps you going?

NIGEL COX

I love it and there's nothing like standing up from the machine and thinking, 'I did it. Never mind tomorrow, today I solved that problem.'

DAMIEN WILKINS

Or maybe you deferred it? For now the problem is gone but tomorrow, a new one?

NIGEL COX

Yes! *Skylark Lounge* I kept pushing it away. *Tarzan Presley*, once I got it going, it was written in a hot fever of *I'm doing this!* I was very excited about it.

DAMIEN WILKINS

I remember you saying to me when you were working on *Skylark Lounge* that it was an unfashionable subject, that you yourself were unfashionable, that no one was going to like it, but who cares? As it turned out the people who read it, loved it. And it turned up in lots of people's favourite novels of the year lists, so it was a success.

NIGEL COX

That book was really written out of desperation because I had thirteen years when I hadn't managed to come up with anything I thought was good enough to publish and

I'd drifted into that bad habit a writer can get into of just kind of writing, starting another novel and writing for a bit and saying, 'This is writing, I am writing something', and all the time thinking, 'This is crap.' I had got so far away from writing for publication that I wasn't able to bite down hard and not be afraid of the results and to really throw myself into it. With *Skylark Lounge* I decided 'I am going to show this to a publisher' before I even started on it. 'I am going to write this book and I am going to show it. I am going to do it because if I don't do it now I'll never do it again.' So it was written in a kind of fear that I was going to have to show this alien novel to someone and on the other hand that did give me the drive and lift to get it there.

DAMIEN WILKINS
Were you surprised at people's response, or did you just feel relief?

NIGEL COX
I knew it was good. I think it's my best novel and when I finished it I knew I had done it.

DAMIEN WILKINS
Why do you think it is your best novel? Because it's the most complete, because it's the most successful in what it does?

NIGEL COX
It's the most successful at what it does. It gets the most out of its material and I think it's original. I think that *Tarzan Presley* is the biggest novel but that's a different quality. I think *Skylark Lounge* is a small novel that packs a very good punch. And I suppose I also think that everyone I wanted to like it liked it and that's very important.

DAMIEN WILKINS

One of those people of course was Bill Manhire and there's that word that he's used about your most recent books: wisdom. He's called them wise books. But it's not the wisdom of vast intellectual heft, where the reader learns great facts about the world, is it? I think one of the things that's crucial to our sense of those novels' wisdom is the voice they're told in and I wonder whether you have a way of characterising how you came about that voice, which *Skylark Lounge* does beautifully and *Tarzan Presley* does beautifully and *Responsibility* does as well. That first-person voice which is confiding, slightly self-deprecating but not overly so . . . but a guy who is sifting through the material. The voice speaks to you as it thinks itself through the material of the novel. A mind in action almost.

NIGEL COX

What happened was, way back a friend said to me, 'I wish you'd write the way you talk.' And that is actually not a simple thing to do. That got me into thinking about writing in the first person, and so that started *Dirty Work* off. That book has its good points and its bad but then a lot of water went under the bridge and I think the thing that really shocked me was the whole business of getting cancer in 1996 and for the first time an oncologist talked to me about how 'this cancer I think will probably kill you in the end' and similar things. I had never thought about this before and the whole of *Skylark Lounge* was written in the kind of shock of mortal knowledge. I wouldn't exactly call that wisdom. I suppose the other thing that happened was that I got my confidence up in life. I had had a very long and I think successful period at Unity Books, where I knew what I was doing and I tried some things out and they worked and we made money. I had had a very good experience at Te Papa where I made a good contribution and then later on the whole business of the Jewish Museum in Berlin. This all worked and I came out of it with a kind of self-belief. I got loose enough to find a way to make this New Zealand blokey talk. That was what I wanted and I think one of the most interesting things about fiction is this whole business about how intelligent is the guy, how educated he is on the one hand, and how much does he know on the other. There are these books that seduce you because the characters are so fantastically intelligent, but actually I am not fantastically intelligent. I just sort of go along through life like anyone else and I wanted to find a way to find a voice that showed that. I do think that male culture in this country mostly consists of quite interesting people who have their enthusiasms and their specialities and their weaknesses and their drives and so forth and I really felt that in *Skylark Lounge* I managed to find a little bit of it, a voice that managed to catch that mood or something.

DAMIEN WILKINS

Can we pick up a thread there? You started at Te Papa as a writer—you were Senior Writer, I think—but then what happened? Did they recognise that you had other skills? What is it you've ended up doing in museums?

NIGEL COX

These days I'm a senior manager—my title is Director (visitor) Experience—and I just manage like every other manager, following your nose and trying not to be an Important Jerk. It's hard to say, from the inside, why my original role expanded, but it did. I guess there were some occasions when I solved a few problems that were not strictly to do with writing and I became this problem-solving guy. Then it turned out I was okay at talking to people and so I was asked to facilitate some big talk sessions where we addressed things that weren't working. Then I had a hand in making some exhibitions and at one point it was entirely unclear what I actually did, except that I was flat out. Then I was asked to go with Ken Gorbey to Berlin to work on the Jewish Museum Berlin and all of a sudden I was an international museums consultant, being hugely wise in Bremen and Bonn and then Ottawa and Liverpool, as well as directing, with Ken, the development of the JMB. Which was an extraordinary success, achieved under massive time pressure and, you know, all the attendant cultural dislocation. I was given a chance to learn a huge amount in Germany and in some ways it really was the making of me, professionally. I sort of feel, after that, anything's possible. And of course I wrote two and a half novels while I was there—*Skylark Lounge* was finished before I left New Zealand—so I came home with a grin on my face.

Yeah, and what do I do in museums? That is so hard, if you mean *really* do. I'm tempted to say, 'Apply common sense', which is not a million miles from the truth. The thought-out answer is probably closer to something like, 'Try to find a way to make a huge, complex organisation find a way to engagingly communicate its expertise to very broad audiences who don't necessarily have too much specialist knowledge as a base to build on.'

I guess being not so well educated myself, and having a feel for pop culture, which has to engage or die, has been a help. The communication skills learned at the advertising agency, the commercial realism I learned running the bookshops, the thinking that went into and came out of the novels—all helps. I'm always thinking, at the museum, of the ordinary person I try to write about, who is usually not well educated, but not stupid, is interested but to a degree, who knows more than is apparent but not yet enough . . . I guess that's where the two connect, if at all.

DAMIEN WILKINS
Berlin was a great personal success of course. You might have stayed on there.

NIGEL COX
I've been lucky. Somehow I've fitted in the museum world. One of the happy days of my life was when, after four and half years at the JMB, one of my senior colleagues said at lunch, 'Nigel, I just can't imagine the JMB without you—I want you to consider taking a permanent contract here.' And the other guy who we were lunching with, who early on had fought with me, said, 'You are the only one who can get us all to work together.' But it was time to come home.

DAMIEN WILKINS
You once said that you thought fiction writing came from the dumbest part of your brain, and it was almost as if the lesson there was that caution was the enemy. If you became too self-aware or too self-conscious about the kind of noises you were making, the note would be false. There's a conundrum here though, right? Because when you're writing, everything is self-conscious. You're conscious about sentence-making. You're conscious about structure. You're conscious about consequence. 'What's the consequence of having that happen to the character at that point?' and so on. So you're suggesting an impossibility, aren't you? Or you're suggesting a way of tricking yourself into the belief that really you're involved in quite a casual act—writing. And I think that is

where a good deal of the charm and even the wisdom of your books lies—the pretence that this is a kind of casual act and the stuff unfolds in a rather kind of loose way but if you look at the books there is a structure, there are controlling ideas, there's craft. What do you think of that business of the balance between control and letting loose?

NIGEL COX

I'm very determined to try the hardest I can to be a skilful writer and that means thinking very much about the chapters, the pacing, the character development, everything you just talked about—I think that's underrated. That's what I call the professionalism of writing. I think there is a huge number of very colourful writers and expressive writers and imaginative writers but in my judgement a lot of writers haven't really slaved away at the whole business of getting to be a professional, which means the pacing is right, scenes are the right length, that jokes come off and all that sort of stuff. You've got that side of it but then you talked about that thing of being dumb. Somehow you have to let yourself loose. I had an awful experience where I once planned a novel and this was going to be chapter one and this was going to be chapter two. It was like homework and I hated it and the book was dead, dead, dead. So now I write the complete opposite of that, thinking all the time—where's this taking me, where's this taking me—in terms of structure and so forth, but being prepared to write practically anything for a sentence to see where it goes to in an effort to make it actually come alive. I do think that I have got more interested in this—you can see it beautifully managed in Saul Bellow where he manages to be what one of my colleagues in Germany called *associatif*—he manages to move back and forth between different ideas with immense fluidity. You can see it in Bill Manhire's poetry too. The focal length changes very quickly and ideas are connected by the most strange connections sometimes but somehow it moves across a territory in a very nicely worked way where you finish up thinking, 'Crikey, we covered a lot of ground there.' I've really tried to learn a little bit about how to do that. I've read a lot of Bellow, trying to think 'What's the secret?' and perhaps learnt a little bit of that.

DAMIEN WILKINS
You mentioned the failed novel there and one of the features of your writing career is your ruthlessness in dispatching unwanted projects. How do you feel about the books which are abandoned? They do exist still, don't they? You don't burn them, so they exist as a kind of marker or something. What is your attitude towards them, is it a fondness or contempt or what?

NIGEL COX
Contempt. There are three novels I didn't publish before *Waiting for Einstein*, and *Waiting for Einstein* is also a book I am fairly contemptuous about.

DAMIEN WILKINS
You've said that *Waiting for Einstein* isn't a book you've been able to read all the way through. Presumably you read it once! I guess one of the things that publishing a first book does, even though you feel contemptuous about it, is clear the deck, make other things suddenly possible?

NIGEL COX
That was the case with that book. What happened there was I was really trying to rewrite a novel which unfortunately was a bad novel of Hemingway's called *Islands in the Stream*.

Especially in the beginning of *Waiting for Einstein*, you can see it's just about lifted from *Islands in the Stream*. The whole idea that the hero of the book is a painter and he is this kind of romantic figure and he's living alone. I suppose the whole experience of writing that book got me over Hemingway. I realised that was a complete dead end and there's nothing there for you and forget about all that because I had been very interested in him and read him very closely, and of course again this was still part of this identification I made with him early on as a heroic writer figure. Also because he was actually a pop star. He was one of the most famous men in the world. My great aspirations of being a pop star were sort of all connected to that. *Waiting for Einstein* got that over with, got it out of me, and the next book—I had actually started *Dirty Work* before *Waiting for Einstein* was finished and that was a completely different kind of book. So I do connect *Dirty Work* to the books that have come later. *Waiting for Einstein* is sitting there all on its own.

DAMIEN WILKINS

VUP is reissuing *Dirty Work*. How does that make you feel?

NIGEL COX

Very strange. I wrote a little author note to go at the back of it and it says, 'Reading your old stuff is like coming upon a wardrobe of clothes you used to wear—everything looks so quaint and, pooh, that musty smell.' It is like that. On the other hand I always had affection for the book and I still do. People liked it, and I liked it. It was my first book that was the sort of book I had in mind. God knows if anyone will take the slightest notice of it being reissued, I suspect not, but personally I am very pleased to see it being done.

Such a nice edition has been made of it because I thought the early edition wasn't a nice object. This is going to be quite a nice object, I think. Fundamentally I am just chuffed to see it come out.

DAMIEN WILKINS

It occupies a funny position though, doesn't it, because it's the book that stopped things, or it's the book at which things stopped for those thirteen years.

NIGEL COX

What happened was that I had in my mind that I was going to be this writer person and it was simply a matter of time. *Dirty Work* was quite a good success in its own way. *Waiting for Einstein* had done all right too. The reviews had been mixed but on the whole generous. It got me going but actually *Dirty Work* was a success. The reviews were very good and more than anything else the book had been noticed. And talked about. It was shortlisted for the prizes and so forth and then when I had finished it I remember thinking, 'So that's a success? So you made about four and a half thousand dollars so that's success? What are you going to live on?' That really threw me into a tailspin. I started thinking, 'Well, maybe you could write a thriller, or some kind of big-selling genre thing', and that led into a quagmire.

DAMIEN WILKINS

You can't have been innocent of the economic realities, surely? Working in the book trade must have armed you with all that knowledge.

NIGEL COX

Exactly right. I was the complete opposite of innocent because I was, as you say, working in the book trade. I knew more about the realities of numbers and figures than anybody. It was that the whole thing had essentially been a fantasy. Now the reality hit me. It was one of those moments where you had to just face the facts even though you already knew them.

DAMIEN WILKINS

I want to pick up something there in your description of the sort of attention your first two novels received and it relates also to some things you've been saying recently about the drift of our national culture. You recently gave the keynote address at the Going West Festival where you suggested that things might be heading back to the dark days of the fifties with fewer and fewer outlets for serious criticism and conversation. Your argument is that at the time of publishing those two books, in the 1980s, there was more supporting literary culture than there is now. And that this shrinkage is happening at a time of an explosive growth in publishing. Are you saying that books just come out and disappear?

NIGEL COX

I don't think the books matter much any more. That is the thing that is really shocking. The reviews for *Waiting for Einstein* and *Dirty Work* were, if anything, longer, much longer, and there were a lot more of them. My last three books have had a fantastically good run with the reviewers. I have no complaints about that. But by and large it is in a book culture that seems hermetically sealed or of no great interest to anybody. There's a time come upon the book culture, I think, which means that a book is a sensation or nothing. Ninety-nine per cent of good books are not sensations. They're good books. And then there's a whole lot of bad books of course. Most good books are not sensations, they are just good books. Every now and then there's a sensation. That's a terrible book culture. I think that within five years there will be no book reviews in newspapers. I think they're already on the way out—relegated to supplements or bright coloured little boxes. The whole business of novel writing, which was once the most commercial part of literature, is probably going to finish up where poetry is now. Which is in some ways wonderful because it's written for pure reasons, there's no money in it. But on the other hand the whole business of what that means for the working writer is pretty worrying. Even perhaps more seriously for the culture. Books don't really matter.

DAMIEN WILKINS

In a way you could argue that it's part of the health of the culture, that we don't depend so much on so little, that we are not focused all of us on the same three things per week. That the culture has got more various and so we can now pick and choose our enthusiasms. Isn't there a sense in which it is maybe better to be free of a kind of weird focus on the novel or what the latest Maurice Gee novel means to us?

NIGEL COX

I think you're right in one way in that when *Waiting for Einstein* came out, I have to guess, but I wouldn't be amazed if maybe eight novels came out that year. Now there are probably sisxty or something. I think that's extremely good and that's part of what you are saying and also there's been an immense rise in all other products, you know DVDs, and pop music that is really worth listening to and so forth, from this country and that's all great. It has reduced something which I was bored by, which was the heaviness of the great cultural book, you know, all that crap about the Great New Zealand Novel. Thank god we are all over that. But on the other hand I think it has produced a tone in books which very often is playful and frivolous and not much else because that's their place in the culture—to be pure entertainment. And I guess that's all right. I always want anything I'm writing to be very entertaining. I mean very entertaining and lively and fun to read, but actually I want it to be more than that too. It's almost as though the culture is going—oh no we just don't want that other bit. I mean if I was to turn into a tedious old bore it is shocking to me how the whole thing of market values is what rules everything in this country now. And everybody is prepared to use that as the one way to measure the value of anything—the market value. I know I sound like an old fart but it's pretty shocking to me.

DAMIEN WILKINS
Did you notice that more when you came back from Germany?

NIGEL COX
I did. There are many tedious things about German culture but when it comes to the arts there's something you just don't get here—a formal consideration in tandem with a personal questioning of, 'What does this work say about us and what does it say about me and what am I to it?' And this has very little to do with money, with success culture. Now someone might say, 'Nigel, you just want your work to matter more, a bigger place in the sun', and, you know: could be. But when you go to the Berlin Philharmonic there's a kind of release from material culture happening in that hall that I don't see so frequently here. There's a sense in Germany of the arts being part of me, of the thing that I am, not as something I'm

going to have to talk about at dinner parties or cafés, but as something that is part of my inner person, that affects who I am. I just wonder how far we are moving away from that here.

DAMIEN WILKINS

One of the striking things about, say, that keynote address, and your willingness to go on TV, or to talk to people about larger public issues, is that maybe having the job at Te Papa first and then having the job in the Jewish Museum Berlin—you talked about the confidence that gave you—but there's also that feeling that because museums intersect with the public life of the society, you became drawn into this sphere. I mean, every day a museum asks, 'Who are we, where are we going, where have we been?', all that sort of stuff. And I couldn't really imagine the Nigel I knew in 1990 being so prepared to say those things.

NIGEL COX

Two things—one was that in Germany I got interviewed to death. I got interviewed a bit about being a writer, but at the museum when they wanted someone to speak English, and we had journalists from Spain or Italy or South Korea so English would be the lingua franca, I was always rolled out. After a certain point I got fantastically used to being interviewed. It would happen at least once a week and often more often. Once a TV crew turned up and the museum PR person said, 'We want you to talk to this TV crew', and I turned up and the director said, 'Now what we are going to do, we are going to be about three or four hours and you are going to walk through the museum and talk while you walk', and I thought, 'You are out of your mind! You want me to talk and walk?' But then I thought, 'Okay, it's not my programme', so I just did it. I got very used to that, I got used to talking publicly about things and being a public spokesperson. So I was very much in practice. The other thing was—and it was quite deliberate and I was conscious of seeing it that way—I knew I would be something of a nine-day wonder when I came back to New Zealand and I decided to go for it. When people say, 'Be on TV', I'll be on TV. When people say, 'Give an address', I'll give an address. I knew it would last about six months and absolutely to the day it did. Then the phone stopped ringing and it was great. I got a call from breakfast television and they said, 'We'd like you to come and talk about charity fatigue.' I said, 'Charity fatigue?' I'd never heard the expression before! I said, 'But I know nothing about that', and they said, 'But you're a good talker', and I said, 'Oh well.' And I'm always keen to go on TV to practise my skills because I'm horrible at it so I went along and did it and they said that was great. And a week later the TV woman rang me again and said, 'Would you like to comment on the upcoming election?' and I thought, 'No I don't want to do this', and she rang twice more and then the phone stopped ringing. I suddenly thought, 'I don't want to be this kind of pundit.' But I was happy to raise my profile—no question.

DAMIEN WILKINS

You were away five years in Berlin. One of the established paths for New Zealand writers, of course, is to get out of the country and then look back, reflect on New Zealand. Was that the case? Did you have time to think about us?

NIGEL COX

The first novel I wrote there was *Tarzan Presley*, which at its launch, you, Damien, described as a sort of love letter to

New Zealand. And I think that was the state I was in—in love with a country I wasn't in, more every day. The main New Zealand part of the novel is set in the part of New Zealand I love best, in the coastal bush at Mataikona, twelve miles north of Castlepoint on the Wairarapa Coast—my family have had baches there forever. The openness of the New Zealand sky, the general sense of possibility in this country, the sense that a great deal is still to happen.

On the other hand . . . You do see what a real city is like to live in, that we don't actually have any cities in New Zealand. And what it's like to live somewhere that culture rather than the money economy is what matters. I mean, I'd lived overseas before. But working at the JMB took me into the heart of European history and what I got was a sort of crash course in that. In some ways it was the education I'd never had and I just drank it up. On the other hand I talked about New Zealand every day—drove my colleagues mad. I can remember long lunches where I explained who Hone Tuwhare was and our James Brown and Blam Blam Blam and why *Hicksville* was so great—they were very patient. And all the time you're thinking, 'They'll never hear of these people.' One day I walked down the corridor and asked the first twenty people I met, 'Have you heard of the All Blacks? Crowded House? The America's Cup? Colin McCahon?' All negative. But they had seen and loved *An Angel at My Table* and, some of them, *The Piano* and *Once Were Warriors*. The movies break through. *Lord of the Rings*, of course. When I sang 'Four Seasons In One Day' they said, 'Oh, they play that before the weather on TV.' Kiri Te Kanawa, yes. But that was about it. So you had this sense of being invisible. And maybe that made me feel free? Certainly in some of the New Zealand scenes in *Tarzan Presley* I felt free to play with our culture in a way that might have been hard at home. Maybe I was trying to write a bigger book that might find a place in this bigger world? But that's only half true. I was in love with the idea of Tarzan and Presley. It was a love song to everything I cared about and I just happened to write it there.

DAMIEN WILKINS

You talk in the 'Boys on Islands' essay, written in the late eighties, about being uninterested in New Zealand things and New Zealand books and in fact of wanting to get away from all that local stuff. You speak of this task you imagined you had as a writer of bringing the 'over there world of fiction' into the immediate present of New Zealand everyday reality. I want to ask about that interest in New Zealand because when I interviewed Geoff Cochrane (*Sport* 31) he had a similar ambivalence about his inheritance. Well, it was hardly ambivalence. For Geoff it was an unqualified disaster to be born in New Zealand! I wonder if that is actually a defining New Zealand thing, to feel like escaping? Is it one part of us that feels a little bit unlucky?

NIGEL COX

I agree with that. I think that I'm infinitely happier to be a New Zealander now than I used to be. I think what is happening in this country is interesting and positive, and I also think we are very lucky. The tension of being in Europe was palpable compared to being here. It's a very easy life. I think that is a kind of curse too. It is too easy and everyone takes it easy. Anyway, I do think it is a curse to be a New Zealand writer but that is a fact of life. In many ways one of the defining things about your writing is place. The number of times you are going to get English readers interested in New Zealand is once a decade. One book once a decade. And American readers one book every thirty years. Therefore the big markets are closed to you. I am talking about survival and commercialism. The idea that you are going to make a standard living as a novelist when you have this handicap—it's hard. So what we do is we all go off and write about being in England but on the other hand we are struggling desperately to keep up so I think it is a curse but I have also always thought that New Zealanders are very romantic and there is a romance about writing here because there's no money in it. And that I like. When I was growing up I thought there was a paucity of event and a paucity of interest here. I'm not sure if that's true any more. I don't think it is. It is probably just naïveté that I thought that then.

DAMIEN WILKINS

I wanted to ask you about the way you use public places in your books. Whereas a lot of fiction writers would use the family as their locus, the place as the starting point of their book, often you use a space, like a hotel, or a pool hall or a museum. *Responsibility* is a more domestic book than the others, but even there you've got the museum. These are quite impersonal public places which often become characters in the books. Is that a conscious decision, a wish to move things away from family?

NIGEL COX

I do like to have an arena for the action to take place in but I think that is a comparatively simple thing. I think much more difficult and important—the best fiction in my opinion is reduced to a little phrase—is what happens between people. It is the hardest thing to write about. So there are books about shipwrecks and there are books about aliens and there are books about Tarzan's great career and all that stuff but what actually happens between people is the hardest thing to write about. The best writers, like Alice Munro, write about that brilliantly and that is why we think she is the greatest living writer of prose in English. In many ways what happens between people in families is the ultimate subject. I hardly ever read any great family books but a great family book is a really great book. But I find it very very hard to get away from my own family when writing about families. So I tend to focus on those neutral spaces so I don't fall into that because I find it too scary.

DAMIEN WILKINS

People in your novels often find substitute families. Strangers bump into one another, and suddenly they start to function as parents to each other or siblings. There is quite a lot of that, isn't there?

NIGEL COX

I guess. Basically it's because I don't feel I have permission to write about my parents or my sister. I did start recently to write a book from the point of view of my sister, who is a religious obsessive. It came out something like Flannery O'Connor, very powerful, and I was amazed at how much more sympathetic towards her view of the world I was once I'd made myself go inside that, instead of being outside where I am personally very unsympathetic. I couldn't go on. It was like an experiment. I had to stop after about twenty pages but it had a roaring life in it that I was actually afraid of. I knew if I wrote any more I wouldn't be able to stop. I felt it was unfair to write about her. She never asked to be written about and she wouldn't like it.

DAMIEN WILKINS

But isn't a writer an opportunistic user of other people's lives?

NIGEL COX

Is that true? Maybe that's a limitation in me as a writer. It's fabulous material, your own family. It's so intimate and so much the real stuff and it's never in films and so forth—you see crap in films about it—there are exceptions but it is just not an easy subject and yet it's *the* subject. It's where we all live.

DAMIEN WILKINS

So you think the sensitivities of family, of people who are alive, outweigh any kind of aesthetic kick you can get? You write a brilliant novel but you'd censor it if there was the chance it was going to hurt someone?

NIGEL COX

I suppose I think I could be cruel enough to write about someone who wasn't in my family because I don't have that intimate knowledge of them. There's a trust about being in a family, not a trust that's asked for or negotiated, there just is and people don't want you to do that to them. You can't write about them without judging them. They don't invite you to. I think that's that.

DAMIEN WILKINS

Responsibility though came closest to the autobiographical use of fiction, didn't it?

NIGEL COX

Oh, yes it did!

And that was a book that almost prodded the reader to make all those assumptions. It wasn't a subtle performance. It was as if you were saying, 'You want my life, I'll give you my life', or at least a facsimile or a shadow portrait or something.

NIGEL COX

Someone called it a personal satire and I did quite like that. I sort of fell into that book by accident. At first I didn't even take it seriously as a novel. What happened was that I had two or three projects that I was mucking around with. I had written *Tarzan Presley*, which was this sort of big effort, and so I wasn't even conscious that this might be a novel and every day I used to work on whatever I was working on. I was also trying to rewrite kind of seriously a long novel version of the story Rapunzel because that's a story with immense pressure in it, the weirdest of events and strangest things. Grimm's version covers years in half a sentence so I decided to expand it all and make it like a realist novel. I was quite enjoying that and I was doing some other thing as well. Every day I would work and I'd send whatever I'd done to the Jewish Museum by email and then at work I would look over what I had done, a couple of pages or a paragraph, make some fiddles and send it back home. Because Susanna was in Germany and she was bored, she used to read them and one day she said to me, 'You know that Rapunzel, that's just shit. But you know that novel about the guy who comes in and he's wet and he sits on the couch, that's great.' And I thought, 'Really?' And so I started taking it seriously as a novel. And then I started to think, 'Hang on, this New Zealander that's in Berlin, like no one is not going to believe that's me.' And suddenly one day I thought, 'I don't care. I'm just going to take whatever's to hand and what fits fits, and I'll go back now to this whole professional thing of a story that's told at the right speed, with chapters and characters and implications and the fact that it's quite close to my family I don't care.' And so I just let it happen that time and several people have said to me, 'I wonder what your wife thinks of this book.' But she's never really complained. I don't think I'd do it again.

DAMIEN WILKINS

Earlier you mentioned the success you had as a bookseller at Unity Books, first in Wellington and then setting up the Auckland shop with Jo Harris (now McColl). And one of the tendencies is to romanticise bookselling, to think if you like books that is what you want to do, work with them. My guess is a lot of people start in a bookshop and leave rather quickly because they realise it's all about—

NIGEL COX

Being a grocer.

DAMIEN WILKINS

Right, being a grocer. But Unity Books was very special because it got very close to the romantic notion of a bookshop. If you imagine a bookshop in the idealised way, as a place where you could not only find books but also have a conversation about them—that was how you ran it. Is that why you stayed ten years?

NIGEL COX

Yes that's right but what was interesting was what preceded those ten years. I had done roughly ten years in other bookshops in England and New Zealand so I knew what bookselling was all about. I knew what it was all about. And then I fell into this marvellous little bookshop, Unity

Books at 42 Willis Street. All the other Unity Books since then have disappointed me. That little bookshop had that romance and it was small enough to manage easily and big enough to be big, and it had this wonderful window that I always thought of as a TV screen that broadcast to the footpath. We were successful enough to be able to do unusual things and secondly I think it coincided luckily when something was happening in New Zealand books, which was exemplified by *the bone people*'s success, but there were a lot of other things too. Bill Manhire was publishing marvellous books at that point, Ian Wedde was published quite strongly, there were a whole bunch of great new writers being published—Barbara Anderson and so forth. And Fergus Barrowman was at VUP. There was a sense of something happening. Because I was passionately interested and also because I was trying to write and be in it, and because I knew how to be a good bookseller, it all came together. The final element was the weird philanthropic generosity of Alan Preston, who allowed us to do strange things with his foot both on the accelerator and the brake at the same time.

DAMIEN WILKINS
Was he ghosting around behind the scenes? What was his role?

NIGEL COX
He was in every single day and he was astonishing in the way he gave us a free hand, and he was a shrewder businessman than a lot of people gave him credit for. I used to run the wilder ideas past him and he would look at the ceiling and then say, 'Do you think so? Well if you think so', and he'd kind of leave it on you and sometimes we got it wrong but he

was very forgiving, and I think a great deal of the romance came from him.

DAMIEN WILKINS

You also liked the idea that writers were coming in. It was a writers' kind of shop, wasn't it? It was a readers' shop as well of course but writers came and they didn't have to buy a book, they could just talk about what they were doing.

NIGEL COX

I found that very exciting. I set out really to attract writers. For example we were the first bookshop to give a discount to writers. We did various things like that. This was the beginning of something that was very strongly articulated later and which I think is fantastic, which I would suggest is something called the Wellington writing community. It was just gathering—of course there had been earlier Wellington writing communities centred around Baxter and Louis Johnson and so on. Anyway this was a new one and it was in certain ways I suppose centred around Bill. And VUP, that was sort of the centre of it. And we were its shop window. I can remember doing a window with a great big Lands & Survey map of Wellington and then I cut letters saying 'Wellington Poets' and putting all the Wellington poets in it, one book each, and then right down the front because he had just published a book that day, a book by Tony Beyer called *Brute Music*, right at the front of the window. It went in on a Friday, late night in those days, and Tony happened to come along the street with his family. They stopped outside the shop and there it was, a centrepiece in the middle of Wellington poets. He was quite cool and he gave me the thumbs-up from outside and they walked on. On Monday he came in to see me and he said, 'I can't tell you what that was like. Walking along the footpath and my books have never really sold, I'm with my family and suddenly I see this whole window lit up with this bright light with my book in the middle of it, Wellington poets!' He said, 'Man, that was one of the big moments of my life.' You know there was a whole sense of being able to actually do that. That was what was amazing. It was free to be done. I had a ball.

DAMIEN WILKINS

One of the dreams of the character in *Responsibility* is to open a poetry bookshop and that sounded like you.

NIGEL COX

It is a little dream of mine because I have been a commercial bookseller and I've been successful. I've done it, I know I can do it and I am bored with it. The idea of opening a poetry bookshop, which I've had for some time, is so stupid and so quixotic and impossible that I really would like to have a go. It's like really setting yourself a hard challenge. I'd love to do it.

DAMIEN WILKINS

You've written a few poems yourself of course.

NIGEL COX

A couple. I published one not long after Kate, our first child, was born called 'Our Apples'. It was published in *Metro* and then there were a couple of others. I have written some poems but I am not a poet. I am clear about that, but I would like to be. I don't read a lot of poetry but I get a lot of pleasure from it and I think I have learnt a lot too. There was a period when I read Bill and Ian really intensely. Over and over again, trying to think what that might mean in prose. I can't write poetry, unfortunately.

DAMIEN WILKINS
Speaking of difficult fits, I wanted to ask about music and how to get it into fiction. Musical enthusiasms are not a great fit with fiction usually. It's really hard to communicate what is so good and interesting about music in words, isn't it?

NIGEL COX
In fact it is impossible. I have never read a decent rock'n'roll novel. There have been quite a few and they're all crap. It's kind of like the impossibility of making a museum about sports. They're boring too. Music is just music and you don't need to write a novel about it. I can't help writing about it because I'm so involved in it. I've tried to find ways to bring some of the charm of the music and what I like about it across into books knowing you can't really write about it. The first successful moment in doing that is in *Skylark Lounge* when the aliens talk to Jack Grout in the voice of Dusty Springfield. I suddenly thought, 'Yeah, got it! Now I've got the pop music in there in a way that works for the book.'

DAMIEN WILKINS
So there might be a kind of off-hand comment in the novel that the character listened to, say, Ray Charles all morning. You do it as fast as you can, you check the name and you check the mood and you're out of there, rather than stay and try to develop a kind of argument about why Ray Charles was important to that character.

NIGEL COX

Totally. I think Maurice Gee is a very great writer but what I sometimes think is missing from Maurice's writing is some stupid phrase like the solace of art, or the whole way that culture, and especially in my case pop culture, is actually around you. Something happens to you and a little tune happens in your head. Or you're driving along and the weather is just so and the car is just so and everything and then the right song comes on the radio and you go, 'Aha.' I think that is very very important to the ordinary people I like to write about. They don't read novels actually, they don't go to conceptual art shows, actually what they love and what they passionately care about is pop culture and they have it in their heads, it's floating about in there like big hunks of cloudy furniture and I want to sort of catch that. Yet you don't want a big kind of critics' discussion about it, like why Ray Charles?

DAMIEN WILKINS

Do you mean that the characters in Maurice's books are written in such a way that they're not allowed to put their heads up? They're caught in the problems of the book? A circumscribed life or something?

NIGEL COX

That's true but I also think that Maurice—he is an artist and a great artist . . .

DAMIEN WILKINS

He thinks it would be bad manners . . .

NIGEL COX

Yes. He doesn't grant the parallel even at a much lower level to everyone else and I think it is there.

DAMIEN WILKINS

The way you're describing it is that it is a formal problem. How to get the crappiness, the messiness we all experience in the world, into this made thing we call a novel?

NIGEL COX

It is a formal problem. And you can't go on about it. It doesn't make it better to have pages of it or a Greil Marcus-type analysis. That's hopeless. It's little things that happen in the back of your head all the time.

DAMIEN WILKINS

You've written the last few books while holding down rather high-powered full-time jobs. You've been getting up early in the mornings to write these books and from a distance it is astonishingly productive. We all say, 'How does he do it?' But you said once it probably affected the kind of books you were writing. There was a certain kind of novel you could write at six in the morning before everyone got up, which you could leave behind for the day, then pick up again the following morning. Maybe that kind of book came easier under those conditions.

NIGEL COX

I hope, taken collectively, there is something distinctive about my books, but one of the things that is a weakness about them is that you would never call them meditative. And I suppose I have in my mind that I would really like to write a quieter book about what happens between people in a family, and I don't feel that I have the mental space and the writing time with the life I've worked with in the past few years to write that type of book. It may be that I am not good enough to write that type of book. I've got in mind something that's better than Chekhov, of course. I have a sense of a book I could write but I don't have the mental space to write that book.

DAMIEN WILKINS

That brings us to the space you are in at the moment which probably doesn't allow you to do much of anything because of your illness. I came across a line recently from Saul Bellow's novel *Mr Sammler's Planet,* where it's said that Sammler has 'the luxury of non-intimidation by doom'. You don't have that luxury do you? You are intimidated by doom at the moment.

NIGEL COX

Yes, I am.

DAMIEN WILKINS

Physically it probably means you are not writing because you get uncomfortable and things like that. In one sense, when you were first diagnosed it was the best thing that happened to you for writing. You actually started writing. When the cancer came back did you feel the same kind of impetus or did you think 'Fuck it'?

NIGEL COX

No, it was completely different. The first time, I never felt cancer-sick at any point. I had some treatment that made me feel sick but I never felt sick. At that time they couldn't find the primary site and so effectively there was no cancer. There was the secondary in my shoulder that they took out. People said very serious things to me, and the weight of those words hit me like a freight train. 'Your cancer'—when someone said that to me the first time I really got a shock.

The oncologist said, 'This will probably kill you', and a few other things. But that wasn't what I was living. This time it is very different. They've found a big cancer in a vital organ and it doesn't sound all that recoverable from, and I don't feel well. It's been much more sobering. In fact it has taken up my imaginative space. I think that is the biggest problem for writing at the moment. I am physically discomfited but I think I can get over that because I have always got over that, the kids are always shouting in the next room, there's always something. But it instantly rendered the book I was working on trivial. You don't want to be writing a gloomy book but it just took me away from the whole mood I had been in and I haven't found my way back there.

DAMIEN WILKINS
That was the amazing thing about *Skylark Lounge*, that it wasn't an expected book from someone who had got that diagnosis, but nevertheless it was a book that in disguise talked about a lot of that stuff, didn't it? It was a brilliant, lovely roundabout way of dealing with it. I guess behind the first question was whether you grieved for yourself at that point and then wrote this wonderful book which somehow negated all that, set it apart a bit. It was a wonderful solution to that, wasn't it?

NIGEL COX
It was. It was a way of asserting being alive. I also thought it was a piece of skill and cunning on my part to have been able to deal with that material in that way. I think that is what is good about those last three books—*Skylark Lounge*, *Tarzan Presley* and *Responsibility*. They have found cunning solutions to those sort of problems. This problem right now is bigger.

DAMIEN WILKINS

Unlike a lot of writers you don't seem to have a great capacity for envy, or for self-pity, which often goes with envy. Those are feelings which, of course, can penetrate a writer and distort his work. You know, the conviction that you're better than the other guy, so why him and not you? Or, 'I hate that guy for getting that film deal.' You don't seem prone to that sort of thinking and I wonder if you're aware of that yourself. It's a silly question—are you aware of being a saint?—but do you wonder why you don't feel that way?

NIGEL COX

I think it's about dignity. I think it is all disgustingly undignified to think like that really. I'm not a saint. I do every now and then think, 'Oh, they won the prize and my book was better.' I think it is disgusting though to express it. And it's really disgusting to feel it. Fundamentally I am unbelievably grateful to be a writer. It was what I wanted and I got it. And that's enough. Recognition and so forth is very nice but it is not what matters. My books matter immensely to me. I am ambitious for a big audience but the other thing, that they matter to me, is much more important.

DAMIEN WILKINS

At your father's funeral last year, when you spoke about his life and what sort of man he was, there was that amazing thing you said where I think you'd observed your father when he didn't know you were seeing him—he was sitting at a piano—and I remember you said that you thought he was a happy man. It was a lovely observation. It wasn't a social moment. You didn't summon your father in a scene of, say, swinging you round in his arms when you were a boy, or anything like that. What you saw was a private contentment.

NIGEL COX

It was the inner person.

DAMIEN WILKINS

Yes, and I remember you saying to us afterwards that that was the hardest thing you had done, to talk about your father in that setting. Was it hard for the obvious reason that it was at your father's funeral? Or was it hard to find the right things to say, the right tone?

NIGEL COX

The right tone. I wanted desperately to avoid standing there saying he was the greatest dad on earth. 'He was a wonderful man.' That is horseshit. He was but you can't say that. The hard thing was to try and find a way to do him justice and to talk about him personally. I talked earlier about how I think that the life of the family is so important and I was the person from our family. My mother couldn't speak for obvious reasons; my sister is not a person who speaks, so it was me. I am used to speaking. I have now talked on various public occasions many times and I had that to fall back on. Most of all I just wanted to get it right. That was the terrifying thing. It is so easy to fall into sentimentality. To not find the right words. I knew I was really speaking for my mother and for my family and that someone had to say what it was like to be around him. That's the hardest thing and yet it is what really matters.

DAMIEN WILKINS

In some ways was it a literary task?

NIGEL COX

No. I had a little piece of paper and I had written on it one opening sentence so that I could get off to a decent start and I had something I wanted to put at the end. I wanted to just talk and that was the most frightening thing to do.

DAMIEN WILKINS

I think of you as happy in that way too. As a happy person. Do you feel that about yourself?

NIGEL COX

Yes I do feel that. I was an unhappy young man and I suppose in a certain way it wouldn't be true to say I studied happiness but that I worked away at it. I worked away at my writing and I have worked away at trying to enjoy who I am. As you get older you start to know yourself a bit and you realise you are not like that, you'll never be able to do that. You'll never be the lead guitarist, you just haven't got it, so relax. On the other hand I have had a little bit of public success. It's been enough for me. Maybe I am not a very ambitious person. It's been enough and I have just got happier as I've got older. I get immense pleasure from my family and underlying all that I am just in a pinch-me situation that I am a writer. I wanted to be one and it seemed impossible but then gradually it became more possible and then I got better at it. It has been an immense source of satisfaction and pleasure to me.

What
I Would
Have Written

We all have days when it seems the rain might not stop falling and for me this is one of them. So I thought I'd just get a few things down, see if it cheered me up.

All going well, I'm about, oh, two weeks from the end of some kind of a first draft of my next novel, *The Cowboy Dog*. With luck, I'll be able to follow through with my plan to tidy it and then—well, the usual things—more work, publication, and the world keeps turning with one more speck added to its burden.

However, I love my books and no matter what anyone else thinks of them, I for one will be pleased to see it.

With luck that'll all happen: *The Cowboy Dog*. Then there's quite a well-developed plan, between me and Fergus Barrowman, my publisher and close friend, to put together a book of some of my short pieces, most of them published

---

28.05.06, previously unpublished

before, that might be made together into a coherent whole. No name for this yet, but a first cut has been made. If he's forced to, Fergus might have to put this together by himself—no worries.

And then . . .

That's when it gets interesting, for me anyway. Obviously I've had lots of time to stare out the window over the last few months. And at night: so many ideas, as though they all want to get their oar in. One that has been stinking around for a year or two is 'a big family novel'. This is called *Half Time at the Woburn Pictures*, and consists mainly of smoke and the vaguest of thoughts. The idea is that this one wouldn't be (too) weird, though I don't seem to have much control over that; they get weird.

Then there's a plan to write a novel set in the Masterton of my boyhood. This one has also been around for ages—stinking. Reeking!—and for some reason the title has the word *Backyard* in it. *Backyard Oblivion?*

That's a couple of weeks' work, easy.

Then you come to a different category of thought. No plot, no location, no shape, no name, but I always wanted to invent my own superhero. It's a childish notion, and the existing ones from my boyhood—*Superman*, *Batman*, etc—have all been thoroughly postmodernised. But I always had a huge amount of time for *The Phantom*, *Captain America*, etc, and anyway I just want to—a figure modern and real, a genuine character, in a serious novel (I regard all my novels as serious). Same goes for an alien novel. I know I had a flirtation with aliens in *Skylark Lounge*, but that one kept itself very well within 'acceptable' boundaries. My desire is to go further out.

Some of that sounds a bit immature, and it is, I accept that. But there was a point where I decided not to be too constrained by the notions of what I thought I should be writing, and my writing got better.

But what I'm also thinking about here is (ta-dah) Nigel Cox at sixty-five. At eighty! I always thought I would live until I was seventy and in my mind I'd get better as a writer and become mature (ha!). But definitely improve. And know more and know how to write it. Contemplating it, it's such a fantastic idea that I have to laugh out loud. But it would have been inevitable, wouldn't it? Doesn't everyone? I guess, looking at some writers, the answer is, not necessarily. But I was in hope.

And I still am. Despite all the evidence to the contrary, I do expect to get these books written. I can see them sitting on my bookshelf, my impulse to write played out.

In the computer industry they call it vapourware. So, when you think of me (and do it often) please think of my vapour novels. Thank you.

My Father's Radios

Always had their batteries charged
He had a little machine
A voltmeter maybe and tested them
Then moved them down the food chain

A little black one in the toilet
Same in the bathroom
One in every room in fact
At least three in the shed

In the later years he was stuck
On the National Programme
But in the fifties it was more likely
The cricket

Manhire at 60: A Book for Bill, edited by Fergus Barrowman
and Damien Wilkins, Victoria University Press, 2006

Or something with music
He liked to sing as he worked
The long tines sliding in
To the depth of the carrots

His special ladder hooked over
The ridge line
Painting himself
Into a corner

Which had been his intention
Scything, though this is not correct
No transistors back then
So probably he just sang

He showed me how to sharpen
The dark pitted blade
Curved like a wing
With the stone and a blob of spit

The fescue falling smoothly
His brown arms making
Measured arcs

I can hear him singing
Any time I listen

THANET
AT WAR
1939-45

ROY HUMPHREYS

ALAN SUTTON

First published in the United Kingdom in 1991 by
Alan Sutton Publishing Limited · Phoenix Mill · Far Thrupp · Stroud · Gloucestershire

First published in the United States of America in 1992 by
Alan Sutton Publishing Inc · 83 Washington Street · Dover · NH 03820

First published in this paperback edition in 1992

British Library Cataloguing in Publication Data

Humphreys, Roy S.
  Thanet at war.
  I. Title
  942.2357084

  ISBN 0–7509–0297–3

Library of Congress Cataloging in Publication Data applied for

Typeset in 11/13 Bembo.
Typesetting and origination by
Alan Sutton Publishing Limited.
Printed in Great Britain by
The Bath Press, Bath, Avon.

Contents

Day by day contemplate your country's power
till you grow full of passionate love for her.
And when you realise her greatness, remember
that it was the dead who won it for you.

Thucydides

Glossary

AA (Ack-ack)	Anti-aircraft guns
AC1	Aircraftman Class 1 (RAF)
AFS	Auxiliary Fire Service
ARP	Air Raid Precautions
Aufklärungsgruppe	Reconnaissance Wing, *Luftwaffe*
ASR	Air Sea Rescue
CD	Civil Defence
CHL	Chain Home Low (Radar)
Cdr	Commander (RN)
CO	Commanding Officer
DFC	Distinguished Flying Cross
DSM	Distinguished Service Medal
DSO	Distinguished Service Order
FAP	First Aid Post
FO	Flying Officer (RAF)
Flt. Sgt.	Flight Sergeant (RAF)
Flgr	*Flieger* (Aircraftman 2nd class), *Luftwaffe*
Fw.	*Feldwebel* (Sergeant), *Luftwaffe*
Gefr.	*Gefreiter* (Aircraftman 1st Class), *Luftwaffe*
GOC	General Officer Commanding
HAA	Heavy Anti-aircraft guns
HE	High Explosive
Hptm	*Hauptmann* (Captain), *Luftwaffe*
IB	Incendiary Bomb
JG	*Jagdgeschwader* (Fighter Squadron), *Luftwaffe*
KG	*Kampfgeschwader* (Bomber Squadron), *Luftwaffe*
kg	kilogram

LDV	Local Defence Volunteers
Lt.	Lieutenant (British)
Lt.	*Leutnant* (Pilot Officer), *Luftwaffe*
NFS	National Fire Service
Obfw.	*Oberfeldwebel* (Flight Sergeant), *Luftwaffe*
Oberst.	*Oberstleutnant* (Wing Commander), *Luftwaffe*
Oberlt.	*Oberleutnant* (Flying Officer), *Luftwaffe*
Obergefr.	*Obergefreiter* (Leading Aircraftman), *Luftwaffe*
RA	Royal Artillery
RNR	Royal Naval Reserve
Staffel	Squadron, *Luftwaffe*
Uffz.	*Unteroffizier* (Corporal), *Luftwaffe*
UXB	Unexploded Bomb
WVS	Women's Voluntary Service

Acknowledgements and Picture Credits

It may well be that even as we are now able to review and profit from the experiences of our forebears, so our descendants might gain from the record of the 1939–45 war.

That the suffering of both civilians and military personnel should not be in vain, it is necessary that the history of them, that may be read, should without doubt be founded on fact. But fact is elusive. Information is sparse within the pages of official documents and those purporting to record events of local significance are often unreliable. To all those who helped in the preparation of this book I am indebted.

Colin Wilson, MBE, BEM, Museums Officer, Margate; John T. Williams, Museums Assistant, Margate; Ken Owen, Secretary to the Kent Aviation Historical Research Society; Winston G. Ramsey, Editor of *After The Battle*; Mike Pearce, Editor of the *Isle of Thanet Gazette*; John Guy, Secretary to the Kent Defence Research Group; David Collyer, Archivist to the Kent Aviation Historical Research Society; Diane Chamberlain, General Secretary to the Maritime Museum Ramsgate; Herbert R. Evans; A.E. Bridgeland; W.H. Bishop; Lionel A. Kempe; Phil Townsend; Mick Twyman; W. Barnes; Richard Foat; W. Stone; Colin S. Cuthbert; Dr Alan Kay; W.H. Lapthorne; Gina Guescini; Gwen Devereux; Rosalie Green; Tom White, Curator to Kent Fire Brigade Museum; Dorothy Culmer.

I have already acknowledged my indebtedness to those people who have helped in the preparation of this book, but here I would like to acknowledge, where possible, the sources from which illustrations were obtained. The majority of the photographs came from a private collection belonging to Mrs Gina Guescini, whose late father George E. Presland, Detective Sergeant Margate Borough Police Force, was officially permitted to take photographs of bomb damage. Many other illustrations would not have seen the light of day had it not been for the diligence of Gwen Devereux, Dorothy Culmer, Lionel A. Kempe, W. Stone, Herbert 'Hank' Evans, A.E. Bridgeland, Richard Foat and John T. Williams. I have made every effort to trace the original sources of other illustrations used, but if I have made any errors or omissions, then please accept my apologies.

Preface

The subject of Thanet's war years is vast and can be chronicled in many different ways, but should, I believe, be recorded before it disappears into the shadows of obscurity. Since nearly fifty years have elapsed facts are elusive. Much of the material used to unfold this narrative to its conclusion has, inevitably, been derived from the existing records, newspapers and survivors. I have done my best to set down here something of the chronology of those last war years, while being conscious that to outline the whole course of events would be too great a burden on the reader.

It is to the citizens of the Isle of Thanet who so unselfishly gave their services to the cause of freedom that this book is dedicated.

CHAPTER ONE

1939

Prelude to War

After the Air-raid Precautions Act was passed in 1937, the chief constables of the Thanet towns immediately sought responsible citizens to form the nucleus of an ARP system in their respective areas. There was no shortage of applicants. Those who enrolled were entered in a register and were given a number so that they would not be confused with others with a similar surname.

The chief constables were in sole charge of the organization until the chief air-raid wardens were appointed. Even so, they remained in overall charge of events and were responsible for a complex arrangement of emergency systems which, in everyday life, would have confounded the best managerial minds.

Quietly and efficiently they organized the distribution of thousands of civilian respirators. At the Duke Street police store, Margate, they unexpectedly discovered a crisis. They needed another four thousand small-sized gas masks. No one it seems, had considered the rise in the baby population. By January 1939, almost everyone had received a fitting and a home storage container.

All sorts of leaflets were pushed through letter boxes and one of the first urged that members of the public should look to their street wardens for all the information they required. The warden became an important member of the Civil Defence structure. In Margate, nearly five hundred were recruited in the first year and were to occupy over eighty-one warden's posts. Each man, and in some cases woman, was to receive instruction in how to detect poisonous gases, how to deal with incendiary devices, what kinds of protection were possible against high explosives, how to fit and maintain the various types of respirator and how the air-raid system was to operate. Then there were the positions of the fire

HRH, the Duke of Kent, accompanied by Ramsgate's mayor A.B.C. Kempe, inspects the Civil Defence Services in 1939. The Duke of Kent was killed in 1942, when a Sunderland flying boat, in which he was a passenger, flew into a Scottish hillside.

hydrants to memorize, also the water emergency tanks, and how the Auxiliary Fire Service operated, not forgetting the elementary first-aid lectures.

Initially both wardens and members of the AFS carried out household visits to check that everyone was in possession of a respirator, and at the same time made the first census checks of the occupants. Regular census checks were made throughout the war period. Census details were extremely useful to the authorities, not only for the obvious reason of knowing precisely who was living where, but also to filter out any 'residents' who might have had sinister or obscure reasons for being there.

This was not without some foundation either. As early as 1935 Herman Goertz, a former *Luftwaffe* pilot, and almost certainly a member of German Intelligence, occupied a bungalow in Stanley Road, Broadstairs. Incriminating evidence was later found which included detailed sketches and plans of the Royal Air Force Station Manston. There was also the Nazi spy, Dr Arthur Albert Tester, a familiar figure in Broadstairs. When

Tester disappeared quite suddenly just before the war it was suggested he had been whisked away to Germany in a U-boat. As we shall see, such suggestions were romantic nonsense.

All the same, Hitler was surprisingly ignorant of the true state of affairs in England, especially after the Dunkirk evacuation when, relatively speaking, the country was unarmed. If an invasion of the British Isles was seriously contemplated, one must assume German espionage was vigorously carried out. In any event, the German authorities seem to have been singularly ill-informed about our defences, despite Hitler's Directive No. 9, dated 29 November 1939, which said, 'Efforts will be made to secure the co-operation of the Sabotage and Fifth Column organizations.'

One of the first ARP demonstrations in Thanet was given to the general public at the Casino Car Park, Margate, in February 1939. A wooden hut containing furniture and other household oddments, to represent an ordinary room, was set up and an incendiary device was placed to ignite it. It failed to go off. Someone thought of throwing cans of petrol over the hut – flames began to lick the walls and firemen began to spray water over it. But a light breeze had got up and instead of the fire lessening it actually increased. Chief Officer Twyman was giving a running commentary over

Ramsgate Carnival in 1939 included a contingent of the town's Auxiliary Fire Service. Standing nearest the pump is Lionel Kempe, son of the mayor A.B.C. Kempe.

an amplifier system when the innocent demonstration began to look decidedly dangerous. A chemical fire extinguisher was hastily brought in to play. The onlookers thought the whole proceedings were quite hilarious and actually applauded every effort to extinguish the flames. While the demonstration might have looked like a Guy Fawkes gala night few, if any, realized that in eighteen months' time, fire fighting would no longer be a joke.

In July a test black-out demonstration was held. Hundreds of volunteers had already filled thousands of sand-bags and had painted white bands round trees bordering the streets. When the air-raid siren sounded at intervals between 22.00 and 22.20 on the 8th and 9th – wardens, firemen and policemen rushed all over the place in a pre-arranged exercise. There were many lessons learned, of course, not least the screening of windows with black-out curtains, putting brown sticky paper over the glass, the partial hooding of road traffic lights with sacks and motorists being obliged to drive with sidelights only. Before long, however, the judicial system was snowed under with black-out summonses.

Towards the end of the year over nine hundred steel air-raid shelters, called Andersons, had been distributed; an ARP Control Centre had been set up at Dalby Square, Margate, and extra fire stations storing trailer pumps and associated equipment were now strategically *in situ* around the towns. The AFS personnel manning the telephone emergency exchange were sleeping on just mattresses in their buildings.

And then, on the morning of 3 September, the BBC news bulletins told the nation to stand by for an important announcement at eleven o'clock. At eleven fifteen the Prime Minister, Neville Chamberlain, spoke to the nation. Huddled round their wireless sets families heard the last sentence of his speech which included the famous words that were to change their lives so dramatically one way or another,

> This morning the British Ambassador in Berlin handed the German Government a final note stating that unless we heard from them by eleven o'clock, that they were prepared at once to withdraw their troops from Poland, a state of war would exist between us. I have to tell you that no such undertaking has been received, and that consequently this country is at war with Germany.

The harbours were taken over by the Admiralty and the Isle of Thanet became a restricted area, only to be visited by special permit issued by either the police or military commanders. When Ramsgate was chosen as

No. 1 Contraband Control Base, it was not unusual to see huge convoys of ships held up off the shore. They were all searched for spies and contraband, and cargo vessels of various nationalities were sometimes brought into the inner harbour where confiscated goods were taken off and piled on to the quayside.

When orders went out for general mobilization, six herring trawlers sailed out of Hull and were part of the original six hundred vessels of 'Harry Tate's Navy', a nickname for the weather-beaten fishing boats, officially known as the Royal Naval Patrol Service. The six wooden steam-drifters, after conversion into minesweepers, took up their station in Margate Harbour. They were formed to undertake special mine-recovery duties for HMS *Vernon*, the Royal Navy's shore-based research establishment at Portsmouth. *Silver Dawn*, *Ray of Hope*, *Jacketa*, *Lord Cavan*, *Formidable* and *Fisher Boy*, had been fitted with mine-recovery equipment at Dover. The object of their hazardous job was to recover, intact, magnetic mines. They were causing too many shipping losses.

The following examples will give some idea of the treacherous sea lanes off the Isle of Thanet.

Pamphlets galore dropped through letter-boxes – 'What to do if . . .'. Few people read them, although the more discerning put them away in their living room sideboards and chiffoniers for safe keeping, just in case.

On 7 October the SS *Mahratta* struck a mine off Ramsgate and her cargo of tea chests floated ashore in their hundreds. Somehow or other dried tea eventually reached the local households – despite the salty taste. Then on 13 November two cargo ships were sunk by mines off Margate – the 1,346-ton *Ponzano*, and the 8,000-ton *Matra*. Two days later the 794-ton *Woodtown* sank off Margate with the loss of eight of her crew.

Coastal lights in the Thames Estuary were extinguished on 21 November, because it was discovered they assisted accurate mine laying by German ships and aircraft. On 28 November, the 1,041-ton steamship *Rubislaw* was sunk off the Tongue light-vessel with the loss of thirteen crew. Almost every day mines of one sort or another, and not only German ones, sank a formidable tonnage. Some were dislodged from their cradles by the heavy winter seas; many of them were being washed up onto the beaches and the shore-based Admiralty mine-recovery teams were almost continuously on call.

South-west of the Tongue light-vessel the cargo ship *Dalryan* struck a mine on 1 December. She was soon followed by the tanker *San Calisto*, almost at the same position, and six of her crew were lost in the explosion. Eight days later off Ramsgate, the steamer *Merel* blew up with the loss of fourteen lives. Two days later the Belgian ship SS *Kabinda* also struck a mine and sank.

In December the mine-recovery flotilla, now working out of Ramsgate, were sweeping in and around the 'war-channel' used by the convoys. *Ray of Hope* got her sweep tangled up on the sea-bed during one patrol. The skipper tried in vain to dislodge the obstruction, but unfortunately the ship had drawn over a magnetic mine. It exploded. *Silver Dawn* was close by and only managed to rescue the skipper and the second mate, the rest of the crew perished.

One of the most astonishing disclosures, however, was that soon after war was declared Admiralty officials came down from London to interview Stanley Rowden, the Port Fishery Officer, at Ramsgate. Naval authorities were anxious to recover a magnetic mine which had been dropped at night in Pegwell Bay. Local fishermen Bob Solly, Bob Cannon, William Towner and George Gorringe were persuaded to look for it. They set out in their motor trawler *Volante*, rigged with just an ordinary trawl. It had been suggested they might locate the mine by dragging the trawl along the sea-bed! Although they failed to find it, the mine was eventually located with tragic consequences. The Admiralty Service tug *Napier* had dropped her anchor in the bay on 20 December. By an unlucky coincidence, she was riding over the mine – later there was a

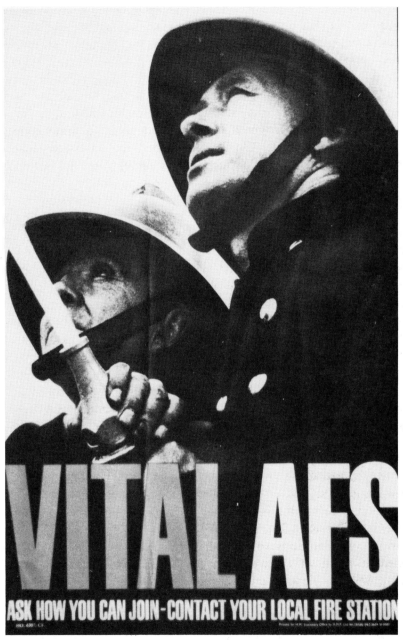

The Auxiliary Fire Service weas formed in 1938 and quickly outnumbered the regulars when, following the Munich crisis, thousands of men and women signed up. A plan to nationalize the fire service was eventually made law on 13 May 1941, and the independant fire authorities were absorbed into the National Fire Service (NFS) on 18 August 1941.

tremendous explosion. The 155-ton tug was blown clean out of the water with the loss of all hands.

Trapped in a net, another mine was bobbing up and down in the swell just inches from a Margate boat, crewed by three youths. They were saved from their predicament, when Jack Hawkes and Arthur Verrion, in their boat *Corona* came alongside. Hawkes and Verrion quickly transferred the net, complete with mine, to the *Corona*, towed it some distance away, put a flag on it, then cut it adrift. The naval mine-disposal team blew it up later.

At the onset of war all fishing was stopped and every boat came under Admiralty orders. Special permits were later issued to enable the fishermen to operate. At that time there were six trawlers operating from Ramsgate, the *Tankerton Towers*, *Kestrel*, *Treasure* and *Provider* – all steam driven, and the motor-trawlers *Thyme* and *Volante*. The *Kestrel*, incidentally, had attended HMS *Blanche*, a destroyer which had struck a mine and sank on 13 November. John Pocock and Ben Richards of Margate, also attended the *Blanche* incident in their boat *Golden Spray*. They had picked up over seventy sailors from the water, and both men were later mentioned in the *London Gazette*, commended by the king.

The War Emergency Committees had already been conceived for each town and the police responsibility seemed endless. The Borough Force was ably assisted by the Special War Reserve Constabulary, and the whole were intensely active in the preparation and enforcement of the black-out restrictions, checking lighting regulations for motor vehicles, and eventually rounding up aliens. Even the positioning and maintenance of air-raid sirens was a police matter.

With three harbours to look after, Margate, Broadstairs and Ramsgate, they assisted in the additional work-load of investigating the individual foreign nationals arriving by sea. They were constantly reminded by their chief constables of the fifth-columnist menace. Liaison with immigration and customs officials became paramount in heading off Hitler's spy network – if it existed at all.

The trouble was, however, fruitless hours were spent by the police investigating false reports. Some concerned illicit wireless transmissions, others reported low-flying aircraft being signalled from the ground. But of all the spurious reports, perhaps the most serious were those mentioning small boats being run up on to beaches at the dead of night. At one stage the duty constables were cycling around the resorts at night, carrying ·45 revolvers tucked into their trouser belts. But that was the time when a full military presence in Thanet was yet to be imposed, and even the Local Defence Volunteers had not been thought of.

When the situation on the Continent looked bleak a few thousand troops were suddenly billeted in Thanet. There were already detachments of the Royal Engineers in the harbour areas, but before long the Hampshire Regiment arrived. Landladies who had not decided to evacuate their boarding-houses, found dozens of troops standing on their doorsteps, wearing full battle order and carrying rifles. Although they were apprehensive about the hob-nailed boots pounding their staircases, at least they were still in business.

In Margate, over 50 per cent of the 14,000 properties had been used to accommodate peacetime visitors. There had been 30 first class hotels; 60 smaller hotels; 150 private hotels; 1,300 boarding-houses; 1,500 apartment houses and lastly 3,500 private dwellings which took in visitors. By the time peace was declared there were just four hotels available. Ramsgate was similarly disorientated by the war, its 35,000 population at the outbreak was eventually reduced to 12,000 and then rose to 17,000 by 1945.

The Isle of Thanet was to endure almost every known form of aerial warfare, ranging from the various high-explosive bombs – parachute mines and incendiary devices, to a few long-range shells and fighter-bomber attacks.

The seaside resorts of Margate, Broadstairs and Ramsgate were unfortunate to have been in an area over which enemy bomber formations flew to their targets further inland. Time and again records show without any doubt that bombs were jettisoned over the towns from aircraft hastily beating a retreat from the shores of Britain.

The Messerschmitt and Focke-Wulf fighter-bombers which made the 'hit-and-run' attacks, were usually briefed to strike at military targets, gasworks, electricity sub-stations and railways, but more often than not, their attacks fell wide of their targets.

CHAPTER TWO

1940

'The Horrifying Swiftness of Air Assault'

Friday 5 January

Nine brick and concrete warden's shelters were to be built at Margate immediately at a cost of £43 15s. each. Rationing of sugar, butter, bacon and ham would begin on Monday 8th. Rationing of meat was to be announced later, but meantime the registration for meat continued. The public were told they could choose any butcher they liked, and the procedure was the same when registering for other foods. The rationing scheme involved the control of all slaughtering through the meat trade. Farmers who ordinarily killed livestock for their own households were given permits to enable them to continue. Tripe, liver, heart, kidney, tongue and sweetbreads were not subject to rationing and, provided they conformed to certain requirements as to content, sausages, brawn, meat pies and pasties were also exempt.

★ ★ ★

Rescued unhurt after falling 20 ft down the air shaft of an ARP shelter at Birchington, a Guernsey cow was immediately milked by the owner and given a bottle of whiskey!

★ ★ ★

A large number of motorists were in trouble after the introduction of the black-out regulations and their names filled most of the charge sheet at

Margate Police Court. They were usually summoned for inadequate screening of their headlights, and for failing to paint their bumpers and running-boards white.

★ ★ ★

'Not Evacuating' – was the headline to a piece in the *Isle of Thanet Gazette* for Friday 19th. It went on, 'There is a rumour prevalent in Thanet that school children are to be evacuated. Fortunately, like so many war-time rumours, there is no truth in it. It is absolutely without foundation.'

★ ★ ★

General instructions for air-raid warnings were posted to the general public, and pasted-up on bill-hoardings in the towns.

AIR-RAID WARNINGS

In the event of threatened air raids, warnings will be given in urban areas by means of siren or hooters, which will be sounded in some places by short intermittent blasts and in other places by a warbling note changing every few seconds. The warning may also be given by short blasts on police whistles. No hooter or siren may be sounded except on the instructions of the police. When you hear any of these sounds – take shelter.

Keep off the streets as much as possible – to expose yourself unnecessarily adds to your danger. Carry a gas mask with you always. Make sure that you and every member of your household, especially children able to run about have on them their names and addresses clearly written. Do this on either side of an envelope or something like a luggage label, not an odd piece of paper, which might get lost. Sew the label to your children's clothes where they cannot pull it off.

Do not leave your shelter until you hear the 'raiders passed' signal which will be given by continuously sounding the siren or hooters for two minutes on the same note.

All cinemas, theatres and other places of entertainment are to be closed immediately until further notice. In the light of experience it may be possible to allow the re-opening of such places in some areas. They are being closed because if they were hit by a bomb large numbers would be killed or injured.

Sunday 7 January

The 2,888-ton steamer *Towneley* was sunk by a mine off Margate, then just north-east of the North Goodwin lightship, the cargo ship *Cedrington Court*, carrying wheat from Buenos Aires to Hull, was also sunk by a mine.

Tuesday 9 January

The Union Castle Mail 10,000-ton passenger liner *Dunbar Castle*, en route to South Africa, struck a mine off the North Foreland and quickly sank with the loss of only seven lives. Among the survivors was a party of nuns and one small child. They were rescued from the sea covered in fuel oil. A valuable racehorse on board unfortunately perished when the liner went down. For many days after the tragedy the sea-shore was littered with stationery, boxes of pencils and pens, cartons of Keatings powder, carpets, leather cushions, bar stools and even a grand piano.

Tuesday 30 January

Despite the heavy shipping losses, the sounds of mines exploding and the steady trickle of merchant seamen brought ashore by the lifeboats and other small craft, the citizens of Thanet were yet to see the effects of aerial bombardment at close quarters. And so the sinking of the 1,178-ton steamer *Highwave* north-east of the Kentish Knock by enemy bombers, became a talking point in the local pubs. Nevertheless, the true significance was not yet fully realized.

Tuesday 13 February
17.00 – Heinkel Shot Down in Sea

While German activity on land during the period known as the 'phoney war' remained quiet, nevertheless the opportunity was seized to operate reconnaissance patrols and direct air attacks against allied shipping.

The Heinkel bomber shot down north east of Margate, by the Spitfires of 54 Squadron, carried as a crew member *Oberst*. J. Stollbrock, a navigation specialist. Although wreckage was picked up by HMS *Brilliant*, the crew were never recovered.

SALE OF ANDERSON STEEL SHELTERS

Notice is Hereby Given that applications can now be entertained for persons resident in the Borough of Margate for registration for the purchase of 'Anderson' Steel Shelters. The purchase price for these shelters ranges from £7 10s. to £12 6s. if the payment is made by instalments, and from £6 14s. to £10 18s. if payment is made in full, according to size of shelter.

★ ★ ★

A report dated 6 February 1940, said that British authorities in the Mediterranean had seized the *Lucinda*, a 245-ton steam yacht belonging to Dr Arthur Albert Tester, of Naldera, Cliff Promenade, Broadstairs, and had ordered the yacht to be taken to a naval base. In Broadstairs Dr Tester, a doctor of philosophy of a German University and a member of the Fascist movement, was a familiar figure until about a year previously. Well-built and monocled, he was frequently seen in the town in one of his two luxurious cars. Dr Tester left England in the *Lucinda* with his wife and five children and was reported to be in Rome marketing a new oil for use in submarines. Naldera, his former home on the North Foreland, was closed, although the house was well kept and fully furnished. Barbed wire protected the gates. A national newspaper stated that Dr Tester was met at Lisbon by a Charles Paquet, a Belgian company director, who at one time was refused entry by immigration officials at Croydon when he attempted to come to London.

★ ★ ★

Because of black-out conditions Broadstairs Council decided to investigate a suggestion that the town should follow the example of Margate and whitewash the street corners.

★ ★ ★

In February a large number of soldiers were billeted in the Thanet towns. An assurance that holiday-makers were not to be banned from the towns where troops were in training was given by the Chairman of Broadstairs Council. After an alarming report appeared in a national newspaper he instructed the Clerk to write to Captain H.H. Balfour MC, MP. Captain Balfour replied that he had been in touch with the Minister of Labour immediately, and was assured that the statement was without any foundation. Referring to a Sunday newspaper's statement that some resorts were not preparing for visitors because they were in a danger zone, Councillor Nobbs denied that Broadstairs was in a danger zone. 'War or no war,' he said, 'ice cream will be sold as usual on Broadstairs sands next summer.'

★ ★ ★

The newly completed air-raid shelters in Margate were left open in case they were needed in a hurry. It was, however, discovered they were being misused. The Emergency Committee decided to lock them up. They arranged for the key to each shelter to be placed in a glass-fronted box and fixed to the wall outside the entrance.

★ ★ ★

It was a Sunday afternoon when Chief Officer Twyman and Fireman Harrison, of the Margate Fire Brigade, locked themselves in a derelict house at Dorset Place. They then set fire to the building. Within seconds flames were crackling and dense smoke was pouring from the windows. Using breathing apparatus, they had nearly exhausted their oxygen supply when auxiliaries eventually broke in and carried them to safety.

   The fire was one of nine separate incidents staged in a mock air-raid situation. ARP teams and first aid teams combined to test their efficiency in coordination techniques. The tests were quite unrehearsed, and no one knew what to expect. Ambulances raced through the town answering emergency calls; over one hundred firemen, eight women telephonists and more than a dozen boy messengers worked flat out without any knowledge of what to expect.

This general purpose fire appliance with a Leyland engine, carried a 40-ft Ajax extending ladder but no pump apparatus. A speed limit of 30 mph, shown painted on the chassis member, was a warning that the trailer pump fitted to the towing bar was apt to prove awkward on corners or sharp bends. Dick Milgate is in the driving seat, and the men are seen wearing steel helmets and civilian clothing, indicating the photograph was taken before uniforms had been issued to the Auxiliary Fire Service at Margate.

Margate's gas decontamination squad pose for the photographer in their newly obtained rubber suits at their Kings Street fire station.

The ARP incident board reported almost every type of emergency – indicating that high-explosive bombs and incendiaries had fallen all over the town.

When Chief Officer Twyman had set fire to straw and wood under the staircase he thought, as any self-respecting fireman would have, that rescue was only minutes away and they would be carried promptly to safety. What actually happened was that the 'victims' watched more than one fire tender dash past the burning house without so much as a glance. Each one that passed left it to the one following! Oxygen nearly exhausted, the two intrepid firemen were eventually rescued by red-faced auxiliaries who had axed their way through four locked doors.

Some ingenious ideas were thought up by the umpires and one of them indicated burst water mains near the harbour. As it turned out the harbour firemen were too smart for the umpires. The incident involved fires at the old Metropole and Ship Hotels. With a high tide conveniently lapping the quayside they drew sea water unhindered.

Despite the inevitable mishaps, by and large, the firemen and ARP teams learned from their experiences.

Saturday 24 February
EXPLODING MINE

Windows at two hotels and several private houses were shattered when a loose mine exploded on the rocky shore near Broadstairs at midnight. Pieces of the mine were found on the golf course. At Margate another mine was spotted from the pierhead. Naval experts put out in a surfboat, looped a rope around it and then dragged it ashore where they rendered it harmless.

Sunday 31 March

NOTICE
SIREN TEST

An air-raid siren test is to be carried out at 9.30 a.m. on Sunday March 31st, 1940. At Margate, Westgate-on-Sea and Birchington, the test signal for steam sirens will be a short blast, and for electric sirens "Commencing with a steady note for thirty seconds, followed immediately by warbling notes for twenty-five seconds, and concluding with a steady note of one minute." Police Officers and Air Raid Wardens will not blow their whistles during the test, and the blowing of whistles, followed by the sounding of sirens, will indicate not a test, but an actual warning.

An optimistic Margate Council issued the following message:

JUST IN CASE – ARP shelters for visitors. Despite war difficulties, Margate hopes and expects a reasonably good summer season this year, and in addition to providing games and entertainments, the Corporation are to build ARP shelters for their guests – just in case. The existing shelter accommodation, already considerable, is to be increased by surface shelters for 725 people at various points along the sea-front.

'I cannot see any reason why Thanet should not have its visitors, and be able to give, and they to receive, a safe, happy, and healthy holiday,' declared Captain Balfour, Under Secretary of State for Air and MP for Thanet, when he addressed a meeting at the Winter Gardens.

Sunday 21 April
RAMSGATE

Minor damage was caused to property by heavy calibre shell shrapnel at a time when gunfire was heard at sea. There were no casualties reported. Both the Kent and Essex coasts were, at the time, under a yellow warning.

A letter to the *Isle of Thanet Gazette* said:

> Presumably large notices will show the purpose of the new brick and concrete wardens' posts that are being dotted about Margate. Architectural frills are too expensive in war-time, but it is a pity they look so much like public conveniences.

Tuesday 23 April
STEAMER SUNK BY MINE

The SS *Lulworth* struck a mine off the North Foreland with the loss of two of her crew – twenty-three others were saved.

Saturday 4 May
FIRST HOSTILE AIRCRAFT SEEN

Although no enemy action was officially recorded on this day, heavy gunfire was heard from several places along the coast between the hours 23.00 and 02.00 and hostile aircraft were seen and plotted at Deal, Broadstairs and Margate. One of the aircraft was identified as a Heinkel III, which made an impudent, but graceful inspection of the North Foreland lighthouse. A group of fishermen on the pier just stood and watched it fly by at no more than fifty feet above sea level. A Mr Newton recalled: 'As it banked to clear the lighthouse we could see the two black crosses on the wings. I ran to the police station to report it, and from a chart they showed me I was able to identify the plane as a Heinkel III bomber.' Another eyewitness excitedly exclaimed: 'It came so close that I could read every letter on it. The plane was aluminium in colour and had two engines.' They were to see many more, coloured a sinister black and demolishing row upon row of houses, maiming and killing the occupants before the year was out.

Friday 10 May
HITLER LAUNCHES HIS ATTACKS ON BELGIUM AND HOLLAND.
WINSTON CHURCHILL BECOMES PRIME MINISTER

Saturday 11 May
KENT POLICE MOVE TO ARREST ALIENS

An order was made, following a conference of Home Office Officials,
Chiefs of Police (Special Branch) and Senior Officers of the Military
Intelligence Department, which stated:

> The Home Secretary has authorized and directed the temporary intern-
> ment of Germans and Austrians belonging to the following category,
> namely, all males over the age of sixteen and under the age of sixty –
> excluding the invalid or infirm.

There then followed a long list of east coastal areas of the United
Kingdom from the Isle of Wight in the south, to the Moray Firth in the
north. The order further stated:

> Every male German or Austrian must take care not to enter this area
> until further orders unless he has the express permission of the Secretary
> of State. The Home Secretary has also ordered directing that all other
> male aliens of whatever nationality over the age of sixteen and under the
> age of sixty, if living in the areas described above, shall be subject to the
> following restrictions, namely, they shall report daily in person to a
> Police Station – They shall not make use of any motor vehicle, other
> than a public conveyance, or any bicycle – They shall not be out of
> doors between the hours of 8 p.m. and 6 a.m.

The *East Kent Times* had run an article entitled 'Enemy Aliens and
Conscientious Objectors' in their Wednesday edition.

> A report of the Margate Council in Committee, presented at the
> meeting of the Council on Tuesday, stated that a letter had been
> received from the Town Clerk of Lytham St Annes, asking the Council
> to give their support to the following resolutions passed by this
> Council: 'That in the opinion of this Council, the present procedure
> regarding the internment of enemy aliens is not compatible with the
> security of the nation, and that the procedure should be reversed by the

internment of all enemy aliens, without exception, such internment being thereafter subject to appeal in special cases, and that such appeals should be dealt with by local authorities throughout the country.

'That in the opinion of this Council conscientious objectors should be compelled to carry out work of national importance at rates of pay no higher than, and under conditions no better than, those of HM Forces.' It was recommended that the Council support the resolution.

When the recommendation came before the Council, Councillor F.W. Mellanby, said he still intended to maintain that it was beyond the authority of the Council to support such a resolution. The Council were not yet asked to give the Government their advice, he said. Machinery had been set up to ensure that the cases of these objectors were heard, and the resolution before the Council set to over-ride the law. The various tribunals decided the conditions under which men were exempt from military service and it was now suggested that the Council should over-ride their decisions.

Councillor Mellanby went on:

Recruiting for Home Defence units was still open to men of certain ages, but he had not noticed any great desire on the part of those who had supported the resolution to move in that respect. He proposed that the resolution be differed in order that its supporters should have an opportunity of taking action. Councillor Munro-Cobb, reminded Councillor Mellanby, that England was still a free country and every-body had the right to express their opinion. Councillor F.W. Padget, said: The point of the resolutions was that men concerned should receive the same rate of pay as soldiers. The resolution did not aim at preventing men from being conscientious objectors.

There was no seconder to Councillor Mellanby's proposal and the recommendations of the Council in Committee was approved.

Sunday 12 May
ALIENS ROUND UP AND CURFEW IMPOSED

At 8 a.m. police moved to arrest several hundred aliens in Thanet. Both civil and military police called at homes of all male aliens and by 10 p.m. that day those arrested were taken under escort to internment camps. In the whole of Kent about eight hundred were apprehended and fewer than twenty were discovered in Ramsgate, some in residence while others were on a visit to the area. National Registration identity cards had already been issued to everyone residing in the country and anyone found without one would be detained for questioning.

Tuesday 14 May
RADIO APPEAL BY SECRETARY OF STATE FOR WAR

The Secretary of State for War, Anthony Eden, broadcast a message on BBC radio for men, between the ages of eighteen and sixty-five, to come forward and join a new force of Local Defence Volunteers. It was the beginning of a Home Defence Force which eventually was to total many thousands, and produced a remarkable effect upon the population who, almost to a man, acted on impulse to join the long queues outside the Police Stations to sign up. Scarcely had the broadcast finished before there were floods of applications for enrolment forms. In some areas the authorities were taken completely by surprise. By Wednesday morning the organization was running at full tilt, and by Friday morning it was estimated that close on two thousand had offered their services. At Ramsgate enrolment was undertaken by the Special Constabulary, and because of the number of people involved it was decided to open the premises in Cliff Street, previously used by the Conservative Club. Eager volunteers were besieging the police stations. So crowded were the inquiry offices there was nowhere to fill in the forms. It was an astonishing sight. Dozens were standing in the street using walls, pavements and one another's shoulders as writing desks. Every class of resident was among the applicants. Workmen in hob-nailed boots and greasy overalls stood cheek by jowl with professional men. Many drove up to the enrolment centres in their own motor cars and one of the first to offer his services at Ramsgate was the harbour master, Lt.-Com. H.J. Maynard. A retired naval reservist, he declared an acquaintance with firearms ranging from automatic pistols to 12-inch guns.

Of course, the great majority of applicants were ex-servicemen. All ranks were represented, from ex-lieutenant-colonels to privates. Cavalry-men, artillerymen and infantrymen, were all eager to join up. Many of them were disabled from wounds sustained in the First World War. A common plea after they were rejected was, 'I just want to have another go at them!' Although the age limit was sixty-five, many applied who were much older. It was believed the oldest applicant was a man of eighty-one who tried to enrol at Margate. He was quite indignant when his declaration that he was only sixty-five years of age was questioned.

Similar astonishing scenes were witnessed at Margate Police Station, where the old aliens office had to be opened for the enrolment procedure to operate without causing too much pressure on the ordinary police administration. It was estimated that at Margate over eight hundred men had enrolled in four days. Almost all of the town's council volunteered as they had in nearby Ramsgate. But at Minster the situation became embarrassing – there was no police station there. Local constables dealt with over fifty enrolments much to the disturbance of their domestic lives. A similar situation was experienced at Broadstairs where over two hundred offered their services.

A week later it was announced in Ramsgate that Lt.-Col. G.A.M. Sceales, DSO, late of the Argyll and Sutherland Highlanders, had been appointed Commandant of the Ramsgate Local Defence Volunteers. Within only thirty-six hours of his appointment section commanders had been selected and the whole administrative organization was in operation. However, there were no uniforms or arms – on their first parade they wore LDV arm-bands and carried pick handles!

The Ministry of Home Security had issued instructions to local newspapers throughout the country that areas subjected to enemy attack, in any form, would be banned from mentioning the specific town involved. It followed, therefore, the same conditions were also to apply to parish magazines, factory newsletters and any printed matter, and no mention was to be made of troop movements, or the locality of searchlights and gun emplacements. In Thanet and along the south, and south-east coast, towns would get mentioned only as a 'south-east town'. The principle of denying the enemy information was sound enough, but it was neutralized by the publication of names and addresses of Thanet's Civil Defence organization, which appeared in the *Isle of Thanet Gazette* on 17 May 1940.

Margate – Major C.S.F. Witts, to take command of Margate Local Defence Volunteers, and was released from his duties as Head Warden. Mr W.R.H. Gardener, is now acting Head Warden.
No 1 Platoon – CO, Major F. Mervyn Cobb, HQ Fitt's Garage, Cliftonville.
No 2 Platoon – CO, Mr T.F. Pettmann, HQ ARP House, Dalby Square.
No 3 Platoon – CO, Captain A.C. Hatfield, JP, HQ Bushell's Garage, Westbrook.
No 4 Platoon – CO, Mr W.G. Stewart, HQ ARP Post, Minster Road, Westgate-on-Sea.

No 5 Platoon – CO, Major E.L. Hunter, MC, HQ Grey Bungalow, St Mildreds Avenue, Birchington.

The 6th Company (LDV) HQ is at 218 Northdown Road, Margate. The Company Sergeant Major is Mr R.F. Walbourn, who was a musketry instructor at the Hythe Small Arms School, before he became Town Sergeant of Margate. Each platoon is divided into four sections with section commanders, and each platoon commander has one platoon sergeant.

Broadstairs – Major R.L. Payne, DSO, of South Cliff Parade, Broadstairs, has taken temporary command of the Broadstairs LDV. His second-in-command is Mr Philip Moss-Vernon, of Kingsgate, well known in Thanet for his Crazy Show productions. Temporary HQ is at 130 High Street, Broadstairs.

Ramsgate – Lieutenant Colonel G.A. McLaren Sceales, DSO, of Cliffsend Hall, Cliffsend, Ramsgate, has been appointed to command Ramsgate's LDV. The Borough Treasurer, Mr Oliver Jones, is acting as adjutant.

Sunday 26 May
OPERATION DYNAMO

At 18.57 in the evening the Admiralty made the signal 'Operation Dynamo is to commence'. A drama, as great and tense as any to beset our island history, was soon to occur. It became known as the 'Miracle of Dunkirk'. The evacuation of the British and Allied Armies from French soil, under the command of Vice-Admiral Bertram Ramsey, began at dawn on 27 May and ended in the late afternoon of 4 June. The German Army divisions had moved swiftly to sever the Allied lines of communication. Soldiers waded into the sea up to their armpits at Malo-les-Bains, Bray-Dunes and La Panne Sands, while others filled the port of Dunkirk to congestion.

Monday 27 May
OPERATION DYNAMO

The sequence of events which were to affect the Isle of Thanet began at 02.40 on the morning of this day. Chief Inspector H.B. Fleet, Margate Borough Police and Deputy Sub-controller of the ARP service was awakened by the night duty officer at the ARP headquarters, which was then at the Winter Gardens. He was told to report to the military commander, Lt.-Col. B.C.T. Freeland, Royal Engineers, at his office at

Cecil Square, Margate, at 03.00. Also required to be present at the meeting were the mayor, Alderman G.B. Farrar; the town clerk, P.T. Grove, and the chief constable, W. Palmer. It was the first indication that all was not well with the British Expeditionary Force in France.

Shortly after the secret meeting Chief Inspector Fleet took up his duties at Margate jetty as the liaison officer to the Royal Navy, which had established its headquarters at the Droit Offices. Military personnel had already occupied the Concert Pavilion at the end of the jetty, but within a few hours the local commanders had been ordered to withdraw their troops from the town. Three thousand left to take up positions at St Nicholas, although a small contingent of Royal Engineers remained behind to blow up the jetty, should an invasion be imminent. Thankfully this did not happen, but the mines, fixed to the undersides of the structure the day before, remained *in situ* throughout the disembarkation of troops.

Chief Inspector Fleet was soon to organize the ARP, FAP, police and special constabulary, and the AFS services, who were to work continuously for very long periods with little rest.

No one knew what to expect. All the military transport had gone with the troops to St Nicholas. There were no stores to speak of or equipment. The civil authorities had to supply all requirements. Alderman W.C. Redman was asked to bring his car. He had no sooner arrived at the Casino when he was detailed to fetch and carry supplies to the Winter Gardens and the railway station. When the first batch of evacuated troops arrived from France they came in a variety of vessels – peacetime paddle-steamers which had brought thousands of holiday-makers from London to Margate, pleasure-steamers converted to minesweepers, coastal cargo boats, tramp-steamers, barges and even mud-hoppers.

The small vessels pool began to operate by sending everything that could float down the River Thames and from other ports, to assemble at Sheerness under Rear Admiral A.H. Taylor. They were joined by the small craft section of the Ministry of Shipping, and the whole gamut of little ships arrived off Ramsgate.

At the height of the evacuation there were as many as fifty-two ships lying off Margate jetty, some so overcrowded that they appeared as a mass of khaki on the waterline. The first to arrive brought with them all their equipment. They were lined up on the jetty then marched to the end of it where they were relieved of rifles and ammunition pouches. They then boarded East Kent coaches and buses which took them to the railway station. There were no waving, cheering crowds to welcome them as the public had been banned from the sea-front areas. During the evacuation period Margate was allocated seventy-five trains and Ramsgate eighty-two.

Everyone expected the Germans to attack the ports of disembarkation. Had they done so the only defence available against an aerial attack was a few Bren guns manned by the London Irish positioned at the pier-heads.

Tuesday 28 May

The armada of ships was on its way by 07.30. The first ship to arrive at Margate jetty was the paddle-steamer *Sandown*, which berthed at 14.20 and disembarked 201 men. An hour later the *Gracie Fields* brought in 281.

Wednesday 29 May

At 06.00 the minesweeper *Ross* came in with 383 troops on board. From then on there began a steady stream of ships, large and small, and shortly after midday the *Royal Sovereign* landed 1,173 men, including five German prisoners.

The paddle-steamer SS *Sandown*, equipped as a minesweeper, was the first ship to berth at Margate jetty at 14.30 on Tuesday 28 May. She had brought 201 troops from the Dunkirk harbour.

Thursday 30 May

Another pleasure-steamer led a flotilla to Margate. The *Golden Eagle* berthed at 05.30 with 500 men and was followed by the *Royal Eagle* with another 808. Later the *Royal Sovereign* arrived again with 1,200, then another Thames paddle-steamer the *Medway Queen* berthed with 450.

Friday 31 May

Between 00.05 on the Friday and 22.15 on the following day, 49 ships berthed at Margate jetty, landing 21,845 men. Daily arrivals for Margate were: 28 May, 482; 29 May, 6,996; 30 May, 8,016; 31 May, 7,834; 1 June, 14,011; 2 June, 2,525; 3 June, 3,758; 4 June, 3,150. The 75 special trains sent to Margate shifted 38,000 troops during the evacuation period, and Ramsgate's special trains moved 42,783.

★ ★ ★

The wooden herring drifters of 'Harry Tate's Navy' or 'Vernon's Private Navy' were still in Ramsgate harbour when 'Dynamo' began. Lt.-Com. A.J. Cubison had been gamely trying to improve the flotilla's system of

Other survivors of the British Expeditionary Force rescued from the Dunkirk beaches, head for Ramsgate in a herring drifter of the mine-recovery flotilla.

communication. The response was encouraging when, after a week of flag signalling the drifters of the mine recovery flotilla were spread out in line ahead from the North Foreland to Dover. Soon after the small coasters, trawlers and scoots, arrived from Belgium and Holland carrying refugees, Commander Cubison was observed waving a couple of white handkerchiefs from the steps outside his harbour office. The semaphore message read: 'All ships raise steam immediately and prepare for sea.' Joining the drifter *Lord Cavan*, Cubison hoisted his signal 'A' – 'Form single line ahead'. The flotilla, with other ships that had since crowded Ramsgate harbour, steamed out to take route X – the shortest mineswept route to Dunkirk. Once there, they were instructed to go into the harbour and bring off troops then to off-load them on to larger ships lying outside.

Fisher Boy and *Fidget* edged into the Mole. With 250 troops crowding the decks they had come out looking for a suitable transport ship, but the only ship they saw had been sunk and abandoned, and so they set course for Ramsgate. After disembarking they were immediately ordered to reload with stores and return to Dunkirk. They took with them scaling ladders which had been made by Ramsgate carpenters to help soldiers climb down from the quayside. By then Dunkirk harbour was continuously being shelled by German artillery. *Fisher Boy*, loaded to overflowing with soldiers until it was impossible to move anywhere on deck, steamed back to Ramsgate at four knots. On every trip they exceeded their quota (officially put at 100) and the astonishing numbers brought back was made possible only by the generously calm sea. The drifters of 'Vernon's Private Navy' made their last journeys on 2 June – *Fisher Boy*, *Fidget* and *Jacketa* all survived, but *Lord Cavan* was totally destroyed by a shell just before she was due to sail back to Ramsgate. At the final analysis Commander Cubison's herring flotilla had rescued no fewer than 4,085 men: *Fisher Boy* in 7 trips brought back 1,350, a remarkable one-third of the total.

★ ★ ★

On 30 May the Lifeboat Institution received a message from the Admiralty to send as many boats as was possible to Dover, the main port for vessels engaged in the Dunkirk withdrawal. However, the two Thanet lifeboats, Margate's *Lord Southborough* and Ramsgate's *Prudential*, sailed direct to France. *Prudential* was the first away, with coxswain Harold Primrose Knight at the helm, but at first in tow of a Dutch barge to save fuel. Under constant attack from the air she lay off the beaches and

The Margate lifeboat *Lord Southborough*, under coxswain Edward Drake Parker, remained off the beaches at Dunkirk for over twenty-four hours, ferrying troops to the larger vessels.

Under coxswain Harold Primrose Knight, Ramsgate's lifeboat, *Prudential*, was the first RNLI boat to reach Dunkirk.

eventually managed to ferry 2,800 troops to the larger vessels standing off.

The Margate lifeboat crew were summoned to the boathouse by their coxswain Edward Drake Parker. There was not a moment's hesitation – to a man they all volunteered, and in the late afternoon wearing naval-issue tin helmets they stood to their positions as the *Lord Southborough* glided down the slipway on its errand of mercy. Under the leadership of Parker were T.D. Harman (second coxswain), H.E. Parker, the coxswain's brother (bowman), E.J. Jordan (mechanic), W.B. Mackie (assistant mechanic), J. Letley, A. Morris, A. Ladd and D. Grice. Also with the crew were two merchant seamen who happened to be at home when the call came – E.E. Parker, the bowman's son, and W.G. Hopper. The *Lord Southborough* arrived not long after the *Prudential* and lay close to the beaches for over twenty-four hours, ferrying troops to larger vessels.

It has been difficult to find an official record of the number of troops taken on board the lifeboats. Each boat could take between sixty and eighty men on each trip, and as they operated continuously for over eight hours, it is probable that the number saved was in fact much larger than some records reveal. The historian is hampered by the typical reserve and modest nature of the two coxswains and their crews, and the brief report provided by them.

One report reveals that part of one night's operation was spent ferrying wounded troops from La Panne Hospital, where they were floated out to the lifeboats on rafts and also carried head-high over the waves. The lifeboat crews saw smaller craft go under by the sheer weight of their human load. They also saw soldiers wading out up to their armpits, only to be knocked over by the surf and drown within sight, many almost within reach of the boats. A tribute to the Margate lifeboat crew was paid by Lt.-Com. E.G. Roper, of HMS *Icarus*, who said in a letter to the RNLI, 'On behalf of every officer and man on this ship, I should like to express to you our unbounded admiration of the magnificent behaviour of the crew of the lifeboat *Lord Southborough* (Margate) during the recent evacuation from Dunkirk. The manner in which, with no thought of rest, they brought off load after load of soldiers under continuous shelling, bombing and aerial machine-gun fire, will be an inspiration to us as long as we live. We are proud to be the fellow countrymen of such men.'

Both coxswains, Knight and Parker, were later awarded the Distinguished Service Medal. They both stated that the medal was not for them personally, but for the whole crew. The RNLI house-flag which had flown at the masthead of Ramsgate's *Prudential* was later laid up in the parish church.

★ ★ ★

The job of tackling the disembarkation of the wounded cannot be better described than by quoting a report made by a supervisor of one Margate first aid party.

> Personnel worked from sunrise to sunset, their only rest was in a deck chair. Ships arrived and several berthed at one time. Captains – through megaphones, announced the number of men on board, adding the number of wounded – stretcher cases and corpses, also prisoners if any. By this time, we knew which ships to board and what to take with us. We quickly learned where to find the more serious cases. Invariably they had been taken to the engine rooms for warmth. On the destroyers, minesweepers, tramps, pleasure-steamers and dredgers, the only entrance and exit was by a perpendicular iron ladder.
>
> Our work in general terms was this – board ship as required, take approximate number of stretchers and blankets, first aid treatments – loading stretchers – carrying stretchers, many of them had to be passed over two, three and four ships abreast before landing, and loading the ambulances; assisting the walking wounded using the hand-seats; distributing old clothes and blankets to the naked and taking round the water bottles. Finally – the removal of the corpses to a mortuary.
>
> One of the hardest things I found to do was to diagnose the injuries of the French and Belgians, which was largely due to language difficulties. Some of them had been in as many as three ships – all of them subsequently had been sunk. They were covered with thick, black fuel oil, and we had great difficulty in handling their slippery bodies. I recall twenty-three men were dead on arrival at Margate and another twenty or so died in hospital.

There were unforgettable scenes at Margate railway station where the troops entrained. Military provisions were pitifully inadequate but, under the leadership of the mayor, over fifty townswomen ran free canteens. Even the fire brigade had a mobile canteen operative at the pier-head. It was soon realized, however, that it would be impracticable to leave it there and it was moved to the railway station. Thousands of cups were obtained from local catering establishments and every shop in the district, as far away as Canterbury was searched every day for provisions such as meat pies, biscuits, bars of chocolate and fruit.

No record was ever made of the quantity of food distributed, and no one stopped to consider the costs. One estimate was that over 100,000 cups of tea were served in the 8 days. But amid the chaos and confusion there came another call; a call to organize the evacuation of children from the Isle of Thanet.

Sunday 1 June
EVACUATION OF CHILDREN

The special trains earmarked for the 'Dynamo' undertaking were increased when the Government Emergency Act was introduced. Distress in the area was great especially as the evacuation came when thousands of troops were being transported in haste from the area. Many could not bear to see their children off at the stations. There was something very sinister about the urgency of it all.

But to the majority of the children it seemed as though it was going to be a holiday – an adventure that few had experienced, some had never been out of their own town.

The county of Staffordshire had been selected as the reception area, and in just over 5 hours 3,255 children, fully labelled and all carrying their gas masks in cardboard boxes, together with 241 staff and helpers, left for the comparative safety of the Midlands.

Had there been a hint that invasion was imminent, there were plans to move a further 25,000 people in 2 days. Although the residents of Thanet who remained behind in 1940 were aware that evacuation was likely, the details of this scheme were kept secret. The Thanet coast was to be cleared of all non-essential civilians to allow troops freedom of movement in dealing with any enemy forces. The 25,000 people would have gone by train to Surrey and Hertfordshire in just 48 hours, leaving behind 3,000 Local Defence Volunteers, firemen, civil defence workers and officials.

Dr B.W. Armstrong, medical superintendent at the Royal Sea Bathing Hospital, Margate, remembered the Dunkirk episode with remarkable clarity. The number of beds at the hospital was raised from approximately 324 to 520, when it became part of the Emergency Medical Service. It was done by putting extra beds into wards with veranda accommodation and by removing pews from the chapel.

IMPORTANT NOTICE

EVACUATION

The public throughout the country generally are being told to " stay put " in the event of invasion. For military reasons, however, it will in the event of attack be necessary to remove from this town all except those persons who have been specially instructed to stay. An order for the compulsory evacuation of this town will be given when in the judgment of the Government it is necessary, and plans have been arranged to give effect to such an order when it is made.

You will wish to know how you can help NOW in these plans.

THOSE WHO ARE ENGAGED IN WORK OF ANY DESCRIPTION IN THE TOWN SHOULD STAY FOR THE PRESENT.

OTHER PERSONS SHOULD, SO FAR AS THEY ARE ABLE TO DO SO, MAKE ARRANGEMENTS TO LEAVE THE TOWN—PARTICULARLY

MOTHERS WITH YOUNG CHILDREN
SCHOOL CHILDREN
AGED AND INFIRM PERSONS
PERSONS WITHOUT OCCUPATION OR IN RETIREMENT.

All such persons who can arrange for their accommodation with relatives or friends in some other part of the country should do so. Assistance for railway fares and accommodation will be given to those who require it.

Advice and, where possible, assistance will be given to persons who desire to leave the town but are unable to make their own arrangements.

Information about these matters can be obtained from the local Council Offices.

(*Signed*) AUCKLAND GEDDES,
Regional Commissioner for Civil Defence.

2nd July, 1940.

(393/4177A) Wt. 19544–30 70M 7/40 H & S Ltd. **Gp. 393**

Throughout the first winter of the war no very serious strain was placed upon the hospital accommodation, though upwards of five hundred cases of German measles, from troops billeted in various parts of East Kent, were received and treated. When the evacuation of Dunkirk commenced the hospital was immediately flooded by large numbers of casualties. During the period 29 May to 6 June some five hundred passed through.

The hospital acted, in the main, as a casualty clearing station, and the larger proportion of the patients was evacuated to inland hospitals after a stay varying from a few hours to a few days, during which time the effects of shock, exhaustion and exposure were treated, wounds and burns dressed – in many cases under anaesthetic, and splints applied to fractured limbs.

The greatest pressure of work occurred on 4 June, when some eighty cases of great severity were admitted, the majority of whom were from the French destroyer *Jaguar*, which had struck a mine off Dunkirk harbour at a time when her decks were crowded with standing men, mainly French sailors and marines and French colonial troops from North Africa.

The effects of the explosion upon these men was to produce multiple fractures of one or both of the lower limbs, pelvis and spine in a very large proportion of the casualties, due to the sudden upthrust of the deck under their feet. The effect, indeed, was comparable to what might have been produced by jumping from a height of 20 or 30 ft.

The resources of the hospital were taxed to the utmost, and only the fact that the hospital had a staff of highly-skilled splintmakers enabled it to cope with these casualties. Much help was received during the latter hours of the night by the arrival of a mobile theatre team from Canterbury, with whose aid all the casualties were eventually dealt with.

Many of these cases were too ill to be transferred for some time, and a number were still in the hospital when it was eventually evacuated on 21 June 1940.

Matron of the Margate General Hospital, Miss A. Garnett, recalled:

The routine of hospital life was suddenly broken by a telephone call to prepare for wounded soldiers, but before any preparations could be made the men were arriving in taxis, buses and private cars.

From my first sight of the wounded men lying in the hall on stretchers, each giving the 'thumbs up' sign, and assuring us that 'We'll beat them yet – just wait until we are re-equipped,' I knew that no enemy could conquer this amazing spirit. We had not heard of the 'Dunkirk spirit' then, but all the staff of the hospital felt it in the behaviour of the soldiers and the magnificent response of the Margate people in gifts and service.

The service of the medical and nursing staffs at this time is well known. No praise of mine could be high enough for the skill and devotion to duty that I witnessed. The late Mr W.G. Sutcliffe, the medical superintendent, did yeoman service. The vicar of Margate, the Revd Donald Beckingham, had an encouraging word for all, supplying half-crowns and postcards to the men.

Many of the Margate people gave unstinted service during this period, and Mrs Venner was a great help with telephone and refreshments. The call for linen and blankets through the broadcast relay service had a great response, and soldiers billeted in the town were working as stretcher bearers.

Ex-mayoress and founder member of the Margate WVS, Mrs B.M. Hoare, wrote:

None of us that first day of the evacuation from Dunkirk, realized exactly what was happening. There had been much activity and organization in the town. The seafront was closed from the harbour to the station, and all the businesses were at a standstill. Then the 'Armada' of ships of various shapes and sizes began to arrive, and lay off the jetty waiting their turn to land their tired, hungry and wet human cargoes – a mass of closely-packed, khaki-clad figures, each boat full to capacity, and more.

The whole picture presented a sea of khaki and faces – the faces of some of the bravest men this country will ever know, men who had so recently faced the terrible horrors of war . . .

But they were not defeated or downhearted, they proved that when they boarded the East Kent coaches, which were to take them to the station, by giving the 'thumbs up' sign and a grin to the people of Margate whom they passed on the way.

I wonder if they knew how much that sign and the spirit of optimism which they showed, helped to cheer us up, and to give us renewed courage to face that period when we had to fight alone.

As the soldiers entrained each was given a view postcard of the town on which to write to his loved ones to tell them they were safely back in England.

Margate's Dreamland in the Amusement Park, well-known to thousands of peacetime holiday-makers, lived up to its name during Dunkirk, and became a real 'dreamland'. Len Mancey wrote:

> The Popular Restaurant was transformed into a first aid casualty station. The procession of stretchers and walking wounded seemed endless, and willing workers were soon busy sending away postcards and telegrams. The Sunshine Cafe lived up to its name, for it became a rest centre and club for both troops and civilians.
>
> Dreamland Ballroom was a huge dormitory. Beds and bedding were brought from firms hostels and hotels and borrowed wherever possible, and the settees, upon which in happier times dancers relaxed, now gave ease and comfort to weary limbs.
>
> I remember an old Frenchwoman. She had walked miles along the dusty roads of France, dragging her few belongings – which ultimately she had lost, except her little dog. Somehow, she got on to a boat with him, and arrived at Margate clutching this last vestige of her homeland. But she had retained her indomitable spirit, for she continually cried out 'Vive la France'. When the quarantine officer separated her from her dog, she broke down and wept bitterly.

Len recalled her wrinkled and tear-stained, bemoaning the loss of her canine friend. Then there were the two young Belgian girls who somehow had made their way to Dunkirk, anxious to reach England. They had 'acquired' two soldier's uniforms, and thus arrayed found themselves in Dreamland, which to them was a real fairyland.

The story of the Dunkirk evacuation: the bravery, the enormous loss of life, the carnage and horrific scenes of drowned soldiers, has been told in great detail many times. The courage and determination of both the rescued and the rescuers was evenly matched by a spirit of camaraderie that somehow rubbed off on to the citizens of the Thanet towns.

There is little space here to encompass the breadth of unselfish assistance, given for the most part spontaneously to the wounded and dying.

Perhaps the spirit of the townspeople can be judged, if anyone was ever

Ramsgate's war-time lifeboat crew of the *Prudential* who did such sterling work at Dunkirk. Back row, from left to right: E. Cooper, E. Attwood (master mechanic), A.Liddle, J. Hawkes, J. Goldfinch. Front row: C. Knight, A. Moody (acting 2nd coxswain), Howard Primrose Knight, DSM (coxswain), T. Read (asst. motor mechanic).

in doubt, by just one small incident which grew into a plethora of kindness. It all began with one old lady in Kent Place, Ramsgate who opened her front door one morning and saw the street full of soldiers. Concerned for their well-being she immediately brought out her teapot and then emptied her larder. Within minutes her neighbours followed her example and, before long, the whole town had rallied. The other housewives responded and their efforts were nothing less than outstanding. They came with food – gallons of hot tea and thousands of sandwiches – and clothing.

The citizens of the Thanet towns were to receive the highest commendation for their part in one of the most poignant operations of British military history when, against all odds, 338,226 men were brought safely back to England. The following is a list of the ships which put into Margate Jetty, and the number of troops they brought:

Sandown, 201	*Kingfisher* (3 trips), 458
Gracie Fields, 281	*Scottish Operator*, 325
Ross (2 trips), 683	*Dundalk* (2 trips), 730
Leda (5 trips), 2,218	*Hopper V 24* (2 trips), 980
Pangbourne, 400	*Twente*, 350
Kellett (3 trips), 1,055	*Antie* (2 trips), 450
Royal Sovereign (6 trips), 6,370	*Brighton Queen*, 160
Albury (4 trips), 1,137	*Plinlimmon*, 900
Patria (2 trips) 1,400	A motor boat, 23
Caribia, 300	*Saltash* (2 trips) 750
Leus, 200	*Westward Ho!* (3 trips), 1,686
Horst (2 trips), 1,150	*Lady Southborough*, 350
Royal Daffodil (2 trips), 3,203	*Galleons Reach*, 123
King George V (5 trips) 3,582	*Queen's Channel*, 52
Golden Eagle (2 trips), 1,750	*Whippington*, 2,500
Royal Eagle (2 trips), 2,058	*Foremost*, 200
Lydd (3 trips), 850	*Oriel* (4 trips), 2,020
Princess Elizabeth (3 trips), 1,344	*Vincia*, 108
Aegir (3 trips), 835	*Queen of Thanet* (2 trips), 2,350
Medway Queen, 450	*Halcyon*, 58
Oranje (2 trips), 600	*Rapid 1*, 25
Delta, 203	*Offenia*, 50
Dogger Bank (2 trips), 708	*Tangelle Maria*, 25
Wolverhampton, 50	*Trawler AD389*, 64
Adventuress, 85	*Guillemont*, 460
Stella Durado, 22	*Trawler L.2*, 85

The following is a list of the ships which put into Ramsgate Harbour during the Dunkirk evacuation:

Yewdale	*Haste Away*
Pangbourne	*Burton*
Batt	*Shannon*
Bonny Heather	*Royal Daffodil*
Wolsey	*Sun IV*
Swallow	*Horst*
Marlborough	*Fisher Boy*
Haig	*Fidget*
Wolfe	*Jacketa*
Pudge	*Sundowner*

Foremost No. 101	*Rosaura*
Kestrel	*Ciel de France*
Tankerton Towers	*Ave Maria Gratia Plena*
Provider	*Jeanne Antoine*
Minotaur	*Arc en Ciel*
Prudential	*Racia*
Massey Shaw	*Pascholl*
Silver Dawn	*Mermaiden*
Lord Cavan	*Letitia II*
Westerly	*Madame sans Gene*
Naiad Errant	*Tigris I*
White Heather	*Rian*
Prince	*Fishbourne*
Princess	*Sun III*
Duke	*Ada Mary*

★ ★ ★

We shall go on to the end. We shall fight in France, we shall fight on the seas and oceans, we shall fight with growing confidence and growing strength in the air. We shall defend our island whatever the cost may be; we shall fight on the beaches, we shall fight on the landing grounds, we shall fight in the fields and in the streets, we shall fight in the hills.

We shall never surrender, and even if, which I do not for a minute believe, this island, or a large part of it, were subjugated and starving, then our Empire beyond the seas, armed and guarded by the British Fleet, would carry on the struggle, until, in God's good time, the New World, with all its power and might, steps forth to the rescue and the liberation of the Old.

WINSTON CHURCHILL, 4 June 1940
★ ★ ★

After Dunkirk, plans to counter any invasion threat by Hitler were implemented. Orders were issued that all signposts throughout the county be taken down, all milestones were to be uprooted, and the names of streets, roads and railway stations, were to be obliterated.

The first line of defence had already begun and temporary road barricades were hastily erected at strategic positions around the towns. The original makeshift barriers of disused farm implements and anything the local authorities could lay their hands on were eventually

The Ramsgate coastal battery, installed in June 1940, consisted of two 6-in naval guns first used on ships during the First World War. Manned by men of the Royal Artillery the guns were situated opposite Wellington Crescent.

Wellington Crescent, Ramsgate, showing the fortified bandstand, a pillbox, and the concrete structures erected to house the two 6-in naval guns. The tower standing at the end of the crescent was the battery observation post.

replaced by the more permanent concrete structures.

Beach areas were already put out of bounds to the public and were cordoned off by rolls of barbed wire. Hundreds, if not thousands, of anti-personnel mines were planted in the sands and on the cliff faces, beneath which were miles of defence structures made up of scaffold poles and old railway track.

Concrete pillboxes and machine-gun emplacements appeared almost everywhere – some of them cleverly disguised as bathing huts, petrol stations, cafés and newspaper kiosks. In the beach and cliff areas the whole became more or less a complete and unbroken barrier against landing craft. Given hindsight, they would have easily been blown up had invasion forces struck.

If nothing else, it gave a sense of confidence to the civilians who were left behind and who were required to negotiate the concrete anti-tank blocks known as 'dragon's teeth', erected across roadways and fields.

While a strong labour force of civilians under the supervision of the Royal Engineers was busy erecting the barriers and all manner of defence works, another force was engaged in erecting the concrete emplacements to house the coastal gun. Margate's two 6-in naval guns, positioned at

These 3-in guns were first used in 1914 and became the main armament of the Territorials in the 1930s. Using 'open-sights' they were largely innaccurate in performance and their 'bite' was far less fearsome than their 'bark'.

Fort Crescent, arrived by rail in June. No. 335 Coastal Battery, 549 Regt. RA, was ready for action in August.

Two 4-in naval guns were installed at Kingsgate, Broadstairs, manned by No. 408 Coastal Battery, and were ready a month later. The Joss Bay guns, four 5.5-in naval, were installed near the North Foreland lighthouse and, under No. 410 Coastal Battery, was finished by August. A pair of 5.5-in naval guns were positioned at Dumpton Point, manned by No. 230 Coastal Battery, but were not ready for action until October.

Ramsgate already possessed two 12-pounder guns which had been erected in June at the very end of East Pier, manned by No. 297 Battery, RA. In July, the Royal Marine Siege Regiment arrived with two 6-in naval guns, complete with turrets, and installed them at Victoria Parade next to the bandstand and in front of Wellington Crescent. When completed they were handed over to No. 336 Coastal Battery, but were not ready until September.

The Little Cliffs End battery, erected in July, possessed two 4-in QF (quick-fire) naval guns. They were manned by No. 914 Defence Battery, RA, and were also designated as 'X' Static Battery, but in November 1941, the guns were replaced with two French 75-mm guns.

Two 6-in naval guns were installed at Pegwell Bay, and became known as the Bethlehem battery under No. 413 Coastal Battery. They were ready for action in September and a year later they set up their HQ at St Augustine's Hotel.

In addition to the coastal guns, two 75-mm field guns were set into the grass bank at Richborough Castle, and dummy gun-sites were erected at West Cliff close to the ornamental gardens and at Vincents Farm.

Heavy coastal artillery was responsible for the defence of the coastal areas and its primary role was to engage and sink enemy shipping, in the event of an invasion, before it could be beached and land troops. All coastal batteries possessed searchlights, positioned one on either side of the gun-site. Their effective range in good visibility was estimated at 6,000 yd.

Heavy ack-ack batteries had been installed around RAF Manston in early May. No. 308 HAA Battery began with 3-in guns at Chalkshole (D8), and at Ozengell Grange (D9). The Cleve Court site (D10) possessed four 3-in guns, which were of the high traverse type – 1914 naval, under No. 306 HAA Battery, RA. By 1941, most of the ack-ack guns had been replaced by the 3.7-in mobile units, and gradually the 40-mm Bofors light ack-ack units which were also mobile, increased in numbers as the Messerschmitt fighter-bombers became a menace at low level. In the

One of the four 5.5-in naval guns installed at Joss Bay. They were, in fact, almost in front of the North Foreland Lighthouse. The role of these guns was, like other coastal artillery in the Isle of Thanet, to engage enemy shipping attempting an invasion.

One of several of the 3.7-in heavy ack-ack guns used for air defence in Thanet, and especially to protect RAF Manston. This particular photograph is thought to show the gunners and their 'God of Thunder' at Chalks Hole – known officially as D8.

weeks of early June there were many scares. There were rumours of
German parachutists in fields behind Minster; German troops fighting
their way up the cliff faces, and the sea set alight in Pegwell Bay. None
were true, of course. The police had the code-word, 'Tarcon', ready and
wondered if they would be able to give sufficient warning to allow
anyone to be evacuated.

The hurried plans of 1940 were constantly being updated and one
tentative arrangement was that Margate citizens should be taken to the
Ramsgate tunnels. Another system would have made use of the Royal
School for the Deaf as a communal centre to accommodate those essential
services left behind.

Saturday 8 June
ALIENS – A NEW ORDER

Under the provisions of the Aliens (Protected Areas) Order, aliens in
Margate and Ramsgate were told to leave for areas beyond a radius of
20 miles from the east and south-east coast. The number of aliens affected in
Margate was 238 and at Ramsgate only 59. However, these figures included
people who were natives of Margate and Ramsgate who were in business or
residents in the towns for many years. In some cases the chief constables
were authorized, in certain circumstances, to grant exemptions to any alien
when they were satisfied that this would not prejudice the national interest.

Wednesday 12 June
GERMAN AIRMEN SAVED FROM SEA

The Ministry of Home Security Intelligence report states:

> Activity of friendly aircraft last night gave rise to yellow warnings to
> Ipswich and Norwich at 20.39. The white message was given at 20.43.
> London South, Maidstone, London Central, Portsmouth, Canterbury,
> Boston, Lincoln, Grimsby, King's Lynn, Norwich, and Boston and
> Canterbury again, were in turn under yellow warning at various times
> between 23.40 and 02.49 hours. No reports of effective enemy action
> over the British Isles have been received.

The *East Kent Times*, however, had a quite different story to tell its
readers:

> Kenneth Rice, a sixteen-year-old boy and two fishermen, Jack Pocock
> and Ben Richards, were concerned in the rescue of two German airmen

whose machine was brought down off the Kent coast last Wednesday 12 June, 1940.

The trio were on a fishing trip in the motorboat *Golden Spray* and when about ten miles off the coast they saw a Heinkel III bomber being chased by three Spitfires. After twisting and turning to avoid the Spitfires, the German machine suddenly nose-dived into the sea.

According to a statement made by Jack Pocock, who was skipper of the boat, they hauled in their nets and made a dash for the damaged plane. They had almost given up hope of rescuing anyone when two heads appeared and they hauled the Germans aboard. Both Germans, one an officer, were injured, and Pocock tore off his vest for bandages, and the rescued men were given mugs of hot cocoa. Two other crew members were trapped in the wreckage and another drowned whilst swimming around. The injured Germans were eventually taken to hospital.

Tuesday 18 June

The events which have happened in France in the last fortnight have not come to me with any sense of surprise. Indeed, I indicated a fortnight ago as clearly as I could to the House that the worst possibilities were open, and I made it perfectly clear then that whatever happened in France would make no difference to the resolve of Britain and the British Empire to fight on – if necessary for years, if necessary alone . . . What General Weygand called the 'Battle of France' is over. I expect that the 'Battle of Britain' is about to begin. Upon this battle depends the survival of the Christian civilisation. Upon it depends our own British life and the long-continued history of our institutions and our Empire. The whole fury and might of the enemy must very soon be turned on us. Hitler knows that he will have to break us on this island or lose the war. If we can stand up to him all Europe may be free and the life of the world may move forward into broad and sunlit uplands. If we fail, then the whole world, including the United States, and all that we have known and cared for, will sink into the abyss of a new dark age made more sinister and perhaps more prolonged by the light of a perverted science. Let us, therefore, do our duty and so bear ourselves that if the British Commonwealth and Empire lasts a thousand years men will still say, 'This was their finest hour'.

WINSTON CHURCHILL, 18 June 1940

Wednesday 19 June
MARGATE 02.15 – HEINKEL CRASH AT SACKETTS GAP

The Home Security Intelligence summary No. 580 records that between
18.00 on 18 June and 06.00 on 19 June, the first full-scale air attack on
Great Britain occurred. Over one hundred enemy aircraft were engaged in
this operation but reports suggest that most of the bombs were jettisoned
at random with no particular target in mind. The newly sited searchlights
probed the night sky and the anti-aircraft guns fired off a few shells. RAF
squadrons had been alerted by radar.

When Hitler came to power in 1933, the British Government looked
seriously at the defences of the British Isles. The air staff became interested
in a radio-wave system, which it was hoped would either kill or maim
aeroplane crews or even stop their engines. Although scientific calcula-
tions soon proved the 'death-ray' impracticable the off-shoot of the whole
experiment confirmed that radio beams of sufficient power could actually
detect an aeroplane in flight. A chain of radar stations was eventually set
up around our coasts and were known as chain home stations. Later, a
series of chain home low stations were introduced, primarily to detect
aeroplanes flying at very low level. The first of these CHL stations, using
a rotating aerial system, and having a cathode ray display tube upon
which a 'blip' signal would indicate an aircraft, was erected at Foreness
Margate.

It was over Colchester that FO G.E. Ball in a Spitfire of No. 19
squadron, engaged a Heinkel IIIH bomber of 6.KG4, and severely
damaged it. *Lt.* H.J. Bachaus, the pilot, set course for the French coast but
his engines were already overheating by the time he had reached the Isle of
Sheppey.

Gliding towards the sea the Heinkel narrowly missed hitting the Grand
and St George's Hotels, and almost took the flag pole from the cliff edge
opposite the Palm Bay Hotel, before plunging on to the submerged rocks
at Sacketts Gap.

A Local Defence Volunteer platoon, Corporal Spiers, Colin Cuthbert,
Roy Addison and Archie Brown, armed with an assortment of rifles but
with little ammunition to speak of, had watched the prowling searchlights
with fascination.

Then suddenly a large black shape shot over their heads and crashed on
the rocks beneath them. The German crew began to climb out of the
fuselage and on to the wings. One of the platoon ran for help to the
nearest military post. Both Corporal Spiers and Cuthbert waded out into

the water as the three airmen drifted towards the shore in their inflatable rubber dinghy.

The platoon learned there was a fourth member of the crew who had attempted to bale out just as the Heinkel came down. Without any hesitation and quite unaware if there were any bombs on board, Cuthbert, only seventeen years old, volunteered to wade out again in search of the missing airman. He found him dead, still attached to his parachute, face down in the water.

The survivors *Lt*. H.J. Bachaus, *Uffz*. T. Kuln and *Uffz*. F. Boeck, were taken by the police into custody. The body of *Fw*. A. Reitzig was buried with full military honours at Margate cemetery on 21 June.

The following notice appeared in every local newspaper:

It was officially announced that the ringing of church and chapel bells is forbidden. The military authorities have decided that it is essential to use church bells for giving warning of the approach of parchutists or other air-borne troops, and their use for any other purpose must now be prohibited. Only the military or Local Defence Volunteers will be entitled to ring the bells in future.

A week later another notice appeared:

It is believed that there may be a number of persons that have firearms or ammunition in their possession without proper authority and that they would be willing to surrender these to the police but for the fear of being prosecuted. As the Home Secretary explained in answer to a recent question in the House of Commons, it is already the practice of the police to accept without formalities any firearms or ammunition voluntarily surrendered, and there is, therefore, no reason why people should be put off by apprehensions of this kind. The Commander-in-Chief Home Forces had already asked all who have 12-bore cartridges to hand them in to the nearest police station, for distribution to their Local Defence Volunteers.

Pasted on telegraph poles, tree trunks and window shutters were many posters warning the public of their obligations.

All persons are warned that they should only approach aerodromes, factories and other prohibited places, including field works, gun and searchlight emplacements by the recognized entrance where they will be stopped and called upon to identify themselves. Failure to observe this warning may result in offending persons being fired upon.

Wednesday 3 July
FIRST HEs (High-explosive Bombs) DROPPED ON ISLE OF THANET

Civilians left behind in the Isle of Thanet had yet to experience the *Luftwaffe's* bombing raids, and had very little idea of the devastation engendered.

BROADSTAIRS 16.18 – HEs & UXBs (Unexploded Bombs)

Eight high-explosive bombs were reported dropping in a line across the Eastern Esplanade and Reading Street. Two houses Kingsmead and High Elms, were damaged, but there were no casualties recorded. Two bombs failed to explode. The Bomb Disposal Unit was sent for and the missiles were made safe.

MARGATE – WESTGATE 16.55 – HEs

Members of Westgate's ARP saw about fifteen 50-kg bombs, fall from a low-flying Dorner 17. Harry Fuller recalled, 'The plane was flying so low and its pace seemed so leisurely that I mistook it for one of ours until I saw the black specks detach themselves from the machine. I jumped over a garden wall and laid down.' Warden Moseley at his post, received a telephone call to say his house had been demolished by a bomb. His house and offices in the building with a workshop and a small petrol filling station attached, were completely wrecked. Bricks, masonry and furniture, were flung hundreds of feet, but the Vicarage next door was undamaged. A bungalow called Bampton in Canterbury Road, Westgate, was also wrecked when a bomb exploded in the front garden. Normally the bungalow was occupied by Mrs Harvey and her daughter Mrs Churchman, but they had left town the day before. Another bomb missed the church by just a few feet, leaving a huge crater in the road. The plate-glass windows of three shops were blown out. The post office, a bank and several houses were damaged. The windows of a bus, which had just drawn up and discharged its passengers, were also blown out. 'If I had nine lives there can only be eight left,' recalled Ernest Nunn, the conductor. 'I was just getting out of the bus when I heard the bombs screaming. I threw myself to the ground. The driver managed to dash into a shop doorway.'

Several policemen had narrow escapes. One was standing outside the Town Hall, and had the presence of mind to fling himself down. Another was cycling when he heard bombs falling. He went through a hedge and the bombs burst just a few yards away. The only casualty was a gardener, whose face was cut by flying glass when a summer-house was completely destroyed. Only a few minutes before it had been occupied by a doctor. He said, 'I was sitting in my summer-house, and when the siren sounded I immediately went into the house for shelter. I told my maid I thought a cup of tea might cheer me up, but before the tea came Jerry arrived. It did not cheer me up.' Showing concern for his heavy garden-roller which was missing, he said, 'If it had not been for the sirens I should have been in that mess', pointing to a large hole where the summer-house had stood.

RAF MANSTON 23.15 – HEs & UXBs

Activity had increased at the nearby aerodrome during the Dunkirk evacuation when our fighters were operating beach patrols. Now detachments of the London Irish Regiment had moved in for airfield defence and assisted the Royal Artillery to dig in their anti-aircraft guns. This raid, while little material damage was sustained, was the first of many air raids to pound the aerodrome into a frightful mess. The Royal Engineers were busy digging trenches and erecting pillbox gun emplacements, road blocks and all manner of defences using hundreds of miles of barbed wire.

RAMSGATE 03.00 – HEs & IBs (Incendiary Bombs)

Over fifty incendiary missiles were plotted in the Cliffs End area and at Manston village, and one high-explosive bomb falling just outside the harbour. Damage was slight and there were no casualties reported. Later that same evening a Heinkel 59B seaplane was forced to make a landing on the Goodwin Sands.

Sunday 14 July
WINSTON CHURCHILL SPEAKS TO NATION

In the course of his broadcast the Prime Minister said, 'Should the invader come, there will be no placid lying down of the people in submission before him as we have seen – alas! – in other countries. We shall defend every village, every town, and every city.'

Bombs and missiles dropped on Thanet were principally, of the high-explosive type used by Germany throughout their assault on the UK mainland. the *SC* (*Sprengbombe – Cylindrisch*) was a thin-cased general purpose bomb sometimes called the Minenbombe. It had a high charge for maximum blast effect and usually contained over 50 per cent explosive, used mainly for demolition purposes. Published sources reveal that eight out of ten HE bombs dropped on the UK were of the *SC* type, between 50- and 2,000-kg in size. A device called the 'Trumpets of Jericho' was sometimes fitted to the *SC* type which was either made from thick cardboard or First World War bayonet scabbards. Approximately 14 in in length they were shaped like organ pipes and as the bomb fell, the wind blew through the tubes causing them to give a fearsome shriek. This screaming device caused the greatest stress and fear in the civilian population designed to undermine their morale.

The *SD* range (*Sprengbombe – Dickwandig*) also called the *Splitterbombe*, was designed as either an anti-personnel or semi-armour-piercing bomb with a load of about 35 per cent explosive. The fragmentation was more efficient than the *SC* although it possessed greater penetration ability, largely due to its streamlined casing.

The armour-piercing *PC* (*Panzerbombe – Cylindrisch*) was usually, because of the heavy hardened cast-steel casing, used against shipping targets or fortified buildings such as concrete gun emplacements. The explosive loading factor was only about 20 per cent.

One of the most devastating weapons used by Germany, especially when dropped on to land targets, was the aerial mine (*Luftmine*). Originally designed for coastal waters and shipping lanes, it was attached to a parachute and was often used against land targets. With a high charge ratio of between 60 and 70 per cent explosive, the land mine, as it became known to the British, caused considerable blast damage over a very wide area.

The Incendiary Bomb (*Brandbombe*) was by far the most damaging weapon used by any air force. Usually of the 1- and 2-kg magnesium type, each had a thermite filling which burned sufficiently to melt steel. One investigation revealed that one ton of incendiaries could devastate over three acres; against only half that area if HEs had been used. Incendiaries were dropped from aircraft in large containers, blown open at a predetermined height by an air-burst fuse, releasing hundreds of missiles over a wide area.

There was a larger type of incendiary similar in appearance to the *SC* type of bomb, but this was not widely used. The British called them 'Fire-pots', and they ranged in size from the 50-kg phosphorus-filled *Sprengbrand*, to the 250- and 500-kg oil-filled *Flammbombe*.

One must not forget, however, that specific types of bombs loaded on to German bombers and destined for a particular target, were often jettisoned on the Thanet towns as a last resort, having been thwarted in their attempts to reach their destination by our defences.

In July a curfew had been imposed under the Defence Regulations Act which further restricted certain people still living in the sensitive areas. It prohibited their movements outside their homes between half an hour before sunset and half an hour before sunrise, unless they had police permission. Spy mania was constantly in the news, aided no doubt, by the film showing at the Parade Cinema, Margate – *The Three Silent Men* – about Fifth Columnists.

In the *Reynolds News*, dated 19 May 1940, the journalist George Darling, named several well-known members of the Anglo-German Association and a similar organization called 'The Link'. The latter was reputed to be the most outspoken pro-Nazi group in Great Britain. Under Section 18b, of the Apprehension of Aliens Act, Captain Robert Cecil Gordon Canning, MC, who had recently left his home near Sandwich, and who was a member of 'The Link', was arrested in London, on Friday 19 July.

★ ★ ★

A neat figure in her blue and red uniform, an ARP ambulance driver successfully conducted her own defence when summoned at the Cinque Ports Police Court, Margate, for driving her ambulance 'without due care and attention' in Queen's Road, Broadstairs. During a midnight air-raid alert, the ambulance mounted a foot-path and struck a telephone kiosk. The accused pleaded that fog obscured her view and that she mistook the kerb for a white line. Miss Piggott said, 'The ambulance was so beautifully sprung that I did not feel it mount the kerb'. The Chairman of the Magistrates urged her to be more careful in future.

Monday 22 July
MARGATE 22.35 – HEs

Twelve high-explosive bombs were thought to have been released by a returning bomber en route to France. One of the most popular boarding-house districts in Margate suffered considerable damage, but although No. 34 Athelstan Road was wrecked and many other dwellings damaged by the blast, there was not one casualty. A year previously the hotels and boarding-houses on either side of the street where most of the damage occurred were crowded with hundreds of holiday-makers. At this time most of the buildings were closed and empty. However, one bomb fell on a house that was still occupied, but two people escaped with their lives. Hearing the scream of bombs approaching they flattened themselves against a wall of the downstairs passage. The house collapsed around them. Their cat crawled out of the ruins without so much as a scratch.

BROADSTAIRS 23.38 – HEs

Four high-explosive bombs fell near the town and were assumed to have been dropped from a returning German bomber. There were no reports of damage or casualties.

Tuesday 23 July
MARGATE 22.22 – HEs & UXBs

Fourteen bombs were dropped but four did not explode. Shipping was attacked in the Channel. No further information available.

★ ★ ★

Alderman Redman, chief pot collector in Margate, was deeply impressed by the self-sacrifice of housewives in the town, Westgate and Birchington, during his drive to find aluminium for aeroplanes. Many of the pots and pans donated to him were brand new. Some had been the pride of the kitchen, so beautifully burnished that he could see his face in them. Copper, brass and pewter were also collected. Alderman Redman explained, 'Everything has been smashed and already Margate has given more than enough aluminium to build a fighter plane and the collection is well on its way to bomber dimensions.'

★ ★ ★

A Thanet naval 'old comrade', blackened a medal ribbon he had worn on his chest since the king of Italy rewarded his rescue work in the Messina earthquake of 1908. As Italian decorations were no longer fashionable, he said he had put the medal into mourning for Mussolini.

★ ★ ★

Whether Margate should keep the fine iron railings round Hawley Square gardens or cut them down was debated by the Emergency Committee, whose responsibility it was under the intensified scrap-iron campaign. The railings weighed over 56 tons.

Wednesday 24 July
MARGATE 13.00 – MESSERSCHMITT FIGHTER SHOT DOWN

In the streets there were dozens of people watching an aerial battle over the town – the Battle of Britain was on. Spectators found themselves just as excited as the BBC commentator, who the week before, describing a similar combat over Dover, had caused so much trouble when the incident was broadcast on the radio. It was suggested he might have been describing a cricket match. The roar of diving and twisting aircraft over the town was the first indication that combat was in progress. 'The sky seemed full of wheeling planes and the chattering of machine-guns,' said one eyewitness. Clutching their shopping baskets women stood in the streets spellbound. 'In an ordinary raid,' one observer said, 'they would have prudently run for shelter – but this was too exciting – too exhilarating. I would not have missed it for the world.' Convoys steaming through the English Channel were the main target during July, and our fighter squadrons were heavily engaged on protection patrols.

'The sky was full of wheeling planes and the chattering of machine guns . . .' an eyewitness said. *Oberleutnant* Werner Bartels, wounded in the left wrist and right thigh, managed to crash-land his Messerschmitt Bf 109 in a cornfield at Northdown, Margate, at 13.00 on 24 July 1940. Bartels' service revolver was later mentioned in the Cinque Ports Police Court, where a man was charged with stealing it.

Oberlt. W. Bartels, the pilot of a badly damaged Messerschmitt fighter, managed to force-land in a field of corn at Northdown. Five minutes later another crashed in the middle of Byron Avenue. *Lt.* J. Schauff had baled out, but his parachute failed to open. His mutilated body was later discovered in a playing field.

★ ★ ★

Local authorities were now given the unenviable task of seeing that lofts were cleared of inflammable rubbish. The job was made all the more difficult because hundreds of properties were now unoccupied.

One of the most astonishing revelations to appear in the local newspapers concerned some of the aged evacuees who had left their homes to take up residence in what were called 'safe areas'. The majority had been persuaded to leave, not because they were afraid of bombs, but because they felt their age or infirmity might prove a nuisance. Leaving home, many for the first time in their lives, was a bitter wrench, but they were prepared to endure that if they were treated with sympathy and understanding. Instead, as was revealed in their letters of complaint, they were treated like tramps and paupers.

Although the evacuation was on a voluntary basis it was, after all, a Government-sponsored exercise and local clergy and others with an interest in old people urged them to go. Perhaps the most startling disclosure came from a Miss Emma Miller, of Westgate-on-Sea who accompanied her aged parents, and recalled:

It all seemed like a bad dream. After reading about how refugees handicapped the soldiers in France and Belgium we thought it only right to go, thinking we should be put into private billets. Our trouble began when we arrived at Tredegar, Monmouthsire. On arrival at an institution we found it like a prison. A grey uniform and hobnailed boots were given to the men, and there was a blue frock and coarse stockings for the women. Husbands and wives were separated, and they could meet only at mealtimes, if the wife was willing to eat with 'casuals' and other inmates.

Bedtime was 7.30 p.m. I was in the infirmary, but there were three imbeciles in the ward. Once I tried to escape with my mother and father, to go for a walk and buy food. The institution food was atrocious. Two porters were guarding the gates and they told us we could not go out.

Emma's bad dream ended three days later when she and her parents came back home, paying their own fare of £6.

Friday 2 August

The passenger-cargo liner *City of Brisbane* was bombed and went ashore on South Long Sand, where she burned for three days.

★ ★ ★

Although exiled wives were trickling back to Margate, the population of the borough continued to fall quite rapidly. A census taken during the last week of July showed that 11,516 people were living in Margate, Westgate and Birchington, compared with 12,391 at the beginning of the month. A year previously when the holiday season was in full swing there had been over 100,000.

★ ★ ★

Most of the valuable prints and books in Margate's local collection were taken to Cheltenham in July.

★ ★ ★

Yachts and motor boats from Margate Harbour were towed away to the Thames by a tug, while smaller craft were loaded on to a lighter.

★ ★ ★

The appearance of white crosses on house gates was mystifying until the Margate Borough Surveyor explained that dustmen could distinguish between houses still occupied and those deserted.

Thursday 8 August
SPITFIRES AND BLENHEIM CRASH

The convoy 'Peewit' was being attacked in the English Channel by a strong force of enemy bombers just before midday. Our fighter squadrons were in the area on convoy patrol. Twenty-one-year-old Sergeant-Pilot David Kirton, whose home was at Dover, was shot down in flames and perished in the crash near Manston after combat with

Messerschmitt fighters. He was followed by another member of
65 Squadron five minutes later when Flt.-Sgt. Norman Phillips also
succumbed to the Messerschmitt's guns. At 11.55 a Blenheim of
600 Squadron was shot up by a Messerschmitt fighter over Thanet. The
Blenheim began to burn fiercely as it approached Ramsgate. Pilot Officer
D.N. Grice, however, succeeded in steering the stricken aircraft away
from the town. Had he not done so there would have been a crash with
disastrous results. The Blenheim exploded on impact with the sea, killing
the pilot, Sgt. F.J. Keast and AC1 J.B.W. Warren. But the gallant action
by Grice did not go unnoticed by the citizens of Ramsgate – not least the
Mayor, A.B.C. Kempe. From funds obtained from a subscription list a
piece of plate, a solid silver hand-carved cake basket, was purchased, and
was later presented to the unfortunate pilot's wife, Margaret, at a private
ceremony in London.

The following inscription, under the Borough Arms, was engraved on
the silver plate:

> Presented to Mrs Margaret Grice by the
> Mayor, Corporation and Citizens of
> Ramsgate, as a tribute to the bravery
> of her late husband, Pilot Officer Grice,
> 'He died to save others.'

Friday 9 August
MARGATE 23.00 – HEs

Wailing sirens sent townspeople scurrying for shelter in their back
gardens carrying blankets, thermos flasks and hurricane lamps. Searchlights flicked on and began moving across the night sky. Then, as the
droning of an enemy bomber came ever closer, the anti-aircraft guns
opened fire. ARP wardens and policemen were at their allotted posts and
telephonists waited for the onrush of calls for assistance. A black,
sinister-looking Heinkel III, altered course to avoid the searchlight beams
and flew over Birchington towards Margate. The Heinkel released its
bombs from about 8,000 ft which fell in the business quarter of the town,
shattering hundreds of windows in offices, shops and houses.

Casualties were amazingly light and only five people were treated for
cuts caused by flying glass splinters. Damage was far less than expected.
One house was demolished by a direct hit, the interior of another was
completely wrecked and an empty public house and four shops took a
battering from the blast.

The brickwork of the Weigall & Inch solicitors office had cracked like an egg shell, windows were blown out at the *Isle of Thanet Gazette* building and the post office in Cecil Square, King Street and New Street fared little better when shop frontages collapsed on to pavements. Two people who received medical treatment were a postman and his wife, who lived in the flat above the Cosy Corner Restaurant on the corner of Hawley Street and New Street. They had been standing outside and had just gone in and closed the door when the bomb fell only five yards away. The door blew in knocking them off their feet. A greengrocer and his wife, living next door, almost as close to where the bomb exploded, had taken refuge in their basement and were unhurt. Bomb fragments hurtled through the windows of another shop, but fortunately the occupier and his wife were in the back room. Auxiliary fireman Brockwell, lived in the house that was demolished, but had left the town to visit his evacuated wife. Mr White, who lived across the street, thought he was the luckiest man alive. His wife and two daughters had run to the Anderson shelter in the tiny back yard while bricks, tiles and masonry fell all around them. Mr White was still in the kitchen when the ceiling collapsed on him and he was unable to move. Mr and Mrs Dixon who were leaving a club were saved by an obstinate petrol lighter. Before going out of the building Mr Dixon paused to light his pipe and those few seconds delay saved their lives. One bomb exploded next to the Old House, the sixteenth-century farm-house in King Street, bought by Margate Corporation for restoration as a museum. Although all the windows were broken and plaster fell off the walls and ceilings, the stout oak framework of the building withstood the shock without so much as a tremble.

★ ★ ★

What happens to bomb-damaged buildings was explained to the general public through leaflets:

It is the duty of the local authority to carry out such 'first aid' works as to make the dwelling reasonably fit for habitation and includes such things as repairing roofs and windows with the object of preventing further damage to the contents. 'First aid' repairs may be carried out without giving prior notice to the owner. The cost of any work is registered as a charge on the premises and the question of the recovery of this charge will not be dealt with until after the war. When houses are damaged those in which people are living are the first to be repaired, and then houses which are occupied only by furniture. In the latter case the repairs are only to protect the furniture and may consist of rendering a part of the house weatherproof and storing the furniture in that part. Claims for compensation should be submitted within thirty days, but the extent of compensation will not be decided until after the war, and no payments will be made meantime. No claims should be made if the loss or damage does not exceed £5.

★ ★ ★

Thanet was extremely fortunate when Anderson shelters were first issued, but an awkward situation developed when thousands of people left the towns, leaving shelters neatly erected in their gardens. There were many thousands in other vulnerable districts who were clamouring for shelters. In the end, the government told local councils to recover as many as they could from the gardens of unoccupied houses.

Margate was expected to recover about 1,000 of the 6,000 put up. The proportion was said to be low, for two-thirds of the population had left the town. 'Those remaining,' the report went on, 'are mostly those who were not entitled by reason of limited income to have a shelter.'

Public street shelters all told, could accommodate 7,000 people, and those built for schools would take a further 3,000. Shelter parties were becoming quite common in Thanet, and some of the communal surface shelters put up by groups of neighbours had been furnished with rugs, chairs and tables.

Over 400 Andersons were recovered from gardens in Broadstairs.

Sunday 11 August
MESSERSCHMITT SHOT DOWN

Stuka dive-bombers were attacking shipping in the Channel. One of the escorting Messerschmitt Bf 109s was shot down and crashed into the sea off the North Foreland. The remains of the pilot, *Fw.* H.H. Heise, were buried with full military honours at St Lawrence Cemetery, Ramsgate.

Monday 12 August
RAMSGATE 12.45 – HEs – Oil Bomb

The *Luftwaffe* were now to intensify their attacks on targets in the south and south-east of England. It was the prelude to the *Adler Tag* offensive, destined to take place, officially, on the following day. But just after first light Messerschmitt fighters were winging their way over Kent followed by the massed bomber formations who had been briefed to knock out radar stations and smash our 'front-line' aerodromes.

Documents reveal that over twenty high-explosive bombs dropped at Ramsgate, Sarre and Monkton – among them one oil bomb that sprayed burning oil for a distance of over seventy feet.

One of the first casualties was fifty-eight-year-old Arthur Smith, who at Ramsgate had run into the Boundary Road lavatories to escape the raid, unfortunately the building received a direct hit. Arthur was killed and two other people were slightly injured by the blast.

Five bombs straddled the village of Sarre where over two hundred troops were billeted in Sarre Court, Sarre House and the Kings Head. They had been engaged in setting up anti-invasion devices under and above the A28 main road to Canterbury, and included a novel system of running barrels filled with a petroleum mixture out over the road from the upstairs windows of the Kings Head on a cable.

This Messerschmitt Bf 109E-4, of III/JG54, was damaged by FO H.J. Woodward of 64 Squadron during an escort sortie over Dover. It made a forced landing in a field near Hengrove at 18.00 on 12 August 1940. *Oberlt.* A. Dresz, the pilot, was captured and taken to hospital.

The Christian family of six had just finished their midday meal when they heard the scream of falling bombs. They were unable to escape before Nos 4 and 5 Chalk Pit Cottages received a direct hit. Soldiers were quick off the mark and arrived at the scene in just a few minutes. Even so a long time elapsed before they could effect a rescue of forty-nine-year-old Elizabeth Christian and her eleven-year-old daughter Dorothy. Both died later in hospital. The husband, son and two other daughters were also injured and were taken to hospital for treatment.

The Coleman family at No. 4 were slightly more fortunate, although they all suffered injuries. Despite the cottage collapsing in a heap of debris Mr Coleman was able to crawl out of the wreckage and direct soldiers to where his wife and children lay buried. Kitty Coleman and her four children, including twins, were all found in one area.

At Manston, twenty-seven-year-old Ivy Impett saved her two-year-old son by lying over him when their cottage at Foster's Folly, World's Wonder, was demolished by another direct hit. Rescue teams worked

The Heinkel IIIH-2, of 6/KG53, was attacked by 242 Squadron while attempting to bomb Radlett aerodrome. The pilot, *Fw*. F. Eckert, was killed and the observer took control of the aircraft. The bombs were dropped in the sea and the Heinkel made a forced landing at Goodmans Farm near Manston at 16.35 on 30 August 1940. *Gefr*. H.G. Kohler was captured severely wounded, and died three days later at Ramsgate hospital. *Gefr*. A. Klapp, *Gefr*. F. Gluck and *Fw*. K. Stockl were taken prisoner.

continuously for three hours before finding the victims. The boy was found still breathing, but Ivy had suffocated. A large wooden beam had fallen diagonally across the cellar and had prevented them from being crushed.

RAF MANSTON 12.50 – HEs

The traumatic events outlined above, were the result of a strong formation of Messerschmitt Bf 110s and Dornier 17s attacking RAF Manston. Spitfires of 65 Squadron were already taking off when the first wave hurtled over the airfield. There was damage to hangars and workshops, and one civilian clerk was recorded killed. Two convoys, 'Agent' and 'Arena', were also being attacked off the North Foreland.

At 18.00, a damaged Messerschmitt Bf 109 crashed at Hengrove near Margate. The pilot, *Oberlt.* A. Dresz was captured unhurt.

MARGATE – LIFEBOAT RESCUE

The Margate lifeboat picked up PO A.G. Page who was trying desperately to swim with severely charred and blistered hands and a face scorched and swollen beyond recognition. Page's experiences, when he and other pilots were treated by the legendary plastic surgeon Sir Archibald McIndoe at the special burns unit near East Grinstead, are outlined in his book, *Tale of a Guinea Pig.*

Tuesday 13 August
BIRCHINGTON 07.30 – DORNIER SHOT DOWN

It was the day set for *Adler Tag* (Eagle Day), the all-out blitz on British military targets, especially RAF aerodromes and the radar stations. Shortly after first light the *Luftwaffe* bombers were heading for Eastchurch airfield on the Isle of Sheppey. At 07.30 a Dornier 17Z of 7/KG2 was shot down by Hurricanes and crashed at Birchington. The crew, *Fw.* F. Dannich, *Fw.* K. Schwerdtfeger, *Obergefr.* E. Nitzche and *Gefr.* A. Beck, was killed.

Wednesday 14 August
RAF MANSTON 11.59 – HEs – MESSERSCHMITTS COLLIDE

Another low-level raid, this time made by Messerschmitt Bf 110s escorted by the indomitable Me 109 fighters, destroyed more hangars and buildings. There were so many aircraft diving and manoeuvring, dropping bombs and machine-gunning that sooner or later a collision was inevitable. It happened at 12.10, two Messerschmitt Bf 110s collided over the airfield, one of them exploded in the air while the other crashed on the actual aerodrome. Two incendiary bombs, later picked up in the village of Manston, were thought to have come from this mid-air collision. Out in the English Channel the South Goodwin lightship was sunk by a Stuka attack.

Thursday 15 August
RAF MANSTON 12.45 – MACHINE-GUN ATTACK

Since the severe battering had taken place only one squadron of Spitfires was available on this day. They were fortunately on patrol when there was another sharp low-level raid by Messerschmitt Bf 110s.

The station personnel suffered sixteen casualties and lost two Spitfires. In the afternoon, a Hurricane squadron was in frenzied combat right over Margate. A Messerschmitt Bf 109 fighter was seen to ditch into the sea three miles off the coast. The pilot *Fw*. O. Steigenberger was picked up by the relief lifeboat from Margate, the *J.B. Proudfoot* at 15.30. Half an hour later a Dornier 17Z, crashed in the sea off Ramsgate. The four crew members were all captured unhurt. Another Dornier was seen to hit the sea with a resounding splash near Reculver.

Friday 16 August
RAF MANSTON 15.50 – MACHINE-GUN ATTACK

In an effort to tie down RAF fighter squadrons the *Luftwaffe* launched a number of independent, low-level group raids. As an example of this tactic in the late afternoon eight Messerschmitt fighters swept in over the North Foreland and set course for Manston, where they strafed the airfield buildings and parked aircraft. Cannon shells and bullets tore their way through aircraft servicing equipment and sent ground crews diving into the nearest slit trenches. One Spitfire and one Blenheim were destroyed.

Sunday 18 August
RAF MANSTON 15.30 – MACHINE-GUN ATTACK

There was so much intensive activity going on that no clear local warning was given when another low-level raid happened. This time airmen were caught out in the open and many of them suffered wounds when Messerschmitts raked the airfield and aircraft were destroyed. But the *Luftwaffe* was also experiencing many casualties. At 17.30 a Heinkel III settled on the sea off Ramsgate. The crew took to their dinghy and were eventually captured after twenty-six hours at sea. The crew of a Dornier which landed in the sea off the North Foreland was not so lucky. Only one of them was picked up, the others perished when the aircraft sank.

Tuesday 20 August
RAF MANSTON 14.30 – MACHINE-GUN ATTACK

During the afternoon several enemy formations at low level attacked the anti-aircraft gun sites around the airfield. This snap raid on Manston destroyed another Blenheim, but there were no casualties reported.

Thursday 22 August
RAF MANSTON 18.55 – BOMB ATTACK

The convoy 'Totem' was hugging the English coast off Thanet when it came under a heavy shell barrage from the recently installed German long-range guns situated near Cap Gris Nez. Although the shelling lasted for over one hour there were no reported shipping losses. Failure of the intensive artillery barrage brought out the *Luftwaffe* to try their luck. But they were beaten off by our fighter squadrons. However, eight bombers escorted by about fourteen fighters arrived over Manston. Anti-aircraft shells pock-marked the skies while the bombs cratered the area. Fortunately there was little damage to speak of and only one person was injured. Nevertheless, the aerodrome was gradually being pounded into a state of chaos.

The Prime Minister, Winston Churchill, wrote in an 'Action this day' memo on 21 August, 'The important thing is to bring down German aircraft and win the battle . . .' Three days later the Air Ministry over-stated its victories by 25 per cent, claiming fifty German aircraft brought down when post-war figures reveal that the *Luftwaffe* had actually lost forty-one.

Take for example the exploits of HM trawler, *Arctic Trapper*. After bringing down at least two enemy bombers off Ramsgate on 24 August, an Admiralty communique said:

When HM Trawler *Arctic Trapper*, skippered by W. Hilldrith, RNR., was attacked by enemy aircraft this afternoon she shot down two enemy bombers in to the sea and probably damaged two others. HM Trawler *Arctic Trapper* was machine-gunned by German fighters which were escorting a force of bombers. The trawler opened fire, the first shell burst between two bombers, and it is probable that both aircraft received damage. The second shell scored a direct hit on another bomber and this aircraft crashed into the sea. The third shell burst very close to another bomber and this machine was seen to turn over and come down into the sea. There were no casualties on HM Trawler *Arctic Trapper*.

Fact or fiction? Four Junkers 88 light bombers, are known to have been lost in the English Channel off Thanet, on this day, but none were ever credited to HM Trawler *Arctic Trapper*.

Saturday 24 August
RAMSGATE 15.35 – HEs – OIL BOMB

The raids on this day were estimated to be both severe and wide-spread and almost continuous. The impending raids were visible on radar before 06.00 and the first of these came in between Dover and Deal, and flew towards Thanet. Over eighty bombers and their escorts were plotted and the formations were partly broken up by our fighter squadrons whose airfields were the priority targets. Other targets of importance were the docks and harbours, and one assumes that is the reason for Ramsgate's most devastating air raid. It was the town's heaviest raid of the whole war. The *Luftwaffe* bombers had already attacked the RAF aerodrome at nearby Manston, while Defiants of 264 Squadron were being re-fuelled. Junkers 88 bombers at low level caused their own type of mayhem by using the anti-personnel bombs which burst into hundreds of jagged pieces of hot metal.

It was estimated that over five hundred high-explosive bombs fell on Ramsgate, the east side of which suffered severely, in particular the gasworks, Camden Square and the Margate Road districts. Gasholders, purifiers and stores were set alight, and even while the flames were being tackled by the Auxiliary firemen, they were subjected to machine-gun fire from escorting fighters. Among the buildings destroyed was the Queen Street premises of Vye & Son, the largest grocers in the town. The manager, forty-six-year-old Miles Leach, was killed when he was thrown through a plate-glass window. The mayor, Alderman A.B.C. Kempe, who was standing with others outside the Council Offices overlooking

All that remained of the air-raid warden's post at Camden Square, Ramsgate, which received a direct hit by a 50-kg bomb on 24 August 1940. Warden Mayes, who was inside, received a broken leg.

the harbour when the first bombs fell, was blown down the entrance passage into the basement. Members of the borough surveyor's department had taken shelter beneath their offices in a reinforced basement. The whole structure collapsed on them and they were buried. The staff of seven managed to clamber out of the rubble. The mayor recalled, 'We all looked pretty ghastly. I made my way to what remained of the mayor's parlour and a glass of whisky helped to restore us to normal.' The area around the Ramsgate viaduct was extensively damaged. Terraced houses in Margate Road and Woodford Avenue received direct hits and the blast wrecked many more.

Sixteen-year-old Charles Wesley was killed at No. 8 Woodford Avenue. The viaduct, however, remained standing and miraculously escaped any severe damage to its structure.

A concrete warden's post in Camden Square was split like a water melon. Peggy Walter and her sister Jose, ran out of their wrecked home to help rescue the dazed and badly injured warden. Local journalists were watching the approaching bombers through telescopes and binoculars.

Ramsgate's gasworks was devastated in the first blitz of the war on 24 August 1940. There were six large raids on that day and Ramsgate suffered twenty-nine civilians and two soldiers killed. A prominent American journalist, H.R. Knickerbocker wrote, 'The horrifying swiftness of air assault was never better demonstrated.'

One of them was blown down a stairway to the street below. Fifty-two-year-old Ernest Howland, an ARP warden, and forty-nine-year-old Sidney Cooper, both gasworks employees, were killed while running for shelter at the Boundary Road gasworks. Ben and Mary Kember, with their three-year-old son Brian, were hurrying towards their home at No. 16 Margate Road. They had reached Hudson's Mill when they were all killed.

A member of the police force, thirty-six-year-old Frederick Ticehurst, was killed outside his home at No. 25 Station Approach Road. He had sent his wife and child away to Tunbridge Wells only the day before. Six other policemen were rendered homeless. The ARP incident board was swamped with urgent messages.

Forty-two-year-old Ivy Lilley, wife of a newsagent at No. 15 Margate Road, was killed because she stopped to serve a customer before seeking shelter. The customer was seriously injured in the explosion, but a young newspaper boy escaped injury. A retired corporation employee, fifty-seven-year-old Albert Chantler, was killed when the blast of one bomb threw him through the doorway of the Railway Tavern. Joseph Tuckley, a one-legged warden, and his wife Rose were both killed at No. 15 Newlands Road. The driver of a tradesman's van, outside the Dawson Hotel, ran into a doorway for safety. He later found his van buried beneath a ton of rubble: his sixteen-year-old helper, William Birch, had been crushed.

Auxiliary Firemen E. Moore and Herbert Wells were cycling to duty when they were both injured by bomb splinters. Wells was the most seriously injured and while Moore was attending to his wounds, machine-gun bullets spattered around them where they lay. Although weak from loss of blood Moore dragged his companion, a heavily built man, to a more sheltered position. He then went off for help. Climbing over masonry, broken glass and telephone wires, he reached a first-aid post. Wells later died of his wounds.

The now famous tunnels in the town had been plunged into darkness when a bomb cut through the electric cables. Those people inside sheltering from the raid, soon brought out the emergency hurricane lamps, stored in special cupboards. The town was without a gas supply for the next twelve days. On the following day, however, Peete's Baker's shop, at the rear of the gasworks with windows and doors blown out and not a ceiling intact, held hundreds of joints of meat in the ovens. Mr Peete had offered to cook and baste the joints for anyone without cooking facilities.

There were over 78 houses destroyed in the raid and more than 1,200 were damaged in one way or another. The Rest Centre at the Old Constitutional Club, under the care of Mrs Sutton, was opened by Mr and Mrs Wood and members of the WVS. They cooked nearly 3,000 meals on just 6 primus stoves in 12 days. In one night 140 people were accommodated. Alderman Kempe observed:

> When I stood outside of what remained of the Council Offices and looked around the town, I did not think there was much left intact. But after our rescue services had done their work and the Borough Surveyor's men had been at work, it was amazing the amount of the place we salvaged. We were badly scarred, but even so, we had our chins up. This was not the way to subdue British people – it only brought out the bulldog breed in us and made us all the more determined to stick it out.

Altogether thirty one people lost their lives – twenty nine civilians and two soldiers: ten were seriously wounded and a further forty nine slightly injured.

Terraced houses in Woodford Avenue, Ramsgate, just behind Margate Road, and beside the railway viaduct, received extensive bomb damage when the Germans attempted to destroy the viaduct during the big raid of 24 August 1940. Sixteen-year-old Charles Wesley was killed at No. 8 Woodford Avenue.

Among the many buildings destroyed in the 24 August 1940 air raid upon Ramsgate was the Queen Street premises of Vye & Son. Altogether thirty-one people – twenty-nine civilians and two soldiers were killed, ten were seriously injured and forty-nine slightly injured.

A prominent American journalist H.R. Knickerbocker wrote in a report to New York: 'The town looked badly enough damaged but revealed the depth of its wounds only under expert guidance. The horrifying swiftness of air assault was never better demonstrated.' He was so impressed with the tunnels he thought they were the best air-raid shelters in the world. 'Tunnels sixty feet underground are proof against the largest bombs in existence. London has no such protection . . .' he went on, '. . . and throughout England few surface air-raid shelters could stand a direct hit from even a small bomb.'

World-wide publicity of Ramsgate's fearful air raid gave birth to the phrase 'Hell Fire Corner', a phrase which has been always associated with south-east Kent.

BROADSTAIRS

The 'Record of Missiles Dropped by Enemy Aircraft' in the Urban District of Broadstairs and St Peter's states:

> 24.8.40 03.39 hrs 5 HEs Dumpton Park, superficial damage and no casualties. (3 UXBs). 11.38 and 13.00 hrs 60 HEs & Oil Bombs (approx). Ryson's Road Airport and the surrounding area, superficial damage over wide area. No casualties treated at F.A.P.

Another report says:

> Soon after 3.30 a.m. five high explosives fell in Dumpton Park, but only two of them burst, causing superficial damage. 'Planes which had carried out the heavy raid on Ramsgate in the morning and early afternoon dropped sixty high explosives and oil bombs inside the Broadstairs boundary at the airport and surrounding areas. Although the damage was comparatively slight, windows and roofs were shattered over a wide area.'

Many of the Ramsgate families who were forced to move to other accommodation after the Saturday air raid, pinned their new addresses on the wreckage of their former homes.

RAF MANSTON

While Ramsgate was being bombed another strong force attacked Manston airfield. The living quarters almost completely disappeared under the weight of the bombing. Communication with the outside world had been cut, telephone and teleprinter lines were down and the whole airfield was littered with unexploded bombs.

No. 11 Group Controller at Fighter Command HQ requested the Observer Corps at Maidstone to try and make contact with the airfield. The nearest observer post was A1 – over one mile away from the airfield. Observer Foad volunteered to cycle to the striken Manston. When Fighter Command eventually heard Foad's report they decided to evacuate the station. Administrative personnel were moved to billets in Westgate, and remaining serviceable aircraft were sent further inland. Before that happened, however, Margate Fire Brigade and the RAF fire unit joined forces to control many fires. Under the leadership of Chief Officer Albert Twyman, they fought in teams – not only to douse the fires, but to remove weapons and ammunition from blazing stores. Both Twyman and Fireman Watson, were later awarded the George Medal. Alex Robinson, who farmed land close to the airfield, had already moved a group of women out of the danger zone.

Collecting a roll of linoleum from a shop in Ramsgate, Eric Ovenden had stuck it through the sun roof of his Austin Seven. It looked for all the world like a mobile anti-aircraft gun. A German pilot must have thought the same thing and strafed the car as it passed the airfield boundary.

★ ★ ★

Leading Fireman Herbert Evans of the Margate AFS, based at the main fire station, Kings Street, wrote a brief account of his experiences. The following is an abridged version.

On Saturday 24 August, 1940, we had been standing by for most of the morning since the sirens had sounded their early morning signal. This was nothing unusual, as the alerts had got more and more numerous and more protracted that summer as the Battle of Britain hotted up.

Around midday on this particular Saturday we became aware of enemy aircraft approaching Manston from the West – about two miles away. Before long we heard the sound of explosions and saw plumes of smoke rising from what was evidently the airfield, and from the vantage point of the top of our drill tower – about forty feet high, it was clear that Manston was receiving a battering. I saw one plane rise into the air to about a thousand feet, then plunge straight down again. It was a British plane trying to escape the bombing.

Our Chief Officer tried several times to contact the airfield by phone, but had no success, and he ordered me to go to the scene on my motor cycle and size-up the situation. I had a Royal Enfield machine which was quite nippy for those days, and I rode off at top speed through the deserted streets towards the scene, where I could see large clouds of smoke rising. It appeared that the enemy attack had ceased for the moment, and I concentrated on wending my way through debris and bomb craters, sometimes leaving the road to try riding over grass to a position where I could see the position more clearly.

Near the guardroom I saw a man, dressed in slacks and an army type pullover, leaning over a gate and surveying the scene gloomily. He was smoking a pipe, and it was with difficulty I could get any answer to my questions. He seemed to be stunned by the destruction wrought by twenty minutes or so of bombing. I asked him if there was a phone working. But he stared at me as if in a daze and just shook his head.

I remounted my bike and rode back towards Margate to where I knew there was a farm about a quarter of a mile from the airfield. When no one answered the door I walked in, found a phone and managed to inform our Chief Officer of the position and the best route to take to avoid the heaps of debris and roads blocked by bomb craters.

I then returned to the airfield and saw the main hangars were completely flattened and the debris was burning fiercely. Nearby there was a long wooden hut with smoke pouring out of the open door. An RAF airman then came out, tears running down his face and coughing from the effects of the smoke, carrying two Browning machine guns under each arm. I joined him, and between us we made several journeys through the heat and smoke, and brought out about twenty or thirty. These weapons were spare guns kept in the armoury for use in the aircraft, and at the time were worth their weight in gold, when arms and machinery of all sorts was in such short supply.

We sat on the ground beside the rescued pile of guns, coughing and our eyes streaming, and as we did so, the hut collapsed with a roar and shower of sparks. It was then that I noticed the fire crews had arrived from Margate. We found one large crater which was partly filled with water from a broken main, and embedded in the side of the crater was a large unexploded bomb, its fins standing clear of the mud and water. We tried to dislodge it with a view of getting it out of the way, since we wanted to use the water for firefighting. Despite our efforts, the bomb remained stuck fast, and we gave up after a while. Looking back, we all realized what a silly thing it was to ever have tried to move it. It could have exploded at any moment. We found out later it was an incendiary oil bomb designed to explode and scatter burning oil in all directions.

Presently, the lookout who stood on top of one of the appliances, blew his whistle. We all looked up to see a number of planes approaching from the North. We scrambled for shelter in a slit trench where we crouched in terror as the enemy turned and headed back towards us, releasing their bombs and firing their machine guns and cannon. Throughout the five minute attack we had noticed a GPO man slung at the top of a telephone pole about a quarter of a mile away. When we emerged from the trench after the attack he was still perched up there and working. Although we had yelled to him to take cover he apparently decided to carry on working – I reckon to this day he deserved a medal! We broke open our emergency rations, mostly biscuits and slabs of chocolate and crisps, and sat and just gazed at the scene around us. Late in the afternoon, we returned to our home station.

Once there our Chief Officer gathered us together and warned us not to reveal any details of what had happened at Manston. It was vital that the enemy should not know just how much the airfield had been put out of action. There can be little doubt that we were all very apprehensive about our knowledge of the complete destruction of an important airfield in the front line of defence, and it was a long time until Manston could be effectively used again.

We lived in fear of invasion in those days, and it was at least a year before complete confidence was restored. In the meantime we set about our own procedures in the event of an invasion, including a secret codeword only to be used in the event, and provisions for destroying petrol supplies and other essential commodities on receipt of the codeword.

Monday 26 August
MINSTER 13.09 – HEs

Seventeen bombs fell between Iron Bridge and the railway station, but no casualties were recorded. Formations of Dorniers and Messerschmitts were flying over the whole of Thanet at varying heights. The ack-ack guns were in action almost continuously and produced a vast canopy of black smoke as the shells exploded.

BROADSTAIRS 12.30 – HEs

Eleven bombs were reported falling on the foreshore at Joss Bay, near the 5.5-in coastal gun battery. At 12.27 according to one document, a Messerschmitt Bf 110 medium bomber was seen to crash in Percy Avenue. This incident, however, is unconfirmed. At 12.55 a Dornier 17 bomber was forced to land on the rocks at Foreness Point. *Uffz.* P. Haupt was rescued by a motor boat from Herne Bay, and the pilot *Lt.* K. Eggert, was rescued severely injured. He died of his wounds two days later. Two other crew members also died in the crash. *Uffz.* F. Buchner, pilot of a Messerschmitt Bf 109 fighter, died when his stricken machine crashed and bored through chalk on Shuart's Marshes near St Nicholas at Wade at 12.20. Another German pilot *Obergefr.* W. Malecki, was captured near Acol when his Messerschmitt fighter crashed and burned out at 15.15.

Wednesday 28 August
RAMSGATE 12.40 – HEs & IBs

Waves of enemy bombers were active over Thanet just after 08.30 en route to targets further inland. But at lunchtime ten bombs fell in the harbour and straddled York Street. The Popular Hotel was seriously damaged and its proprietor, Mr J. Marzetti, was seriously injured. The harbour offices were also damaged and several buildings which spread out along the Harbour Parade.

WESTGATE 12.30 – HEs & IBs

High-explosive bombs and incendiaries were scattered over the Queen's Down Estate, and Quex Park area. There are no recorded details of damage or casualties.

A Dornier 17 bomber had been damaged by our fighters over the Thames Estuary, and with both of its engines crippled it jettisoned its bomb load into the sea before crashing into the waves two miles off Foreness Point at 12.45. *Lt.* P. Krug, *Gefr.* A. Burghardt, *Gefr.* W. Gailer and *Flgr.* A. Bruckmann, were picked up by the fishing boats *Persevere* and *Golden Spray*. The crew were later transferred to the Margate lifeboat, *J.B. Proudfoot*, which brought them into Margate harbour.

The highlight of the day must have been the visit of the Prime Minister, who arrived with the then Chancellor of the Exchequer, Sir Kingsley Wood, and reached Ramsgate just after an air raid. Churchill expressed concern about payments of compensation for the bombed-out shop-

Fishing boats *Persevere* and *Golden Spray* picked up the crew of a Dornier 17 bomber which crashed in the sea two miles north of Foreness at 12.45 on 28 August 1940. *Lt.* P. Krug, *Gefr.* A. Burghardt, *Gefr.* W. Gailer and *Flgr.* A. Bruchmann, were transferred to the lifeboat *J.B. Proudfoot* and landed at Margate. Above, the Dornier pilot P. Krug is taken into custody.

keepers – then the alert sounded again. The mayor promptly suggested that the Prime Minister should take shelter in the nearest chalk tunnel. Churchill was handed a steel helmet. He lit one of his famous cigars and strode towards the entrance in Queen's Street. It was there he was informed that smoking was not allowed in the shelter. This cigar then came into the possession of a workman; whether he handed the cigar to him when the workman was standing closeby, or threw it to the ground where it was picked up it is unclear.

Churchill eventually reached RAF Manston where he saw an airfield that was completely covered with flags denoting unexploded bombs. While he might have shown a nonchalant attitude at Ramsgate he was, nevertheless, visibly disturbed by the unserviceability of one of his front-line airfields. The very next day, back in London, he wrote a letter to the Secretary of State and the Chief of Air Staff, to suggest that a mobile airfield company should be formed, properly equipped, to undertake the repair of damaged airfields.

Friday 30 August
MARGATE 18.35 – ENEMY BOMBER CRASHES

A Heinkel III bomber which had attacked Radlett aerodrome was severely damaged by our fighters. The pilot was killed in the attack and the observer took over control of the machine, dumping the bomb load into the sea, then he made a forced landing in a field near Goodmans Farm, Manston. Three of the crew were taken prisoner. *Gefr.* Kochler was severely injured and died of his wounds on 2 September.

Saturday 31 August
MARGATE 09.05 – ENEMY AIRCRAFT CRASHES

A Messerschmitt Bf 110 sustained crippling damage from our fighters when over the Thames Estuary and, burning furiously, it got as far as the Foreness Point before ditching into the sea. The pilot *Lt.* K.J. Eichhorn, was eventually rescued from his rubber dinghy by a fishing boat which brought him into Margate harbour. *Uffz.* Growe was never found and believed drowned. At 13.45 ack-ack guns opened fire when a Dornier 17Z was seen in difficulties above the town. Both engines had stopped and it was touch and go whether it would reach the sea area. Everyone expected the crew to bale out, but the bomber kept going in a glide until it eventually crashed into the sea near the South Goodwin lightship. *Uffz.* H. Blasche, *Fw.* E. Gudat and *Uffz.* W. Sonntag were rescued, but *Fw.* B. Nickel was presumed drowned.

The first fitting tribute to the ARP teams and other groups such as the AFS and police, appeared in the *Isle of Thanet Gazette*, dated 30 August, 1940. It read:

> By their sterling work in the raids of the past week, the men and women of Thanet's ARP and AFS organisations have proved beyond doubt that civil defenders in the front line are trained and fit to play a big part in the Battle of Britain.
>
> As recently as a few months ago street corner loungers sneered at the elaborate exercises to co-ordinate fire-fighting, rescue work and first aid. Special Constables were called snoopers and wardens were laughed at.
>
> And then it happened, just as the experts predicted. The years of planning, training and back-breaking exercises were justified in a moment. Everyone knew what to do. Nobody flinched from the heart-breaking sight of homes blazing and in ruins. Girl ambulance drivers, some of them seeing serious wounds for the first time, went deftly and rapidly about their work. There was no panic. At Ramsgate the organisation was so good that it was not considered necessary to call in the County Mobile ARP Reserve. They stuck to their posts despite enemy aircraft machine-gunning them whilst they fought the gas works blaze.

★ ★ ★

A warning to souvenir hunters was given at the Cinque Ports Police Court, Margate, when a man was fined £2 for stealing a revolver from a German airman. The prosecuting solicitor said:

> At about 12.30 p.m. on July 24, a German fighter aeroplane shot down in an air battle, made a forced landing in a cornfield. The sole occupant *Lt.* Werner Bartels, was wounded in the left wrist and right thigh.

The Chairman of the Magistrates said,

> We regard it as essential that those who may be near an aeroplane when it comes down should do nothing in the way of souvenir hunting. As this is the first case of its kind we are dealing with it more leniently than we should otherwise be inclined to do.

Tuesday 3 September
MARGATE 06.07 – RAF WHITLEY BOMBER CRASHES

The Kent War Diary records that a Whitley bomber of No. 58 Squadron made a forced landing in the sea 200 yd west of Margate Pier. It had run out of fuel while returning from a raid on Genoa, Italy.

The dramatic rescue of Pilot Officer Richard Hillary, a pilot with No. 603 Squadron, and a descendant of the founder of the Royal National Lifeboat Institution, Sir William Hillary, was made by Margate Lifeboat. Scrambled from their base at Hornchurch, 603 headed south-west and engaged with Messerschmitts. It was while Hillary was actually shooting down one of them that he was attacked himself by *Hptm.* Bode of II/JG26. It was about 10.00. Hillary's Spitfire, shot to pieces, began to burn. As the blazing fighter spiralled towards the sea his cockpit canopy jammed. He managed to bale out with extreme difficulty, but not before he received terrible burns to his hands and face.

Coastguards, after seeing his parachute descending, picked him up at 11.45. Margate's relief lifeboat, *J.B. Proudfoot*, launched down the ramp. The crew searched in a dense sea mist for over an hour before they spotted the white parachute fifteen miles north-east of Margate. The crew carefully brought the pilot on board. A.C. Robinson, the honorary secretary to the lifeboat, put up an awning to keep the sun off Hillary's burned face.

Alongside the Margate Pier Hillary was seen by a waiting doctor, then taken to hospital. The lifeboat crew, who had so patiently searched for Hillary, did not forget him and visited him in hospital throughout his slow recovery. Richard Hillary lived not only to fly again, but to write his own story – *The Last Enemy*, which appeared in 1942, a graphic account of his flying experiences. Unfortunately, he was killed in a flying accident in 1943.

Thursday 5 September
MESSERSCHMITT CRASHES

During a 'freelance' sortie over the English Channel a Messerschmitt fighter, damaged in combat, made a forced landing at Monkton Farm at 15.45. The pilot, *Hptm.* W. Meyerweissflog was taken prisoner unhurt.

Friday 6 September
MESSERSCHMITT CRASHES

Another German fighter on a 'freelance' sortie over Dover was severely damaged in combat and attempted to land at RAF Manston at 18.39. *Uffz.*

H.G. Schulte, the pilot, could only manage to force land his machine on Vincents Farm. He was taken prisoner unhurt.

Saturday 7 September
MESSERSCHMITT CRASHES

This was the day when Goering launched his massive attack on London. Nearly one thousand aircraft had been amassed in one huge tactical unit and advanced towards the Thames Estuary at heights varying from 14,000 ft to 23,000 ft. It was an armada of colossal strength, a tidal wave of bombers and fighters that hitherto had only been imagined in the minds of pre-war writers.

One of the escorting Messerschmitt Bf 110s was shot down in combat and ditched in the sea off Birchington at 17.20. Margate's lifeboat, *J.B. Proudfoot*, rescued *Oberlt*. W. Brede.

Monday 9 September

Two drifters – *Alfred Colebrook* and *Harvest Moon* were sunk as blockships in the Richborough Channel.

Wednesday 11 September
16.24 – MESSERSCHMITT CRASHES

A Messerschmitt Bf 110 on escort to a bomber formation was shot down in combat over Thanet and crashed into the sea about three miles from the coast. The crew perished, and the body of only *Fw*. Joseph Radlmair was washed ashore a month later.

Friday 13 September
RAMSGATE 22.28 – HEs & IBs

An unidentified German bomber released high-explosive bombs and a few incendiaries at Foads Hill, Cliff End. One bungalow was demolished and six others damaged. Casualties were not recorded.

Monday 16 September
RAMSGATE 22.00 – HEs

Two bombs fell on the Marina Bathing Pool and just outside the Granville Pavilion. Another four bombs fell just off the harbour. Damage was given as slight. There were no casualties.

Although it had been open only a fortnight, the Kent County Spitfire Fund had already reached the splendid total of £7,000 and, as the estimated cost of a Spitfire was £5,000, the remainder of the monies was put towards a second fighter. Many Kent towns and private citizens and organizations had started their own Spitfire funds and large sums of money had been raised. Lord Cornwallis, President of the Association of Men of Kent and Kentish Men which had launched the County Spitfire Fund, suggested that all efforts throughout the county should be co-ordinated to provide a Kent Spitfire squadron of twelve aircraft, including three reserves. He thought it would be a noble gesture if a whole squadron of Spitfires could take to the skies under the banner of the 'Rampant White Horse' – the county emblem.

Hitler surely could never have expected that his *Luftwaffe* would help in raising money for the Spitfire Fund. One enterprising Margate fireman was particularly expert in making fine trinkets and jewellery from aluminium and perspex obtained from crashed enemy aircraft which all AFS units were obliged to attend. He was once heard to say while looking into a clear sunny sky, '. . . could do with a Messerschmitt today – I'm running out of material!'

Whenever there was an air-raid warning the Revd Donald de Meredith, of St Peter's, took the opportunity to give his parishioners gas-mask drill. Men, women and children all took part in races to see who could be the first to don their gas mask. Those who arrived first at the shelter were given either sweets or chocolate. It was never explained how he got his 'extra' rations of confectionery!

★ ★ ★

A warning to amateur photographers was given at the Margate Police Court where a Westgate ARP Warden appeared on a summons for taking a photograph of a crashed German aeroplane without a permit. The accused explained that as the aeroplane was being moved past his ARP post, he took the picture as a memento of something that had happened near his home. Being the first case of its kind brought before the magistrates they dismissed the charge with a warning.

★ ★ ★

Despite the wartime difficulties pigeon fanciers still operated in Thanet – 'Air raids seem to hurry them along,' an enthusiast explained, when his favourite bird arrived home from a 134-mile journey from Lymington, Hampshire. Although pigeon racing was abandoned in late September 1940, their value as messengers in a clandestine communications network was not fully understood by the general public.

★ ★ ★

The Chief Constable of Margate, W. Palmer, emphasized once again the danger of souvenir hunting among crashed aircraft which littered the Isle of Thanet. His constables had recently recovered four machine-guns from local youths. One boy had pulled the trigger of one of the guns which he had taken home to show his mother – quite unaware a bullet was still in the breach. The bullet struck the skirting board in the kitchen, terrifying his mother.

Tuesday 24 September
BROADSTAIRS 11.15 – HEs & UXB

Two high-explosive bombs were dropped from a high altitude, one fell and exploded near Ramsgate Airport at Bromstone Corner, while the other failed to explode at Park Avenue. Damage was confined to shattered windows and roof tiles. Casualties nil.

Wednesday 25 September
BROADSTAIRS 13.11 – HEs & INCENDIARIES

Houses in Salisbury Avenue were extensively damaged by the blast when about a dozen high-explosive bombs and one canister of incendiaries fell at midday. Further information is unavailable.

RAMSGATE 12.19 – HEs & UXBs

Bombs also fell at Warten Road, and others on the railway track near Dumpton. Two houses were demolished and others seriously damaged. Four bombs failed to explode at Dumpton Race Track. Casualties nil.

MARGATE – CLIFTONVILLE 12.45 – HEs

More than twenty high-explosive bombs were dropped indiscriminately, but only three fell in the Cliftonville area. A cinema was heavily damaged and a shop in Northdown Road lost its plate-glass windows. One bomb fell at the rear of Nos 36–38 Harold Road, which tore down the brickwork but left the front standing. A member of the Home Guard was in bed suffering from gout when the brickwork and all the upstairs furniture of the house next door collapsed into his house, missing him by about 10 ft. His sister was cleaning the front doorstep at the time. She was thrown to the ground but only suffered slight scratches. Another bomb fell at the rear of Montrose School.

MARGATE 15.00 – HEs & UXBs

More bombs descended upon the town in the afternoon. The Grand Hotel Ballroom was wrecked, the Oval Bandstand was also damaged as were houses in Norfolk Road. Casualties nil.

★ ★ ★

The playful tricks of a wandering balloon caused more than a passing disturbance at Margate. The trailing cable dragged through the town,

Painted light grey all over this Morris Commercial light van was converted by members of the Margate fire brigade into a mobile canteen. It was first used during the evacuation of the BEF from Dunkirk in June 1940, and attended most of the major air-raid incidents. From left to right: F. Watson, 'Duker' Saxby and Mr Rains.

tapping on roofs and doors, dislodging a fence or two and even knocking over a five-gallon oil drum, which was sent spinning down a street with a resounding clatter. Everyone thought they were being showered with incendiaries. AFS crews had been sent out, but they stood and watched the balloon's progress until it was brought down by a well-aimed burst of machine-gun fire.

The runaway balloon had come from the RAF Leaflet Balloon Unit that was stationed at Birchington, and which remained there for nearly two and a half years. The unit was responsible for sending thousands of leaflets to the enemy-occupied countries, and when first introduced as a propaganda weapon it baffled the Germans completely. The Germans were puzzled because, on the nights when no British aircraft were reported in their areas, shoals of leaflets were strewn all around without any trace of how they got there.

The answer was both simple and crude. When the wind was in the right direction – and everything depended on that – and the moon was up, the residents watched balloons continually rising by the dozen above the roof-tops and drifting away in an easterly direction towards Belgium, Holland and Germany – sometimes south-bound for France. Every day Birchington residents saw lorry-loads of gas cylinders arriving and leaving at a secluded spot, almost hidden by trees. Although they eventually discovered that they were used to fill balloons with gas, it was a long time before the real purpose of the exercise became known and whispered abroad. On some nights the work was carried on for hours, and the hissing noise caused by the release of gas from the cylinders into the balloons was so loud and persistent that people living in the vicinity of the launching site were kept awake until the early hours of the morning.

Occasionally a balloon would not go where it was supposed to. Some got caught in trees or telegraph wires, and a few came down in the Margate area. The balloons were specially made of a rubberized fabric. They varied in size, depending on the target, the distance and number of leaflets to be carried. A small charge was used to get the balloons away to a flying start, but when in flight there was practically no noise, just a gentle swish as it continued to rise into the night sky. Underneath the balloon was a basket-weave framework on which the leaflets hung, tied in bundles, which was connected in turn to a fuse. The fuse varied in length according to the distance to be travelled before the leaflets were to be released. They were so arranged that by the time the balloon reached the target area where the first bundle was to be dropped the fuse would have burnt round the frame to where the bundle of leaflets was hanging.

It was, by any standard, a bit of a Heath-Robinson design, but allowing for wind currents and speeds, a simple formula was worked out for the fuse settings and it was said they were quite accurate.

Saturday 28 September
RAMSGATE 17.40 – HEs & UXBs

High-explosive bombs fell from a high level. The aircraft was not identified as it was above cloud. Dumpton Park, the Greyhound Track, Wallwood Road, Warten Road and Hereson Road all received a bomb and one oil-bomb was reported falling on allotments near Dumpton railway station. Although four bombs failed to detonate one exploded late in the evening causing considerable damage to nearby houses. Casualties were not recorded.

Monday 30 September
RAF MANSTON 16.50 – HEs

A sharp 'tip-and-run' attack caused only minor damage to some outlying buildings. The ack-ack guns thwarted a second wave of fighter-bombers who changed course and headed for Broadstairs.

Wednesday 2 October
MARGATE – GARLINGE 06.22 – HEs

High-explosive bombs fell in the Garlinge area but most of them struck open land. Two AFS telephonists were cycling home from night duty and were knocked off their bicycles when one bomb hit the road just 20 yd in front of them. Both girls picked themselves up, brushed the dust from their uniforms and cycled home without a scratch.

MARGATE – WESTBROOK 11.30 – HEs

Another German bomber decided to jettison its bombs over Westbrook. Thought to be the 50-kg type they straddled houses in Wellis Gardens and Grove Gardens. One couple was returning home from a walk and discovered their home at No. 22 Wellis Gardens in ruins. Their little car in its garage was crushed by a collapsing wall. Damage – three houses wrecked and several badly damaged. Casualties – one slightly injured.

Monday 7 October
RAMSGATE 06.35 – HEs

Ten bombs were dropped in the sea off the East Cliff, and a further four in

Pegwell Bay. One or two bombs were reported having exploded near the Merrie England. Damage unknown – casualties unknown.

BROADSTAIRS 06.40 – HEs

About a dozen bombs fell in the Holy Cross Convent area and one damaged the railway track and several houses close by. Damage was said to be extensive although there are no recorded details. Casualties – one slightly injured.

Tuesday 8 October
BROADSTAIRS 07.33 – HEs

A bungalow at the junction of Park Road and Stone Road was completely demolished and there was considerable blast damage to surrounding property when two bombs exploded in the area. Lanthorne Road was also affected by blast damage. A further three bombs fell near Bromstone Road at 15.50. Confusion exists here, for times logged by the police, ARP and military do not indicate the actual time of the incidents. Unfortunately, log-book entries were sometimes made many hours after the incident and any cohesive chronological pattern has been lost.

Friday 11 October
RAMSGATE 13.43 – HEs

Most of the daylight raids in the Thanet area were now being made by bomb-carrying Messerschmitts. The bombers were now operating at night to attack specific targets in the cities and larger towns. The Messerschmitts usually carried either a 250- or a 500-kilo bomb slung beneath their fuselage and more often the fragmentation type was used. On this occasion, however, the railway was the target. Five bombs were dropped at the Ramsgate railway station where two sidings were extensively damaged. Unfortunately, two houses were demolished in the raid and ten others seriously damaged with a further sixty-four being slightly damaged. Although there were eight casualties reported among the civilians no one was killed.

Perhaps one of the most extraordinary incidents of the day involved Mrs Doris Finch. She had been alone in her cottage home when it received a direct hit. The ARP rescue team arrived very quickly on the scene of utter devastation. They found Doris buried up to her neck in rubble. They were astonished to find she was alive, despite appalling injuries.

Thursday 17 October
MARGATE 09.20 – HEs

Messerschmitt fighter-bombers were responsible for releasing bombs over Margate and Broadstairs. They were being harassed by our own fighters and had been turned back from their original objectives further inland.

In the first raid there were estimates of ten aircraft making shallow dives when most of the bombs fell on open ground. There was very little damage done and no casualties recorded. The second, and more serious raid, was made about half an hour later. Thirteen bombs were dropped, and one of them caused cuts and bruises to six women and four men who were all treated at a first-aid post.

The front was torn out of the Lloyds Bank building in the main shopping centre at Cliftonville. A county council clinic and at least thirty houses were damaged. Although no particular building received a direct hit several were later pulled down as unsafe. Machine-guns chattered before the attack and our own fighters were observed corkscrewing through the enemy formation, driving them towards the coast. People stood and watched the combat and one of the onlookers later remarked, '. . . they were dancing like moths in the sunshine'. People soon flung themselves down to the ground when they heard the familiar sound of Messerschmitts in a dive. After the scream of the engine came the whistle of the bombs. Each fighter-bomber followed the same pattern in rapid succession.

At Lloyds Bank, Mr Witts, the manager, had just collected his post when he heard the whistle of falling bombs.

> I ordered my staff to take shelter in the strong room. We had just reached it when there was a terrific explosion. A bomb had fallen in the road outside, blowing out the front of the building. Large girders were slipping from the masonry a few feet away as we crawled out of the wreckage. Everyone was marvellous, especially Miss Jones. All she said was, 'That was a near one.'
>
> When I found no one was hurt I dashed upstairs to see what had happened to my talking budgerigar. Its cage was completely covered with plaster, but a small voice said, 'Hello darling'. The bank caretaker was shaving at the time. He said, 'It was the closest shave of my life.'

Within one hour all the important documents had been transferred to another bank across the street. Normally, the shopping area would have

Mr Witts the manager at Lloyds Bank, Northdown Road, Cliftonville, ran upstairs after the dust had settled to find his pet budgerigar. He was greeted with 'Hello Darling!' from within a plaster-covered cage.

Mrs Beard of Prices Avenue looks out at the chaos caused by Messerschmitt fighter-bombers at 9.15 on 17 October 1940. She cheerfully scrubbed her hall floor and made tea for the council workmen repairing the damage.

been quite busy, but fortunately it was almost deserted when the raid happened. The bomb which caused the most damage fell at the rear of Connaught Road.

The oldest casualty was eighty-three-year-old Harry Edis, who had just returned to the town to see his sons. He was in the kitchen when the ceiling collapsed; one of his sons was later rescued from the rubble. Other casualties included Mrs Cawson and her son, who had also returned from London where they had been bombed out. They had just managed to reach their Anderson shelter before the blast sent fragments flying everywhere. Mrs Whitehead was cleaning her living-room grate when the blast of one bomb flung her through the doorway and into the kitchen. She had the presence of mind to crawl over the debris and turn off the gas tap. A few minutes after one bomb had made a huge crater outside her house in Princes Avenue Mrs Beard cheerfully scrubbed out the hall.

Saturday 19 October
MARGATE 11.45 – HEs

Twenty high-explosive bombs fell on the town centre, demolishing four houses and two works, with a further fourteen houses badly damaged, including the Mission Hall. A Heinkel III bomber, which suddenly appeared out of low cloud, just before the scream of falling bombs sent people scurrying for shelter, was said to be responsible for the damage.

After the terrific explosions came the rattle of machine-guns as our fighters latched on to the raider. The main damage was to working-class dwellings, five of which were demolished in Dane Park Road, Grotto Hill and Milton Avenue. Among the terraced houses savagely torn apart, families just stood in the roadways, stunned and unbelieving.

Clarence Hyde, summoned from his work in a clothing store, helped a rescue squad search the ruins of his home at No. 46 Thanet Road. After some hours of painstaking work they eventually found the bodies of his forty-year-old wife Doris and sixty-year-old Miss Maud Cox. Only ten days before Mrs Hyde had returned from Staffordshire, where she had been working as a helper among the evacuated children. She had left behind her own two children.

While the ARP rescue teams were systematically searching among the heaps of bricks, plaster and smashed furniture, they heard a dog whine. Crawling through a hole tunnelled in the rubble, a warden rescued the family pet – Jill. The warden was bitten for his trouble!

The bomb which wrecked three small houses in Milton Avenue, killed

A single Heinkel bomber jettisoned its bombs on Margate at lunchtime on 19 October 1940. Three women became the first fatalities caused by an air raid in the town. At No. 46 Thanet Road Mrs Hyde and Miss Cox lost their lives, when their house received a direct hit from a 250-kg bomb.

Mrs Warren was the third air-raid victim when a 250-kg bomb wrecked Nos 55–9 Milton Avenue, at midday on 19 October 1940. Her pet dog, Jill, was rescued unscathed.

Sifting through the rubble at the Penial Mission, Milton Avenue, demolished on 19 October 1940.

seventy-three-year-old Mrs Maria Warren. Five girls and the manager at the Kodak workshop at Grotto Gardens had a narrow escape as the bomb which exploded outside the building took away half of it. The girls inside flung themselves down against the walls just as the manager shouted a warning.

Among the many heroines of the day was Miss Lena Bing, a young ARP telephonist. Despite bombs exploding around her little sandbagged post, she realized the importance of her job and stayed at the switchboard. Although all the doors and windows were blown in, she calmly took messages from wardens who rang in to report the damage in their areas. Her only emotional outburst was when she later discovered her bicycle had been wrecked.

In the streets of shattered houses neighbours were soon bustling about with pots of tea and friendly offers of help to those who were now homeless. Among the babble of voices came one which cheered everyone, 'I dunno wot me old man will say when 'e finds 'e aint got no pyjamas! – I left 'em on the line and Hitler's made 'em a military objective.'

Damage was estimated as severe. Casualties – three killed, eleven injured.

Sunday 20 October
BROADSTAIRS 14.30 – HEs & Oil Bomb

People in Magdala Road, St Peter's, had a narrow escape when a Heinkel dropped three bombs, two high-explosive and one oil. At one house two women and a man rushed to their Anderson; they had no sooner taken refuge when their home suffered a direct hit. Another bomb fell in Pierremont Avenue, causing only slight damage. The oil bomb fell in the grounds of St Peter's School. Four people were slightly injured, but there were no fatalities. Later an unexploded bomb was discovered in the garden of Salisbury Lodge.

Tuesday 22 October
BROADSTAIRS 06.37 – HEs & UXBs

Early risers in Broadstairs saw a huge, black-painted Heinkel loom out of the mist at just a few hundred feet above sea level. The aircraft was seen to regain height almost at the same time that seven bombs were released. Two of them faileld to explode and fell in the gardens of Fig Tree House, Callis Court Road. There was extensive blast damage to many other houses in the immediate area but there were no casualties reported.

No. 15 Dane Park Road was completely demolished by a direct hit on 19 October.

Red-hot tracer bullets were observed curving towards the bomber, and the military were convinced that many strikes had been made on it before it reached the safety of low cloud.

Thursday 24 October
BROADSTAIRS – GERMAN PILOT WASHED ASHORE

The body of *Oberfw.* Georg Weiss was washed ashore at Joss Bay, and was buried at Margate New Cemetery. The mortuary report of the Broadstairs & St Peter's Urban District Council also records another German airman being washed ashore at the Broadstairs Jetty on the same day but there are no documents which state his identity. Georg Weiss had been shot down in his Messerschmitt Bf 109 in combat with fighters over the Channel off Dover on 14 August.

Friday 25 October
BROADSTAIRS 12.18 – HEs

A few seconds after an East Kent bus had passed along the Broadstairs to Ramsgate Road a bomb exploded in Dumpton Close. Damage was given as slight. Just after 16.30 a convoy off the North Foreland was under attack from enemy bombers, escorting destroyers put up a fight and no ships were lost.

Sunday 27 October
RAMSGATE 17.10 – HEs

A formation of Messerschmitt fighter-bombers swept in over the Pegwell Bay area and released their bombs. Seven houses were demolished and a further four seriously damaged with forty-eight receiving slight damage.
    The only casualty was seventy-year-old Samuel Filer, who was buried alive beneath his home, Garfield, in Pegwell Avenue. When the ARP team finally dragged him out of the rubble they were relieved to find him still breathing. The casualty figure would have been quite high had not most of the residents been evacuated. Mrs Harvey had just left to go shopping when the bombs fell. She had not reckoned on stretching her length on the pavement, more especially as she was wearing her new coat.
    Mr and Mrs Butcher were having tea in a room at the rear of the house when a bomb exploded not far away. Mr Butcher quickly made a grab for his wife and bundled her through the french windows and into the garden. He almost threw her into the Anderson shelter. He was scrambling through the entrance when another bomb exploded at the front of

the house. The Anderson was completely buried in rubble. Leaving his wife behind Mr Butcher managed to crawl out and, on his hands and knees crept over the debris to discover a ruptured gas pipe. Even more alarming were the red-hot embers from the hearth. Resting on bits of broken furniture they had started a fire. Although badly shaken up by the explosion he emptied the coal scuttle and scooped up the burning pieces before another explosion occurred.

When all the hullabaloo had died down the couple looked at their devastated home in sheer bewilderment. The lawn, for example, was now covered with roof tiles which had been embedded in the turf, on edge, and in perfect rows. They looked for all the world as if they had been planted there. Then there was the valuable grandfather, long-case clock. It had always stood in the hall. It was smashed to pieces. The front of the piano had been ripped off, and everywhere bits of furniture, china, pictures and glassware were scattered.

But that scene was not an unfamiliar sight in Thanet. That night, what few possessions could be salvaged were put on a hand-cart, and pushed to another part of the town. But was there anywhere in the town regarded as safe?

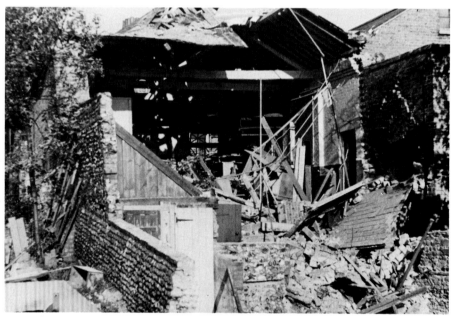

Five girls and the manager at the Kodak Works, Grotto Gardens, escaped with their lives when a 250-kg bomb exploded at the rear of the premises on 19 October 1940.

Tuesday 29 October
RAF MANSTON 10.45 – MACHINE-GUN ATTACK

Nine enemy fighters were plotted flying over the airfield but bombs were not dropped on this occasion. There was increased enemy air activity for most of the daylight hours. One report states that over fifteen Italian bombers and Fiat bi-plane fighters, took part in a raid on Ramsgate. A 'South-east coast town' was bombed and machine-gunned said one report, which described two houses being demolished by bombs. The same report suggests there was a fourth raid on the town when people were buried beneath the ruins of their battered homes. The trouble is, however, none of these reports can be confirmed by any official documents.

Wednesday 30 October
MARGATE 12.10 – MACHINE-GUN ATTACK

Messerschmitt fighters were reported shooting-up the town, but bombs were not released anywhere in the vicinity. Bullets and cannon shells ricocheted between buildings but there were no casualties recorded.

★ ★ ★

So far the German High Command were disillusioned by their failure to overpower the Royal Air Force, even though the pressure on the British defences was maintained in both daylight and night raids. And so, once again, Adolf Hitler was forced to abandon his invasion plans and suggested a spring offensive instead. This decision was communicated to the German forces in October. The result of that decision was, according to long held views of British historians, the end of the offensive which became known as the Battle of Britain. The Germans have never understood that particular view, for they maintain that their aerial offensive continued well into 1941.

Since the battle started in July the *Luftwaffe* had suffered the loss of over 2,600 crewmen with a further 950 made prisoners of war. Their total number of aircraft destroyed was 1,800. This can be set against the RAF total of 1,000 aircraft with a loss of 541 lives.

★ ★ ★

Two Thanet telephone engineers were mentined in the Civil Defence Honours List: Mr Arthur Shepherd of Birchington and Mr Cyril Box of

Ramsgate. Together with Inspector Goodwin, they had volunteered to
restore communication to RAF Manston when the lines were severed in a
heavy air raid on 24 August. They were still at work when bombs were
falling on the following day. They carried on splicing the hundreds of
wires in water-filled craters and beside unexploded bombs dangling from
telegraph poles in their leather harnesses while Messerschmitts made
low-level machine-gun attacks. When the job was completed they were
highly commended by the Air Ministry.

Friday 1 November
BROADSTAIRS 13.18 – HEs

The Isle of Thanet had been on red alert for some time. Everyone
expected to hear enemy aircraft in the area and they were not disappointed. The dreaded Stuka dive-bombers were being deployed in the Thames
Estuary, the first time since the middle of August. But even so, the raids
were on a moderate scale, and they were met by our fighter squadrons

The caption on the back of this photograph says bombs were dropped at about 19.00 on
1 November 1940. In fact, the stick of bombs fell at 13.20 and St Margarets in Foreland
Avenue received a direct hit.

Dreamland Amusement Park, which had brought joy to thousands of holiday-makers in peace-time, was used to billet troops during the Dunkirk evacuation. It received a direct hit at midday on 1 November 1940.

before they could get anywhere near their targets. The 'all clear' signal sounded and townspeople went out shopping. Workmen began to repair the damaged properties, to mend the water pipes and gas mains, and to clear the streets of rubble. But suddenly enemy aircraft approached the coast from the North. Observer Corps personnel counted over thirty bombers escorted by fighters. They had been turned back from an attack. High-explosive bombs began to fall on Dundonald Road and the junction with John Street, where a bakery was demolished. The bakehouse belonged to Mr W.E. Lawrence, and was completely wrecked when a stick of seven bombs fell in the area. The adjoining Royalty Cinema, which had been closed for some time, was badly damaged. One bomb detonated in the grounds of the Rectory and windows of the Broadstairs Parish Church, were blown in. Other buildings in the Crow Hill and Stone Road areas suffered damage. Fortunately there were no casualties.

MARGATE 13.20 – HEs

A stick of bombs fell in Northdown Road, Cliftonville, Tivoli Brooks, Reading Street, Foreland Avenue, Marlborough Road and Dreamland Park. Spumes of sea water rose into the air when more bombs fell into the sea.

Three motor coaches, three lorries, a private car and an old horse brake, which had taken thousands of holiday-makers for country rides in peacetime, were all destroyed at Sayers Yard, Marlborough Road. The damage was later estimated at £7,000. One bomb went through the roof of the Dreamland Amusement Park, wrecking one side of it. Although unoccupied at the time, a large, semi-detached house called St Margarets in Foreland Avenue, had the front blown out. Two more houses were seriously damaged and a further twenty suffered minor damage.

RAMSGATE 13.20 – HEs

Only one high-explosive bomb is recorded falling at Dumpton West. There were no casualties reported.

Saturday 2 November
RAMSGATE 11.25 – HEs

The Thames Estuary had been the target for a considerable force of bombers, escorted by fighters, which set off the red alert in Thanet early in the morning. For almost an hour the heavy drone of enemy aircraft was heard. Occasionally the chatter of machine-guns was also heard, but the anti-aircraft guns remained silent. Our own fighters were everywhere. Then the 'all clear' sounded. The citizens of Ramsgate, like those in Broadstairs and Margate, came out of their shelters and were seen rushing about the town shopping before the next alert sounded. They were still shopping when about sixteen bombers, escorted by about twenty fighters, approached Ramsgate. This particular raid is recorded as the second most severe to effect the town. About sixty bombs were dropped, most of them falling in the gasworks area: Denmark Road, Church Road, Alma Road and the cemetery. In the latter hundreds of graves were destroyed, tombstones and masonry were flung in every direction. It was a macabre sight which engendered feelings of intense hatred towards the Germans. Over fifteen houses were demolished, one hundred seriously damaged and almost one thousand were slightly damaged. When the alert warning signal was sounded for the second time ARP rescue teams were

Members of just one of Margate's first aid parties who gave such sterling work to the local community throughout the Second World War.

Motor coaches, lorries and an old horse brake were crushed beneath tons of rubble when Sayers Yard, Marlborough Road, Margate, received a direct hit at midday on 1 November.

already at work recovering bodies from the wreckage. Within hours there
were seven lifeless forms covered by blankets beside the kerbstones.

Two churches and two schools were damaged, while many businesses
in the main shopping area sustained window and roof damage. One
report mentioned that the bombs were of a larger calibre than usual. One
of them demolished two houses in Hollicondane Road, one of them
unoccupied, but four occupants in the other lost their lives. Fifty-two-
year-old Catherine Williams at No. 37 Hollicondane Road, her eighteen-
year-old daughter Margaret, and two grandchildren, Alice Shiel aged four
and Georgina Shiel aged one year, were all killed. Mrs Shiel, the children's
mother, was still out shopping and returned to find the house demolished.
The victims had taken shelter in the nearest tunnel, away from the home
during the first alert. They had returned home before the second attack.

In another road three houses were also demolished. Edward Ruffell and
his wife Ethel, were sheltering under the stairs in the first house when
they were buried. The body of sixty-five-year-old Edward was found
later that morning, but that of his sixty-six-year-old wife was not
recovered until Monday 4th. Mrs Day, next door, was also under the
stairs and, although her home collapsed in ruins she was found suffering
only from shock. Mrs Robbins, in the third house, was still out shopping.

In Denmark Road fifty-two-year-old Florence Saffrey was killed when
No. 29 was wrecked. At No. 7 Cecilia Road, seventy-year-old Herbert
Lawbuary was running towards his Anderson when he was blown into
the garden next door. Herbert died, but his wife Emily survived as she
was out shopping at the time.

Customers in a butcher's shop threw themselves to the floor when they
heard the first explosions. An assistant was putting stuffing into a chicken
– he returned to the counter later to find the chicken filled with ceiling
plaster. At Maple's, another butcher's shop, father and son took refuge in
the large cold-box. They emerged unhurt, but considerably shaken. The
sixteen-year-old son, an ARP Messenger, immediately reported for duty.
Both the chief officer of the fire brigade and his deputy were among those
listed as injured, when they received burns while attending a fire in the
town.

In the vicinity of the gasworks, Mrs Peete had left her baby in its pram
outside a house while she went to the shop opposite. When the bombs fell
she rushed out of the shop, snatched the baby and ran down some steps
leading to a basement. There she crouched as glass splinters and masonry
fell on top of her. The pram was flattened beyond recognition. In the shop
the proprietor and his wife were serving half a dozen children – they all

rushed for the safety of the stairs. They were packed like sardines in a tin when the shop collapsed. But miraculously they all survived. The rescuers found them later and whisked them all to hospital for treatment – they were in shock. One document states there were eighteen seriously injured and a further five slightly injured. Fatalities totalled eight.

Tuesday 5 November
MINSTER 11.25 – HEs

Messerschmitt fighter-bombers were making low-level sweeps in the south-east from as early as 9.30, some formations totalled fifty aircraft. Two bombs fell in the Minster area but there were no casualties recorded. Guy Fawkes celebrations had been banned but the *Luftwaffe* provided plenty of fireworks.

RAMSGATE 11.16 – HEs

A dozen Messerschmitts sneaked in below the radar detection systems and dive-bombed the town. Four high-explosive bombs struck Camden Square, Queen Bertha Road, Southwood Road and St Lawrence College. Five houses were destroyed and a further six were badly damaged. Thirty-year-old Emily Horten of No. 8 La Belle Alliance Square ran into her house for shelter. It received a direct hit. Her body was not recovered until Friday. Another thirty-year-old woman, Louisa Taylor, was also buried beneath her ruined home next door, but was fortunately rescued in a very short time and rushed to hospital.

In another part of the town a bomb scored a direct hit on a house where the occupant had gone into his garden. He ended up blown across the lawn and into his shed. At No. 23 Southwood Road, eighty-year-old Mabel Miall was recovered from the wreckage and taken to hospital where she died two days later. Her husband, seventy-five-year-old David, was found with serious wounds, and was taken to West Malling hospital where he died three weeks later.

Among the injured was twenty-one-year-old Jean Day, a Wren. She was in her room at the top of the building, four storeys from the ground, when the bomb struck. Each floor collapsed consecutively, one upon the other, until the whole mass of debris reached ground level.

The rescue teams held no thoughts of Jean surviving that ordeal. They sawed through dozens of floor joists and rafters and used powerful hydraulic jacks to lift the heavy stone masonry before they could get anywhere near her. Several hours passed before they could release her from what they supposed to be her tomb. Miraculously, when they finally lifted her on to a stretcher, except for a slight cut on her forehead she was otherwise unscathed. She told her rescuers she did not know what all the fuss was about as she was all right.

Last to be dragged from the rubble was sixty-three-year-old Maud Heizman. Although injured, she insisted on having a cup of tea before she would allow the ambulance men to take her to hospital.

Police Sergeant Buddle, together with John Todd and George Baker, had attended the incident at No. 9 La Belle Alliance Square, and succeeded in locating Louisa Taylor. Later, when Sergeant Buddle was inspecting the wreckage with Mrs Taylor's husband they were surprised to find that a large wooden elephant, an ornament, had actually survived the blast. It was entrusted to Sergeant Buddle who promised to return it to the family when they were re-housed. Jumbo was eventually returned to its former owners in August 1945!

BROADSTAIRS 11.40 – HEs

In the same air raid one bomb fell in the grounds of Bartrum Gables School. There were no casualties recorded.

RAMSGATE 16.05 – HEs

Over forty Messerschmitts were plotted attacking a convoy in mid-Channel, between Deal and Ramsgate. But another formation was seen further inland who were turned back by our fighters. They were less manoeuvrable with a bomb slung beneath their fuselage, so to give themselves a chance, the German pilots released their bombs. Some of the missiles were said to have fallen on the town, but there is no existing record of either damage or casualties.

The citizens of Birchington, however, were treated to a thrilling display when the Messerschmitts were attacked by Spitfires. At the first sound of machine-guns the onlookers began to rush for shelter, but stopped in their tracks to observe one German under attack. They forgot the danger in their excitement and watched a Spitfire attack the swerving fighter-bomber. When only about 300 ft above ground the German pilot seemed to just fall out of his cockpit. He had almost reached the roofs of houses before his parachute opened. He fell into the branches of a small tree in Albion Road, which broke his fall. Soldiers suddenly appeared as if from nowhere. They helped the pilot down and after attending to his cut lip, they bundled *Fw*. E. Scheidt into a police car and took him away.

Scheidt's Messerschmitt, that he had vacated so quickly, had careered on, missing chimney stacks by just a few feet, to eventually crash into an allotment behind Crescent Road. Two Spitfires circled overhead and were seen performing victory rolls before flying off in the direction of Manston.

★ ★ ★

Almost all the entertainment facilities in Margate had closed down. There were one or two small clubs where dances were still held, and most of those were jam-packed with military personnel. Suggestions to open the Winter Gardens were frowned upon by the Emergency Committee, not least, because it came within the restricted area. Some relaxation from the worries of the war was, however, necessary to keep up the spirits of the 12,000 civilians. 'Margate' said one Councillor, '. . . is about as dead as any town could be.'

At Ramsgate, however, the Corporation had shown sufficient initiative to open the West Cliff Hall for regular dances and up to five hundred people had been attending, including many Margate residents. In addition to the civilian population there were upwards of 5,000 soldiers and airmen to consider. Only two cinemas were operating by this time, the Regal and Parade.

Wednesday 6 November
MARGATE 21.22 – HEs & UXB

A sudden explosion in the marsh area outside the town was later confirmed by the military to have been the detonation of an unplotted, unexploded bomb. A parachute was recovered from the area by the AFS, confirming that a 'G' Mine had been dropped.

★ ★ ★

The following notice appeared in the *East Kent Times* newspaper for 6 November:

Now that the sounding of the air raid sirens is intended to be interpreted as an 'ALERT' instead of, as previously, being a warning to take immediate cover, it has been necessary to revise the terms of the recent Order making it an obligation that horses on roads where the 30 mile an hour speed limit applies shall wear a halter, and that persons in charge of horses shall secure them when the sirens sound. While the provision of a halter remains obligatory, the horse need not be secured when the air raid 'ALERT' is sounded, but when the driver is instructed to do so by any police officer.

Thursday 7 November
MARGATE 10.00 – UXB & Parachute Mine

A parachute mine floated down on to Little Brooks End Farm at Birchington but failed to explode. The area was immediately sealed off by the military until the Bomb Disposal Unit came to defuse it. At 15.00 hrs four Spitfires of 603 Squadron shot down a Messerschmitt Bf 110 into the sea off Margate. *Oblt.* H. Kopetsch and *Lt.* H. Veil were never recovered.

Friday 8 November

The naval tug *Muria* was sunk by a mine off the North Foreland.

Sunday 10 November
BROADSTAIRS 07.30 – HEs

The *Luftwaffe* were operating single aircraft in the Thanet area and documented sources fail to identify what aircraft dropped eight high-explosive bombs in the sea.

RAMSGATE 15.15 – HEs

Two houses were demolished and a further eight seriously damaged in Newington Road when two bombs fell from another unidentified aircraft. Blast damage affected more than one hundred properties. Casualties recorded – two slightly injured.

Monday 11 November
MONKTON 12.20 – HURRICANE CRASHES

A Hurricane fighter belonging to No. 17 Squadron based at Martlesham was shot down while the squadron was attacking Junkers 87s (Stuka) over a convoy off Ramsgate. The Hurricane, with Sgt. R.D. Hogg still in the cockpit, crashed into the road opposite the church. Sgt. Hogg had already been credited with three enemy aircraft shot down.

RAMSGATE 13.15 – HEs

There was strong enemy activity in the Thanet area with fighter sweeps heading towards London. In the Thames Estuary ships were being herded into convoys. Tankers, cargo ships and tugs, stretched along the Sheppey coast towards the North Foreland. Ack-ack guns were heard letting off a few rounds at intervals, but most of the early morning sorties seemed to be of a reconnaissance nature and were usually flown above 15,000 ft.

At lunch-time, when people were beginning to appear out of their shelters, three Messerschmitt fighter-bombers suddenly dived out of low cloud. Their 500-kg bombs fell in Beresford Road, Portland Court and Irchester Street. Seven houses were blown to pieces in just one minute, a further seven were seriously damaged and eight hundred suffered slight damage. The Municipal Offices, Public Library, ARP headquarters, Police Station and the Old Fire Station were on the damaged lists. The mayor, A.B.C. Kempe, and his clerk, Miss Christine Cook, were blown down the shelter steps. Except for their pride they were otherwise unhurt. Thirty-six-year-old Miss Annie Verrion, standing at the bus stop outside the Municipal Offices, threw herself down when the bombs were falling. She was seriously injured by the blast and died of her wounds two days later. A total of eight people were injured.

Tuesday 12 November
RAMSGATE 16.45 – HEs

Eyewitness accounts suggest a single Junkers 88 bomber was responsible for dropping a couple of bombs when no siren had sounded. The south-west corner of the Granville Hotel was shattered by one very large bomb. Others fell on the Post Office garage, near Bellevue Cottages and Sussex Street. Eight houses and one garage were destroyed, fifteen houses seriously damaged and a further two hundred and fifty slightly damaged. It was at No. 22 Sussex Street that a couple lost their lives in tragic circumstances. After the all clear had sounded, Mr and Mrs Stredwick, who had been sheltering in the tunnel nearby, returned to their home. It received a direct hit. In the same street two sisters were sitting in their basement room when part of the house collapsed on them. Neither was injured.

Wednesday 13 November
BROADSTAIRS 03.00 – HEs & OIL BOMB (UXB)

In the early hours an oil bomb was dropped on open ground near

Broadstairs Road. It was about three feet long and was marked FLAM.C.5001940. It failed to detonate and provided an opportunity for the local policeman to write the details down in his little black book. A high-explosive bomb fell at the Eastern Esplanade and another blew a huge crater close to the railway station. Damage slight – casualties nil.

Thursday 14 November
MARGATE 14.25 – HEx & UXBs

The sting associated with enemy action was missing in a report in the *Isle of Thanet Gazette* on Friday 15 November. It began:

> There were only a dozen casualties, most of them of a minor nature, when a number of Messerschmitt 109s released about twenty bombs on a south-east town yesterday [Thursday] afternoon, but one proved fatal.

Journalists were becoming complacent, after all, it was just another 'tip-and-run' raid. They, like the townspeople, were getting quite used to the bombs, the crack of ack-ack guns, the sight of row upon row of terraced houses without roofs or windows, and watching the rescue teams sift through tons of rubble to reach those victims buried beneath. If an actual raid did not take place there was the steady drone of enemy aero-engines overhead.

In this particular instance twenty-three bombs were released by the Messerschmitts in as many seconds. Before the anti-aircraft gunners could bring their weapons to bear on a target the raiders had gone, leaving behind them devastation and carnage. Four houses were demolished ten houses, six shops and one public house were seriously damaged. Major damage occurred at one school, a hotel and a warden's post. 'The damage was not extensive having regard to the number of bombs', wrote one journalist.

Five people who had heard the whistle of falling bombs were huddled together in a small passage in a basement at No. 1 Clifton Gardens. The building received a direct hit. Everyone was trapped. A couple of workmen nearby picked themselves up and ran to the house. Before the rescue teams had arrived, they had already found fifty-nine-year-old Louisa Kingsley's body in the rubble. Mr and Mrs Stokes, and their two children, Gladys aged fourteen and Nellie aged ten were found, all suffering from superficial injuries.

A report for this raid on 14 November states, 'There were only a dozen casualties, most of them of a minor nature . . . but one proved fatal.' 'Romany' in Hartsdown Road, Margate, collapsed like a pack of cards when a 250-kg bomb was released from a Messerschmitt fighter-bomber just after 13.00.

The back of Marine Gardens towers above the Empire Garage in Eaton Road, where a bomb wrecked the premises and Auxiliary Fireman Holt was injured on 14 November 1940.

It was not until the autumn of 1941 that the steel Morrison shelter was introduced to protect families who refused to leave their homes. At No. 1 Clifton Gardens, five people were sheltering in the basement when it received a direct hit. Mrs Louisa Kingsley was the only fatality on 14 November.

The new Catholic School, Salmestone Grange, received a direct hit, and when another bomb exploded at the rear of Empire Garages, Auxiliary Fireman Holt was injured. But Mrs Halliday and her daughter Patricia Holness had the most remarkable escape. A bomb went careering through the roof and top floor of the house next door, then passed through the dividing wall and ended up unexploded in a cupboard under the stairs at Romany, Hartsdown Road. Total casualties were one dead, five seriously injured and thirteen slightly injured.

While rescue teams worked among the ruins, the convoy 'Booty' was attacked off North Foreland. Two Stuka dive-bombers were shot down and each sank with a crew member inside. Two others were picked up by a naval torpedo boat.

One of the Messerschmitts which had attacked Margate succumbed to the guns of a couple of Hurricanes. The fighter crashed in flames at Sacketts Hill Farm, St Peter's and the charred remains of *Flgr.* E. Vortbach were later recovered from the wreckage. One report says the pilot had been shot in the head. He was buried at St Peter's churchyard a week later, the Revd D. de Meredith of St Andrew's Church, conducted the service.

In the evening of 14 November *Luftwaffe* formations unleashed their heaviest raid of the war upon the city of Coventry. Hundreds of bombs and incendiaries devastated large areas causing a huge loss of life.

Saturday 16 November
MARGATE 10.04 – HEs

A single Junkers JU87 Stuka dive-bomber released two heavy calibre bombs on St James Park Road, Garlinge and although the target was the railway line, six houses were demolished and a further twenty-three suffered damage. Fortunately, only two of the houses were occupied, but in them were four people, two of whom lost their lives.

Commendable coolness was shown by a fourteen-year-old baker's roundsman. Robert Clifford was delivering bread and had just left the front door of a house called Edwyn, occupied by Mr and Mrs Wooderson, when he heard the Stuka diving. His employer, Clifford Barnes, was on the opposite side of the road. Barnes shouted a warning. Mrs Wooderson went inside and closed her front door. Robert ran across the road to the baker's van. He and Mr Barnes climbed in. There was a terrific explosion. The van was showered with bricks and masonry which almost filled the vehicle when the roof was blown off. Covered with dust and debris the two managed to scramble out with just a few cuts and bruises.

Thirty-five-year-old Winifred Wooderson waved goodbye to the baker's roundsman and closed the front door of Edwyn in St James Park Avenue. She never reached the kitchen. Two heavy calibre bombs were dropped by a Junkers 87 Stuka and Edwyn disappeared, as did five other semi-detached houses on 16 November 1940.

A huge cloud of dust and smoke hovered over the area. When the dust cloud settled they were confronted by a scene of devastation that would have passed for a film sequence in H.G. Wells' *War of The Worlds*. Where just moments before there were six houses, there were now just six heaps of rubble. They walked towards the wreckage as if in a dream. They could not believe their own eyes. Bewildered by what they saw they stood at the kerbside. Robert heard a cry for help which came from a pile of bricks that a few moments before had been the house Edwyn. Seconds later he was digging his way through the rubble. Trapped beside an overturned gas stove, which had no doubt prevented him from being crushed, they found Mr Wooderson, clutching in his arms his three-year-old daughter. The child was passed through a hole made by Robert and his employer, and Edward Wooderson crawled through shortly afterwards, suffering from slight abrasions and shock. Rescue teams arrived and were helped by soldiers to move the rubble piece by piece, in their search for thirty-five-year-old Winifred Wooderson. An hour passed before they found her. Faint signs of life were detected, but she died on arrival at hospital.

At what was left of San Pan, the house next door, sixty-five-year-old Blanche Lamb was found too late. She had died of multiple injuries. John Lamb, Blanche's husband, a retired coastguard, had been at the back door when the explosion occurred. He was blown down the garden path and only received a cut hand.

Adjoining houses and those on the opposite side of the road sustained heavy blast damage. Twenty-three-year-old Louise Wood, delivering meat in the road, was blown several yards into a passage between two houses. Her meat basket was filled with mortar and dust, but she miraculously escaped injury.

Monday 18 November
RAMSGATE 13.35 – HEs

The town's gas supply was seriously disrupted when a sneak fighter-bomber attack fractured the mains at six separate points. Bombs were jettisoned in the East Cliff district where one house was demolished and twenty badly damaged. Casualties totalled five injured.

Wednesday 20 November
MARGATE 12.55 – HEs & UXBs

Although six bombs were dropped by a Dornier 17 bomber, harassed by our fighters, there were only two casualties. The raider came in from the direction of the Channel and jettisoned its complete bomb load in a line less than half a mile inland from the shore – from St Paul's Road to Omer Avenue. The alert had not sounded and people watched the Dornier being chased by two Spitfires. An extension to Clifton Church Hall, built just two years before, received a direct hit by a 50-kg bomb which blew out the doors and windows and wrecked the roof. Only the day before the building had opened as a YMCA hostel, but at the time of the incident just two people were inside. Half an hour before there had been half a dozen workmen having a cup of tea in the corner of the hall where the bomb struck.

'I had only been in the premises about two minutes, and was in the ante-room, when I heard the zooming,' Mr Avery, the treasurer recalled afterwards. 'I backed against a wall and everything seemed to fall in on top of me. The door blew in and a sheet of glass about five feet by eighteen inches fell in front of me.' Mrs Wilson, the caretaker, was washing up in the kitchen. Six oil stoves were knocked over in the blast and although paraffin spilled out of them they did not catch alight.

Thursday 21 November
BROADSTAIRS 01.10 – HEs

There was slight damage to property when twelve high-explosive bombs fell in the Dumpton Gap area. They were thought to have been released by a returning bomber. Casualties nil.

★ ★ ★

The Mayor Making Day at Margate's Town Hall was marked by the disclosure by the new Mayor, Alderman George P. Hoare, that local government change would probably include a united Thanet. His prediction was realized soon after the war. The mayoress began her term of office by becoming the head of the town's Women's Voluntary Service, an organization which had eluded the town until now.

Her burning ambition was to rally the women of Margate to do useful work under the banner of the WVS. In the first week of its existence nearly one hundred women had enrolled for the various activities such as knitting, needlework, store-keeping, canteen and clerical work. Their headquarters was at the Royal School, Victoria Road, where there were offices, bedrooms and dormitories intended for use of the homeless. Perhaps the most important work was the creation of a body of partially trained women in each warden sector who were to assist in looking after the elderly or crippled, those suffering from minor injuries, and the people made temporarily homeless.

The Mayoress was soon asking questions of the council regarding the increase of schoolchildren in the town. It had been estimated that four hundred were now running about the streets without any chance of going to school. It was suggested that they either opened some schools or made evacuation compulsory.

Sunday 24 November

Minelaying in the Thames Estuary was almost a daily occurrence. In the Barrow Deep area of the estuary the cargo ship *Alice Maria* loaded with coal, and the naval trawler *Amethyst* were both sunk by mines, and before long another cargo ship, the *Ryal* struck a mine. Nine of her crew lost their lives.

Wednesday 27 November
RAF MANSTON 15.45 – MESSERSCHMITT CRASHES

Following a combat with our fighters over Thanet a severely damaged fighter-bomber made a forced landing at the airfield. The pilot *Lt.* W. Teumer, was taken prisoner unhurt and his aircraft was eventually repaired by the RAF and flown by our Enemy Aircraft Flight with the designated number DG200. This particular Messerschmitt can now be seen at the Royal Air Force Museum at Hendon.

Friday 29 November
RAMSGATE 15.37 – HEs

The gun emplacement at the East Cliff came in for special treatment when the *Luftwaffe* attacked it with Messerschmitt bombers. Thirteen bombs were plotted on the eastern foreshore near Brockenhurst Road, and one of the raiders was brought down in the sea with the loss of both crew members. Damage was caused to the Promenade and six houses suffered slight damage.

Saturday 30 November

The naval trawler *Chestnut* was sunk by a mine off the North Foreland.

★ ★ ★

Unique to the history of local government was an unforeseeable problem relating to the Ramsgate tunnel system. When they were first conceived and designed it was to provide the townspeople with an absolutely safe refuge from enemy air attack. But such immunity from the attentions of German aircraft resulted in the transformation of the safe haven from shelters into a permanent refuge. It was reported in local newspapers that the townspeople were rapidly becoming troglodytes.

People, unable to find or provide for themselves a suitable refuge, began to spend nights underground on council deck chairs. Before many weeks had passed the 'tunnel bed' had arrived, some of them ingeniously constructed from bits of wood and made into a sort of home-made folding couch. Others were cunningly contrived from available deck chairs and transformed into the most elaborate camp beds.

More and more people for one reason or another chose to spend long hours of darkness in the tunnels and their make-shift beds gave way to the ordinary sprung bedsteads. So there began in Ramsgate's troglodyte city a sort of unwritten law which recognized the sanctity of each 'pitch', where whole families and groups of friends came to look upon sections of the tunnel as their own particular property. Eventually the problem of cooking was overcome by the installation of small oil stoves, and old-fashioned oil lamps supplemented the meagre lighting system. When the desire for privacy began to assert itself, family pitches were screened from neighbouring groups by hessian partitions. In some cases quite elaborate structures had blossomed into two and three bedroomed apartments. In this unfamiliar world of semi-darkness, hundreds of men, women and children lived in some degree of comfort, assured of complete safety. The authorities, however, were not content with the situation and, while they had no wish to disturb the tunnel dwellers, they were asked to consider such problems as sanitation and hygiene. Not the least of the town's concerns was the welfare of the children. The danger of fire in the tunnels had not been considered by the troglodytes.

When His Royal Highness the Duke of Kent, paid a visit to Thanet to inspect the coastal defences, the Ramsgate tunnels were cleared for his inspection. After seeing much of the war damage in the town, he was visibly impressed with troglodyte city.

This German *Luftmine* failed to explode when it drifted on to the Cliftonville School playing fields on 13 December 1940. PC Bridgeland of the Margate Borough Police, was most concerned when Captain Hopkins, RN, billeted at Second Avenue Cliftonville, arrived on the scene and poked the mine with a walking stick!

By the KING'S Order the name of

Herbert Reginald Evans,
Leading Fireman,
Margate Auxiliary Fire Service,

was published in the 'London Gazette on

13th December 1940,

as commended for brave conduct in
Civil Defence.
I am charged to record His Majesty's
high appreciation of the service rendered.

Prime Minister and First Lord
of the Treasury

Thursday 5 December
RAMSGATE 07.42 – HEs

Eight high-explosive bombs were plotted falling in the sea off East Cliff. One document suggests they may have been long-range shells fired from the Cap Gris Nez area, but this has not been confirmed. Damage nil – casualties nil.

Sunday 29 December
RAMSGATE 15.03 – HEs

As far as Ramsgate was concerned this was the last air raid of 1940. Two high-explosive bombs fell near the railway station, and caused serious damage to over thirty-six houses. One happy point, outlined by the mayor, was that there were no casualties.

MARGATE 16.12 – HEs & IBs

Whether a German bomber found itself in difficulties over the town may never be known, but it dropped its complete load of missiles; eight high-explosive bombs and a canister of incendiaries. The districts affected were Northdown Road, Warwick Road, Wyndham Avenue, Laleham Gardens, Northdown Hill, Montrose School Grounds, First Avenue and Walpole Road. Damage was quite serious to many houses but there were no casualties.

Tuesday 31 December
MARGATE 15.05 – TRAIN MACHINE-GUNNED

The 12.55 train from Victoria station, London, was attacked on the Reculver Marshes. Casualties – one seriously injured, one slightly injured. William Debling of Ramsgate, was shot through the mouth.

CHAPTER THREE

1941

They Heard the Sound of a Baby Crying

Thursday 2 January
BROADSTAIRS 12.41 – HEs

Wellesley House, an evacuated private school, was damaged when two high-explosive bombs fell in the grounds at midday. Blast damage affected a wide area but there were no casualties reported.

Saturday 4 January
RAMSGATE 14.40 – HEs

Weather conditions had deteriorated in south-east England. There was a cold east wind blowing accompanied by snow flurries, and the whole of Thanet looked bleak and uninviting. German air activity during the daylight hours was intermittent and largely confined to reconnaissance patrols and attacks on shipping. But Ramsgate was to receive a severe bombing attack, even before the alert had sounded.

Townspeople were about their daily business when a single Junkers 88 bomber dived out of low cloud. PC Coughlan, on duty in the Market Square, saw the raider making its approach and blew his whistle for all he was worth. His prompt action sent shoppers scurrying for shelter. Three shops including Woolworths, received direct hits. It was perhaps fortunate, that the bomb which struck Woolworths, actually exploded on the top floor and at the rear of the building. Casualties would have risen alarmingly had it exploded near the front and at ground level. A grocery store in the main street belonging to Messrs Saunders also received a direct hit. It was next to Dewhurst the butchers, where shop assistants ran into the large, cabinet refrigerator. Nineteen-year-old Edna Honess, a grocery store assistant, ran into the butcher's shop for safety. She was met at the door by the manager Albert Dennis. They had almost reached the cabinet refrigerator when the bomb exploded. The massive door crushed Edna, and Albert was buried beneath the rubble. Rescuers later pulled him from the wreckage, but he died in hospital that same night.

The Police station, Ambulance station and the ARP offices, were all seriously damaged. Elizabeth Hougham, out shopping with her seven-year-old son Norman, ran into a nearby yard when she heard the commotion. Three bombs exploded near them. Norman was killed instantly and Elizabeth was eventually taken to hospital with serious injuries. Mrs Clara Kay was just walking past the ruins of the former Messrs Vye's premises, in Queen Street, when a bomb exploded on it. She was killed. The Chief Constable of Ramsgate, S.F. Butler, was among those injured when the police station was all but wrecked, and he was unable to return to duty for a month. Casualties totalled twelve seriously injured and eight slightly injured. Among those injured was twelve-year-old Derek Smith, who was trapped for twenty minutes under a house which had been partially demolished. Covered with blood and dirt, and his legs firmly pinned together by crushing forces, he kept saying to his rescuers, 'I'm all right, I'm all right!' They eventually released him by sawing through dozens of wooden joists.

People who had rushed to the scene of destruction were amazed to find an off-duty policeman, wearing only a singlet and trousers, with a toothbrush clenched firmly in one hand, standing on what was left of the upstairs landing where the front of the house had been torn away.

Sunday 5 January
BROADSTAIRS 21.30 – HEs

One document records six high-explosive bombs falling at Buddle's Farm area, where slight damage occurred. There were no casualties reported but a number of chickens died.

MAYOR'S APPEAL
TO PARENTS OF ALL CHILDREN OF
SCHOOL AGE IN MARGATE

The recent census which was taken of the number of children in the Borough gives me much concern, not only because of the possible intensification of enemy action in the air and the danger of threatened invasion, but more particularly because of the children themselves.

Margate is a 'DEFENCE AREA'. The possibilities of what can happen in the spring with such large numbers of children in our midst is an alarming outlook. Parents who from selfish motives have refused to allow their children to proceed to our Educational Centre are penalising them to an extent that may react in after years in a very serious manner.

Can you visualise the effect which the lack of education will have on the children if perchance the war continues over a lengthy period of years?

This is a serious matter and one that is causing much concern to me. I am constantly receiving reports from Staffordshire of the happiness of the pupils and of the progress they are making in their studies. Are you doing your duty as parents by depriving your children of the enjoyment and benefits of the educational facilities which are readily being granted?

It will be my privilege in the early weeks of February to visit Staffordshire in company with the Mayoress so that I can pay my tribute, on behalf of the people of Margate, to all those who are so loyally looking after the welfare of the children.

Will you help at once by registering your children to take up their studies when schools reopen. Call at the Town Clerk's Office. It is your duty. Please respond. I appeal to you.

G.P. Hoare – Mayor, Town Hall, Margate
7 January 1941

Friday 10 January
MARGATE 08.15 – IBs & UXBs

As enemy aircraft, flying at a high altitude, returned towards France, some of them released their bomb loads over St Nicholas, Birchington, Margate and Cliftonville. There was a mixture of oil bombs and incendiaries. Over twenty-five incendiaries were counted over the railway track on the marshes, and another forty were discovered at Coldharbour. Some of the incendiary canisters failed to open when released and had burst open only when they hit the ground. Missiles were scattered all over the area but did not ignite. One high-explosive bomb fell at No. 32 Cliftonville Avenue, but failed to explode. There were no casualties and very little damage was reported. One oil bomb failed to detonate at Dumpton Gap.

Saturday 11 January
RAMSGATE 13.55 – HEs

Two Messerschmitt fighter-bombers made their appearance before the alert signal was sounded. One 500-kg bomb fell at Ellington Park and threw up tons of earth. Fifty-one-year-old Olive Walls heard the commotion and both she, and her fifteen-year-old son, ran down the garden to the shelter at No. 80 Manston Road. Unfortunately the next bomb beat them to it. They were both killed in the explosion which seriously damaged four houses and slightly damaged a further fifty-three.

RAF MANSTON 16.10 – HEs

Messerschmitt fighters sneaked in to drop bombs on the airfield. Damage was estimated as slight and there were no casualties.

Monday 13 January
BROADSTAIRS 01.00 – HEs

Two high-explosive bombs exploded on open land during the night. Damage nil – casualties nil. Although searchlights were sweeping the night sky no aircraft was seen in the immediate vicinity and the ack-ack guns remained silent. It was suggested that the explosions were caused by unexploded bombs which detonated.

Wednesday 15 January
RAMSGATE 23.59 – HEs

Eight high-explosive bombs were dropped on the town close to midnight. It was a cold, frosty night when the bombs fell in Boundary Road, the High Street, Chapel Place, Elms Avenue and Beresford Road, seriously damaging twenty houses, twelve shops, two garages and partly demolishing St Mary's Church. The alms houses were damaged and also the Council Offices. Other bombs damaged houses in Upper Dumpton Park Road and exploded in the Chatham House grounds. Mrs Suzanne Flowerden was the only casualty when her house was all but destroyed at No. 125 High Street. She was taken to hospital suffering from severe shock.

Saturday 18 January
RAMSGATE

The Kent War Diary has no entry for this incident which is recorded elsewhere as one high-explosive bomb in the grounds of the Convent of the Daughters of the Cross, High Street. There were no casualties. The drill hall of the old 234th Battery, RA, was partially wrecked. Due to deplorable weather conditions, only a few reconnaissance sorties were operated by the *Luftwaffe*. Snow covered most of the country.

Sunday 19 January
RAMSGATE 01.41 – HEs

The old drill hall, mentioned in the previous day's incident, is recorded in the War Diary as demolished on this day, with five houses listed seriously damaged, and no casualties. Although the *Luftwaffe* operated shipping attacks during the day around our coasts, and bombed London and Southampton at night, no Thanet town gets a mention in other documents. It is probable that the explosion which wrecked the drill hall was a delayed action bomb, which had lain undiscovered since the attack on the 15th.

BROADSTAIRS

An unexploded bomb was discovered 40 yd west of the coastguard's hut at Joss Bay.

Wednesday 22 January
MARGATE 08.10 – HEs & UXBs

Although the Kent War Diary lists ten high-explosive bombs falling on Margate for this day, the Home Security summary states 'There were no reports of bombs anywhere in the British Isles.' Damage was slight – casualties nil.

Tuesday 28 January
MINSTER 13.30 – HEs & IBs

Over forty incendiaries were dropped near Marsh Farm and seven bombs fell on Golstone Marshes. There were no casualties or damage to property.

MARGATE 14.05 – HEs

Four bombs fell at Street Court, Westgate, to where the RAF had moved when they evacuated Manston. Street Court was known as 'Z' Point, where the infants' school had been taken over, and the Officers' Mess occupied a large house on the opposite side of the road. The Lodge which stood at the main gates was completely demolished. Rumours circulated among the RAF personnel that a Fifth Columnist was responsible for the attack. The secrecy surrounding service casualties remains to this day. There were no known civilian casualties. The aircraft responsible was recorded as a Junkers 88.

Monday 3 February
BROADSTAIRS 09.34 – HEs

Stuka dive-bombers attacked shipping off the coast and sunk a naval patrol vessel, and damaged HM trawler *Arctic Trapper*, a former Grimsby boat, built for the Iceland fishing grounds. She sank eventually in shallow water close to the shore. A memorial service was given on Sunday 16th, and was dedicated to the men who had lost their lives in the attack.

RAMSGATE 09.40 – HEs

Four bombs fell in Hardres Street and Broad Street, and one other of a large calibre, buried itself in a road without detonating. It was not made safe until a week later. Fifty-two-year-old Alice Oates and her friend thirty-two-year-old Lottie Pritchard were both killed when a bomb struck No. 5 Hardres Street. The same bomb wrecked the Wesleyan church, and seriously damaged the new telephone exchange. Six houses were badly damaged and a further fifty-eight were slightly damaged. Several people received injuries. Four bombs fell harmlessly in Pegwell Bay.

Wednesday 5 February
RAMSGATE

The wreck of the *Arctic Trapper* was once again bombed as it lay in shallow water about 300 yd from the shore. The 641-ton trawler *Tourmaline*, standing off the North Foreland, also came under attack and was eventually sunk.

Many people watched the demise of one of the attacking Stukas which was fired upon by a Spitfire of 92 Squadron. The machine was set alight and crashed rather spectacularly at Cheeseman's Farm, Minster. Both crew members died in the crash.

Ten high-explosive bombs were plotted at Cliffs End, but there were no reported casualties, although several bungalows received damage.

MARGATE 20.45 – HEs & IBs

A lone Junkers 88 dropped a flare, then made its attacking run on Cliftonville with bombs and incendiaries. They spread over Leicester Avenue, Gloucester Avenue, Avenue Gardens, Northumberland Avenue, Omer Avenue, Cornwall Gardens and Devonshire Gardens.

The recent fire prevention measures taken by Margate were put to the test when several small fires were started over a very wide area. So rapidly and efficiently were the incendiary bombs dealt with that many residents were quite unaware that any had been dropped until next morning.

One fire started at an empty hotel, which perhaps was the most serious, because it was some time before it was discovered. A cluster of small high-explosive bombs fell along the promenade and foreshore, and a further batch fell on open ground. Householders and soldiers helped the wardens, policemen and firemen to smother the fizzling missiles with the recently distributed sandbags, which had been placed round the town as part of the fire precautions. Despite the frantic activity there were no casualties reported.

Saturday 8 February
BROADSTAIRS 17.05 – HEs

A south-bound convoy was attacked off the North Foreland. Hooters, whistles and sirens went off in rapid succession, but the German aircraft remained over the convoy.

Wednesday 12 February
RAMSGATE 12.35 – SHELLING

This was the first occasion when German long-range shells actually reached Thanet, after being fired from the French coast. A ranging shot fell in the harbour, but the next shell wrecked the bungalow called Shanghai Lodge in Whitehall Road, where Mr and Mrs Cullen, and Mr and Mrs Lewis, were having their midday meal at the rear of the building. The front was completely blown out. Another shell exploded close to No. 21 Wilfred Road. Although six buildings were reported damaged and a further seventeen slightly damaged, there were no casualties recorded. A German official news agency reported that '. . . important military objectives were shelled.'

Saturday 15 February
MARGATE 19.50 – HEs

Four plumes of spray were plotted in the sea off Margate, but as there was no alert in operation at the time and no aircraft was heard in the vicinity, it was later suggested that the plumes of spray might have been caused by shells.

★ ★ ★

In response to the continued appeals of local authorities over seventy children left Margate for the evacuation area during the month. They were conveyed in special coaches which took them from one terminus to the other; meals were provided on the journey. The town clerk, Mr P.T. Grove, later received a telegram announcing their arrival.

But the authorities felt that this number was an unsatisfactory response to their appeal. It was regretted that the parents of the 750 schoolchildren who remained in the borough had not thought fit to send their children away to what was considered a comparatively safe area. It was further suggested that those parents would have no cause to regret their decision.

Saturday 22 February
RAF MANSTON 12.30 – HEs & UXBs

A strong formation of Messerschmitt fighter-bombers swept in to release their bombs and machine-gun the aerodrome. One airman was killed while he ran for shelter. The decontamination centre and the sick bay were both damaged. Bombs also fell wide of their mark and exploded near Minster.

MARGATE 12.33 – HEs

The original fighter-bomber formation had split into two separate groups, one reaching Manston while the other scattered eleven 500-kg bombs near Margate. No futher information available.

Saturday 1 March
MARGATE 05.35 – HEs

The 'tip-and-run' type of raid was increasing along the Kent coast. The Messerschmitts penetrated our defence systems before the radar could spot them by flying low over the sea. It became almost routine for alert warnings to be a few minutes late. In some instances the sirens never sounded at all. Five high-explosive bombs fell on Millmead Road and Northdown Way, where at the latter, The Yet was extensively damaged.

Sunday 2 March
MARGATE 21.45 – HEs & UXBs

The twenty or so high-explosive bombs which fell on the golf course and into the sea, were thought to have been dropped by a returning bomber. High density cloud stopped the searchlights from finding their quarry.

Monday 3 March
RAMSGATE 17.10 – HEs

Improved weather conditions increased enemy activity, and a large formation of Messerschmitt fighter-bombers headed towards Thanet. One section flew inland to attack RAF Manston, while the other jettisoned their bombs over the town. The council estate at Whitehall was the recipient of many high-explosives and so were Bradley Road, Newington Road, and the grounds of St Lawrence College. There were three fatalities: Arthur Impett, James Woodcock and E.A. Davey.

Impett and Woodcock were both agricultural workers and were on their way home from the fields in the back of a lorry when the attack began. The driver quickly drove the lorry into the nearest field where everyone got out. They lay on the ground beside the vehicle but a bomb exploded quite close to them, killing Woodcock immediately, and so seriously injuring Impett that he died while being taken to hospital. Davey was employed at RAF Manston and was killed by another bomb explosion. In a greengrocer's shop belonging to a Mr G. Carson, were three women customers, one of whom had with her a baby in a pram. When the bombs were heard falling Carson pushed the pram into a far corner of the shop. A bomb exploded nearby and sent the shop window into a thousand pieces. Florence Rose was the only one hurt and was taken to hospital for treatment.

At an adjoining shop two women and a girl, owed their lives to the prompt action of the proprietor Mr Rogers. He sent them rushing into his garden shelter just as the shop collapsed. The heavy chimney stack landed on top of the Anderson and the area around it was completely covered with bricks and rubble. All four occupants eventually clambered out quite unscathed.

RAF Manston 17.10 – HEs

About a dozen bombs fell on the aerodrome but as the ack–ack defences threw up so many shells in the path of the raiders many bombs fell wide of their target. A number were plotted at Gray's Hole, Philpott's Field, Foster's Folly, Grove Farm, Chapel Farm, Haine Brickfields and Manston Court. RAF casualties are not known.

Saturday 8 March
Broadstairs 23.09 – HRs, IBs & UXB

Although six bombs and over one hundred incendiaries were scattered over a wide area they were all located in open ground on the outskirts of the town. But one especially heavy bomb, probably a 1000-kg, buried itself in the ground near the Links Hotel, Reading Street, but failed to explode. A large number of small fires were started by the incendiaries, but a laundry was the only building extensively damaged.

The burning incendiaries were promptly pounced upon by the AFS crews, policemen and wardens, and were extinguished in rapid succession. But the whole episode was described by one warden as '. . . a nice bit of fun'. He was the Revd Donald de Meredith who, with another warden, each extinguished about twenty missiles within the space of a few minutes. 'It was the best picnic we've had for weeks,' he said, '. . . we've been out here night after night on duty and have had nothing to do.' He went on, 'We saw the incendiaries glowing so we jumped on our bikes and went to find them. We just pulled them out of hedges – pushed them into the ground and stood on them!' There were no casualties reported.

★ ★ ★

The *East Kent Times* ran the following article in its 8 March issue:

CHILDREN AT WAR

The minds of local authorities, on the south-eastern coast of England are much exercised as to the position of children of school age during the present period. In spite of repeated appeals, there are many parents who have either neglected to send their children away to a place of comparative safety, or having sent them away, have now brought them back again.

The result is, that the towns which are subjected to the most direct attacks by the enemy are literally swarming with youngsters who, not being subjected to any form of education are running wild. Moreover, they are living under conditions which cannot be but detrimental to them, both physically and mentally. The numbers are staggering. It is estimated that at Ramsgate there are about 680 such children. Recently Alderman W.C. Redman, Chairman of the Margate Education Committee, said that there were about 700 children still remaining in that town while at Dover the number is put at about 1,000. None of the authorities has been blind to the situation, and from time to time representations have been made to various government departments regarding the problem.

Sunday 9 March
RAF MANSTON 07.25 – HEs & UXBs

The aerodrome, after its devastating raids of the year before, was now operating as a forward striking base from which squadrons based further inland, arrived to be refuelled and pilots briefed before operating against targets on the Continent. It was because of these 'intruder' operations that Manston was being singled-out for sharp, fighter-bomber attacks.

Minster, Acol and Monkton were the recipients of scattered bombs released during these airfield attacks. On this day there were over thirty bombs dropped over a wide area, three of them failed to explode, one of which was plotted in the rural area of Margate.

Friday 14 March
RAMSGATE 00.40 – HEs

Searchlights stabbed the night sky looking for enemy bombers which were flying inland to their targets. Whether the pilot of one aircraft was hoping to hit them with his bomb load will never be known. Nevertheless, eight high-explosive bombs fell between Ramsgate and Minster. Margate Road received the most damage where four houses suffered severely and a further thirty received slight damage. Three people were treated for shock.

Tuesday 18 March
MARGATE 07.15 – HEs & UXBs

No one saw or heard the aircraft which dropped a couple of bombs early in the morning. One of them fell at Hartsdown Park, killing two sheep, while the other buried itself in a field at Twenties Farm, Shottendane, and failed to explode. Henry Willis was rolling the field in readiness for planting. Quite undisturbed at the thought of an unexploded bomb in the field he carried on rolling as if nothing had happened. 'I heard the whistle of the bomb and then saw the crater about twenty-five yards away', he said, 'I just went on rolling as otherwise this year's crop will be late.'

RAMSGATE 07.17 – HEs

Another bomb, thought to have been jettisoned by the same unknown aircraft, fell at the top end of Winstanley Crescent, burying Alfred Wood, an ARP Warden, and his wife Jessie. Both were seriously injured. Seventeen-year-old Vera Gardner was sleeping in a upstairs room when a wall collapsed and the ceiling fell on her. She emerged unscathed. Her grandmother, Jessie White, who was in the kitchen, was injured and taken to hospital for treatment. Mrs Johnstone, who was in bed next door, pulled the bedclothes over her head as the ceiling fell on top of her. She managed to crawl out unhurt, but was extremely upset when she later found all her clothes riddled with splinters. Thirteen houses were damaged.

Wednesday 19 March
BIRCHINGTON 01.25 – HEs

Three bombs were plotted falling in a direct line from Plum Pudding

Damaged houses in Winstanley Crescent, Ramsgate, being repaired after a high-explosive bomb wrecked them on 18 March 1941.

The high-calibre bomb which fell in Rutland Gardens on 19 March 1941 wrecked this quality residence. The only casualty was a mouse.

Island to Great Brooks End Farm. There were no reports of casualties or damage to property.

MARGATE 04.55 – HEs

A single bomb exploded at Rutland Gardens where one house was partially demolished and a further twelve seriously damaged. Mr Joseph Fusco, his wife and a family friend, Miss Oclee, who had already been bombed out of her own home, were all sleeping in the rear of their house. The only casualty was a mouse which was later found dead with a piece of glass in its side. Mr Fusco recalled, 'We were asleep at the time and the explosion threw me up in the air. I hit my head on the ceiling then rebounded back on to the bed. I had a mouthful of plaster, and when my wife asked me if I was all right, I could not reply. She thought I was dead!' Miss Oclee thought the house had caught fire but it was a gas main out in the road.

Thursday 20 March
RAMSGATE 11.00 – HEs

Severe damage was caused in Addington Street and Adelaide Gardens, when bombs fell on the area. Six houses are listed as being demolished, a further twelve seriously damaged and eight slightly damaged.

Two Messerschmitt fighter-bombers made a lightning attack – the usual 'tip-and-run' type of raid. They appeared suddenly out of low cloud, dropped their bombs, and were gone before the ack-ack could bring their guns to bear on a target. More tragic accidents occurred when civilians were subjected to heartless bombing by *Luftwaffe* pilots who knew there were no military targets in the area.

Mr and Mrs George Crompton, at No. 63 Addington Street, were sitting quietly at home, unaware that their lives were in any danger. Their home suddenly collapsed when it received a direct hit. As the house fell apart the Cromptons were shunted into the basement with the debris and buried. Rescuers were doubtful that anyone could have survived, but they moved with the greatest precision amidst the rubble – painstakingly picking away the bricks, lumps of plaster and shattered timber until, at last, they were able to locate the area where the victims lay.

Buried deep in the wreckage the Cromptons were oblivious to the frenzied activities going on above them. Forty-six-year-old Mrs Crompton was found first two hours later. Still conscious she was able to direct the rescue team to where she believed her husband to be. Another two hours passed before they found George. He had died.

Mrs Woodfield had left to go shopping, leaving her sixty-two-year-old husband Bernard working in his printing shop at No. 69 Addington Street. When the raid started she took shelter. She returned home to find the house in ruins. Rescuers faced the terrible frustration of locating the victim and then being unable to get close enough to save his life. Escaping gas was always a serious problem, and water mains often filled basements before they could be turned off. They eventually found Bernard three hours later; he also had died.

Alfred Moyes and his friend George Smith, had been gardening at No. 8 Prospect Terrace, when they heard the first bomb explode. They ran into a shed and the next bomb struck the back of the house before exploding in the back garden. The rescuers were unaware if anyone was under the rubble. Then someone found Alf's jacket, still hanging on some railings. In one of the pockets they found his identity card. His lifeless body was pulled from the debris two hours later. George Smith was found with just a broken arm.

When No. 63 Addington Street, Ramsgate, collapsed on 20 March 1941, Mr and Mrs Crompton suddenly found themselves buried deep under rubble in the basement of their house.

At No. 69 Addington Street, Ramsgate, on 20 March 1941, Mrs Woodfield went out shopping, leaving her husband working in his printing shop. On her return she found the house in ruins. Rescuers found her husband Bernard dead three hours later.

On Thursday 20 March 1941 Alfred Moyes had been doing a spot of gardening at No. 8 Prospect Terrace. Rescuers, unaware if anyone was in the rubble, found Alf's jacket hanging on a post. His lifeless body was found two hours later.

Tuesday 8 April
MARGATE 12.55 – MACHINE-GUNNED

Pocock and Richards wondered why they were being singled out for target practice when their fishing boat, *Golden Spray*, was attacked by an enemy fighter. After all, they had rescued a number of German airmen from a watery grave. Was this the German way of repaying them? Time and again the Messerschmitt made low-level passes. Pocock put the unarmed boat through 360 degree turns while bullets and cannon shells splintered the woodwork. Tying up at the quayside an hour later they were both whisked off to hospital suffering from bullet wounds.

BIRCHINGTON 23.00 – IBs

AFS telephonists were swamped with calls when, just before midnight, canisters of incendiaries scattered over the cabbage fields west of Birchington. Fire trucks and trailer pumps left their depots at high speed. The whole area was reminiscent of a mismanaged firework display, but it was soon realized that the job of tackling all the burning missiles was beyond the capabilities of the existing services. Someone had counted over 150 around Gore End Farm, and then there were more of them fizzling on the ground near Monkton Road Farm.

Ack-ack commanders were conscious of the fact that German bombers could mistake the display for a target area, and jettison high-explosives all over the place. One lieutenant reported on the phone, '. . . there are thousands of the bloody things burning all around us!'

Wednesday 9 April
MARGATE 02.00 – HEs

Two high-explosive bombs screamed into the putting green at Devonshire Gardens, Cliftonville, but caused little damage. There were no casualties reported.

RAMSGATE 23.40 – HEs

Although a number of people were trapped under debris when two more bombs fell at Abbotts Hill and Albion Place, rescue parties worked with such speed and determination that all were saved except one, an eleven-year-old boy, Alan Battersly. He died before reaching hospital.

One of the bombs fell in the centre of a row of boarding houses, completely demolishing one of them, which fortunately, was unoccupied. The other bomb exploded in a narrow thoroughfare demolishing three small homes. Rescuers worked desperately among the rubble to find people whom it was feared were buried, and who were in further danger from flooding in the basements. Forty-nine-year-old Miss Margaret Taylor was the only one detained in hospital.

The Peters family had a lucky escape. While mother and father were trapped, both the sons crawled out of the wreckage unscathed. But a narrow tunnel was dug out through which the parents were eventually led to safety. Charles Banbury, a boot repairer, was at his work-bench when his house collapsed. He crawled out from beneath the rubble and set about rescuing his wife. Both escaped without a scratch.

Thursday 10 April
MINSTER 21.40 – HEs

One heavy bomb exploded about 350 yd from the Brook Crossing, where the railway track lifted above a large crater. There is a report which says a train fell into the crater, but no further details are known.

Thursday 17 April
MARGATE 01.50 – PARACHUTE MINES

One of the most formidable weapons of the last war was the parachute mine, which floated to the ground on the end of a parachute, and usually detonated within seconds of reaching the ground. The result was always catastrophic, sending out terrible shock waves over a wide area. Two such weapons, released by a Heinkel III bomber, floated on to Fitzmary Avenue and Audley Avenue, demolishing twenty-eight houses, and causing severe damage to another one hundred and fifty. In total, over a thousand properties received damage of one sort or another. Four people lost their lives, and twenty-six were injured. The stretch of railway line from Margate to Westgate, ran only a few yards behind the devastated area, and was clearly the objective of the Heinkel crew.

The formidable *Luftmine* with a 60 to 70 per cent explosive charge was, without doubt, one of the most devastating weapons used by Germany on land targets. Although designed for coastal water they were often used on land objectives such as railway tracks. The accuracy of a missile dependant on a parachute was often in question because it drifted towards the target instead of falling towards it at high speed. One of two *Luftminen* dropped at 01.50 on 17 April, drifted on to a house at the end of Audley Avenue where Edith Harford was killed.

The second of the two *Luftminen* drifted on to Fitzmary Avenue on 17 April. Over one thousand properties received damage of one sort or another and there were three fatalities.

Damage caused by blast on the eastern side of Fitzmary Avenue, Westgate, on 17 April 1941.

Sixty-three-year-old Councillor George Vanner and his wife Ann, together with a friend, Lily Denham, who was staying the night with them at No. 11 Fitzmary Avenue, were all killed. Also in the same house was Arthur Rhodes. Rescuers found him later seriously injured. At No. 9 Audley Avenue, Edith Harford was found beneath tons of rubble when the walls of her house collapsed on her. Mrs Frost and her son were helplessly trapped by fallen masonry. The pressure of the masonry pressed against their bodies, making it difficult to breathe. The continuing silence after the explosion made them wonder if anyone was aware of their predicament. The crushing pressure increased steadily. The numbness which had spread over their minds, caused by shock, eventually gave way to panic. 'I managed to find a piece of wood, and pushed it through a hole in the wall. Then I waggled the piece of wood about to attract attention,' Mrs Frost recalled. 'We were getting a little desperate for we were being gradually smothered by the sheer weight of the rubble. The whole roof had collapsed on us.' Her son mentioned later, 'The rescue squads had to lift heavy lumps of masonry before we could be released from our beds. Had it not been for their smartness I feel certain that both my mother and I would have lost our lives.'

BROADSTAIRS 04.00 – HEs

Two bombs fell on the golf course. In the *East Kent Times* the following appeared: 'In spite of the fact that enemy action has damaged the 11th fairway at the North Foreland Golf Course, the game is to go on. It has been decided to make good the fairway at a cost of £7.'

At 11.00 a Messerschmitt Bf 110 was shot down into the sea off Ramsgate, with the loss of both crew members. The two Spitfires responsible, flew over the town performing victory rolls. When a Spitfire pilot attempted a victory roll over RAF Manston, seven days before, he spun into the barrack square and was killed.

Sunday 4 May
RAMSGATE 19.25 – HEs

The *Luftwaffe* was flying in large formations over the west of the country, and went on to bomb Belfast. In the Thanet area there was little activity to speak of. The sirens sounded the alert just after 19.00 and enemy aircraft were heard out at sea heading towards the Thames Estuary. Then one high-explosive bomb fell at Lavender Farm, Cliffs End, causing slight damage but no casualties. At Minster three high-explosive bombs fell at

Sevenscore railway crossing, Cottington Hill, and another near the A253 road.

RAF MANSTON 21.15 – HEs & UXBs

Forewarned by radar our fighter squadrons were up and ready for the attempted onslaught on the airfield. Aerial battles raged over Thanet and it was reminiscent of the Battle of Britain period. The streets of Margate and Ramsgate were almost deserted as bullets and cannon shells ripped along the streets ricocheting from one building to another. Young boys peered out from Anderson shelters to identify the aircraft. They were, on the whole, oblivious of Alderman Redman's statement to the Margate Education Committee meeting the previous Friday: 'I should think recent events will make parents think twice before being so stupid as to say their children are going to stop here.'

Monday 5 May
MARGATE 05.15 – HEs & MACHINE-GUNNING

The Westbrook area of the town received an early morning shake-up when two Messerschmitts machine-gunned houses as they headed towards RAF Manston.

RAF MANSTON 06.15 – HEs

The four Messerschmitt fighter-bombers raced over the airfield, released their bombs, and were receding into the distance before the ack-ack guns could take a bearing.

Tuesday 6 May
MARGATE 16.36 – HEs &

This evening attack was similar to the one made the previous day. The Messerschmitts shot over Cliftonville but were not expecting the terrific ack-ack barrage that went up in their path. Doubtless it was the red-hot tracer bullets, curving towards them as they approached the coast which made some of them jettison their bombs. One fell at Zion Place, another on the Fort Promenade, one on the foreshore and the next in Northdown Road. Only three people suffered any kind of injury and the target, RAF Manston, only received a few bombs, which made craters in an already pock-marked area. There were no casualties or damage reported.

This was the result of a direct hit at Zion Place, Margate, when a single 250-kg bomb was released from a Messerschmitt fighter-bomber at 16.30 on 6 May 1941.

BROADSTAIRS DUTCH REFUGEES ARRIVE

Earlier that morning military observers were taken aback by the sight of a German Heinkel seaplane landing just a few yards off shore and then taxiing into the harbour. The crew of four were Dutch nationals, and a white flag was frantically waved from the rear cockpit. While some observers were surprised by it all, a small contingent of RAF personnel, who had arrived an hour earlier by lorry, greeted the Dutchmen like long-lost brothers. To a policeman standing nearby it seemed both tantalizing and suspicious as he watched the hand-pumping and back-slapping on the quayside.

Wednesday 7 May
RAMSGATE 11.24 – HEs

Two explosions were heard at sea off Government Acre but they did not cause any damage to property, and no one saw or heard an aircraft in the vicinity. German long-range shells might have been responsible but there are no records to confirm this.

Thursday 8 May
MARGATE 23.25 – HEs

Four bombs fell near the harbour sluice and a further four were plotted near the town boundary, close to the railway line. Three others fell on open marsh land and one plopped into the sea. It seems likely that this particular incident resulted when a Heinkel III bomber, which might have lost its way because our own electronic defence system 'bent' the German beam used by the *Luftwaffe* to find targets, and released its bomb load before returning to its base. No damage or casualties were recorded.

Friday 9 May
MINSTER 23.30 – HEs

Five bombs were plotted having exploded in a line from St Nicholas to Minster. Among them was one said to be a parachute mine. No further information available.

Saturday 10 May
RAMSGATE 23.55 – HEs, IBs , UXB

In the previous month the people of Thanet were formally introduced to the Compulsory Fire Watching Order, that was included in a Civil Defence Duties (Compulsory Enrolment) order which had been applied to a large area of Kent and Sussex by the Regional Commissioner for the South-Eastern Region. In a nutshell it meant that local authorities could direct men between the ages of eighteen and sixty to register for fire prevention duties for periods not exceeding forty-eight hours a month, thus supplementing volunteers who had already enrolled in the service.

London had been the target for the bombers this night, but Ramsgate had its very own little blitz. Over one hundred incendiaries fell on the town starting twenty-three fires in Cliff Street, Effingham Street and Cavendish Street. Seven shops and six houses were seriously damaged, and then more incendiaries fell in King Street and Queen Street. One 2,000-kg high-explosive bomb buried itself in Government Acre and failed to detonate. The casing of this huge missile was later exhibited at Littlewood's stores during the 'Wings For Victory' week. The fire-fighting teams, men and women, had a real taste of action which affected the three major towns. Incendiaries were scattered everywhere, but so

Ramsgate's firemen, seen here at Newhaven, Sussex, were on detached duty there. The administrative organization of the NFS eventually evolved to provide the necessary back-up to other areas where they gave valuable assistance during the coastal shelling period.

energetically did the teams work that not one fire was allowed to reach serious proportions.

The bombing began just before midnight and lasted about two hours. Fires broke out at shops, a cinema, many private houses, a garage, two public houses and a number of stores and workshops. The most severe fire occurred at a garage where a lorry loaded with provisions was destroyed, and six other lorries were severely damaged.

A surgeon walking the grounds of the General Hospital began smothering incendiaries within seconds of them falling. He was joined by the sister and other nursing staff. 'They all behaved splendidly,' he remarked, '. . . and there was no panic among the patients.'

Sixteen-year-old Brewster Lowing, an ARP messenger boy, climbed up on to a roof at Allah Cottages, at the rear of Queen Street, picked up a burning incendiary, and threw it down into a courtyard where it was soon extinguished by firemen. From his high vantage point Lowing noticed smoke coming from Blinke's stationer's shop. When the fire team entered the premises and went upstairs they found a store-room well alight. Firemen broke into a number of properties to get close to the seat of the fires, and because of the hundreds of incidents, four additional auxiliary pumps were called from neighbouring towns. At the end of the day, the newly formed fire teams came through with many commendations from the authorities.

BROADSTAIRS 23.55 – HEs, IBs, UXB

A 1,000-kg bomb fell in the grounds of Lyric, Park Avenue, but fortunately did not explode. Over one hundred incendiaries were plotted falling in the Dumpton Gap area, causing only slight damage and no casualties. Small fires were tackled with gusto, and the newly formed fire-fighting teams in that particular area, seemed to produce from nowhere stirrup pumps, small hoses, buckets and sandbags. They climbed into lofts, tore up floor-boards, and threw hundreds of squib-like, white-hot magnesium ingots to the ground outside.

Monday 12 May
MARGATE 01.45 – HEs & IBs

The bombs and incendiaries which rained down on Margate in the early hours were thought to have been released by a Junkers 88 bomber which had missed its original target further inland. Searchlights stabbed the night sky and the ack-ack guns opened fire at a rapid pace. The area affected was Selborne Road, Dane Valley Road, Arlington Gardens and Ramsgate Road. It was the second night of furious fire fighting.

BROADSTAIRS 01.50 – HEs & IBs

Scores of townspeople took shelter when the siren sounded, and before bombs and incendiaries fell in a line from Westwood to Lindenthorpe Road, starting many fires. There were, surprisingly, no casualties reported. Seven houses were damaged by the blast and extensive fire damage occurred at many properties.

Sunday 25 May
MINSTER 21.40 – HEs

Two bombs fell near Thorne Farm, causing slight damage to agricultural buildings, but there were no casualties.

★ ★ ★

6   ISLE OF THANET GAZETTE.   MAY 30th, 1941.

THANET WAR WEAPONS WEEKS

OVER £250,000 SUBSCRIBED

FIGURES FOR FIRST FIVE DAYS

	MARGATE	BROADSTAIRS	RAMSGATE	WESTGATE (Included in Margate Total)	BIRCHINGTON
Saturday	£25,489	£35,955	£65,881	£2,382	£4,725
Monday	£23,486	£11,900	£12,776	£213	£1,077
Tuesday	£18,221	£3,420	£10,288	£656	£2,716
Wednesday	£21,505	£2,635	£11,796	£1,461	£1,154
Thursday	£27,587	£6,151 (up to 8 p.m.)	£10,750	£1,450	£2,763
Totals	£116,288	£60,063	£111,494	£6,165	£12,435
Aim	£150,000	£30,000	£75,000		£5,000

TOTAL FOR THANET, YESTERDAY (THURSDAY) EVENING

£287,845

TWO MORE DAYS TO GO

GO TO IT, THANET
EVERY PENNY MEANS ANOTHER
BULLET FOR HITLER

When the final figures were made available they showed that Thanet, with a war-time population of about 32,000, had raised the astonishing amount of £393,756. Ramsgate subscribed £165,626, Margate £157,122 and Broadstairs and St Peter's £71,008.

The well-known actor Naunton Wayne, compèred an Entertainments National Service Association show at the Regal Cinema, Margate, that evening. There was an impressive list of film stars, including Lily Palmer, Constance Cummings, Ursula Jeans, Judith Furse, John Clements, Roger Livesly, Rex Harrison and Lew. D. Ayres.

Thursday 29 May
ST NICHOLAS 00.15 – HEs

Four bombs were plotted falling in the fields near Hale Farm, but there were no casualties or damage. Another report stated that two parachute mines floated down into fields without causing any damage. The report did not say if the mines exploded or not.

Saturday 14 June
RAMSGATE 03.29 – HEs

Enemy mine-laying aircraft were still operating in the Thames Estuary at night. A strong north-east wind may have been the reason for three 'G' mines to descend upon the sleeping town. Fifteen houses were demolished

Dropped from a lone German raider on 14 June 1941, a parachute mine severely damaged Wilfred Road, where James Holt and his wife Sarah were killed at No. 26, and John Godfrey and Clifford Aste died at No. 28.

in Wilfred Road, where four people lost their lives in as many seconds: James and Sarah Holt at No. 26, Clifford Aste at No. 28 and his friend John Godfrey at the same address.

Eight houses were partly demolished, forty seriously damaged and a further two hundred slightly damaged. When the first explosion occurred the Mayor, Alderman Kempe, was in bed and recalled seeing a large greenhouse toppling towards his bedroom. He covered his head with the bedclothes. He said later that it was the third time he had experienced a narrow escape. Another high-explosive bomb exploded at Warre Recreation Ground, and ten people were injured in the chaos.

As expected, considerable damage was done over a very wide area. The Young family seemed to have had a guardian angel looking after them. Husband and wife, together with their two daughters, Marjorie aged seventeen, Beryl aged four and their baby son aged fourteen months, owe their lives to the fact that they were sleeping under two heavy dining-room tables:

People used to laugh at us because we made our beds up under the tables. But there is no doubt that it was the tables which saved our lives. We used to sleep the baby in his cot beside our bed so that we could drag him into shelter if any danger threatened. On Friday night, for the first time in his life, he crawled out of his cot and tried to get into bed with us. My wife dumped him back into his cot, but he crawled out again. When the bomb almost completely wrecked the house, several hundred-weights of brickwork came crashing down on to the tables. One large piece of masonry fell plumb into the cot.

The machine-gun platoon of the 6th (Thanet) Battalion Home Guard, seen here at Ramsgate in 1941. Commanded by Major F. Wale, they had progressed from the earlier Local Defence Volunteers, when they paraded in civilian clothes – their only visible sign of belonging to anything at all was the LDV armband. Now they were a competant fighting force equal to any regular Army unit.

Members of the 6th (Thanet) Battalion Home Guard, Margate Company, took over the coastal gun battery of two 6-in naval guns at the Winter Gardens, Margate, when the Royal Artillery were required for the D-day invasion build up in 1943. Captain A.C. Hatfield, JP, seated at centre of front row, was the commanding officer. A local farmer, he had served with the Royal Flying Corps during the First World War in No. 101 Squadron later joining the Royal Canadian Mounted Police.

The eldest daughter Marjorie, sleeping in the next room, although her room was practically demolished, sustained only slight injuries. But she was more concerned about her clothes. Not one piece of clothing could be found afterwards.

The ARP teams faced up to their work with remarkable courage, and at many incidents, sheer physical strength. There was never any romance in their work. As soon as they had arrived at an incident they set about freeing the victims who had been trapped in the wreckage of their homes. Then there was the upsetting task of recovering the dead. If that was not enough, they were responsible for protecting the public from injury through the possible collapse of shattered masonry by shoring up what was left of the building. Towards the end of their task they salvaged the furniture, personal belongings and treasures from the debris. Most often these were put in little piles where the owners could find them later.

The teams usually consisted of ten men: a leader, three skilled men, five labourers and a driver. The skilled were usually qualified tradesmen in either brickwork, carpentry or plumbing. Their training and experience formed the basis of their suitability for their war-time job, and more especially, if they were bodily strong.

Every one of them had been specially trained in rescue technique; the quick and precise removal of debris, the lowering of injured people from upper windows, and tunnelling through rubble to reach the wounded. Experience had shown that skilful tunnelling was a justified method of saving lives under the inspired leadership of one man selected for his intuitive grasp of a situation.

Monday 23 June
MARGATE 23.40 – HEs

A returning bomber released its bomb load on the foreshore and Pleasant Place. Four houses were demolished by one 500-kg bomb, three of them were empty, and the occupants of the fourth had already taken shelter. The Tutt family had only just reached their shelter when their house was destroyed. Special Constable Smith was the only casualty when he threw himself violently to the ground and injured his arm.

Monday 7 July
BROADSTAIRS 01.30 – HEs

Two bombs were reported having fallen in the sea.

The damage caused at Pleasant Place, Margate, at 11.40 on 23 June 1941, suggests an *SC* 500-kg bomb was the culprit.

RAMSGATE 01.29 – HEs & UXBs

Once again returning enemy bombers released their bomb loads on coastal towns. Townspeople spent many long hours in their shelters, never knowing how close they were to death or injury. Half a dozen high-explosive bombs fell across the town and demolished the Employment Exchange in Chapel Place by their sheer weight – not one of them detonated. There were no casualties reported.

Tuesday 8 July
MARGATE 00.12 – HEs

The siren sounded long before midnight. People took refuge in their shelters, carrying blankets and thermos flasks. The heavy drone of enemy aircraft engines became the accompaniment to conversation before the bleary-eyed townspeople drifted into a disturbed slumber.

Policemen, ARP Wardens and the fire watch teams, waited for the sounds of screaming bombs. The incident board at headquarters had already been wiped clean. In the left-hand columns, picked out in white paint, were the words: STREET, MISSILE, UXB, FIRE, CASUALTIES. The telephones were silent and there was an air of apprehension. Outside the searchlights swept this way and that.

The first of over twenty bombs fell on Edgar Road and the High Street. Others fell in the sea and straddled the Winter Gardens and Margate Hospital. Shops and houses were blown high into the night sky in clouds of brick dust, tiles and masonry.

The rescue teams arrived from their depots and descended upon the stricken streets. They unloaded their paraphernalia: shovels, pick-axes, ladders and ropes, while their leader took stock of the situation. He saw roofs and floors hanging down across basements, trapping people who had remained in their homes – people who had firmly believed, that if 'their number was up', then it would be immaterial where they were when their time came.

Bill Yeoman appeared at a window over his father's shaving saloon with his wife. The staircase and back of the premises at No. 81 High Street, were completely shattered. The Yeomans were helped down a ladder by police officers. Both were injured and were taken to hospital. John Yeoman, the father, had been asleep at the back of the shop. It was some time before they found his body.

A voice from a window over a newsagent's shop at No. 87 High Street, quickly brought response. Twenty-six-year-old Miss Evelyn Edwards,

The sirens had sounded long before midnight, but thirty minutes later over twenty bombs fell on the town of Margate. After Dunkirk the Winter Gardens and Pavilion were in a restricted area of the town, gone were the days when Frederic Hargreaves and his Knights of Swing entertained thousands of holiday-makers. Above, the stage at the Winter Gardens was wrecked by a stick of bombs which fell just after midnight on 8 July 1941.

was helped down to safety in her nightdress. But despite her many scratches and bruises she was able to direct the rescuers to where her employer, sixty-three-year-old Miss Clara Hawkins, was trapped in the debris. She told them she had heard Clara calling her from her bedroom on the second floor. They all stopped and listened. They heard a faint moaning, but after a while it stopped. They eventually found her. Hideously injured, she lay in a coma, fighting to survive. Clara died before reaching hospital.

The third fatality of the raid was fifty-nine-year-old Violet Brown, of No. 85 High Street, a widow, whose sixtieth birthday was only one week away. Wardens were unsure if she had returned to her shop. Their records showed that she had left to visit her daughter. Further enquiries revealed she had changed her mind. When the rubble was painstakingly removed her body was found.

The devastated East Balcony of the Winter Gardens which received a direct hit just after midnight on 8 July 1941.

The early Victorian dwellings of most seaside resorts were not built to withstand blast damage let alone a direct hit by a German bomb. Charlotte Place was wrecked just after midnight on 8 July 1941.

The Brewers Arms, No. 94 High Street, Margate, stands opposite the demolished shops where three people lost their lives on 8 July 1941. Much of Sturtons the builders' merchants disappeared into the huge crater in the foreground.

Dividing walls in these early nineteenth-century buildings in Margate High Street, collapsed like crêpe paper, the lathe and plaster shattering into heaps of dust on the 8 July 1941.

The injured: two seriously and another seven slightly, all suffering from shock, were attended by the first-aid teams before being taken to the hospital.

While the rescue work was feverishly taking place another four bombs fell on Charlotte Place. The stick of bombs took out four houses and damaged a further dozen, with only three casualties.

Monday 14 July
MARGATE 00.10 – HEs

Possibly turned back from its target area by the sheer weight of the ack-ack defences, a Heinkel III bomber arrived over the coast. At no more than 8,000 ft the crew would have seen the English Channel, glistening beyond the dark land-mass of the Isle of Thanet. It was now or never. Why waste their bombs by releasing them into the sea? The release button was pressed. Twelve 250-kg bombs struck in a line across the harbour district. West Ham Homes, the Stone Pier and Zion Place erupted in explosions of plaster and masonry. While the rescue teams were hard at

A returning Heinkel III jettisoned its bomb load just after midnight on 14 July 1941. Above, the Droit Office, Margate, was severely battered when bombs were dropped on it.

work, another Heinkel released two more bombs into the sea off Foreness Point. Then just after three o'clock in the morning a single bomb fell on the town centre.

Tuesday 15 July
MARGATE 23.24 – HEs

Harold Avenue and Hawtrey's School at Westgate went up in a spectacular fashion when five bombs almost demolished thirty houses. A further three bombs fell on Princes Street, where twenty-five homes were seriously damaged, including Bobby's Printing Works. Six more fell off Stone Pier and at Foreness Point, without causing any damage. Casualties over the short space of five minutes totalled one killed and twelve injured. Army personnel worked alongside policemen, firemen and the ARP rescue teams, to recover the trapped and injured. Police Constable Stace was on duty at the sea front when the bombs dropped in that vicinity. Accompanied by a special constable, they found several men trapped in a badly damaged house. Some were pinned down by heavy beams in a ground-floor room. Two of the walls had fallen in and another two were in danger of collapsing. PC Stace climbed through the debris into the room and found three men, one badly injured in the head. While parts of the building were still falling, he moved the beams and masonry to release those trapped. He later received the King's Commendation for Bravery.

Ambulances and sitting-case cars were lined up in nearby streets, ready to take the injured into medical care. The whole organization was extremely efficient. The rescue teams especially, had absorbed not only the lectures and training sessions, but had one year's experience to fall back on. Cats, dogs and canaries, buried beneath tons of rubble, were brought to the surface with as much care as was apportioned to the families.

★ ★ ★

A forty-year-old German woman appeared at Margate Police Court in July, summoned for entering a prohibited area without a permit. She had originally arrived in England from Hamburg in March 1939, and had lived at Birchington until forced to leave the area under the Aliens Act in May 1940. A musician and lecturer, the woman was known to have visited many sensitive areas throughout England, and was aware that permits were necessary. She had been apprehended at Birchington Railway Station by a conscientious police constable. She was fined just £1 by the magistrate.

This was the nearest the *Luftwaffe* had come to blowing up the Westgate railway station, when a stick of bombs fell in Harold Avenue on 15 July 1941. Soldiers were billeted in these houses which received extensive damage and one soldier lost his life.

One of five high-explosive bombs wrecked this flint-walled house in Harold Avenue, at 23.30 on 15 July 1941.

Two 250-kg bombs fell on Pump Lane, at the back of the *Isle of Thanet Gazette* offices, on 15 July 1941.

Sunday 3 August
BROADSTAIRS 13.45 – HEs

The Germans concentrated on night raids while the Royal Air Force was increasingly engaged in shipping strikes in the Channel. Squadrons of Hurri-bombers and Blenheims were now using RAF Manston from which to attack the German convoys, but they were heavily protected by flak-ships which put up a tremendous barrage of shells. Much of the action was heard rather than seen by the local townspeople, nevertheless, they were confident in the belief that it was our turn to harass the enemy.

Few enemy aircraft were seen during daylight hours, but this particular Sunday was an exception. Taking advantage of cloud cover a single Junkers 88 swooped down on Broadstairs. Perhaps it was more luck than judgement, which created one of the most devastating raids yet experienced on the town. Only five bombs were dropped, and yet they caused so much havoc. One bomb fell on the residence of Councillor J. A. Forde, JP, who was killed instantly. Mrs Forde was in a back bedroom at No. 4

Once again, the older-type, working-class dwellings came in for a battering at Princes Street, Margate, on 15 July 1941.

St Peter's Road, and was rescued suffering only from shock. But part of the fire station was demolished, part of the railway station collapsed, the public library and the Post Office were partly wrecked. In all, ninety-four properties were extensively damaged, including forty-one shops in the Broadway area. Although only one fatality occurred there were nineteen other casualties, which included the stationmaster, S. Bishop. A German newsagency said, 'A number of bombers took part in an attack on Broadstairs, near Margate, and made a specially successful attack on the station.'

Wednesday 6 August
MARGATE 00.01 – HEs & IBs

At night neither our fighters nor guns possessed their daylight efficiency. Our ability to track the enemy bombers accurately in the dark was left to the Observer Corps who were dependent on sound. The searchlights and guns relied heavily on their own sound-locator systems which varied in accuracy depending on the weather prevailing at the time. The search-lights were more of a deterrent, for they could neither track an aircraft for a satisfactory length of time, or effectively illuminate above 12,000 ft. Penetrating cloud was out of the question.

Our anti-aircraft guns made a lot of noise but were far from being adequate in performance. The first heavy ack-ack guns to operate in Thanet were the obsolescent 3-in type, used by the Territorial units in the 1930s, and whose height limitations were restricted by the predictor equipment which could not accept a height beyond 20,000 ft. The smaller Bofors light ack-ack guns could deal with aircraft at heights of less than 6,000 ft. It was the Bofors gun that gave admirable service when tackling the fighter-bombers and any low-flying bomber.

The incident of the 6th was almost a carbon-copy of that of 14 July. A mixture of high-explosives and incendiaries was dropped from a single bomber. Three bombs fell on Albion Road, another on waste ground behind Willens Road, then two exploded in Alpha Street, and three more on Cross Road and two on Welborough Road. Incendiaries were scattered over a wide area. Firemen and ARP teams were galvanized into action before the telephones began to ring. Rescue teams were still searching the rubble at daybreak but only one person suffered slight injury.

Wednesday 13 August
RAMSGATE 00.25 – HEs & UXBs

Of the eleven high-explosive bombs dropped by a returning bomber just after midnight, four failed to detonate. Those that did fell in Church

BOROUGH OF RAMSGATE.

FIRES IN CROPS.

A Person on discovering a fire is requested immediately to report the matter to the Fire Brigade (Telephone No. Ramsgate **75**).

A General Alarm in the fire area will then be given by the sounding of a Klaxon horn carried by a motor cyclist.

All available civilians on hearing the Klaxon horn are asked to proceed to one of the following places :--

CLIFFSEND MANOR HUT
MANSTON FORGE
MANSTON COURT
HAINE ROSE FARM

These places will be used as assembly points from which civilians and other helpers will be taken to the scene of the fire.

Fire beaters and flails will be provided, and the earnest co-operation of all people is requested in the prevention of spread of fire in crops.

FIRE BRIGADE HEADQUARTERS,
    RAMSGATE.
    23rd July, 1941.

Road, Truro Road, and the Lord of the Manor. Two houses were demolished including the Continental Bakery, at No. 60 Church Road, and a large section of the biggest hotel on the sea-front, the Granville, fell into the road, exposing the bedrooms and bathrooms on each floor. Over fifty houses and shops received severe damage but there were only two casualties.

Saturday 16 August
RAMSGATE 21.30 – HEs

The Observer Corps plotted two Junkers 88 light bombers flying close to the sea and parallel to the coast, heading from west to east. The guns at Little Cliff End opened fire as the bombers turned towards Ramsgate. Black shell bursts were seen following the raiders but there were no hits.

Bomb-doors open, the two JU88s streaked in over the harbour. Three 250-kg bombs fell close to the harbour wall and then four fell in La-Belle Alliance Square and Hibernia Street. Four houses were demolished and several were so badly damaged by blast that they were considered unsafe. The second JU88 reached Broadstairs.

BROADSTAIRS 21.31 – HEs

It has been recorded that this attack was the most tragic to befall the town throughout the war years. Sandwiched between the larger towns of Margate and Ramsgate, Broadstairs did not receive the battering experienced by the other two. The first four of eight high-explosives fell on Dumpton Park Drive, and the other four dropped at the junction of the High Street and Vere Road. Members of the fire service were standing outside the fire station at Alexandra Mansions, Vere Road, when the bombs detonated. Three firemen were killed instantly: the chief officer, sixty-one-year-old Arthur Bate; William Hammond and Percy Spice. Robert Pemble received such serious injury that he died on the way to hospital. Another fireman Frank White, died in Margate hospital two days later which brought the total fatalities to five. There were eleven others injured. Ninety-eight houses and shops were seriously damaged by blast and the High Street was completely blocked by debris. Military personnel clambered over the rubble and rendered invaluable assistance to the already hard-pressed teams of rescuers.

Tuesday 26 August
MARGATE 21.21 – HEs

Another returning bomber was responsible for the half dozen bombs released over Westgate and Cliftonville. Four high-explosive bombs crashed into St Pauls Road where Cliftonville Hall was wrecked and a further thirty houses were damaged. At Westgate five bombs caused havoc among eight shops and over one hundred houses. No casualties were reported from either area.

Saturday 30 August
RAMSGATE 22.40 – HEs

Ack-ack guns were heard barking from inland but searchlights remained inoperable. It was double summertime, when the clocks had been advanced a further one hour. It was not yet dark, but a high-flying German bomber released its bomb load and five missiles screamed into the harbour area. Damage was slight and two people received injuries.

The attack at 21.20 on 26 August 1941, actually hit the sidings at Westgate railway station.

Sunday 31 August
RAMSGATE RAF BOMB

One document states an RAF plane dropped a bomb at Summerhill, Margate Road. No time was given in the report.

Sunday 7 September
RAMSGATE 22.23 – HEs

It was a brilliant moonlit night when two Junkers 88s diverted from their target further inland and decided to attack the harbour. Conditions could not have been better. There was at the time a spectacle going on over the French coast which had drawn townspeople to the West Cliff area to watch our own aircraft bombing enemy targets. No one suspected that enemy aircraft were in the vicinity. When the throb of German engines was recognized the bombers had already opened their bomb doors. They began their shallow dive towards the centre of the town. Even as the bombs fell people were still scurrying for shelter. It was fortunate that

Adelaide Gardens, Ramsgate, after a moonlight raid on 7 September 1941. Damage was widespread, casualties totalled eight killed and twenty injured.

fewer people were in the public houses. The Foy Boat and the West Cliff Tavern both received direct hits and were wrecked. Edith Evans, landlady of the West Cliff Tavern, was killed instantly, and her husband William received serious injuries. At No. 8 Townley Street, William and Kitty Bowles, were both killed when their home collapsed on them. Further down the street at No. 15, thirty-seven-year-old William Landi, and his sixteen-year-old son, died before rescuers could reach them.

At Sion Hill there were two more fatalities when fifty-eight-year-old George Cossens, an Air-Raid Warden, and seventy-two-year-old Frederick Simpson, were buried alive beneath tons of rubble. When the rescuers reached Joseph Tomalin after four hours of tunnelling at No. 3 Adelaide Gardens they discovered that he must have faced the unimaginable horror of having his skull slowly crushed. With extreme dexterity the rescue team removed the bricks and masonry from his body. A doctor crawled through the tunnel; there was a faint flicker of life. His removal took another agonizing thirty minutes. He died two days later in hospital.

After many hours of digging Mrs Wood and her daughter were found alive in their special shelter built by Mr Wood in the basement. He had kept canaries on the verandah, twenty of which were recovered alive. Damage was widespread: three houses were completely demolished, sixteen partly demolished, twelve seriously damaged and over two hundred suffered slight damage. Total casualties were twenty-six: eight dead, five seriously injured and thirteen slightly injured.

Monday 8 September
MARGATE 00.27 – HEs & UXBs

After the catastrophic events of the previous night at Ramsgate, personnel at the ARP Headquarters, Royal School, Victoria Road, were anxiously contemplating their own fate.

The night shift were playing cards, and the telephonist was ringing round the warden's posts to find out the names of those on duty. Teams of fire fighters were at their posts. Firemen checked their equipment: the hoses, auxiliary pumps, ladders and ropes. On the cliffs a solitary silhouette of a Home Guard sentry could be seen against the backdrop of a shimmering, moonlit sea.

The red alert sounded before midnight when enemy aircraft were heard. Searchlights flicked on and off, and the anti-aircraft gunners stood to in anticipation. ATS girls, manning the predictors, peered over their

Searchlights flicked on when two Heinkels were observed heading towards Thanet in the moonlight. Over twenty bombs fell on 8 September 1941, and a stick of them demolished houses at Upper Grove Margate and damaged Weston's Dairy. The gasworks buildings in the background suggests the target area.

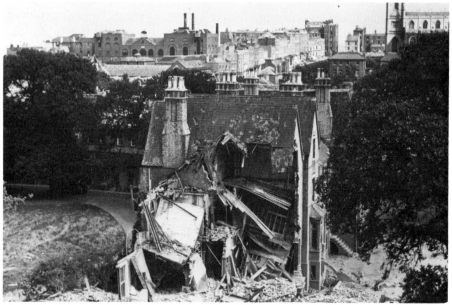

Most of Margate College was wrecked on 8 September 1941, fourteen soldiers were killed there.

sandbagged emplacements, fascinated by the luminescent waves creeping steadily over the Pegwell Bay flats.

Then the Observer Corps post at Foreness Point, saw two, dark shapes heading towards them at about 8,000 ft. Half a dozen searchlights switched on their candlepower as a message was being sent by the Observers. Identified as two Heinkel IIIs, a cluster of twenty-three bombs fell on the town. Weston's Dairy at Upper Grove was almost wrecked and two bakeries partly collapsed.

At Park Place bombs completely demolished two shops and five houses. Maud Denton, with her fourteen-month-old son, had gone next door to her friend, Katie Pilcher. They were all in the front basement room with Katie's two sons, when the houses collapsed on top of them.

Police officers and wardens arrived within minutes at No. 34 Park Place. Piercing the death-like silence they heard a sign of life, the heartwarming sound of a baby crying. Their first difficulty, however, was to locate the room the victims were in beneath the chaos of rubble. Working feverishly, but expertly, the teams pulled away wreckage piece by piece until they came to a door. It led to Mrs Denton's house. But they found the cellar empty. They heard voices coming from an adjoining room, the cellar of Mrs Pilcher's house. Tunnelling an entrance was resumed. They worked at several areas with only the lights of small torches to guide them. One woman was heard to say a gas stove was lying on top of her, but after about an hour had passed the voice ceased. It was daylight before they found the basement door and crawled inside. The delicate task of releasing the victims followed. Rescuers found difficulty in establishing who was dead or alive. The victims had been in darkness for five hours, but gradually they emerged through a small hole in the rubble, but with the ever-present risk of more wreckage falling down and smothering them – yet again.

Katie Pilcher and her sixteen-year-old son, Edwin, had died, but Maud Denton and Alan Pilcher were alive. The most traumatic experience for one rescuer was to find Maud's baby son John, lifeless, but still warm. He carried the little bundle to the waiting ambulance, his head bowed, tears unashamedly staining his smudged face.

Although one of the two shops demolished was empty, in the other, Kenneth Brown, a cycle dealer, and his wife, were buried in the debris of their home for three hours. They had been saved by a door which had fallen across a wall. They were beneath it with over a ton of rubble covering them. Just a few hours before the Regal Cinema received a direct hit, completely wrecking the auditorium, it had been showing to a packed

Newsagents Setterfield & Rogers, No. 158 High Street, Margate, received serious damage during the bombing of 8 September 1941.

house, H.G. Wells' *Kipps*. The three fire watchers were lucky to have been in the small kitchen when the bomb fell. George Atkins and two youths, Derek Hastings and James Savin, hastily beat a retreat towards the foyer. 'As we reached the main doors another bomb exploded, and we were immediately thrown through the doors, landing on the pavement outside.' George recalled. They picked themselves up and ran to the nearest shelter. 'After the bombing had finished,' George said, '. . . we returned to the cinema and found a fire burning among the ruins. We set about it with a stirrup pump to try to get the fire under control. But finding it more difficult than we anticipated we called for the fire brigade.'

Margate College, occupied by the military, received a direct hit, demolishing part of the building and killing fourteen soldiers. Another bomb failed to explode. A member of the First Aid Team, Gwen Devereux, recalled:

> Most of the dead and injured had been taken away when our shift came on duty. We had to stand by while the rescue teams were digging for a soldier feared buried in the ruins. They had reached the cellars when they found a large cache of ammunition and explosives. This delayed the search until the cache was removed to a safer place. Had that little lot exploded there was no way of knowing how many more lives would have been sacrificed. Later we were told the soldier they were looking for had gone on leave.

The total damage in the town amounted to fifty shops and three hundred and fifty houses being badly damaged and a further twenty shops and one hundred and fifty houses receiving slight damage. Casualties were fourteen soldiers killed, three seriously injured and fifteen slightly injured. Civilian casualties were three killed, two seriously injured and seven slightly injured.

Sunday 21 September
MARGATE 20.02 – HEs

This particular attack was almost a repetition of the raid that occurred thirteen nights before. The siren had sounded earlier in the evening when the night shift of the Civil Defence Services was preparing to go on duty. The Kent War Diary states there were twenty high-explosive bombs dropped, five at the junction of Wellis Gardens and George V Avenue, five at the Royal Esplanade, five on the RAF Compound at Foreness

Piercing the deadly silence the police officers and wardens heard the heart-warming sound of a baby crying in the rubble at Park Place, Margate. A 500-kg bomb had destroyed most of this four-storey tenement on 8 September 1941.

Little imagination is required to picture the scene had the bomb dropped on the Regal Cinema just two hours before, when H.G. Wells' *Kipps* was being shown to a packed house on 8 September 1941.

Point, and one in the harbour. Records reveal that Trinity Square and Zion Place also received a number of bombs and so one can assume these were the missing four. Damage and casualty figures were not mentioned.

Friday 31 October
SARRE 11.25 – MACHINE-GUNNING

There was little enemy activity during the month of October, at least the Thanet towns received a well-earned respite from attack. The only incident recorded is the machine-gun attack made on a goods train near Sarre, by low-flying Messerschmitts. Damage nil – casualties nil.

Sunday 9 November
MARGATE 17.57 – HEs & IBs

Two 250-kg bombs dropped near the railway line at the rear of Connaught Road, one on the foreshore, one at St Peter's Road, three in

Cliftonville Hall received its first bomb on 20 November 1940, the day after it had opened as a YMCA hostel. The *Luftwaffe* made certain of its destruction on 26 August 1941.

Written on the back of this photograph is the following, 'At 5.45 p.m. Sunday 9 November 1941, a number of German dive bombers dropped HEs on railway line near St Peter's Road Bridge, Perkin's Yard, College Road and at Canterbury Road.' The picture shows the damage at Perkin's Yard.

Canterbury Road and two on College Road. But that was not all. Two incendiary canisters shed their magnesium missiles over Street Hill, Westgate, All Saints Avenue, Hartsdown Park, Nash Court Farm, Marlborough Road and Albert Road. Sixty incendiaries burned fiercely but were soon brought under control by the fire-fighting teams. Damage was extensive but there were no fatalities, only twelve people injured.

BROADSTAIRS 23.45 – HEs

Greenhouse windows were shattered when three bombs fell on open ground at Sackett's Hill. There were no casualties. An RAF aircraft made a forced-landing near the same spot, and the pilot was seen to walk away carrying his parachute.

RAMSGATE 23.45 – HEs & IBs

Bombs fell on the Barbers Almshouses, Elms Avenue, where eighty-five-year-old Clara White was killed when the roof collapsed on her bed;

Just before midnight on 9 November 1941, a direct hit on No. 16 Church Square, Margate, killed Annie Tranham. Note the emergency water tank on the left. Static water tanks were installed around the towns to provide a source of water for the fire-fighting teams.

the Clarendon House County School; Clarendon Gardens; South Eastern Road and Picton Road. As in other night raids there were many extraordinary escapes. One such case was recalled by Mrs Lucas. With her eighteen-month-old son she was sheltering in the basement of her home in Elms Avenue. The house next door was blown apart and immediately caught fire. Mrs Lucas and her baby were rescued an hour later, and had been saved from certain death by an iron girder which had prevented the roof from falling on them. The Acting Town Clerk fell down a large crater after the Council Offices had suffered damage. At the time of his accident he was helping with rescue work and received facial injuries. A total of seven houses were demolished, twenty more were seriously damaged and a further one hundred slightly damaged. Casualties were one killed and five slightly injured. But that was not the end of the night's proceedings – Margate was attacked again.

Two old-age pensioners, sisters Francis and Ann Riches, were killed here at Buller's Court, when their homes received a direct hit on 9 November, 1941. The photograph shows the Dickensian hovels that existed in many town areas.

MARGATE 23.50 – HEs & IBs

Widespread damage occurred in this second raid and many fires started. Bombs dropped on Edwards Place, the High Street, Invicta Road, Dane Hill, Church Square, and a few in the sea. Over sixty incendiaries were plotted in the Dane Valley area, a further ninety in the Maynard Avenue district, thirty were reported in Westbrook Avenue, thirty more in the harbour area, and many more were scattered across open fields in the Halfmile Ride area. Damage was estimated as 'severe' with one hotel extensively damaged, two more partly damaged, and over three hundred houses and shops receiving a battering of one sort or another. Three women unfortunately lost their lives, sisters Francis and Ann Riches, were pulled from the rubble of their home at No. 5 Bullers Court, and Annie Tranham had been smothered by wreckage at No. 16 Church Square. Her husband Thomas was one of three people treated for serious injuries.

Thursday 27 November
RAMSGATE 17.55 – HEs & IBs

Identified as a Junkers 88 by military observers, a plane flew in over Pegwell Bay, from the direction of Sandwich. Bombs and incendiaries fell on Southwood Road and Grange Road, with others scattering over Gilbert Road, Stanley Road and Station Approach Road. The result of an obvious attack upon the railway station, was the demolition of four houses and severe damage to another twenty-six. Fortunately there was only one casualty.

CHAPTER FOUR

1942

The Victims were Found an Hour Later

The attendances so far registered at the new British Restaurant, opened at the Lillian Road School on Monday 5th January, suggested that the eastern suburb of Ramsgate was not clamouring for the provision of facilities for communal feeding. The class-room converted into a restaurant was attractive and inviting, but the patronage had been poor and the helpers there had a less strenuous time than those working at St George's and Ellington Schools, at each of which average attendances of 150 were recorded daily.

So ran an article in the *Advertiser & Echo*. The Ramsgate Communal Feeding Centre was opened a year before on Monday 13 January 1941, when over sixty people had an excellent meal for 9d. Local authorities had been pressed by the Government to create communal feeding centres, largely to offset the inequality of conditions when people were suddenly rendered homeless by enemy action. Nevertheless, although the centres were designed mainly for emergencies, everyone was welcomed to take their midday meal there.

When the first centre opened at Ramsgate in St George's School, the Mayor, A.B.C. Kempe, and an entourage of local officials, paid their 9d. at the door, were seated at tables, and almost immediately a plate of food was set before each of them – roast beef, three vegetables, followed by stewed apples and ground rice. Bread was ½d. a slice and a cup of tea was an additional 1½d. After the meal the mayor declared the centre open. 'I feel sure,' he said, 'there are many of our citizens who will be glad to take advantage of this very good spot. I have to confess the meal I have had today is a jolly sight better than some of the stuff I have been getting during the past week.' The Mayoress declined to answer questions put to her by a local reporter!

It was in March 1941, that Lord Woolton, then Minister of Food, planned an expansion of the scheme to cover the whole of the country. Winston Churchill, the Prime Minister, minuted Lord Woolton,

> I hope the term 'Communal Feeding Centre' is not going to be adopted. It is an odious expression . . . I suggest you call them 'British Restaurants'. Everybody associates the word 'restaurant' with a good meal, and they may as well have the name if they cannot get anything else.

★ ★ ★

Full-time compulsory education began again in Ramsgate on Wednesday 7 January 1942, and over eight hundred children between the ages of five and fourteen were receiving a normal education. It was estimated that the number of children of school age in the town was about nine hundred and fifty. Each day saw an increase in the attendance rate.

At Margate, Westgate and Birchington, five schools were opened for half-time education. The number of children enrolled was 673, an increase of 130 on the numbers who took advantage of the home service tuition system which had been introduced the year before. At Broadstairs, where there was full-time education, twenty-one boys and fifty-three girls were attending school.

The loss of the destroyer HMS *Thanet*, announced by the Admiralty on the 29 January 1942, caused much dismay among the citizens of Thanet. She had been sunk during an engagement with a superior Japanese force off Endau on the east coast of Malaya.

Naturally, Thanet towns had a close association with the vessel, for not only was the North Foreland Lighthouse adopted as her badge, but both the officers' wardrooms and the men's mess possessed pieces of silver plate presented by Ramsgate and Margate when she was first commissioned at Chatham in 1919.

The Admiralty, however, rejected Thanet's pleas that a new ship commissioned to replace the lost destroyer should retain the name *Thanet*. They even had the temerity to suggest the new vessel should be named *Whirlwind*. This controversial decision was met with loud indignation,

From 2 November 1942, the basic pay of members of the Police War Reserve and full-time paid Special Constables had been increased by 4s. 6d. (23p) a week. They received £3 18s. 6d. (£3.57) per week. War Reserve Constable H. Watson stands on the left with Police Sergeant A.S. Norris, Margate Borough Police, outside Police Box No. 8 at the corner of St Mildreds Road and Westgate Bay Avenue.

and letters of protest were sent to the Admiralty. By November that year
the ex-mayor of Margate, Alderman G.P. Hoare, was able to announce
that the Admiralty had changed its mind and that the new warship was to
be named *Thanet* after all. Doubtless the £400,000 subscribed by the
people during Warship Week was a sum which could not be ignored.

Tuesday 12 February
RAMSGATE – SWORDFISH BLUNDER

One blunder after another compounded the terrible tragedy which beset
Lieutenant Commander Eugene Esmonde, DSO, and his outdated
biplanes, when they attempted to attack the German warships *Scharnhorst*,
Gneisenau and *Prinz Eugen*, sailing through the English Channel in broad
daylight.

It was almost 12.30 when the people of Ramsgate looked skywards to
see through the mist, half-a-dozen old Swordfish torpedo bombers
circling just seawards of the town.

The sound of Bristol Pegasus engines drew attention to the plight of
such aircraft. Every boy of school age knew the differences between
different aero engines and was expert in identifying aircraft before they
were seen by the naked eye. Since the spring of 1941 the RAF had been
engaged in taking the fight to the enemy. Spitfires and Hurricanes,
Blenheims and Beauforts, Lysanders and the rest, took off from RAF
Manston in ever increasing numbers. Clearly, a fearful premonition
evolved that the old biplanes would be no match for the ubiquitous
Messerschmitt fighters lurking over the English Channel. Military commanders and civilians were quite unaware of what was going on. The
rumbling coastal guns at South Foreland were deemed to be firing practice
rounds. A single squadron of Spitfires joined the biplanes and, together
they made off over the sea. All the Swordfish were lost. Only five crew
survived. Esmonde, who only the day before had received the DSO from
the king, led his biplanes through the fire. Lt.Cdr. Eugene Esmonde and
his gallant No. 825 Squadron, disappeared from the radar screens. He was
posthumously awarded the Victoria Cross.

Sunday 26 January
WESTGATE 22.50 – HEs

A reduction in enemy activity had been noticeable for the past three
months. This respite gave the Civil Defence Services an opportunity to
assist local contractors in repairing the damaged properties without being

blown off their ladders. However, just before 23.00 this night, one very large bomb was dropped without any warning and damaged over 173 houses and 11 shops. A further 100 houses were slightly damaged. There were no casualties listed.

Despite the Earl Jowitt's statement, '. . . the Germans throughout the war seem to have been singularly ill-informed about our conditions', it is rather curious, that three days after a large WAAF contingent were billeted in Ursuline Convent, Westgate, one large bomb fell in the grounds of another large house, Eccleston, The Grove, Westgate.

Friday 20 March
RAMSGATE

There had been a slight relaxation in the Defence Zone although the invasion scare was always present in the military sector. Few believed the suggestion that the Germans might still attempt an airborne landing, and try to take RAF Manston, among other objectives. To keep everyone on their toes a new defence system was put into operation. And so everyone at the airfield was given a rifle and ammunition; cooks and clerks were included, and eventually Lieutenant-General Bernard Montgomery, GOC, 12th Corps, paid a visit to the area. There was a lot of time spent visiting the ack-ack sites and the Home Guard. Various aircraft were taking off and landing at the airfield. But at Ramsgate an armour-piercing shell exploded on No. 18 James Street. It caused considerable confusion. No one seemed to accept responsibility for it. In fact, the whole episode was hushed up as the shrapnel was identified as British.

Friday 3 April
BROADSTAIRS 00.26 – HEs

Severe damage was caused at the Lodge, Dane Court, when three bombs fell in the grounds of the estate. Casualties and any specific damage were not recorded.

Tuesday 14 April
RAMSGATE GAS TEST

Local authorities were advised to keep the civilian population alert, and it was proposed to release tear gas in the boroughs. Few people were disposed to carry their gas mask, except the schoolchildren, but the adults had become rather complacent about it all. Nevertheless, wardens and

Peter Jan Schipper, owner of the Dutch fishing boat, stands between PC Bullard and Detective Constable 'Ginnie' Wren, of the Margate Borough Police Force. On 24 March 1942, Schipper with David Davids and Arthur Pay (both the latter thought to be British agents) made the astonishing sea voyage from Ymuiden Holland quite undetected by the Germans.

policemen raced through the streets swinging their wooden rattles as gas was released in King Street, Broad Street and the Plains of Waterloo. People who had not heeded the warning posters which had been liberally pasted about the town, ran into shops to escape the gas. Those who had remembered the warnings had stayed clear of the town, but there were a number of women shoppers who wept copious tears. Their plight was increased when they were tempted to rub their eyes. It only aggravated the condition.

Saturday 30 May
RAMSGATE 01.30 – HEs

There was widespread damage to graves and tombstones when bombs fell on the town cemetery, near Cecilia Road. Houses surrounding the area received great lumps of marble and masonry in roofs and bedrooms. No casualties were reported.

Friday 22 June
RAMSGATE 17.18 – SHELL

A German long-range shell was believed to be responsible for the damage sustained by houses near the harbour. Other shells were seen going into the sea. No casualties were reported.

Thursday 13 August
BROADSTAIRS 03-55 – RAF BOMBER CRASH

Returning from a raid, a damaged Stirling four-engined bomber, had been advised to land at RAF Manston. It had been circling the airfield because the undercarriage failed to operate. It was ordered to make a belly-land when the wheels suddenly came down. The pilot decided to make a normal landing and had just lined-up to make his approach when the engines stopped. He had run out of fuel. Unable to alter course at such a low level the Stirling crashed on to an Anderson shelter in the back garden at No. 132 Rumfields Road.

   Several of the crew received slight injuries, but when they climbed out of the bomber they were astonished to learn there were several children in the shelter. Despite their rude awakening the children began arguing with each other about the type of aircraft which had very nearly killed them all!

Friday 4 September
RAMSGATE 15.15 – HEs

One bomb fell in the sea off West Cliff. There was no damage reported.

Pilot Officer Beaty flying a Spitfire of the American 'Eagle' squadron, No. 133, was making for RAF Manston after scrambling from the airfield to intercept Focke-Wulf 190s over the Channel, when he was attacked and shot down by one of them. Beaty baled out and landed in the sea about five miles from North Foreland. His Spitfire crashed on the old Ramsgate Airport. While Beaty was seen hanging from his parachute the Air Sea Rescue squadron, No. 277, was alerted from RAF Hawkinge. He was located by a Lysander and a message was sent to the ASR launch at Ramsgate who picked him up ten minutes later.

Friday 18 September
RAMSGATE

An anti-aircraft shell fell on St Augustine's Golf Links but failed to explode.

Monday 28 September
BROADSTAIRS 11.00 – HEs

No alert had sounded when a Junkers 88 light bomber released four bombs near St Peter's gasworks. A horse was the only fatality. The water tower and surrounding buildings were seriously damaged and the pumping station was said to have been demolished. One bomb failed to explode and there were five casualties needing medical treatment.

Saturday 10 October
MARGATE 07.39 – HEs   RAMSGATE 07.40

Two Focke-Wulf 190 fighter-bombers, the latest and probably the most successful fighter Germany produced, suddenly and without warning, shot over Westgate at very low altitude to release their 500-kg bombs near the gasworks.

The Bofors light ack-ack gunners heard the distinctive engine noise, and the newly arrived RAF Regiment manning the guns sent up a barrage of shells. One of the raiders was hit almost immediately. Bits flew off it, and as it careered towards St Peter's and Ramsgate, the pilot baled out.

While the other raider altered course and flew out over the sea, *Uffz*. W. Schammert fell out of his burning machine. Baling out at low altitude was risky. The chances of the parachute opening before reaching the ground were slim. He was extremely lucky to have survived the aircraft direct hit, let alone safely drop in an alley behind Denmark Road. One eye-witness recalled he asked for a cigarette in perfect English, and showed little concern for his plight at being captured.

His stricken machine crashed through the rear of No. 27 Wellington Crescent, the bulky radial BMW engine, penetrated right through the building and lodged itself in the railings surrounding the gardens. Bullets and cannon shells began to go off and started a fire in the building, but the NFS personnel still managed to put out the fire. Twenty-five houses had been damaged by the exploding bombs and five people were injured.

Wednesday 28 October
MARGATE 15.50 – HEs

Once again the Focke-Wulf fighter-bombers now occupying the airfields
in the Pas de Calais, made another quick, low-level raid. They usually
flew in groups of four – each carrying either a 250- or 500-kg bomb
beneath their fuselage. Their pilots were, more often than not, keen flyers
with special skills in low-level flying techniques. These were the days
before the German pilots held any feelings of respect for the anti-aircraft
gunners, ranged along our coast-line. Within a few months they were to
change their views, and fly at higher altitudes. Bombs released by this
group of four in the early evening fell in Dane Park and Park Crescent
Road, demolishing one house and partly wrecking another two. Fifteen
houses were seriously damaged by blast with another 482 receiving slight
damage. Casualties numbered fifteen slightly injured.

Saturday 31 October
RAMSGATE 17.15 – MACHINE-GUNNING

There were no casualties reported when a single raider began to machine-
gun the area of Park Road.

MARGATE 20.40 – HEs & IBs

It was close to a quarter to nine when an enemy bomber was suddenly
caught in a searchlight cone over the Isle of Sheppey. Guns opened fire
and the aircraft was seen to dive out of the cone. The searchlights spread
out in all directions but were unable to make contact again. Then
pandemonium broke out when bombs were heard falling on Margate.
Bombs and 'fire-pots' fell in the Royal School grounds.
   There was considerable blast damage and the Lodge caught alight. The
Lodge was almost demolished and the side of the unoccupied headmaster's house was blown out. On the opposite side of the road a church,
which had not been used since the war started, was extensively damaged
by blast and bomb splinters.
   Mrs Florence Lyall, wife of the school engineer, and her mother Mrs
Kate Kyley, were in the schoolhouse when the bombs exploded. At the
time Mr Lyall was at the school entrance with a warden William
Mathews. They were both thrown against the wall by the blast but were
uninjured. Lyall saw his house blazing and partly blown away. He
directed Capt. F.G. Wenham of the Home Guard and Mrs Ovenden, to

While the city of Canterbury was being attacked by Focke-Wulf fighter-bombers a single enemy bomber dropped one high-explosive bomb in Victoria Road, Margate, demolishing the Royal School Lodge, killing Mrs Kyley at 20.20 on 31 October 1942.

the exact spot where his mother-in-law and wife had been sheltering. Policemen, Home Guard and the ARP rescue teams began to search the rubble. Meanwhile the fire service had arrived and had extinguished the fires. The victims were found about an hour later. Kate Kyley was dead, but her daughter Florence was recovered seriously injured. A further six people were injured.

★ ★ ★

Like many other towns in the south east, Margate had the unpleasant task of reducing the number of whole-time members of its Civil Defence Service. As a result of instructions from the Ministry of Home Security, thirty men and women were to receive a month's notice to terminate their employment. Directions to lower the strength from 273 to 139 were received in April 1942, and since then reductions in personnel had gradually been made. Of about ninety who had left, sixty-one had gone in to industry, seven into the armed forces and six to the County Mobile Rescue Service. Ramsgate on the other hand felt intimidated and proposed that the Home Guard should be strengthened in case of invasion.

Sunday 1 November
MONKTON 01.20 – HEs & IBs

A returning enemy bomber released two bombs and eight incendiaries in open land near the village. Damage nil – casualties nil.

Wednesday 2 December
RAF MANSTON 10.05 – AIRFIELD STRAFED

Activity had increased at the airfield during the year and almost daily there were operations sending squadrons to targets in France. Cannon-firing Hurricanes, some equipped to carry a single bomb, were often being used to either attack enemy shipping, or the railway marshalling yards. In addition, there were many training flights engaged in shooting up the Goodwin Sands! Because of the increased squadrons using Manston airfield, defence became all important. A number of light ack-ack units arrived and consisted mostly of the 40 mm Bofors guns. Since their arrival the *Luftwaffe* pilots usually gave the airfield a wide berth, for reasons only known to the enemy, they actually ventured to strafe the airfield in broad daylight on this day. Typhoons of 609 Squadron were approaching the airfield when the snap raid took place. Flight Sergeant Haddon shot one of the raiders down. Damage at the aerodrome was recorded as minor and casualties were nil.

Saturday 5 December
BROADSTAIRS 14.40 – FOCKE-WULF 190s STRAFE TOWN

Four Focke-Wulf 190s strafed the town, and the Holy Trinity church was hit. Another four Focke-Wulf 190s reached RAF Manston but were beaten off by the intensive ack-ack. Damage slight. No casualties.

Almost on the eve of Christmas the fervent curiosity of a fifteen-year-old Margate boy was responsible for a terrible tragedy which resulted not only in his own death but also the death of his sister and two brothers.

Early on the evening of Tuesday 22 December people living in the Dane Hill area heard an explosion. At first they thought a bomb had been dropped, but going into the street they saw no tell-tale sign of enemy action. A couple walking past No. 6 Dane Hill Row, heard the faint cry of a child coming from the basement room. In the room they found the badly mutilated body of Ronald Fruin, his terribly injured sister Iris aged eleven, their six-year-old brother David and two-year-old Peter.

An explosion had shaken the room, in which were found parts of a mortar bomb similar to one which the eldest boy had had in his possession earlier that day.

Ronald had been working for a building contractor at Birchington, and the previous week his foreman took from him a mortar bomb which the lad had found on the rifle range at Minnis Bay. Later that same day he was seen with another mortar bomb and was told to take it back to where he had found it.

On the day of the tragedy, the boy was again seen trying to remove the cap from a bomb which he had placed in a vice on a work bench. Again he was told to return the bomb to where he had found it. Unbeknown to the workmen returning home in a lorry that evening, the boy had in his possession a mortar bomb which was to wipe out his family.

CHAPTER FIVE

1943

Not Knowing if They Were Alive or Dead

Monday 18 January
MINSTER 20.00 – HEs

A German bomber, thought to be a Junkers 88A, was plotted on a course from Pegwell Bay towards Manston airfield. Ack-ack guns opened fire almost at the same time when bombs began to fall from the intruder. They fell near the Minster railway line and reports indicated there were no casualties or damage.

BIRCHINGTON 20.10 – HEs & IBs

The same aircraft released four 'fire-pots' on Westfield Road. One house was seriously damaged by fire, and at No. 66 Westfield Road two women were killed.

Sixty-year-old Edith Hoare and her sixty-five-year-old sister Agnes Millen were sitting by the kitchen fire when a 'fire-pot' demolished their home. Soldiers and police helped the rescue teams to search for the missing women and Edith was found in a short time suffering multiple injuries. Fire had broken out in the ruined house and hampered the rescuers, and frequently throughout the operation a hose was used to put out the more serious blazes which were constantly flaring up. This however, caused serious flooding of the basement as the water filtered through the debris. Agnes was eventually found dead in the cellar three hours later. Buildings on either side of the house were considerably damaged by either blast or fire and the occupants considered themselves very lucky to be alive.

Another 'fire-pot' fell on a large house previously occupied by a doctor, and caused a fire which was quickly extinguished by soldiers who had rushed to the scene from their gun emplacement. The other two 'fire-pots' fell in gardens where they were tackled by the fire-watching teams.

Tuesday 26 January
RAMSGATE 08.34 – HEs

Focke-Wulf bombers came in very low over the sea and turned towards the town from Stoner. The siren raised the alert but the first bomb was already falling on the outskirts of the town. Four houses were demolished in as many seconds when the bomb exploded on Coleman Crescent. Fifty-three-year-old Miss Christina Hiscoe at No. 58, and sixty-two-year-old Louisa Rouse at No. 60 were both killed. Blast damage was extensive and almost wrecked a further ten houses; one hundred and fifty received roof damage and five people were treated for injuries, including an ARP warden, Edward Hougham, who suffered a fractured thigh and severe arm wounds.

In the back gardens at Coleman Crescent dead rabbits were strewn in all directions and their hutches were piled in a heap of matchwood. Birds and chickens were also among the casualties. In some of the partly wrecked homes furniture in upper rooms stood at almost unbelievable angles. Two water tanks seemed to be suspended in mid-air without any visible means of support. Concrete posts which had supported the fencing dividing the gardens, had been snapped off as though they were little more than match sticks. People rendered homeless were quickly accommodated by neighbours, including eighty-seven-year-old Mrs Solly, whose ceiling had collapsed on her.

Saturday 30 January
MARGATE 08.38 – HEs

Telephones began to ring in the incident room when four Focke-Wulf fighter-bombers streaked in over the coast near Herne Bay for another breakfast-time visit. But they soon altered course when the ack-ack guns opened fire. Followed by the exploding anti-aircraft shells the raiders, with no particular target in mind, and with their sinister-looking bombs slung beneath their fuselages, headed for the nearest town. The bombs were released over Cliftonville: one fell in Ethelbert Road, another in Princes Gardens, one exploded at the rear of Cliftonville Avenue, and the other behind Surrey Road.

This is all that remained of No. 23 Princes Gardens, Cliftonville, when a 500-kg bomb struck on 30 January 1943, killing Alderman William Noble and his wife Mary.

Six houses disappeared in clouds of dust and smoke, eleven more were seriously damaged by flying debris. Shops, almost twenty, were seriously damaged and over one thousand received slight damage to roofs and windows. There were four deaths – all at Princes Gardens. Mary and Alderman William Noble at No. 23; Reginald Lambert and his fifteen-year-old daughter Sybil at No. 21. Four others were taken away seriously injured and a further seventeen were treated for minor wounds.

Mrs Noble had been partially buried in her semi-detached home, but finding her husband proved a more difficult problem. The rescue teams were handicapped by not knowing where he was at the time the bomb exploded. He was not found until Sunday morning.

Mrs Ellen Twyman, the wife of the Chief Fire Officer, and her sixteen-year-old daughter Gladys, were lucky to be alive. Ellen Twyman was preparing breakfast for her daughter in the kitchen when she heard the bomb falling. She dived under the table for cover without realizing the flimsy structure had its limitations. Even so, the table protected her from serious injury. She managed to climb out from beneath the rubble, cut and bruised all over, and reached the garden shed where she shouted for help. A passing local bus driver heard her shouting. She eventually was taken to hospital for treatment. Gladys was in her upstairs bedroom dressing when the floor just collapsed beneath her. She was rescued soon afterwards suffering from cuts and shock.

One bomb travelled quite a distance before wrecking a home. It went through the side wall of an empty shop, passed through a communicating wall and the front door into the street. It then apparently crossed the road, passed through another empty shop before exploding at the back of a house which collapsed.

BROADSTAIRS 08.43 – MACHINE-GUNNING

Five minutes after the attack at Cliftonville, a single fighter machine-gunned Stanley Road. There were no casualties reported from this incident.

Tuesday 9 February
RAMSGATE 08.50 – MACHINE-GUNNING

There was no alert in operation when a single Messerschmitt fighter suddenly appeared over the town when everyone was going to work. His attack concentrated on the Manston Cottage Homes. There were no casualties reported.

Tuesday 23 February
MARGATE FIRE GUARD EXERCISE

The town's second Fire Guard exercise took place in Northdown Road on the Tuesday evening, when six incidents were staged, and four Fire Guard groups from business premises were engaged. Street fire parties from Sweyn Road and Princess Mary's homes were also called upon to assist. Three of the 'incendiaries' were arranged in damaged premises so that wet drill with stirrup pumps could take place. In others the full process of dealing with an 'incendiary bomb' had to be operated without actually using water. It was the first time private fire parties had been included in an exercise, and unlike the first one, held in the High Street the previous week, there was no moon to assist the parties. Added to the darkness, the 'bombs', indicated by red lamps, were placed in buildings which were like rabbit warrens, but the Fire Guards found their way about with remarkable agility and enthusiasm.

The next morning an inquest on the exercise was held with the senior fire guards, when a report was discussed regarding the weaknesses and how to remedy them. The Chief Fire Guard, Mr E. Dixon, wrote in his report, 'It is most difficult to get the real effect when you are conscious that what you are doing is an exercise. The sense of real danger is not present. This, I think, led in several cases to disregard cover, and to occupying positions that led to exposure from 'exploding fire bombs':

While the drills proved your capacity to perform your operation with stirrup pump, make your approach to the scene of action in open formation, and almost at the run, to take cover, get to work, make sure no fire was left. I feel that you yourselves were not altogether happy as to co-operation. There is no doubt that team work – inter-team work, co-operation between parties, needs development.

Summing up with a few words of advice, Mr Dixon said:

> You know the shortcomings in your experience. Now get together, discuss them with your team, your party leader and captain. Explore your area and find out all about it. You had the advantage of a moonlit night a week before. I feel sure that with your ability and enthusiasm you can overcome all difficulties, but training and leadership will have to be developed to get the full value of your qualities.

After the Northdown Road exercise it was proposed to have regular exercises, so that all groups throughout the town could benefit from their own experiences. Perhaps the most encouraging aspect of the Fire Guard operating in the Thanet towns, was that they volunteered to serve in that capacity for twelve hours per week unpaid, and that it was considered their duty to turn out for action in the event of bombs falling in their area, whether on watch or not.

Tuesday 2 March
RAMSGATE 22.43 – SHELLING

Four large calibre shells were reported falling in Pegwell Bay.

★ ★ ★

Shortly after the Dunkirk evacuation huge railway guns were brought up to the French coast by the Germans, using the existing French railway tracks. These massive artillery pieces were to operate from the Pas de Calais and provided the heavy bombardment necessary to dominate the Straits of Dover. In 1941 more permanent structures began to take shape, and by 1942, huge concrete casemates had been erected to hold formidable artillery in various calibres.

The *Batterie Lindemann* at Sadgatte for instance, with its three 406-mm Krupp guns, was thought to be the most intimidating of the twenty-four naval gun batteries installed between Calais and Boulogne. Other important installations were the *Grosser Kurfurst* and *Todt* batteries, and as early as October 1940, the first artillery pieces in temporary installations, accurately shelled British convoys almost at will.

"UP HOUSEWIVES AND AT 'EM!"

YOU can have a "smack at 'em." There are war weapons in *your* household waste. Every scrap counts, so save every scrap — of paper, metal, bones. *

Keep them separate and put them by the dustbin every collection day. They are wanted urgently to make munitions. Let's all get right into action *now!*

* *Also put out waste food if this is collected in your district.*

PUT THEM OUT CAREFULLY
Follow the instructions you will receive, care saves time, space, money.

THEY *WILL* BE COLLECTED
Councils in districts with a population over 10,000 must arrange for collection. You can help to see that the collection is well and thoroughly done. Send suggestions to your Councils.

THEY *WILL* BE USED
Every scrap that is put out according to instructions and efficiently collected will be used for victory.

This is what your back door should look like on collection day.

ISSUED BY THE MINISTRY OF SUPPLY

German uniforms brought back from Dunkirk, were used during a street fighting exercise at Ramsgate in May 1943, when the local Home Guard put on a demonstration for Lt.-Gen. Sir Edmund Schreiber, GOC, Commander-in-Chief, South Eastern Command. Before the General's arrival the platoon went into a York Street café. The woman behind the counter ran out into the street believing that Hitler had invaded.

There is little doubt that the German batteries enjoyed, not only superiority in equipment and instant retaliatory capability, but most importantly they possessed an uncanny accuracy.

Our own Siege Regiment long-range guns installed between Dover and St Margarets were active in the counter-bombardment role, and the regiments were confident they could silence the German guns.

Wednesday 7 April
BROADSTAIRS 07.10 – HEs

Light anti-aircraft guns had increased in Thanet, partly to deter the 'tip-and-run' raiders from making their lightning attacks, but also to defend the additional searchlight units and troop concentrations in the rural areas. The Bofors guns barked from all corners of Thanet when three Focke-Wulf 190s dived suddenly from out of cloud. As far as the Observer Corps post at Kingsgate was concerned there were no enemy aircraft in the area. The siren had not sounded either. The raiders did what they always did – dropped their bombs on unsuspecting civilians, and on a course setting which would put them out over the sea long before anyone knew what was happening. One wing of the Holy Cross Convent collapsed under a direct hit while another bomb exploded near the Lodge House. The third bomb demolished No. 1 Seafield Road where there were two casualties. Three other dwellings were seriously damaged by blast and a further three hundred and fifty slightly damaged.

Tuesday 1 June
MARGATE 13.10 – HEs & UXB

Flight Lieutenant Wells and Fg. Officer Davis, of No. 609 Squadron, were taking off in their Hawker Typhoons at Manston, when they saw low-flying aircraft in the vicinity of Margate and Broadstairs. Local defences, in particular the light anti-aircraft Bofors units specially placed around the Thanet towns, had already received a warning from squadron commanders for firing on the Typhoons. Understandably, the ever-alert gunners became trigger-happy when so many low-flying aircraft, of all shapes and sizes, streaked in from the seaward side of the towns quite unannounced. After all, the Typhoon and the German Focke-Wulf fighters looked alike to apprehensive gunners, whose prime purpose was to shoot down anything which looked at all menacing. Coupled with awful weather conditions, it was a wonder they hit anything at all.

This midday raid on Margate was carried out by twelve Focke-Wulf fighter-bombers, who not only released their bombs on an unsuspecting town, but also used their cannons to great advantage. Bombs fell on St Peters Road, Thanet Road, Northdown Road, Laleham Road, Dalby Square, St Mildred Road, St Pauls Road, Milton Square, Warwick Road, Cornwall Gardens, Approach Road, High Street, Athelstone Road, Danes Park and Lower Fort Promenade. Only one failed to explode at Northdown Park Road. But the two Typhoons were too late to stop the carnage and chaos. Had the raid been anticipated and a full squadron of Typhoons had scrambled from Manston, then perhaps the story would have been different.

As it turned out, however, the two RAF pilots quickly latched on to the attackers just as the Broadstairs gasometer went up in flames. The vulnerability of the German fighter-bombers, in the bomber mode was considered disastrous by all who flew the machine. Once the bomb had been released it reverted to the fighter role. Amidst the plumes of smoke and dust twisting above the ruined streets, and the cacophony of bombs exploding and anti-aircraft shells bursting, the raiders beat a hasty retreat – followed by the Typhoons.

At 13.00 on 1 June 1943, a low-level formation of twelve FW 190s swept in to make one of the most serious raids of the war upon Margate. Messrs Tumbers and White Fuller's in the High Street, received the first 500-kg bomb. PC George Bray is in the foreground.

The attack by SKG10 only lasted about sixty seconds, but in that short time eight civilians lost their lives, a fourteen-year-old boy died in hospital later that day and a fire guard died of his wounds a month later. The Penial Mission Hall, Thanet Road, Margate, collapsed in a heap of rubble on 1 June 1943. The mission had already been bombed out at Milton Avenue in 1940.

Soldiers and Civil Defence personnel were still looking for Amy Wellman a day later, when a 500-kg bomb demolished houses in Milton Square, Margate on 1 June 1943.

Civil Defence personnel were too busy to attend the Holy Trinity Church. Margate, on 1 June 1943, when it suffered a direct hit by a 500-kg bomb. Later it was considered unsafe and was pulled down.

Documents reveal that Flt. Lt. Wells shot two of them down before his own machine was hit by ack-ack shells. FO Davies, flying like a demon, pursued another one and shot it down at Lydden near Dover. The German pilot *Uffz*. O. Zugenrucker, baled out too low and his parachute failed to open.

The incident board at the ARP Control Room was too small to register all the occurrences. Chalked messages appeared on the walls and doors. The telephones never stopped ringing. Every available rescue team was operating somewhere in the town. Men and women, not all of them belonging to the rescue squads, were clawing at the rubble with their bare hands to reach those people buried beneath tons of bricks and masonry. The High Street was an absolute shambles.

William Avery, an ARP member, had been standing at the bar in the King's Head when most of the building fell into the street. His body was not recovered until three hours later. At No. 13a High Street Annie Saunders, Violet Butt and Frank Coppins, all lost their lives in the rubble. Fourteen-year-old Bernard Collard-Evans, a butcher's errand boy, was cycling past a house when he was thrown off by a bomb blast. He died in hospital. Nine people had been buried alive when three houses were demolished by the blast. Among the first to be rescued were Lily de Bock, and her fifteen-year-old daughter Joyce. Forty-nine-year-old Amy Wellman, whose husband had died only a fortnight ago, was killed while on a visit to the home of her brother-in-law at Milton Square. The whole house collapsed on them and Mr and Mrs Garland were seriously injured.

Asleep in his bed upstairs Jock Ross, a fireman, woke up with a start to find himself, and his bed, going down with the rest of his house. He managed to crawl out unhurt. His wife had been sitting in a chair in the kitchen. A door fell on top of her, preventing her from being crushed to death. She was also rescued unhurt.

Although the body of Violet Butt was recovered during the afternoon at the High Street, rescue teams worked until late at night with the aid of torches and portable lamps. In an attempt to trace the actual spot where the victims were buried a casualty detector unit was brought into use. The detector unit used a number of powerful microphones and loudspeakers which were placed over the wreckage at strategic points and connected by cable to a transmitter and receiver van. When everything had been connected up the team leader shouted for quiet. Then a message was passed over the loudspeakers to the trapped people. The system was designed to penetrate the rubble. The message was to ask the victims to knock on something hard or shout, which would be picked up by the

St Mildred's Road, Margate, another house demolished on 1 June 1943, during a midday raid by twelve Focke-Wulf 190 fighter-bombers.

A large property in Warwick Road, Cliftonville, demolished by a 500-kg bomb on 1 June 1943.

microphones. In this particular incident not a sound was heard. The rescuers were therefore faced by the formidable task of removing tons of debris piece by piece.

At No. 2 Arnold Road there was another agonizing rescue attempt. Elizabeth and Robert Denchfield were known to have been at home when the bomb struck. Once again the detector system was used, but there was no response. When the site at last was cleared of all rescue teams on the following day, it was thought the bomb had penetrated the actual room where the two victims had been. They were never found. When an inquiry was held at the Town Hall two weeks later, and when the Coroner had heard all the evidence suggesting the couple had been at home a short time before the raid, he came to the conclusion that what little remains were found among the ruins, were those of Mr and Mrs Denchfield.

The bomb which almost destroyed Trinity Church passed through the roof of an unoccupied boarding house, then bounced over more houses before exploding near the altar. The tower remained standing, but stained-glass flew into the houses on the opposite side of the road. Another bomb of the delayed-action type, passed through the roof of a school building, then through a house and bounced twice on the roadway before hitting other houses.

There were many astonishing experiences. Just as an example there was the Larkin family. Mr Larkin was sitting in his living room reading the daily newspaper when a bomb came through one wall and then dis-appeared through the other. His two sisters were washing up in the kitchen when all the ceilings fell down. Yet no one suffered any injury. When Mrs Dadds returned to her partly wrecked home she found her two parrots still in their cages and shouting Hello! Hello! Blast damage was colossal. Twenty-two houses were reported demolished, twenty-nine seriously damaged, seventy-three slightly damaged with a further one thousand nine hundred and forty-one suffering minor damage. There are conflicting casualty records. The Kent War Diary states there were sixteen people killed, thirteen seriously injured and fifty-seven slightly injured. However, the War Graves Commission pages lists only nine civilians dead, the others recorded may have been military personnel.

Sunday 13 June
RAMSGATE 01.52 – HEs

One high-explosive bomb fell in an area close to College Road and shattered windows of St Lawrence College. Casualties nil.

A 500-kg bomb bored down into Warrior House, Dalby Square, Margate and killed several soldiers billeted there. The actual number of fatalities is unknown.

Wednesday 16 June
BROADSTAIRS 00.38 – HEs

Thought to have been dropped by a returning bomber one high-explosive bomb partly demolished a house called Westmount in Seaview Road. One other bomb fell in the sea. A further sixty dwellings were badly damaged by blast. Only one casualty was reported.

★ ★ ★

Five boys in the eleven to twelve age group, appeared at the Margate Juvenile Court in June, charged with stealing thirteen phosphorous bombs. They had been out on their cycles on Easter Sunday when they were suddenly attacked by four other youths throwing stones. The five cyclists entered into battle by throwing stones back at their antagonists. When the skirmish had subsided and the 'enemy' driven off they stumbled upon a cache of twenty cases containing bottle-bombs. The cases had been hidden in a deep trench covered with corrugated sheets of iron and the whole was liberally covered with earth. The magistrates showed concern when it was revealed in evidence that some of the bombs had been taken home to Wellis Gardens and hidden in their parents' gardens.

The whole incident was put down to boyish mischievousness, but a month later an eight-year-old boy was seriously injured when he took the pin out a grenade he had found in a field.

The cache of phosphorous bombs, although not revealed in court, belonged to the Home Guard Auxiliary Unit, several of which were scattered in the rural areas and destined to become the British resistance movement if Hitler had invaded these shores. Soon after the Dunkirk evacuation and when France capitulated, the German Panzer Divisions, poised on the French coast, brought an awareness that invasion and even occupation was a distinct possibility. There was, after all, only the English Channel to deter the enemy from making a lightning strike across the Channel.

Our strategists, enveloped in an aura of out-dated warfare, conjured up a civilian, 'devil-may-care' force of volunteers ostensibly to outwit the Germans. The original auxiliary units were formed in late 1940, made up of civilians who knew their own area like the backs of their hands. Each platoon of about half a dozen men had an underground bunker secretly erected in the countryside. The platoons were to act independently of each other and security was the hallmark of their success. At government level, however, they were officially known as 201 Battalion Home Guard. This secret army formed the nucleus of an armed resistance; guerrillas who were trained to wreak havoc upon the Germans should they have invaded England. Each of their bunkers was underground and well-hidden from prying eyes, and even the local 6th Battalion Home Guard were quite unaware of their secret hide-outs – not to mention the real purpose of their existence.

In November 1944, the auxiliary units disbanded with the Home Guard battalions. These secret resistance groups faded into oblivion and much of the equipment: guns, plastic explosive, phosphorous bottles and all manner of paraphernalia associated with their particular type of warfare, disappeared into barns, lofts and even ponds. The secret bunkers around which a veil of secrecy had been drawn, crumbled beyond recognition, and with them went the anonymity of the men who had been considered outside the rules of the Geneva Convention.

★ ★ ★

A verdict of Accidental Death was returned by the Acting Coroner at an inquest at Margate, looking into the circumstances surrounding the untimely death of seventeen-year-old Barbara Gregory, who died at Margate hospital on Sunday 3 July. She had been shot in the lung by a bullet fired from a Sten gun on 17 June.

The accident happened while she was visiting friends with her mother. They were in the kitchen talking when the son of the house, a member of the Home Guard, came into the kitchen. He was carrying his equipment and a Sten gun, and was almost ready to go on duty that evening. When he dropped his equipment on to the cement floor the gun went off and Barbara was shot.

The coroner said he was satisfied that the fatality was a pure accident and believed the lad had no idea there was a round in the chamber. He said in conclusion, '. . . the Sten gun in its present form is a highly dangerous weapon not only to the enemy but also to the people who have the duty of handling it.' Because of the accidental death verdict Barbara Gregory does not appear on the civilian war deaths lists.

Sunday 20 June
MARGATE 02.05 – HEs

One high-explosive bomb fell on an ack-ack site near the town, killing one soldier and wounding a further nine.

Monday 28 June
MARGATE 23.51 – SHELLING

A shell exploded at Dowlings Chocolate Factory, Eaton Road, just before midnight and caused considerable damage to over one hundred dwellings. There were no casualties, however.

RAMSGATE 23.52 – SHELLING

Long-range shells exploded near the gasworks and this was the beginning of intermittent shelling from the French coast which was to last for nearly one year. Four shells were plotted that night and the first exploded in the roadway inside the gasworks yard, which connected the main gates with the gasholders. Both the gasholders and the main pipes beneath the purifiers were set ablaze for the third time during the war. The whole town was bathed in a red glow, and would have been easily seen from the French coast. As a precaution RAF Manston sent up fighters to protect the rest of the town while the NFS teams battled to bring the fires under control.

Another shell exploded on No.7 St Luke's Avenue, where seventy-year-old Alice Miller lived. In bed at the time of the bombing her lifeless body was later recovered from the chaos which had been her home. The dividing wall had collapsed and had pressed down a heap of plaster and lathes and roof joists. The roofs of the houses on either side had been shorn of their slates and a few rafters remained pointing at the sky. Other walls were crazily distorted with the front doors leaning towards the roadway. Nothing could be seen through the windows but a mass of debris that had once been furniture, ceilings and floors.

Mrs Florence Spice, living at No. 3 St Luke's Avenue, had been standing in her front porch when the shell struck. A large piece of shrapnel hurtled through the fanlight above the front door and tore away part of the passage wall. She was hit about the head by the falling bricks. With her head bleeding profusely she ran out of the house again to reach a dug-out shelter. As she ran towards the recreation ground she fell into the shell crater and injured her hand. Florence was later taken to Ramsgate General Hospital.

At No. 5 St Luke's Avenue, Mr and Mrs Barnes, decided to get out of bed when they heard the first shell arrive. They had just reached the back of their house when their bedroom at the front collapsed into the road.

Another large chunk of shrapnel pierced the side wall of No. 1 Salisbury Avenue. So great was its velocity that it penetrated the partition wall, after scorching the bedroom ceiling en route and sending bricks and mortar into the bedroom next door. Private Gordon Sampson, on leave from a military hospital, was standing beside his bed when the wall caved in. He later emerged unscathed.

Monday 5 July
RAMSGATE 03.03 – SHELLING
Reports differ in calculating the number of shells which fell during the early morning. One report says ten, while another states five, and yet another gives six. Seven can be traced. Two fell in Pegwell Bay, frightening the Royal Artillery manning the coastal gun battery, one other fell at Newlands Farm, one at Jackey Baker's Recreation Ground, and one at The Old Railway Cutting. A salvo of two shells exploded close together, one just outside the Borough in Margate Road, but the other was most significant when it demolished No. 8 Bradley Road, and brought down most of No. 6 next door. Fifty-two-year-old William Roberts and his twenty-year-old son Arthur, were both killed at No. 8, and the rest of the family received serious injuries.

Monday 16 August
RAMSGATE 23.21 – HEs

Five high-explosive bombs fell from an unidentified aircraft just before midnight and straddled the western extremity of West Dumpton Lane, where a bungalow called The Hut was wrecked. The wooden structure had almost disappeared in the explosion. Wreckage was strewn everywhere. Sixty-five-year-old John Twyman was found seriously injured and died later in the General Hospital. His wife Thrisa, although terribly injured, survived the ordeal, as did four others who were injured.

MARGATE 23.22 – HEs

The same aircraft was responsible for the bomb which fell on Lonsdale Avenue, seriously damaging nine dwellings with another two-hundred-and-forty being slightly damaged.

BROADSTAIRS 23.23 – HEs

Another three bombs fell on open ground but the blast damaged eighty houses and two shops in the Northdown Hill area. There was only one reported casualty.

Wednesday 18 August
MARGATE 00.03 – HEs

The bomb which fell at the junction of Foreland Avenue and Holly Lane, Cliftonville, made a huge crater and damaged three hundred dwellings. There were four casualties.

BROADSTAIRS 00.29 – HEs

Searchlights were trying to cone the enemy aircraft which was heard circling the area. Heavy ack-ack guns had been 'cleared' to open fire and our own bombers returning from their Continental targets, were advised to steer clear of Thanet. The second of this night's large-calibre bombs exploded in a field near George Hill Road and nearly hit the Coastal Defence Battery at Kingsgate. In the event, over seventy houses received damage of one sort or another, and only one casualty was reported.

Monday 23 August
RAMSGATE 01.30 – HEs & UXB

Searchlights were trying to pick up an enemy bomber which was heading towards Thanet from the direction of the Thames Estuary. The next thing that happened was the sound of two bombs screaming towards ground. One fell off the East Cliff near the Quern Buoy, and the other exploded just 250 yd from a searchlight unit, on Jackey Baker's Farm. There was no damage reported nor any casualties.

Monday 6 September
MINSTER 22.40 – HEs & IBs

Fourteen bombs are recorded having fallen on Surrey Road, Laleham Road, Invicta Road, Northdown Park Road, Meadow Road and Mill-mead Avenue. Incendiaries fell near the town boundary at the junction of Northdown Hill and Reading Street Road and four bombs exploded in fields. Two boarding houses were demolished, five seriously damaged and a further two hundred and fifty received minor damage. Miraculously there were no casualties reported.

Sunday 3 October
RAMSGATE 22.43 – SHELLING

This was one of the worst shellings to affect the town and lasted for about four hours. Ten high-calibre missiles were plotted. The first, the ranging shot, fell into the sea and was seen only by military observers. Of the remaining nine to hit the town, seven fell in the harbour area, Queen Street, George Street, Chapel Place, High Street and South Eastern Road.

Unlike bombs, shells arrived and exploded before anyone knew they were on their way. Shell warnings were given as a normal procedure in Thanet when other south-east towns, such as Dover or Folkestone were being bombarded, the warning often coming around three hours before the first shell fell into the sea. When nothing happened in the Thanet area on this occasion everyone expected to hear the 'all clear' signal. Then two shells fell in Queen's Street, at the rear of Messrs Banwell & Young's and at the warehouse of Messrs R.G. Dunn & Sons. Damage was severe at Dunn's warehouse and, besides the building, a large quantity of stored furniture was completely destroyed. In Chapel Place huge holes caused by shrapnel pitted the front elevations of a Georgian terrace. Some buildings were rendered uninhabitable for months. Three elderly ladies were later rescued from No. 158 High Street. They remembered the terrible noise as

A number of small-calibre bombs were dropped in the Dane Valley district of Margate, but one large-calibre bomb demolished Strathdene in Warwick Road, on the night of 21 September 1943.

being as shattering in its power as that of a speeding train. Then the house collapsed around them. They were thrown violently into a heap and were covered with bricks, masonry and plaster. Then they lay for what seemed like hours in darkness and silence, not knowing whether they were dead or alive, before being rescued.

The shell which demolished No. 15 George Street and No. 13 next door, crashed its way down through the building and into the cellar before exploding. James Bishop, a photographer at No. 15, was killed instantly. Next door at No. 13, twenty-one-year-old Rosina Cleveland and seven-year-old William Walker, living above Shooter's fish shop, also died, but Rosina's eight-month-old baby was found some hours later still in its cot, unhurt. The rest of the Walker family were recovered from the rubble as was the Bishop family. When dawn broke several houses had been demolished and it was apparent that several more would have to be pulled down. There were sixteen casualties altogether and some families had to be evacuated to a rest centre.

Friday 15 October
BIRCHINGTON 23.00 – JUNKERS 188 SHOT DOWN

From Belgian and French airfields the new Junkers 188 bomber, the successor to the Ju 88, now carrying a single SC 1,000 bomb externally, and ten SC 50s internally, were operating night raids on London. One of them burst into flames after being attacked by a Mosquito of No. 85 Squadron. People heard the commotion when the night-fighter opened fire on the intruder. They were able to watch the stricken Junkers disintegrate before falling near hay-stacks at Great Brooks End Farm. Although the crew was seen to bale out only the pilot survived. When the police arrived on the scene they saw *Lt.* K. Geyer, walking towards them through a cabbage field. He was taken to the farmhouse, but before entering he combed his hair. An immediate search of the surrounding area revealed the body of *Ober.* D. Kretzschmar. He had received fatal head injuries. The body of *Fw.* W. Flessner was washed up on the beach three days later. *Ober.* O. Schmidt was never found.

Wednesday 3 November
RAMSGATE 22.39 – SHELLING

The usual ranging shot fell in the sea before the next shell struck the town. It hit two houses in Grove Road, where at one of them, Chadworth, Emily Holthouse and her mother Elizabeth Wolfe, were both sheltering under the stairs. They received fatal injuries. Charles Holthouse, a church warden at St George's, was only slightly injured in the blast. Three other houses were later demolished as unsafe. Another eighty houses were damaged by the blast.

Saturday 6 November
RAMSGATE 22.57 – HEs & UXB

People sheltering in St Augustines Caves had a narrow escape when an SC 1,000 bomb fell on the promenade, penetrating twelve feet into the West Cliff before coming to rest. Fortunately it failed to explode. If it had done so the effect would have been disastrous for those occupying the caves.

Friday 13 November
RAF MANSTON

WAAFs at Manston were shocked to learn of the death of Flight Officer Pam Barton, who had been killed in a flying accident at Detling. The funeral took place at St John's, Margate, where she was buried with full military honours. Pam Barton is remembered as a famous golfer.

CHAPTER SIX

1944

'What Kind of People do They Think we Are?'

Thursday 20 January
RAMSGATE 22.30 – SHELLING

Once again the German long-range artillery turned their guns on Thanet, but although nine shells were fired, seven fell harmlessly in the sea off the East Pier. Lady Luck was still holding out when the next two shells exploded on dwellings in Finsbury Road and Denmark Road. There were no casualties because the houses were unoccupied, but there was extensive damage to eleven houses.

Tuesday 1 February
BROADSTAIRS

All branches of the Civil Defence Services were represented at Broadstairs Picture House on 1 February, when Alderman E.S. Oak-Rhind, CBE, chairman of Kent County Civil Defence Committee, presented to the town a Civil Defence standard. The standard, the first to be received by any local authority in Kent, had a Union Jack in one corner and a crown and the letters CD superimposed on a blue and gold background.

In presenting the standard to Councillor H. Noble, Ald. Oak-Rhind said the king had approved the award of the standard to local authorities in Kent who had known the horrors of total war during the past four years.

'The London Press was boasting – and perhaps rightly,' he said, and went on, '. . . London had just passed its 700th alert. Broadstairs and neighbouring towns – Margate and Ramsgate, had just passed their 2,700th. You have come through more than the rest of England and have known the fear of invasion in the area.' Ramsgate received their standard on Saturday 11 March 1944.

Friday 4 February
MINSTER – MONKTON 05.20 – HEs & IBs

Three high-explosive bombs fell at Minster and over thirty incendiaries fell on the marshes. Damage nil – casualties nil.

Wednesday 22 March
MARGATE 01.14 – HEs

Blast damage affected over eighty buildings when three high-explosive bombs fell near Westgate. Casualties nil.

Friday 21 April
STOURMOUTH 01.40 – ANTI-PERSONNEL BOMBS

Over 214 anti-personnel bombs were discovered scattered across the marshes from Westmarsh to Stourmouth, and the result was a notice appearing on the walls and telegraph posts in every area of Thanet.

DON'T TOUCH THESE BOMBS
(BUTTERFLY BOMBS)

The public has already been warned in various ways of the danger of touching a small German Bomb weighing about 4 lb. It is usually painted either greyish-green or a bright yellow. This bomb, known as the small anti-personnel bomb, may be found with the outer casing either open or shut. If shut, it looks like a large, round cigarette tin with a short, thick wire protruding from one side. If open, the outer casing expands into four hinged parts at the end of the wire. A number of these bombs have been dropped in the last few days and may be found scattered over a wide area. The public is warned on no account to approach or touch such a bomb but report it at once to the wardens or police. They are liable to explode at the slightest touch.

Rocket-firing Typhoons of No. 198 Squadron based at RAF Manston between January and March 1944, caused havoc in the English Channel, making rocket attacks upon German shipping and shooting down many Focke-Wulf and Messerschmitt fighters.

Tuesday 25 April
RAMSGATE 04.15 – BUTTERFLY BOMBS

A large number of butterfly bombs were scattered over the town and thirty-two were discovered in the Canterbury Road area. Records are vague in their estimation of the actual total originally dropped. It is known, however, that twelve exploded for one reason or another, although there were no casualties recorded, and eight houses were slightly damaged when the small missiles landed on their roofs. The butterfly bombs were usually dropped in canisters, which opened on a time fuse and released the missiles over a wide area. Two unopened canisters were later found on open land near Acol.

Monday 8 May
WESTGATE – BOY KILLED BY SHELL

The theory that a time fuse of a 3.7-in anti-aircraft shell fired at sea during a practice session on the naval off-shore anti-aircraft fort known as

Tongue, the closest fort to Margate, failed to operate, was put forward at the inquest on Victor Patrick Jones. Fifteen-year-old Victor, was killed when a shell exploded in the builders yard where he was employed.

Admiral Robert Bax, RN (retd), then serving as a residential naval officer, said fragments found at the scene had been identified as parts of a 3.7-in shell, and there might have been a fuse malfunction preventing the shell from exploding in the air.

The Tongue fort was one of four naval off-shore anti-aircraft Maunsell forts, named after the civil engineer G.A. Maunsell who had designed them. The four naval forts were positioned in the approaches to the Thames Estuary and a further three army forts were positioned closer in-shore.

Thursday 29 June
MARGATE 16.57 – V1 (Flying Bomb)

The Kent War Diary mentions that a V1 exploded over the sea at Westgate. There were no further details recorded.

RAMSGATE 14.58 – SHELLING

Two long-range German shells were reported exploding on the West Rocks. There were no further details recorded.

Shell bombardment of the coastal towns of Kent had increased by the middle of June 1944, but the towns most heavily affected were further west of Thanet, such as Dover, Deal and Folkestone. When the allies landed on the Normandy beaches on 6 June (D-Day), the citizens of the Isle of Thanet experienced a sense of extreme relief. But when Hitler's new weapon, the V1, began to appear over Kent, carrying its one-ton warhead and propelled by a rocket motor, they were, once again, apprehensive of the outcome.

After one of the most devastating raids by Bomber Command on Lübeck in March 1942, Hitler ordered attacks of a retaliatory nature on non-military targets. The citizens of Thanet, along with others who lived in the coastal towns, would not have noticed the difference. Many bombing raids made on the towns were largely indiscriminate. Back in 1936, on a remote island in the Baltic, at a place called Peenemunde, a secret research establishment had been built. By 1942, Werner von Braun, a leading authority on rocket propulsion was the director of the establishment.

The product of the research was the V1 – *Vergeltungswaffen* (weapon of retaliation) but better known to the British as the flying bomb, doodlebug or buzz-bomb. The flying bomb was launched from easily erected ramps in the Pas de Calais area and flew at a pre-set height, range and speed. Aimed at London most of these bombs flew on pre-selected routes which meant that the majority entered British skies between Deal in the east and Hastings in the west. However, flying bombs often left their course, either by some internal fault; because of ack-ack shells exploding near them; or our fighters attacking them. The V1 which had exploded over Westgate must have been a long way off course. The eventual increase of the V1 menace brought a heavy concentration of ack-ack guns into the coastal areas. The light anti-aircraft guns and patrolling RAF fighters were given selected areas within which to engage the flying bomb. It was, however, fortunate for the citizens of Thanet, that the flying bombs did not bring the devastation and chaos experienced by other towns in the south east.

One of Churchill's famous phrases 'What kind of people do they think we are?' caused some animated, if not analytical discussions in the Isle of Thanet. The main point of discussion was that the local press was still in the doldrums, or perhaps more accurately, remained in the unyielding grip of censorship. When Rome had fallen to the Allies, not so much as a mention was made in the local newspapers. The invasion of Normandy was greeted with a sigh of relief after many months of expectancy. Cherbourg's capture was accepted with typical British phlegm and everything that followed was accepted as a matter of course – even Arnhem!

★ ★ ★

An NFS fireman was summoned for being in possession of a dozen cannon shells, part of a parachute and an incendiary device. Originally taken from a crashed aircraft they were later found under the defendant's bed. Police Sergeant Wren said in evidence that the incendiary was later identified as having a five-second fuse attached.

★ ★ ★

Lt.-Gen Sir Edmund Schreiber, KCB, DSO, General Officer Commander-in-Chief South Eastern Command, awarded certificates for good service to three members of the 6th (Thanet) Home Guard battalion; Sgt. J.J. Wale of 'D' (Ramsgate) Coy, Sgt. P.K. LeMay of 'B'

Ramsgate's sea front had been despoiled, because in the dark days of 1940 Thanet, would have formed the first line of defence had Hitler attempted an invasion. The re-structuring of 1944/45 gladdened the hearts of the townspeople who saw a promise of better things to come.

(Birchington) Coy, and Cpl. H.C. Ladd of 'A' (Margate) Coy. He had paid a visit to Thanet on Sunday 16 July 1944, to view the Home Guard.

Before leaving Thanet Sir Edmund told Lt.-Col. Witts, CO of the 6th Battalion, that he could be proud. The practical work of the men greatly impressed him and he felt they were well trained and ready to meet any emergency.

He first visited the Minnis Bay rifle range, where he saw 'D' Coy, 'E' Coy and 'C' Coy practising. While at Birchington he saw 'B' Coy with Major Hunter in command, engaged in firing Smith guns and Spigot mortars. At Westgate he watched the battalion medical officers and stretcher bearers go through their paces under the instruction of the Civil Defence. At Margate Sir Edmund visited 'A' Coy under the command of Major Jarman, where he was served coffee made at the mobile kitchen devised from kerosene tins.

Major Wale, OC 'D' Coy, had the reputation for street fighting and Sir Edmund said he had never seen a better demonstration than that staged for his benefit. The exercise involved some members dressing up in German uniforms. On Saturday night the 'enemy' dropped parachute troops to sabotage harbour installations, but were dealt with before any serious damage could be done. However, a few broke away from the main group and went to ground.

Special town fighting troops of the Ramsgate company were detailed to winkle them out and destroy them. Led by Sgt. Dyer, they were approaching Leopold Street, when he received word that the 'enemy' had been located in a house at the end of Princes Street. Using an ingenious system of ropes Dyer's section entered the second floor of a warehouse and, by what was called the 'death-ride' method, reached the courtyard opposite the 'enemy' position. Blowing a hole in the roof with a sticky bomb Dyer's assault group entered the house and completed the rout of the 'enemy'.

Sir Edmund was greatly impressed and congratulated Sgt. Major E. Hawkins on a 'really first class effort.' Sgt. Dyer and L/Cpl. Adams, both over fifty years of age, were commended for their agility.

Monday 10 July
BROADSTAIRS 03.10 – V1

It was soon after 03.00 when the first flying bomb to crash on Broadstairs careered into gardens at Broadstairs Road. Its gyro system had obviously been upset by a night-fighter. When the one-ton warhead exploded it did considerable damage to houses. Three dwellings were demolished, forty-eight seriously damaged and a further three hundred and thirty-two received slight damage. Casualties numbered four slightly hurt but there were no fatalities. Nurse Chapman, a midwife, was answering a telephone call when the explosion blew her french doors off their hinges. Despite being severely cut about the face, right thigh and hand, she immediately went out in her battered car to attend a confinement at which twins were delivered. Not until the mother and children were comfortable some hours later, would Nurse Chapman have her injuries attended to. For her splendid action and devotion to duty, Nurse Chapman was eventually commended by the king.

Tuesday 25 July
BROADSTAIRS 00.01 – V1

Just about every ack-ack gun in the vicinity opened fire at a V1 which had approached North Foreland. It was not long before the doodlebug motor stopped. There was now an eerie silence before the robot tipped up on its nose and dived to the ground. It exploded, fortunately, on an unoccupied house called Redriff, which just went up in a sheet of flames. Sister O'Farrell of the St George's Girls School at North Foreland, watched the whole thing and even stood her ground when the bomb dived on to the house next door. She was the only person to receive an injury from the blast effects.

Monday 31 July
MONKTON 23.15 – V1

Another flying bomb came over Thanet and was hotly pursued by a couple of Spitfires, taking turns to blast away at it with their cannon, safe in the knowledge that it could not fire back at them. However, inevitably the motor stopped and it dived to the ground at St Nicholas-at-Wade.

Tuesday 1 August
ST NICHOLAS 07.00 – V1

This flying bomb had been brought down by ack-ack fire and exploded near Shuart Farm.

To combat the flying bomb menace an assembled weaponry of light anti-aircraft guns and 'Z' rocket batteries ran into thousands, although most of them were sited to the west of Thanet, reaching to Hastings in Sussex.

In June 1944 AA Command's guns were largely of the successful Bofors 40-mm unit with a back-up of the 3.7-in mobile which was capable of throwing a shell to 32,000 ft. The lighter 40-mm could only reach 12,000 ft, and had the additional problem that it was necessary to make a direct hit for the shell to explode. When fired at a V1 they often bounced off.

Although the ack-ack performance had improved by July and August, mainly because of a new radar system, the biggest advance in gun technology was the arrival in this country of the proximity fuse. Made in America, but a British invention, it was code-named Bonzo, and changed completely the concept of ack-ack accuracy.

Bonzo VT (Variable Time) proximity fuses were activated by changes in the magnetic field to within 60 ft of the target. The sensitivity of the device enabled it to explode a shell near a flock of birds or anything else within that range. But if the self-destructing safety mechanism failed it could, and often did, cause considerable damage to private property when it fell to the ground.

Friday 1 September
MARGATE 04.25 – SHELLING

The flying bomb and shelling phase was now drawing to a close. The Allied armies' spearhead, consisting of the British 21st Army Group, were from late August just north of Abbeville, and drove the German Flak Regiment 155W from their V1 launching sites between Dieppe and Boulogne. In September the German long-range guns in the Pas de Calais were under siege. Nevertheless, they made every effort to discharge as many shells as possible. Determined to spread their shells as far east as they could before being overrun, the German gunners let fly at distant Margate. Ranging shots fell in the sea and then the next salvo struck Red House in Star Lane, causing considerable damage to surrounding property. There were no casualties recorded.

RAMSGATE 04.25 – SHELLING

The rest of the salvos fell on Ramsgate and effected Station Approach Road, Lorne Road, Wilfred Road, Royal Road, Sion Hill, Bradley Road and Coleman Crescent. There was severe damage caused at Sion Hill where the middle of a high block of buildings adjoining the already bombed Foy Boat, was completely demolished. At Station Approach Road the Simmons family had taken shelter in their garden Anderson. Fifty-seven-year-old William Simmons was fatally injured by a shell splinter. His wife and daughter were rescued unscathed. Thirty-two-year-old Violet Hougham, at No. 26 Bradley Road, suffered internal injuries from which she died in hospital that same day. Three houses were completely demolished and over one thousand received slight damage. There were seventeen other casualties, among them a twelve-month-old baby found still in its cot beneath the rubble. These were to be the last long-range shells to fall on the town.

Sunday 17 September
RAMSGATE 18.50 – RAF FIGHTER CRASH

Two women were slightly injured when an RAF fighter crashed on bungalows in Haine Road.

In the *Isle of Thanet Gazette* dated 29 September 1944, there appeared the following:

Above, Chief Inspector H.B. Fleet, Margate Borough Police and Deputy Sub-Controller ARP is seated in front of the Civil Defence Standard, presented to the Margate CD in 1944. Other members in the group were from Westgate, Westbrook, and Garlinge.

GESTAPO CHIEF SHOT

The Mysterious Dr A.A. Tester

Many Thanet people have read with interest this week reports received from Bucharest and appearing in the national press of the shooting of Dr Arthur Albert Tester, described as Chief of the Gestapo in Rumania. All the circumstances indicate that he was a man of that name and title who, for about six years, lived a somewhat mysterious life at a house on the cliffs at North Foreland, known as Naldera. He also had a house in Spencer Road, Birchington.

According to reports, Tester was killed in Transylvania by a Rumanian frontier guard when trying to escape to Hungary, and that he was carrying a passport signed by Hitler.

Tester was known by Scotland Yard before the war as a Fascist, and it is said that he claimed to be personal aide-de-camp of Sir Oswald Mosley and one of the first members of the British Union of Fascists.

He came to reside at Naldera, North Foreland, about 1933, the house having formerly belonged to Lord Curzon, and evidence of his expensive life style were seen in the lavish furnishings. He became an influential customer of many tradesmen in Margate and Broadstairs, some of the furniture for the 245-ton luxury yacht which he sailed being bought in Margate. Although he paid for many of his purchases, he left the country, no doubt hurriedly, a few weeks before the outbreak of war. He owed large sums and creditors have had no news of him since. He had, however, created an impression of being honourable in those dealings.

When Tester left the country with his German-born wife and children in 1939, and sailed to the Mediterranean, he made no arrangements for the care of Naldera with the valuable furniture it contained, although a local estate agent has kept an eye on the house. It had been derelict, and in 1940, was broken into, some of the contents being stolen. Last month (August 1944) the roof and windows were damaged by a flying bomb which exploded in the garden next door.

Tester, who has been described as being an Irishman, but asserted he was English, was known in London as a mysterious financier. He was interested in several companies, including a wine business and a London restaurant.

According to one report, Tester arrived in Belgrade in 1940, and told a journalist that he was seeking a contact in the Yugoslavian Government. After Yugoslavia had been invaded by Germany he disappeared and was next seen in Athens.

By the end of September 1944 Ramsgate relinquished the claim of being a front-line town. There was a sense of relief and thankfulness to the Canadian 1st Army, who had overrun the German long-range gun positions in France.

The Germans had often said that their powerful artillery was aimed at military installations and invasion ports. But one newspaper journalist wrote, '. . . no one knew better than those who were bombarded that, in the main, the missiles fell in residential quarters, killing and maiming civilians and rendering hundreds homeless'.

Since the first shell fell in Thanet on 12 February 1941, Ramsgate people were among the first to admire, and sympathize with, their fellow sufferers in Folkestone, Deal and Dover, who faced almost the full brunt of this particular form of warfare. By comparison, Ramsgate did not receive the battering meted out to the other resorts further to the west, but nevertheless, it bore many shell scars and ten residents lost their lives as a result. Forty-two shells were recorded falling on Ramsgate while another one hundred and fifty burst in the air, either above the town or near the foreshore.

Only two reached Margate, neither of them caused any casualties. Broadstairs also received two without loss of life. During the shelling ordeal the towns were seriously disrupted. Under the defence orders the Post Office, businesses, cinemas and all forms of entertainment were forced to close until the All Clear was sounded. Buses were also stopped and trains were held up outside the towns.

★ ★ ★

Despite flying bombs and shells affecting other parts of the country and despite the tremendous air activity going on over the south-east of England, the ban on visitors to Thanet was unexpectedly lifted at the end of August. A statement issued by the War Office announced that the removal of the ban affected the whole of the protected area which had extended from The Wash to Lymington in Hampshire. Of course they added a rider:

> The public are warned that the removal of the visitors' ban on these areas does not mean that in the view of the military authorities there is any less danger than heretofore from enemy missiles. These areas will remain regulated and the military authorities will retain or impose local restrictions on access to highways or other places to which the public have access. The bylaws made by the Secretary of State for War on 31st March, 1940, remain in force. Identity cards must always be carried in public places and telescopes and binoculars must not be used anywhere in these areas. Certain beaches in these areas will remain closed to the public because they are unsafe owing to mines.

The main effect of the curfew had been to stop people using the promenades and certain roads on the sea fronts from 22.30 to 06.00. Local bylaws remained in force and dances and public houses still closed at 22.00. Nevertheless, a week later, there were long queues at Victoria Station, London, from where hundreds of people packed into every available train en route to Thanet.

Beach scenes revived memories of pre-war times. The majority of visitors brought their own food, especially those who came for just the one day, but those who elected to stay the weekend caused unforeseen problems. Authorization to supply extra food to restaurants increased the emergency ration cards. It doubled in the first week.

Vacancy notices, almost forgotten, were hastily dusted off and cleaned and promptly displayed in boarding-house windows. The crucial reorganization of boarding accommodation was now a priority.

For the most part, however, merriment was stifled by austerity. Amenity lighting was still as depressing as it had always been. The locals did what they had always done, at least for the last four years, listened to the BBC nine o'clock news bulletin, then retired to a cold, blacked-out bedroom.

In a wartime broadcast J.B. Priestley, contrasting a visit to a deserted Margate in 1941, with one taken a few years before, asked himself whether, had he a magician's power, he would bring back that happier peacetime scene in place of the grisly present. And he answered No. 'For, by making such a choice he would forgo the right to make a better future: a Margate and an England which no man can at present even visualise.'

Saturday 25 November
BROADSTAIRS 04.59 – V1

In a last desperate attempt to carry on the war and under the extreme threat from the allied forces, Germany began launching flying bombs from aircraft. Most of these were aimed at the Midlands, but one of them crashed on to the foreshore beneath the Victoria Homes where considerable damage occurred. There were no casualties recorded.

★ ★ ★

It was in November that curiously shaped 'monster' machines, such as never were seen before the war, roared over the Ramsgate sands. Giant cranes were perched on the cliff tops, and a fleet of lorries travelled to and fro along the promenades carrying away hundreds of tons of concrete rubble and steel girders.

The strongly fortified pillboxes, some disguised as refreshment kiosks, were pounded to destruction by pneumatic drills operated by men of the Cementation Co. Ltd of Doncaster, who, incidentally, had been responsible for the work digging the Ramsgate tunnels before the war.

The contractors were faced with some peculiar engineering problems, not least of which was the removal of the steel scaffolding which ran for hundreds of yards from the Marina end of the sands to the East Pier. Had the structure of thousands of feet of tubular scaffolding been erected on hard ground the task would have been easy. But in 1940 the structure was placed on the sand surface. Because of four years tide action they had been buried in some places to a depth of over 14 ft. Removal of these obstacles called for seven great diesel-driven excavators, each capable of moving

The 'Troopers' amateur concert party sang and danced their way through three years of war, entertaining both military personnel and civilians at RAF airfields, ack-ack gun sites and in village halls throughout Kent. Above, Ramsgate's mayor A.B.C. Kempe, who is seen here making-up one of the artists backstage before a performance, was also compère, and an entertainer extraordinaire.

350 tons of sand each day. As it was cleared gangs of men armed with oxy-acetylene burners began cutting the tube away. It took five weeks to complete. Eventually, Ramsgate's sea front, for over four years a scene of desolation – a spectacle of steel scaffolding, barbed wire and conical concrete blocks, was almost restored to pre-war amenity. The sea front had been despoiled because, in the dark days of 1940, Thanet, like other resorts in the south-east, might have formed the first line of defence against invasion. The structures of defence were, thankfully, not required, but the authorities were aware of the urgent necessity for concrete and steel barriers, and blowing up the cliff paths. This meant that the defences barred access to these areas to such an extent that no maintenance work was ever done. And so for four years the resorts watched their sea fronts deteriorating into a sad state of dilapidation. Grass had grown to enormous lengths on the sands, iron railings had lost their bright paint and became coated with thick rust, as did the coils of barbed wire. Weeds

were free to take root in the pavements cracked through bomb damage. The Ramsgate Marina bathing pool was in a sorry state. A happy rendezvous for many thousands of peacetime holidaymakers, it had been struck by bombs and was empty of water, pitted by craters with the protective railings broken away. As the re-structuring progressed it gladdened the hearts of the townspeople as a promise of better things to come.

There must have been many people in Thanet who had assembled at St Lawrence Cliff, Ramsgate, on Sunday 3 December, who, on hearing the speeches at the final parade of the 6th (Thanet) Battalion Home Guard, wondered if the events of the past four years had all been a mistake. The war had been the main topic of conversation in newspapers, letters of complaint, music-hall jokes, rationing, evacuees, air-raid wardens, gas-masks and shelters. But now the mood had changed. 'Sixth Battalion – for the last time – Dismiss!' Thanet Home Guard heard their commanding officer, Lt.-Col. C.S.F. Witts, TD, give this order at the stand-down parade before Brigadier General H.S.E. Franklin, CMG, CBE, DSO. Appropriately, just before the order was given 'Auld Lang Syne' was played by a naval band.

The parade of the 6th was one of many held in different parts of the country, but over 500 officers and men who took part in it were able to look back on a record of service which was probably unsurpassed by any other unit in the country. From General Franklin they heard unstinted praise for their part in guarding the most vulnerable shores of the country, a task which they had performed willingly, cheerfully and efficiently. He told them they had put in longer hours of duty than any other battalion, and it was a record of which they might well be proud.

The parade started from Chatham House grounds, and as the five companies – Ramsgate, Margate, Broadstairs, Minster and Birchington, headed by the band of the Royal Naval Depot, Chatham, marched through the High Street, and Queen's Street, they were watched by an admiring crowd.

While a Union Jack fluttered from a flag pole, General Franklin stood on the roof of the tennis pavilion at the Royal Esplanade to take the salute. He was accompanied by a party which included the Mayor of Ramsgate, the Revd Harcourt Samuel; the Mayor of Margate, Alderman F.J. Cornford; the Chairman of Broadstairs Council, Councillor H. Noble; Captain Howard; Major Arnold, the Chairman of Minster Council, Councillor the Revd T.A. Keniry; Lady Carson; the Officer Commanding RAF Manston; the Deputy Chief Constable of Kent, W. Palmer, and Chief Inspectors H.G. Butcher and H.B. Fleet. After smartly marching past the saluting base, each company was formed up on the lawns facing the pavilion.

The CO of the 6th said it could be truly said that Thanet had been in the front line since the early days of 1940, when the LDV was formed. Every night since that time 150 officers and men had manned the coast of Thanet under all conditions and in all weathers. At first each man did one night's guard duty in three and, latterly, one in six, and that was in addition to their training, during which they learned to fire many kinds of weapons. The Colonel told them:

> I am aware that I have been a hard taskmaster, and have demanded a lot from you, but you have to remember that the brigade commanders had asked a lot from me. According to the government regulations you were asked to do forty-eight hours duty each month, but that was not good enough in Thanet, and many of you did eighty hours a month. I thank you for your loyal support, especially the NCOs, who have always been the backbone of the British Army.

General Franklin said he did not expect many of them thought, when the LDV was formed that they would still be wearing uniform in 1944. In 1940 they had expected invasion at any moment and he knew they would have done their best and, if necessary, sacrificed their lives for their country. They were not called upon to do so because that enormous body of men, one and a quarter million strong, springing up in the night, must have given the rulers of Germany cause for thought. He continued:

> I would say that this battalion has a record of which you may well be proud. You have planned yourselves into an efficient battalion which has been praised by every brigadier who has commanded in these parts. You have also provided two detachments for the six-inch guns under Captain Hatfield.
>
> His Majesty has given us the order to stand down, but I interpret that order as, 'stand-easy – but stand by'. You are not likely to be called out again, but war is full of uncertainties . . .
>
> In the Home Guard you have learned the value of patience, discipline and comradeship. I ask you to carry these virtues with you into civil life. That spirit of comradeship will be valuable in the difficult days ahead.

CHAPTER SEVEN

1945

People Actually Slept in Their own Beds

When their Majesties King George VI and Queen Elizabeth visited Folkestone in October 1944, to pay a personal tribute to members of the Civil Defence Services, including the Women's Land Army, Thanet's other CD organizations were also represented and paraded on the Cheriton Sports Ground.

There were many speeches praising the personnel as a whole for their very high standard of efficiency throughout the war years. By then, of course, Thanet's CD Service had already seen a decline in numbers, and were to be officially disbanded in June 1945.

The Home Guard had stood down in December 1944, the Fire Watching Parties also, and only a fraction of the ARP Rescue Teams remained. Even the NFS stations who had occupied much privately owned accommodation throughout the emergency had been amalgamated and staff reduced.

No one quite understood this rapid decline for, after all, the war was still on. Despite local government announcements appealing for more housing, more entertainments, new hospitals and ambitious plans for a Utopia on the cliffs above Ramsgate, the ordinary citizens were somewhat bemused by it all.

Air-raid sirens were officially 'sacked' in May, but the last wailing siren was heard at Margate on Sunday 8 April, when someone threw the wrong switch. The 'all clear' signal went off four minutes later. As the weeks went by the silence prevailing in the towns seemed unreal. There were no explosions, either on land or at sea, and people actually slept in their own bedrooms. Schoolchildren had been arriving back home in small groups for the past year, but now there was a sudden influx of boys and girls from Staffordshire. Their return marked the end of the Government's official evacuation scheme.

At midday on 8 May the ancient Town Hall at Ramsgate was once more brought into use when, from the balcony, the mayor addressed many hundreds of people assembled in the old market place. At three o'clock, the Prime Minister made his promised announcement on the wireless. Mr Churchill said '. . . hostilities will cease at one minute after midnight on Tuesday 8 May, but in the interests of saving life the cease fire will begin the previous day'. When he concluded with 'Advance Britannia! Long live the cause of freedom! God save the King!' ships in the harbour ran up bunting with incredible speed.

The sands presented an animated appearance in the glorious afternoon sunshine. Hundreds of deck-chairs were occupied and bathers enjoyed their first peacetime dip. Thanet's celebrations of VE-Day provided something of a mixture. Ramsgate hailed Victory in Europe with ships' sirens, impromptu concerts, street parties, and a liberal display of bunting. Margate, however, was in more sombre mood and there were few outward signs of jubilation. In fact, it was a peaceful day more like an Easter bank holiday when people were more prosaic and restrained. Quite a large number of people were on the sands. The only indications of lively jubilation came from the hotels and soldiers' billets where songs were heard in vociferous chorus. Although one or two flags had been hoisted on public buildings and local government offices, everyone began to wonder where the bunting was. The church bells remained silent. Nevertheless, on the following day hundreds of private houses and shops were gaily decorated with flags and streamers, and just about every kind of patriotic device which could be either found or made.

To mark the occasion all the schools were closed for the two days holiday which was declared, and there was scarcely a child in any street without a red, white and blue emblem. Of course, in the evenings louder signs of jubilation rose to a crescendo from the public houses; a one hour extension had been granted. A few lights were visible, although streets were unlit as restrictions in the coastal towns were still operative until 11 May.

In Ramsgate, by contrast, there were scenes of jubilation in the early afternoon. Soldiers, sailors and airmen formed a huge circle at the crossroads junction and gave a full performance of every known song in the British serviceman's repertoire. The audience at this impromptu concert extended into Harbour Street, High Street, Queen Street and King Street – even the church bells were rung.

Although VE-day was celebrated in various ways in Thanet, possibly the most popular, and successful, were the children's street parties. House to house collections were made to cope with the expenses of providing food and drink but, in spite of the fact that although England had been at war for over five and a half years, there seemed to be no food shortage. Brightly coloured flags and bunting hung from house fronts and stretched across the streets as well as decorating many of the heavily laden tables, the like of which, many of the youngsters had never before seen.

Sunday 13 May was observed throughout the country as a day of national thanksgiving and prayer. At Ramsgate a parade of over a thousand was organized to take place at the St Lawrence Cliffs bandstand in the afternoon.

The blitz on London and other large cities has always caught attention and is well-known, but fire services operating in the provinces went largely unrecognized. To put the record straight with regard to the Isle of Thanet, 'D' Division No. 30 (East Kent) Fire Force, covered an operational area of some 200 square miles, and embraced Margate, Ramsgate, Broadstairs and St Peter's, Sandwich and Deal, not forgetting RAF Manston.

Figures obtained from official records show that in East Kent a total of 1,150 fires and incidents were attended by the National Fire Service (NFS) during the period from 1 January 1942 to 31 August 1944, and if there is added to this figure the attendances of the Auxiliary Fire Service (AFS) from the outbreak of war up to the formation of the NFS the total attendances is easily raised to over 2,000. But these figures, although significant, do not tell the complete story.

Herbert R. Evans, a retired Divisional Officer, Kent Fire Brigade, recalls some details:

In 1938, I was providing the band in the Beresford Hotel, Birchington, when my drummer came up with the information that he had joined the AFS. This was at the time of the Munich crisis, and although we had the startling news about the goings-on in Europe, it seemed far from our shores, and we took the news of 'Johnnies' joining the amateur fire-fighters as weird and faintly amusing. However, we got interested in this idea ourselves as being something to do in our spare time, and three of us joined up and did our training at the Margate Fire Station. We eventually got our badges, a shilling and after some months our uniforms.

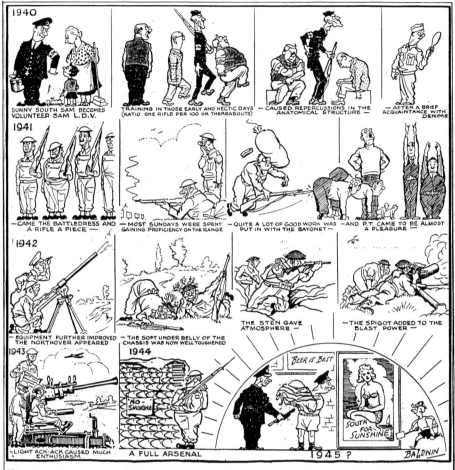

This cartoon, drawn by Mr. A. Baldwin, whose home is at Margate, was published in the last issue of "Southern Home Guard," the journal of the Southern Railway Battalions of the Home Guard, and is reproduced by courtesy of the Southern Railway Company.

By the way, my first wage packet received as a professional member of the AFS in September 1940, was £2 17s. 6d. less deductions (£2.87½). It was in that month that I received a telegram requiring me to report to the fire station AT ONCE! Within a very short time there were about three hundred and fifty AFS men at fourteen stations in the Borough of Margate.

I well remember walking down the road in my uniform for the first time, and seeing the amused looks of my neighbours at the sight of me – fully geared in cap and dark blue serge with buttons gleaming.

The early weeks of the war were fully occupied with issuing fire crews with their equipment and towing vehicles for the fire pumps. We also helped to issue gas masks to the public and showed them how to use them correctly. I also got the job of teaching civilians how to cope with escaping from buildings and rescuing others – lowering people out of upper windows, resuscitation, and going through a gas-filled room with respirators. We had a derelict farmhouse at our disposal for the purpose of these exercises, and lit bonfires of damp hay and straw to fill the rooms with smoke.

I hardly saw my home – we slept rough at the fire station most nights, grabbing food at a nearby cafe, and our duties were mostly preparation and drills. Eventually each of the outlying stations in the town had to be self-sufficient and did their own catering.

The personnel came from all walks of life – carpenters, builders, clerks, mechanics – you name it, we had them. Lorries and vans were either confiscated or given to us as towing vehicles and were fitted with the necessary towing gear and ladder gantries, a large dinghy was given to the AFS who fitted a lightweight Coventry Eagle fire pump for use in the harbour. One large van was converted to a mobile canteen, with storage cupboards, serving flaps, a sink and Calor gas stove. This particular van played a prominent part during the evacuation of the BEF from Dunkirk, and was later used at many of the incidents caused through bombing raids in Thanet.

Gradually the war hotted up, and we began to attend fires and incidents where bombs had demolished buildings and people had to be rescued. I attended many such incidents, and the harrowing sights sometimes required strong nerves – especially the attendances we made to crashed aircraft – both RAF and German.

One in particular concerned a Spitfire which came down almost vertically over Cliftonville, and crashed into an electrical transformer in Omer Avenue. We had to use a lot of care to get near the burning wreckage. We saw the shape of the pilot still in the cockpit and did everything possible to reach him, although he was certainly dead. I have a vivid memory of a hefty AFS man reaching inside the cockpit and trying to get the body out. But it was charred to a cinder.

When a Messerschmitt fighter came down with an ear-splitting shriek to bury itself in Byron Avenue, making a crater some 15 ft deep, we stood by in case the fuel tanks ignited. Then the RAF arrived to take charge. They asked us to recover the cannon guns as they might be of a

new type. We obliged, clambering down into the wreckage to locate
the wing stubs. Despite being fearful that a spark might start a fuel fire
we managed to hack out the guns with our axes.

After Dunkirk came the awful prospect of invasion. We were
instructed to offer no resistance, but merely to do our job. Certain
precautions were to be carried out, however, and upon receipt of a
secret codeword, we were to sabotage petrol tanks and destroy canned
oil supplies.

Some of us were detailed to do a week's service with the London Fire
Brigade – on an exchange basis, and our units were soon confronted by
the first raids on London dockland.

Later we were to experience alarming incidents at RAF Manston,
when the runway had been extended to accommodate the American
Flying Fortresses. We were often detailed to stand by at the end of the
runway during the daylight raids operated by these bombers. I can
recollect one such bomber coming in with only two of its four engines
going and a severely damaged undercarriage. It came in slowly – almost
hovering over the airfield. When it finally touched-down it began to
career all over the place until a wing dug into the ground and it swung
round like a top. Our job was to get in as close as we could, to apply
foam in an attempt to stop any fuel fire whilst the crew got out. They
usually did get out – even before the aircraft came to rest, and ran like
Hell away from it.

Used to working at heights off ladders we were given the task of
making repairs to damaged property in Thanet. Consequently, we
were to find ourselves in Dover doing the same job during the shelling
period in the second half of the war years. Provided with hammers and
nails and roofing felt we proceeded to cover up the damaged roofs and
blown-out windows and make the houses habitable once again. Often,
while we were upon the roofs, the shells would start to come over in
their salvos. Whether we wanted to or not we were made to take
shelter.

Early in 1944, in preparation for D-Day, there was considerably increased
activity in the Kent coastal regions under the codename 'Operation
Colour Scheme'. Substantial reinforcements of NFS personnel, firemen
and firewomen with pumps and all manner of equipment, were drafted
into areas mainly from Yorkshire. They were to form part of the No. 12
Column Overseas Contingent.

Hank Evans recalls:

> I had fifteen firewomen posted to my station in Norfolk Road, where
> we had a large garage and a hotel as a billet. They were far more
> troublesome than the sixty or so men to manage – and you can perhaps
> imagine the goings-on there were with men who had been deprived of
> much of their home life!

That this particular fire-fighting force was not called upon to play a more
active part when the invasion of Normandy took place, was due, as is
now known generally, in great measure to the rapid progress of the Allied
armies through French territory. The administrative organization of the
NFS had evolved to provide the necessary reinforcing moves to other
areas, such as giving valuable assistance to shell-torn Dover and Folkestone. Areas suffering from the flying bomb menace were also included.
'D' Division executed their duties with commendable efficiency and were
held in high esteem throughout the county. The fire crews were in the
forefront of rescue work and in repairing damaged property. Their
courage was never in question.

★ ★ ★

Although the Royal Navy's front line base was Dover, its first reserve
base was Ramsgate and was the only other naval base exposed to the
enemy in Kent. HMS *Fervent* was paid off, to use a naval term, in
September 1945. As the White Ensign was hauled down outside the
Merrie England, once the resort's main fun-fair, it took with it memories
of the Contraband Control, Dunkirk, and most of all, the Coastal Force
Patrol. The base at Ramsgate was started before the war to deal with the
Contraband Control Service in the Downs, and was then responsible for
the whole coast between East Swale and North Foreland.

HMS *Fervent* was commissioned as a shore base on 10 October 1939,
with, according to naval custom, a small motor boat as its 'name ship'.
The large amusement building, Merrie England, where thousands of
holiday-makers had yearly enjoyed themselves, was requisitioned for the
accommodation of ratings and stores. Army-type huts were erected in the
grounds for office and administrative accommodation. It was not long
before the tunnels under the cliffs had been utilized as protection from the
air raids and for the base ammunition magazine.

At first the Contraband Control Service was carried out by six small

Thanet
Advertiser and Echo

incorporating
The Thanet Advertiser, Pullen's Kent Argus,
and The Broadstairs & St. Peter's Echo

Bi-Weekly Chronicle for RAMSGATE, MARGATE, BROADSTAIRS, ST. PETER'S, MINSTER, WESTGATE, BIRCHINGTON AND all THANET
THE OLDEST ESTABLISHED NEWSPAPER IN THE ISLE OF THANET

No. 5225]   Offices: Church-hill, Ramsgate. Phone 1012   TUESDAY, 8th MAY, 1945   Registered at the General Post Office as a Newspaper   [Price Twopence

VICTORY IN EUROPE

THANET HEARS NEWS OF VE-DAY

PRIME MINISTER SPEAKS THIS AFTERNOON

MAYOR ASKS FOR "LAST ALL CLEAR"

THE WAR IN EUROPE IS OVER. VE-DAY HAS ARRIVED.

AFTER NEARLY SIX YEARS OF BLOOD, SWEAT AND TEARS, THE PEOPLE OF BRITAIN LAST NIGHT HEARD THE GLAD TIDINGS THAT TODAY, TUESDAY, THE 8TH OF MAY, 1945, MARKS THE END OF THE FIRST STAGE IN THE BATTLE TO FREE THE WORLD FROM THE TYRANNY OF THE DICTATORS.

The day for which we have prayed at last has dawned. We give thanks to God for a merciful deliverance, mindful of the sacrifice that has brought sorrow and suffering to so many homes in this land which we love. We rejoice that the first stage of the journey has been completed and steel ourselves for the battles which lie ahead.

The confusion which clouded the minds of everyone for the preceding 24 hours was dispelled last night by the official announcement that 8th May was to be VE-Day and that the Prime Minister, the Rt. Hon. Winston Churchill, would broadcast a message to the nation at 3 p.m. But the tension had been eased three hours earlier when it was announced that the German wireless had stated that their armed forces had been ordered to lay down their arms in surrender to the Allies.

Anticipating "the pistol," large numbers of Thanet residents were already flying their victory flags early yesterday, and after the B.B.C. announcement in the evening the chief preoccupations appeared to be the decoration of home and shop fronts with Allied colours.

One of the first ceremonies to be held will be at the Ramsgate Market-place at noon to-day, when the Mayor (Councillor the Rev. Harcourt Samuel), aldermen and councillors, will assemble on the Town Hall balcony for a short service. There will be a hymn, a prayer and a brief address by the Mayor.

Thankfulness will be the predominant emotion in the hearts of the people and it is appropriate that they should gather at the churches throughout Thanet at 7 o'clock this evening to offer prayer.

It is the wish of His Majesty the King that Sunday next should be observed as a day of thanksgiving and prayer. United services are being held in each of the three Thanet towns.

THE MAYOR OF RAMSGATE HAS SENT A TELEGRAM TO THE HOME SECRETARY ASKING FOR PERMISSION TO SOUND "THE LAST ALL CLEAR" ON THE SIRENS. SO FAR NO REPLY HAS BEEN RECEIVED.

While in most parts of the country VE-Night will be celebrated with floodlights and bonfires we, in Thanet, will still be subject to full black-out restrictions, but our rejoicing will be no less restrained.

NOT AN END BUT A BEGINNING

Town's Pride in Magnificent Achievement

A Place in the Grandstand

by
THE MAYOR OF RAMSGATE
(Councillor the Rev. Harcourt Samuel)

THE Day has come; the Day for which we have waited, and not only waited, but worked and prayed. There has been no surprise about it. Even in the darkest hours through which we have passed we believed it would come, and we have watched it draw nearer and nearer. And now it has come, what conflicting emotions surge within us! Thanksgiving to God; pride in the magnificent achievements of our gallant men and our splendid allies; remembrance of those who helped to bring victory at the cost of their lives; recollection that the struggle is not yet completely over; determination that until it is we will continue to put all our energy into it; resolve that the country so battered but so wonderfully delivered from deadly peril shall be rebuilt on yet fairer lines so that greater things in the past the future shall be greater still; these are our thoughts.

FIRST is thanksgiving to God. All 'through these long years we have believed ourselves, as our Prime Minister has said, "The servants of an unfolding purpose," and we have offered our prayers. We have prayed. There are so many deliverances so remarkable that we have been constrained to say "This is the Lord's doing, and it is marvellous in our eyes." Look back now at the course of the war as a whole, seeing how great has been our peril and how narrow our escapes, noting how our enemies' mistakes have contributed to our success, recognising that courage and endeavour, heroism and devotion to duty are Divine gifts, we say again that God has done great things for us, and our first thought is to give thanks to Him.

NEVER before, surely, has the world seen so great a change as we have witnessed. Compare our position in 1940, when we stood alone, almost entirely disarmed, waiting the coming of a foe who had swept through Europe and stood within sight of our own Kentish coast, with the position to-day, with that scene for utterly defeated and by a perfect and more sweeping conquest. It is impossible not to be proud of the men who beat back the foe and then pursued him till he was destroyed; and amongst those men we all of us count husbands, fathers, brothers and sons. Ramsgate's sons have done exploits in all parts of the world theatre of war, and their fellow townsmen are proud of them, keenly looking forward to welcoming them home again.

WE who have had men behind have not been altogether out of the war. We have had a place in the grandstand. From our vantage point we watched the contraband control, at work from our own Royal Harbour; and saw what will almost certainly be regarded as the greatest feat in the history of the war, the masterly evacuation of our army of disembarkation for the heroes of Dunkirk. We witnessed the Battle of Britain fought out in the sky above our heads. We viewed from afar the aerial bombing of the opposite coast that prevented one invasion feet from setting sail, while later we saw another sailing through the Straits on its way to the Normandy beaches. We saw that marvel of engineering, the mobile harbour, in part assembled in Pegwell Bay. Almost daily, at times, we watched our planes go out on their punitive errands, or read the gliders that took brave men to Arnhem. It has been a great experience.

BUT we have had more than a place in the grandstand. We have been in the front line. Nearest to the enemy, we have had our share of bombs and shells. For months we lived under the threat of enforced evacuation at shortest notice. Three-fifths of our population departed, and the depressing sight of shutters appeared in every street. Indeed, it seemed in those days as if the life of the town would be extinguished. But all of us, some of us will always be glad we saw it right through. As one who did, and as one who has had a finger in many a pie, and who is now privileged to hold the office of Mayor at this great moment, I want to thank the men and women who kept things going: the Civil Defence Services, police and firemen, Home Guard and Fire Guard, men of the Works Department, retail tradesmen, nurses, doctors, and clergy, and all who stuck to their posts. Our thanks are due also to the Borough Officials, all of whom carried on greatly increased work with a sadly depleted staff, undertaking many strange and arduous pieces of work and doing them all with their usual quiet efficiency. They have served the town well. Nor must I fail to thank my colleagues on the Council. Elected and co-opted, they have rendered additional responsibilities and shouldered extra burdens, and they have had the great pleasure of seeing prosperity beginning to return to the town they serve. If at this time we are thankful first of all, in Ramsgate we may well be proud also.

YEARS ago when the news came to this country of the taking of Quebec and the death of James Wolfe, "bonfires were lit in every town and village of England, save Wexford, where the hero was born: and there no bonfire was lit, for they were mourning her beloved son." There are homes like that in Ramsgate and up and down the land, it's the homes from which men should like them all to know that we share their sorrow. Victory does not bring only to those of us who happen still to be alive, and we salute the memory of those who have passed on, those who fell on the field of battle and those who died by bomb and shell. To them that victory belongs.

WE do not forget that victory in Europe does not mean the end of the war, for many of us have relatives and friends in the Far East, and we know that there cannot be peace until there is in the West the victor of a few years ago becomes the utterly crushed. We are not losing from

VE-DAY DRINKS

THANET EXTENSIONS GRANTED

At a special sitting on Friday Ramsgate magistrates granted an application for licensed houses to remain open until 11.30 p.m. on VE-Day.

Making the application on behalf of members of the Isle of Thanet Licensed Retailers Protection Society in both the Ramsgate and county districts, Mr. A. R. Young asked that it should be in respect of VE-Day, "whenever that may be."

The chairman (the Mayor, Councillor the Rev. Harcourt Samuel); Can't you tell us when it will be?

Mr. Young: I have no information this morning.

Mr. Young continued: "We are approaching the end of a phase in events in the past five years in respect of which it appears that the nation as a whole thinks the time has come to indulge in the illusion that rejoicing is justified, and rejoicing they intend to have. Whether it will prove an illusion is not a matter with which we in court this morning are concerned. The Government has blessed this idea to a certain extent and they have suggested that magistrates might grant an extension on this day.

Mr. C/I Butcher said he was in favour of and he would be applicable to all licensees who made application for it.

Similar extensions were granted by Margate magistrates on Wednesday.

BLACK-OUT TIMES

To-day ... 10.3 p.m.—5.43 a.m.
Wednesday 10.5 p.m.—5.43 a.m.
Thursday .. 10.7 p.m.—5.44 a.m.
Friday ... 10.9 p.m.—5.44 a.m.
Saturday .. 10.10 p.m.—5.42 a.m.
Sunday ... 10.11 p.m.—5.41 a.m.
Monday ... 10.12 p.m.—5.39 a.m.

HIGH TIDE AT RAMSGATE
	a.m.	p.m.
To-day	10.30	10.52
Wednesday	11.18	11.35
Thursday	0.1	0.15
Friday	12.16	12.42
Saturday	1.4	1.24
Sunday	1.48	2.13
Monday	2.34	2.52
Tuesday	1.27	3.43

PEACE —

(Thanet Advertiser photo)
MINSTER LANE

But the real and lasting victories are those of peace and not of war.—EMERSON.

— AND WAR

(Thanet Advertiser photo)
ALMA ROAD, RAMSGATE

This England never did, nor never shall,
Lie at the proud foot of a conqueror.
—SHAKESPEARE.

pausing to draw breath for the last round or the long drawn out battle. To Ramsgate's sons out yonder we send word that we shall keep on praying and working until the final Cease Fire is heard.

ALTHOUGH the war is not yet fully over, from now on we must turn our thought increasingly to reconstruction. What-ever Government is elected will have to rebuild the institutions of our national life, bringing into them the good things that have marked the struggle of these years of war. Equality of sacrifice has been demanded from all and given by all. Now there must be equality of opportunity for all. The spirit of unselfish service must be kept burning brightly. The legislation for which we look will confer benefits on our citizens, but we must think most of what we can give to our country than what we get from it if we are still to be the servants of an unfolding purpose.

WE have much rebuilding to do in Ramsgate. In the realm of the material, in bricks and mortar and concrete, we have homes to construct, schools to re-make, a hospital to enlarge, streets to widen, fresh public services to provide. In the realm of the spiritual we have much to do also if our town is really to be the city beautiful. The Day for which we have worked and which now has come, is not an end but a beginning. It demands that all that we can give of physical strength, moral energy and spiritual power. Let us give it, and when we seek to build let not forget the words of the wise man:—Except the Lord build the house, they labour in vain that build it." In peace, as in war, let us seek His blessing, and the triumphs of peace will

SUNDAY'S CEREMONIES

Parades in which representatives of the Armed Forces, Civil Defence Services and other organisations will take part will precede Sunday's services of thanksgiving.

The service at Ramsgate will be at the St. Lawrence Cliffs Bandstand at 3.15 p.m. If wet it will be held at Sts. George's Church.

At Broadstairs the service will be held at St. Peter's Recreation Ground at 3.30 p.m., with the Picture House as an alternative in the event of wet weather.

The Victory Parade will assemble in Parrowtree-avenue at 2.30 and Major-Gen. H. E. Kippenberger will take the salute as the procession passes the Broadway.

Margate's thanksgiving service will be held at Dreamland

motor boats requisitioned locally and manned by civilian crews. But this was soon increased to six armed boarding vessels, seven tugs, nine drifters and nineteen other craft.

It was off Ramsgate, in the Downs and the Thames Estuary, that the magnetic mine menace was first confronted. At one time during November and December 1939, the congestion was such that 186 merchant vessels were lying off and trapped in the anchorage. Twenty ships were either mined or in collision and two-hundred-and-fifty survivors were landed at Ramsgate during this period. It will be recalled from earlier pages in this history that the little drifters were the first ships to be given the hazardous job of sweeping for the new and quite unknown enemy weapon.

With the start of export control, the work of the Ramsgate service increased and up to April 1940, 637 import and 336 export ships were searched and 98 seized.

Within a month of the close-down of the Naval Control Service, Ramsgate, like many other ports, prepared for the Dunkirk epic. For nearly a year after this historic event Ramsgate became an auxiliary patrol base, with HMS *Providence* commissioned as the parent ship, and operational offices situated on the eastern pier. During this period six trawlers and a variety of other craft acted as the Navy's first line for alarm and, if possible, defence against the expected enemy invasion. Patrolling just inside the Goodwins, the trawlers knew as they performed their nightly operations that they would have been doomed once they had raised the alarm.

Ramsgate's most important naval duties, however, began in January 1941, when, to relieve congestion at Dover, it became an overflow Coastal Defence Force base. The hectic days of the Dover Command Patrol, saw Ramsgate as the headquarters of the motor gun-boat flotillas, which were engaged in many fierce and fast actions with German E-boats protecting enemy convoys. Many famous Coastal Force 'aces', operated from Ramsgate at various times. At least two of them left the harbour never to return: Lt. G.D.K. Richards, DSO, DSC, RN, the famous 'boarding party' specialist, and his successor, Lt. R.B. Rooper, DSC, RN.

Another MTB 'star' – Lt. P.F.S. Gould, DSC and bar, RN, who was to lose his life in another theatre of war, was previously in command of a Ramsgate flotilla. The full role of honour is an impressive one, and includes not only British sailors, but Norwegian, Polish and Dutch.

The Coastal Force was established in the commodious premises of the Royal Temple Yacht Club from June 1941 onwards, and was later handed over to HMS Fervent as a ward-room.

In September 1940, Captain A.F.W. Howard, DSO, RN, succeeded Captain W.R. Phillimore, RN, as Naval Officer in Command and remained at Ramsgate until September 1945.

For the build-up to operation Overlord – the D-Day landings on the 6th June 1944 – no fewer than eighty-five vessels of various types were hemmed in to the quaysides of Ramsgate's harbour. From the invasion onwards a coastal patrol was operated from the port and can claim with certainty to have sunk nine midget submarines and probably a further eleven.

Security regulations threw a veil of secrecy around the harbour, strongly defended by concrete block-houses and miles of coiled barbed-wire entanglements. Contrary to common belief, the harbour was not taken over 'lock, stock, and barrel' by the Admiralty – there was a little army of civilians who were still employed on the 'prohibited' side of the barbed wire throughout the war years. These civilians performed the vital task of keeping the harbour running efficiently and ensuring that all naval vessels operating from the port were kept seaworthy. Of course, certain buildings and parts of the harbour were requisitioned as the war emergencies dictated, but it always remained under the control of the harbour-master, Lt.-Com. H.J. Maynard.

Defence of the harbour during the invasion scare became the first priority, with the prime purpose of hampering, if not preventing, the enemy from entering the outer basin. For that reason it was decided to sow mines in the approach waters. The mines, primed on board the dredger *Ramsgate* were taken out and lowered over the side from the dredger crane into holes blown out of the sea bed by explosive charges. Each mine was then connected by electric cable running to the control room located in the sea caves. Although a naval officer was in charge of this delicate operation the rest of the men involved were Ramsgate civilians.

★ ★ ★

Alderman Kempe of Ramsgate, already well-known as the top-hatted mayor, was invited to become a military welfare officer in March 1940 and set up offices at Clarendon House with his secretary, Mrs Peete. It became, more or less, an advice bureau which dealt with matrimonial matters, legal and other problems on the lines of the Citizens Advice Bureau set up the same year. In March 1941 Alderman Kempe was given the honorary rank of captain in the Army. As Capt. Kempe he became honorary father, mother and even nurse to service personnel who were billeted in the town and the surrounding area. In addition to those duties he was involved with the Services Fund, which provided musical instruments and sports gear and leisure equipment to the outlying ack-ack gun posts and supplied furniture to the RAF dispersal huts at RAF Manston. He became a sincere friend to the servicemen and servicewomen, supplying to the latter many luxury items which were formally denied them.

It was during this spirit of hospitality that the Troopers concert party evolved. Alderman Kempe recalled:

> I know to some people the Troopers did not always carry the enthusiasm one might have expected but, with the troops, it was always received with spontaneous applause. Even in our wildest dreams we did not expect to travel the distances and entertain the numbers we eventually did and considering conditions in many parts during that time, I take off my hat [and the top hat at that] to all those who carried on, and those who gave whatever time they could to help us.

The Troopers started their venture on 11 June 1941, at the Parish Hall in Broad Street. They typed out their own programmes then went out into the streets to hand them to any servicemen who happened to pass by.

For three years the Troopers functioned, visiting concert halls, parish halls and ack-ack sites, not only in Thanet, but as far afield as Wye College and the Isle of Grain. They continued to operate throughout the winter months, walking through deep snow or mud to acknowledge the requests from aerodromes such as West Malling, Detling and Hawkinge. By the time they had amassed over fifty artists, most of them amateur, the ENSA people had adopted them and actually paid all their expenses.

Capt. Kempe's recollections of those three years included many amusing incidents – like the time they were performing in a tent in the middle of a remote field, when the alarm sounded. Their audience rushed out to take up action stations at the guns, range-finders and predictors. The artists were left on stage alone and wondering if the invasion had started. Then there was the occasion when they performed in a large barn. The only lighting was three Tilley lamps. By the time the National Anthem was being played there was just one left burning! At a gun site near Dover the pianist discovered only three notes could be played on the piano available. But when another piano was found the German long-range guns decided to shell the town. In another remote spot the stage had been constructed of ammunition boxes. It was not until afterwards that the girls discovered they had been tap-dancing on full boxes! The Troopers played to several hundred thousand servicemen and servicewomen throughout South Eastern Command. Their last and 500th show was performed on the eve of D-Day.

★ ★ ★

During the final stages of the war details were revealed of the vital part which the Thanet pigeon fanciers played in assisting, not only the Royal Air Force, but the resistance groups during the German occupation of France, Belgium and Holland. For security reasons, the co-operation of the pigeon fanciers in wartime had hitherto been shrouded in mystery. The general public, by and large, knew nothing of it. After the fall of France and Belgium to the enemy, small resistance groups were formed who, for the most part, were isolated in remote areas of their country. Attempting to harass the Germans with hopelessly inadequate weapons, and later to set up an organization to secretly send back to England, airmen who had been shot down over their country, it was crucial to possess a communication network as a back-up to the inadequate wireless system.

The Maquis – later recognized as a definite part of the Allied Forces, certainly by 1943, was one of the first guerilla groups to use the pigeon service. The National Pigeon Service was formed in 1940, and from it sprang the Army Pigeon Service, a unit of the Royal Corps of Signals. To ensure the success of this service a constant supply of good homing pigeons was needed. This was solved by the goodwill of civilian loft owners, and the first pigeons used were birds previously trained for cross-Channel racing. Ramsgate and Margate were in a geographically advantageous position. Among the first pigeon organizations which co-operated in the scheme were the Ramsgate South Road Flying Club, and the Margate and District Flying Club. From their lofts in peacetime, club members trained their birds in cross-Channel flying and one of the most important events was the race from Bordeaux. For the war effort, they agreed to train their own birds, as well as others supplied by the Government, in long distance flying along the south coast, a route with which they could connect up on returning from 'operations' in France.

Although at first the local clubs were only concerned with breeding and training birds, it was later decided to use local lofts as 'reception stations' to which pigeons would return with their messages. As a result of localizing the service Pigeon Service Officers were appointed: E.C. Mackins of No. 41 Chapel Road, St Lawrence, became the officer for Ramsgate, and W. Fright was the appointed man in Margate. Between them they enlisted the help of their fellow members; at Ramsgate there were eighteen participants, in Margate eleven.

Dozens of wicker baskets containing pigeons were sent to both officers, and after training the birds they were sent by train to towns as far away as Penzance in Cornwall. On average the Royal Signals asked for thirty to forty birds a month, but the fanciers received no compensation from the Government for birds lost. The failure of birds to return was due to a varity of reasons, not least the fact that the Germans were not unaware of the system. They offered substantial rewards to anyone handing them in. If birds were discovered in the possession of French or Belgian patriots the penalty was death.

Sworn to secrecy the fanciers faithfully honoured their pledge and sent off the tiny leg cylinders to the appropriate authorities. Special cards were received by the club members giving the dates of successful missions. One card sent to T. Woodward of Ramsgate, recorded the special mission from Belgium by one of his hen birds on 28 August 1943. Snowball, a black and white hen owned by W. Mackins, returned two days before D-Day, with a message from Sarthe, south of Normandy. Another bird belonging to J. Hoile of Garlinge, made two journeys to France and back quite safely.

Over seven hundred birds were trained by the Thanet clubs, and exhausted pigeons were picked up in Southampton, Yarmouth and many other locations in the southern counties. One of the last missions flown was during the Potsdam 'Big Three' conference between Churchill, Stalin and Truman, when a Margate pigeon flew from Berlin back to its loft, a distance of more than five hundred miles, in ten days.

★ ★ ★

The Home Guard battalions were often the butt of jokes and, even now after all these years have passed, one can still hear disparaging remarks made about them. Laughing and joking, they may have been, voicing their unsolicited opinions to generals and brigadiers alike. But they knew their job well. Sometimes, it was suggested, they outmatched the regulars. The reader will, no doubt, be aware of the BBC's burlesque caricature of the Home Guard, *Dad's Army*, which takes place in a seaside resort, which could easily be mistaken for Westgate-on-Sea.

The TV series was sometimes not that far from reality. No one could make tea at the Broadstairs guardroom quite like the elderly First World War veteran, Private Whitehead. In an adjoining room a young platoon member was practising loading and unloading the ammunition drum of a Thompson sub-machine gun. Whitehead was pouring boiling water into the teapot when three ·45mm bullets suddenly came through the partition wall. He calmly filled the pot, walked into the guardroom, glared at the shocked private and said, 'Well – you nearly didn't get any tea, did you?'

Then there were the Sunday morning parades. These were routine occasions and no one had thought of checking ammunition on a regular basis until a spot check was carried out which revealed several rounds missing. It was usual practice for the men to take home their American Remington ·300 rifles and 120 rounds of ammunition. The spot check gave the game away for one platoon member who had been shooting rabbits in the Hearts of Oak area to supplement his meagre meat ration! A fine of 1s. 6d. was enforced for any round subsequently found missing on inspections.

There is little doubt that platoon members, not only found a new purpose in their hum-drum lives, but found also, an unexpected sense of power. An example occurred one night, just after midnight, at Broadstairs. Private Horton with a colleague on guard duty, spotted a figure in the blackout, shining a torch at a Post Office letter box. They challenged a man who was unable to identify himself officially. He was promptly arrested, and with two fearsome-looking bayonets prodding his back, was marched off to the local police station. Of course, everyone knew it was the local butcher, who explained, in an embarrassed manner, to the police constable that he had suddenly woken up to realize he had not posted his football coupon. Not wishing to risk missing the early morning collection he got up there and then. The magistrate fined him for failing to carry his identity card.

One other story which cannot be left out is, I am assured, absolutely true, the details of which were recounted by a citizen of Broadstairs whose father was a platoon member at the time.

When an unexploded bomb had been reported to 'C' Company, 6th Battalion (Thanet), the CO Major E. Davis, notified his HQ at Margate. He was advised to make the bomb safe by packing it with sandbags.

Sgt. J.E. Brunger, second in command, was ordered to take the bomb to the seashore where there was an unlimited supply of sand. Corporal Robinson, a local builder, supplied a two-wheeled hand-cart, and with others of 'C' Company, set off for the sands. The hand-cart trundled through the deserted streets, watched by anxious police constables responsible for keeping the public at bay. When the intrepid, and profusely sweating 'C' Company had reached Harbour Street, they experienced difficulty negotiating the anti-invasion obstacles erected on the steep incline. Pandemonium broke out when everyone began to give orders Left! – Right! – Stop! – Stop! But it was too late. Unable to hold the heavily-laden cart, its wheels groaning beneath the weight of several sandbags, and not least the quite lethal, unexploded bomb, everyone let go! Inevitably, the cart, free of any restraining influence, ran away down the hill. After striking the stone buttress at the base of York Gate, it overturned shedding its load. The bomb rolled out of the cart and careered down the hill until striking the Droit Office wall. There was no sign of 'C' Company

The Royal Engineers Bomb Disposal Unit defused the runaway on the following day.

Although Thanet's war was considered over, the police were to experience a new problem when banished offspring returned. The outlook of the returning evacuees was totally alien to those youngsters who had remained behind. They had not been brought up in an atmosphere of bombs and shells exploding around them, the nightly excursions to the air-raid shelters or the tunnels. Few knew the daily observation of troops, airmen and naval personnel, the fascination engendered by the proximity of aircraft of every description flying overhead – identified by reference to the sixpenny booklets sold at the corner shop. Bomb sites became wonderful adventure grounds where buddleia and lilac flourished, and where bomb craters filled with rain water; a home for newts and frogs.

In and around the skeletal remains of bombed-out dwellings the children learned to climb over crumbling walls and, Tarzan-like, swung on ropes secured among the branches of trees which had survived the bomb blast.

Top of the youngsters' list of priorities was collecting pieces of bomb casings and bits of crashed aircraft. Bullets, cannon shells, time-fuses, detonators, hand-grenades, mortar-bombs, and 101 objects of war, filled garden sheds to overflowing. A police report described one shed crammed with war paraphernalia as an Aladdin's Cave. Older youngsters had served their country as ARP Messengers. They had seen at first-hand the devastation and chaos left by air raids. They had even rubbed shoulders with the rescue teams, clawing away the rubble with their bare hands to reach the injured and dying victims. The scenes at night, illuminated by the emergency lighting, would remain with them for the rest of their lives. They would remember, in sharp focus, the lop-sided bedrooms where furniture hung in smashed heaps; the tin baths thrown from their garden hooks to land in a crumpled lump at someone else's door; the picture frames still fixed to cracked walls, and gaping chasms where once a floor had been. In what is known as 'the informative years' they had absorbed the lessons of war and had, unwittingly, been a part of it. Some of the lessons were hard to learn, such as a whole family being wiped out in one fearful stroke.

In wartime as in peacetime, there is always a lighter side. Discovered sitting in the cockpit of an American fighter aircraft at RAF Manston, a sixteen-year-old boy admitted to the magistrate at Ramsgate's juvenile court that it was something he had often done. During the proceedings he revealed he had frequented the aerodrome since June 1943! During this time he had removed a quantity of aircraft parts including a dashboard clock, a pair of flying gloves, a bomb-release switch, a wooden box full of microphones and 420 rounds of ammunition, all belonging to the United States Army Air Force.

Inspector Hann said the boy was seen by an RAF sergeant sitting in a Mustang fighter who took him to the guardroom. When asked by Captain Hatfield, the magistrate, if he had anything to say, the boy replied, 'I want to be a pilot'.

Appendices

ROLL OF HONOUR

A permanent memorial in honour of those civilians killed as a result of enemy action was entrusted by Royal Charter on 7 February 1941, to the Imperial War Graves Commission.

The lists of names were submitted to the Commission by the Registrar-Generals from the various counties and these lists formed the basis of several volumes, known as the Roll of Honour.

On 21 February 1956, the Duke of Gloucester, as President of the Imperial War Graves Commission, handed the Roll of Honour to the Dean and Chapter of Westminster Abbey. One volume lies open in a Memorial Case where a single page is turned each day.

The Municipal Boroughs of Margate, Ramsgate and the Urban District of Broadstairs and St Peter's, amalgamated in the early 1970s to form Thanet District Council, have their own Roll of Honour and, like those of other boroughs cities and towns, they are probably incomplete. The reasons for which are complex.

The following lists were provided by the Director-General of the Commonwealth War Graves Commission.

BROADSTAIRS
Bates, Arthur, 61, 16 August 1941
Forde, Joseph Augustine, 65, 3 August 1941
Glover, Samuel Jesse, 17, 26 January 1943
Hammond, William David, 54, 16 August 1941
Pemble, Robert Walter, 35, 16 August 1941
Spice, Percy Charles Ralph, 39, 16 August 1941
White, Frank, 35, 18 August 1941

MARGATE

Avery, William Robert Frederick, 67, 1 June 1943
Barron, Ada, 63, 1 June 1943
Brown, Violet Mary Ann Bessie, 60, 8 July 1941
Butt, Katherine Mary, 76, 1 June 1943
Coppin, Frank Cousins, 41, 1 June 1943
Cox, Maud (Anne), 71, 19 October 1940
Denchfield, Elizabeth Maud, 60, 1 June 1943
Denchfield, Robert John, 60, 1 June 1943
Denham, Lily, 61, 17 April 1941
Denton, John, 14 months, 8 September 1941
Evans, Bernard, 14, 1 June 1943
Gardner, William Dashwood, 56, 14 October 1944
Garland, John Henry, 59, 2 July 1943
Harford, Edith Mary, 54, 17 April 1941
Hawkins, Clara, 61, 8 July 1941
Hoare, Edith Mary, 60, 19 January 1943
Hyde, Doris May, 41, 19 October 1940
Kingsley, Louisa Howard, 59, 14 November 1940
Jones, Victor Patrick, 15, 8 May 1944
Kyley, Kate Catherine Jane, 73, 31 October 1942
Lamb, Blanche May, 65, 16 November 1940
Lambert, Reginald Augustus, 56, 30 January 1943
Lambert, Sybil Eleanor Mary, 15, 30 January 1943
Millen, Agnes Eliza, 65, 18 January 1943
Noble, Mary Blanche, 62, 30 January 1943
Noble, William Robert, 60, 30 January 1943
Pilcher, Edwin Harry, 17, 8 September 1941
Pilcher, Katie Florence, 53, 8 September 1941
Riches, Francis Hannah, 79, 9 November 1941
Riches, Mary Ann, 73, 9 November 1941
Saunders, Annie Beatrice, 70, 1 June 1943
Tranham, Annie Francis, 63, 9 November 1941
Vanner, Anne Matilda, 55, 17 April 1941
Vanner, George Barker, 63, 17 April 1941
Warren, Maria Susannah, 72, 19 October 1940
Wellman, Amy, 45, 1 June 1943
Wooderson, Winifred Blanche, 35, 16 November 1940
Yeoman, John George, 58, 8 July 1941

RAMSGATE

Adams, Frank William, 54, 24 August 1940
Aste, Clifford Henry, 66, 14 June 1941
Battersby, Alan, 11, 10 April 1941
Birch, William Robert Thomas, 16, 24 August 1940
Bishop, James, 67, 4 October 1943
Bowles, Kathleen Florence, 30, 7 September 1941
Bowles, William, 41, 7 September 1941
Boxall, Catherine Ann, 68, 24 August 1940
Brown, John, 19, 24 August 1940
Browning, Sidney Thomas, –, 16 March 1946
Campbell, Kenneth William George, 31, 19 April 1947
Chantler, Albert Henry, 57, 24 August 1940
Cleveland, Rosina Mary, 21, 4 October 1943
Cooper, Sidney, 49, 24 August 1940
Cossons, George James, 58, 7 September 1941
Crompton, George James, 48, 20 March 1941
Davey, Charles Arthur, 34, 3 March 1941
Dennis, Albert Victor, 35, 4 January 1941
Evans, Edith Alice, 56, 7 September 1941
Farley, George Edward, 53, 27 August 1940
Gifford, Albert Richard, 59, 24 August 1940
Godfrey, John, 66, 14 June 1941
Haggis, James Reginald, 16, 24 August 1940
Hiscoe, Christine, 53, 26 January 1943
Holt, James, 70, 14 June 1941
Holt, Sarah Jane, 70, 14 June 1941
Holthouse, Emily Olga, 40, 3 November 1943
Honess, Edna, 19, 4 January 1941
Horton, Emily Hilda, 30, 5 November 1940
Hougham, Norman Edward, 7, 4 January 1941
Hougham, Violet Lilian, 32, 1 September 1944
Howland, Ernest, 52, 24 August 1940
Impett, Arthur Charles, 60, 3 March 1941
Jones, Thomas Arthur Ronald, 26, 24 August 1940
Kay, Clara Gladys, 45, 4 January 1941
Kember, Benjamin, 31, 24 August 1940
Kember, Brian Benjamin, 3, 24 August 1940
Kember, Mary Elizabeth, 31, 24 August 1940
Landi, William, 37, 7 September 1941

Landi, William, 16, 7 September 1941
Lawbuary, Herbert Victor, 70, 2 November 1940
Leach, Miles Wrigley, 46, 24 August 1940
Lilley, Ivy Doreen, 42, 24 August 1940
Miall, Mabel Elizabeth, 80, 7 November 1940
Miall, David George, 75, 23 November 1940
Miller, Alice Maude Mary, 71, 28 June 1943
Morris, Alfred George, 51, 24 August 1940
Moys, Alfred, 61, 20 March 1941
Newland, Albert Edward, 39, 24 August 1940
Oates, Alice Louisa, 57, 3 February 1941
Page, Phillip John, 26, 24 August 1940
Plummer, Frederick Thomas, 56, 25 August 1940
Pritchard, Lottie Winifred, 33, 3 February 1941
Roberts, Arthur, 20, 5 July 1943
Roberts, William John, 52, 5 July 1943
Roddy, Cornelius, 15, 24 August 1940
Rouse, Louisa, 64, 26 January 1943
Rowland, Gladys Joyce May, 20, 24 August 1940
Ruffell, Edward William, 65, 2 November 1940
Ruffell, Ethelwyn, 66, 2 November 1940
Saffery, Florence Frances, 52, 2 November 1940
Shiel, Alice Veronica, 4, 2 November 1940
Shiel, Georgina Catherine, 12 months, 2 November 1940
Simmons, William Henry, 56, 2 November 1940
Simpson, Frederick William, 72, 7 September 1944
Smith, Arthur Albert, 58, 12 August 1940
Stredwick, Clara, 63, 12 November 1940
Stredwick, William Tilbey, 51, 12 November 1940
Ticehurst, Frederick Charles, 36, 24 August 1940
Tomalin, Joseph Richard, 72, 9 September 1941
Tuckley, Joseph, 59, 24 August 1940
Tuckley, Rose, 69, 24 August 1940
Twyman, John, 65, 16 August 1943
Verrion, Annie Kathleen, 36, 13 November 1940
Walker, William Michael, 7, 4 October 1943
Walls, Derek, 15, 11 January 1941
Walls, Olive Jane, 51, 11 January 1941
Wells, Herbert Frank, 32, 25 August 1940
Wesley, Charles Stephen, 16, 24 August 1940

White, Clara Matilda, 85, 9 November 1941
Williams, Catherine, 52, 2 November 1940
Williams, Evan, 47, 24 August 1940
Williams, Margaret May, 18, 2 November 1940
Wolfe, Elizabeth Jane, 70, 3 November 1943
Woodcock, James Thomas, 68, 3 March 1941
Woodfield, Bernard James, 62, 20 March 1941

SARRE
Christian, Elizabeth, 49, 12 August 1940
Christian, Dorothy Beryl, 11, 12 August 1940

MANSTON
Impett, Ivy Doris, 27, 12 August 1940
Jackson, Alfred James, 44, 28 August 1940

GROUP HEAD WARDENS SELECTED IN 1939 FOR MARGATE

The chief air-raid warden selected for Margate by the chief constable, was Major C.S.F. Witts, TD, and his deputy was Major G.H. Boreham. Other area group head wardens were as follows:

Birchington	Head warden, Mr R.L.W. Spurrett; deputies, Mr L.W. Taylor and Mr A.R. Samuels
Westgate-on-Sea	Head warden, Lt.-Col. G.F.W. Anson; deputy Mr H.R. Bright-Betton
Westbrook	Head warden, Captain C.A. Clarke, MC; deputy, Captain W.R.H. Gardener, JP
Garlinge	Head warden, Captain A.C. Hatfield, JP; deputy, Mr R.A. Stokes
Tivoli	Head warden, Mr W.J. Tunbridge; deputy, Mr E. Reynolds
Central	Head warden, Mr A.C. Robinson; deputy Mr E.J.F. Pettett
Cliftonville	Head warden, Mr F.G. Wenham; deputy Mr B.L. Abbott
Palm Bay and Northdown	Head warden, Mr W.G. Judd; deputy Captain A.H. Robinson, MC

The Dane   Head warden, Mr A.J. Stickles; deputy Mr J.E.
                         Saxley

A year after this list was compiled Major Witts resigned as Head Warden,
and became the commanding officer of the Local Defence Volunteers, and
later CO of the 6th Battalion (Thanet) Home Guard.

AIR-RAID PRECAUTIONS SERVICE

WARDENS

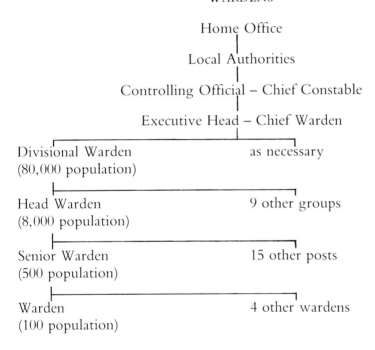

Home Office

Local Authorities

Controlling Official – Chief Constable

Executive Head – Chief Warden

Divisional Warden   as necessary
(80,000 population)

Head Warden   9 other groups
(8,000 population)

Senior Warden   15 other posts
(500 population)

Warden   4 other wardens
(100 population)

Wardens – men or women, to be over thirty years of age

Tasks:

Distribution, fitting and maintenance of gas masks
Reporting bomb damage and presence of gas
Shepherding public to shelters
Lighting restrictions
Liaison between all ARP services, police, fire brigade and public

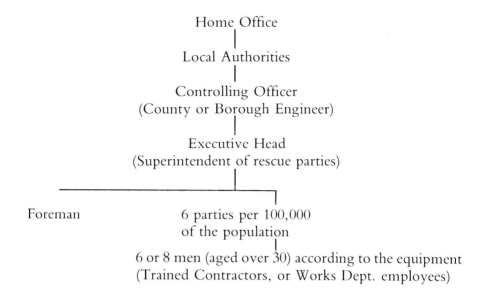

RESCUE

Home Office
|
Local Authorities
|
Controlling Officer
(County or Borough Engineer)
|
Executive Head
(Superintendent of rescue parties)

Foreman   6 parties per 100,000
               of the population
               |
6 or 8 men (aged over 30) according to the equipment
(Trained Contractors, or Works Dept. employees)

Duties: Extrication of casualties from damaged buildings.
Demolition of dangerous buildings – (interchangeable with decontamination squads).

Note – Unexploded bombs to be disposed of by the appropriate corps of the local fire-fighting service's Officers Commanding, which should be notified by Wardens through the police.

LIST OF AIR-RAID SHELTERS IN MARGATE

(Central)
Marine Drive
Marine Gardens
West End Hotel
Imperial Hotel
British Home Stores
Fort Road

Hawley Square Gardens
Zion Place
Saracens Head, High Street
Grosvenor Place
Charlotte Square

(South Margate)
College Road
Dane Park
Milmead Road

(Cliftonville)
Cliff Terrace
Newgate Gap
The Oval
Medical Baths, Cliftonville Avenue
Munro Cobbs, Northdown Road

LIST OF AIR-RAID SHELTERS IN BROADSTAIRS AND ST PETER'S

(The figure in brackets denotes capacity)

Pierremont Pleasure Gardens (130)
Chandos Square (two shelters) (100)
Devonshire Terrace (50)
Wellesly House School, Dumpton Park Drive
Gables School, Dumpton Park Drive
Stone House School, Stone Road
Broadstairs Gas Co. Yard, Albion Street (100)
George Hill Road, Kingsgate (50)
Carlton Avenue (310)
Victoria Gardens (100)
Balmoral Hotel, Albion Street (50)
Rear of Mr French's Shop, Albion Street (100)
Church Street, rear of Harrison's Farm (120)

Bertha Bridge (50)
Reading Street (50)
St Mildred's School, Grosvenor Road (two shelters) (250 and 60)
St Peter's Boys School, High Street (260)
St Peter's Girls School, Ranelagh Grove (80)
Reading Street Infants School (40)
Corner of Crawford Road and St. Peter's Road (50)

ISSUE OF AMMUNITION AND GRENADES

TO 6TH (THANET) BATTALION HOME GUARD AT SEPTEMBER 1942

Battalion had five companies based at Ramsgate, Margate, Birchington, Broadstairs and Minster, consisting of over two thousand officers and men. Their CO was Major, C.S.F. Witts.

Medium and light machine guns issued to Home Guard Units:
Lewis, Browning and Vickers

Grenades issued were type 36 Mills Bomb

Rifles were Canadian Ross, American P14 and P17, and Lee-Enfield

Type

Rifle ·300 (P14 or P17)	Rounds per gun	110
Rifle ·303 (Lee-Enfield)	Rounds per gun	1,100
Sten gun 9mm	Rounds per gun	80
LMG ·303 (Vickers)	Rounds per gun	7,000
LMG ·303 (Lewis)	Rounds per gun	3,000
Revolver ·38 (Webley)	Rounds per gun	9
Revolver ·45 (Webley)	Rounds per gun	9
Revolver ·455 (Colt)	Rounds per gun	9
Grenade, hand Type 36	Rounds per platoon	38
Grenade, hand Type 36	Rounds per man	4
Spigot Mortar 20 lb HE	Rounds per man	20
Spigot Mortar 14 lb HE	Rounds per man	12

RECORD OF THANET CASUALTIES AND DAMAGE PUBLISHED FRIDAY 6 OCTOBER 1944

RAMSGATE CIVILIAN CASUALTIES

Killed or died of wounds	84
Injured	262
Number of air-raid warnings	
(Including 1,193 imminent danger warnings)	3,655
Shelling warnings	86
Aircraft attacks	53
High-explsoive bombs dropped	692
Other bombs	381
Shells	42
Buildings demolished	373
Buildings severely damaged	340
Total damaged	8,891
War damage claims	12,700

Of the 340 houses and business premises badly damaged, 300 had by this time been restored. Many buildings suffered more than once and this accounts for the high total of war damage claims, the number of which is higher than the total of 11,500 premises in the borough. In addition to the 53 aircraft attacks on the town, 25 sweeps on Allied shipping in the Channel were watched by people on the sea front.

BROADSTAIRS CIVILIAN CASUALTIES

Killed or died of wounds	7
Injured	49
Air-raid warnings	
(Including 1,165 imminent danger warnings)	3,628
Shelling warnings	86
Aircraft attacks	52

High-explosive bombs dropped
(16 Unexploded) 278
Flying bombs (V1) 2
Shells 2
Oil bombs 5
Incendiaries 300+
Buildings demolished 17
Buildings severely damaged 114
Total damaged 3,238

Broadstairs was the only town in Thanet to suffer damage from flying bombs. The Kent War Diary lists eight flying bombs within the Thanet Boundary. No shells fell in the town of Broadstairs. The two recorded were located in Pyson's Road and near to the old railway bridge at Haine.

MARGATE CIVILIAN CASUALTIES
Killed or died of wounds 35
Seriously injured 47
Slightly injured 201

Air-raid warnings
(Including 1,078 imminent danger warnings) 3,541
Shell warnings 86
Aircraft attacks 83
High-explosive bombs dropped 595
Shells 2
Parachute Mines 5
Incendiary bombs 2,000+
Buildings demolished 238
Buildings severely damaged 541
Others damaged 8,391
Cases of damage reported 16,776

There were 14,000 properties in Margate and at one time 7,309 of them were unoccupied. The peacetime population of about 40,000 was reduced in 1940 to under 10,000 but many residents returned and by 1944, the population had reached between 18,000 and 19,000.

Maps

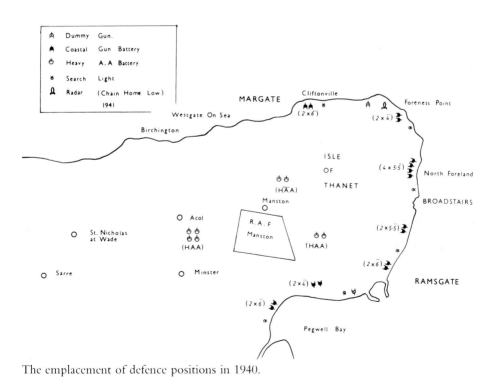

🚩	Dummy	Gun.
🔺	Coastal	Gun Battery
⊙	Heavy	A.A Battery
⚒	Search	Light
♨	Radar	(Chain Home Low)
		1941

MARGATE   Cliftonville   Foreness Point

Westgate On Sea

Birchington

ISLE

OF   (2 × 6″)

THANET   (4 × 5·5″)   North Foreland

(2 × 4″)

⊙ ⊙
(H.A.A)

BROADSTAIRS

Manston
Manston

⊙ Acol   R.A.F
Manston

(2 × 5·5″)

⊙ St. Nicholas
at Wade   ⊙ ⊙
(H.A.A)   ⊙ ⊙
(H.A.A)

(2 × 6″)

⊙ Sarre   ⊙ Minster   RAMSGATE

(2 × 4″)

(2 × 6″)

Pegwell Bay

The emplacement of defence positions in 1940.

Map of Ramsgate's Deep Shelters

Key to Entrances
A   Westcliff harbour
B   Spencer Sq.
C   Liverpool Lawn
D   Queen St car park
E   hospital
F   Ellington Park – two entrances
G   Cannon Rd car park
H   Townley Castle
I   St Georges School
J   St Lukes Recreation Ground
K   Arklow Sq.
L   railway tunnel, south portal
M   Victoria Parade
N   synagogue
O   Scenic Railway, Hereson Rd
P   railway tunnel, north portal

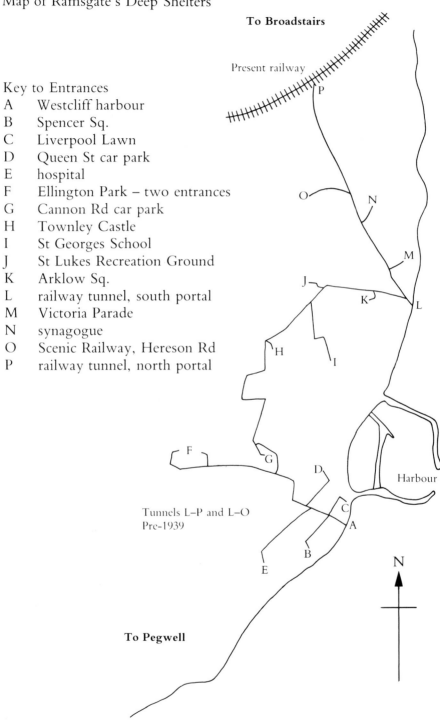

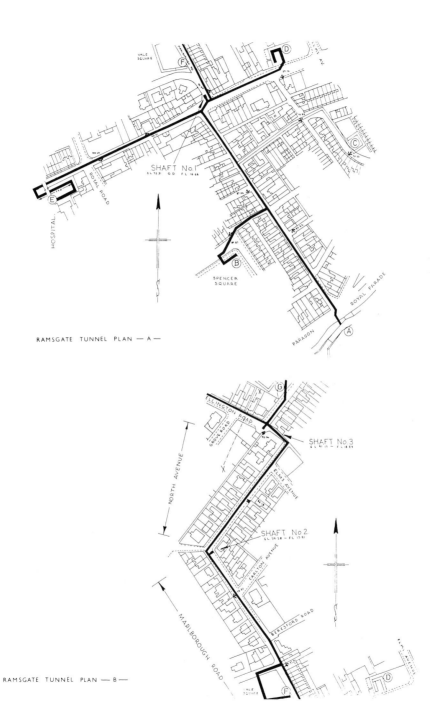

RAMSGATE TUNNEL PLAN — A —

RAMSGATE TUNNEL PLAN — B —

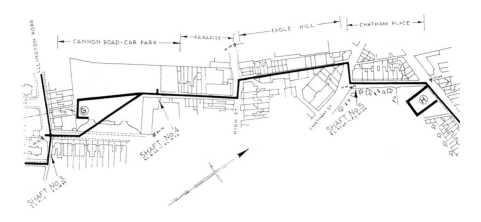

RAMSGATE   TUNNEL   PLAN — C —

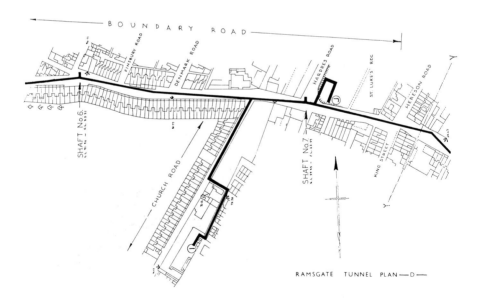

RAMSGATE   TUNNEL   PLAN — D —

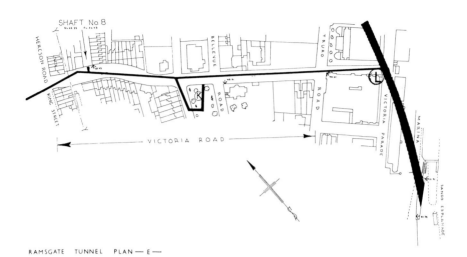

RAMSGATE   TUNNEL   PLAN — E —

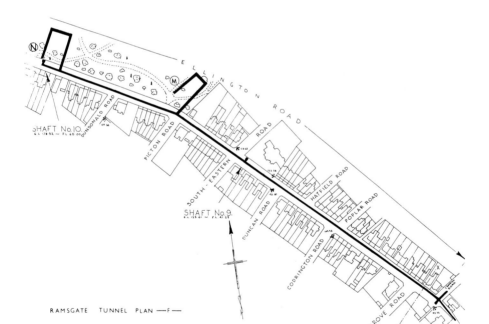

RAMSGATE   TUNNEL   PLAN — F —

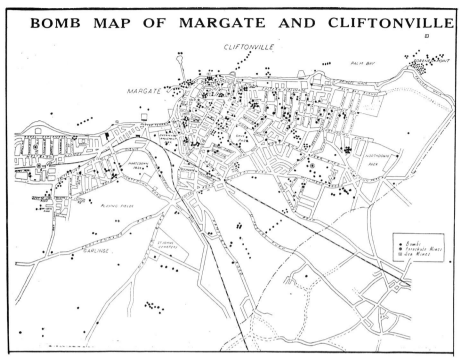

The 'Bomb Maps' prepared at the offices of the *Thanet Advertiser & Echo* in 1944, show the points at which incidents occurred. It is, however, interesting to note that at some incidents recorded by a black dot more than one missile actually fell. Exact representation of the number of bombs or shells was not possible, but an effort has been made to plot every incident accurately.

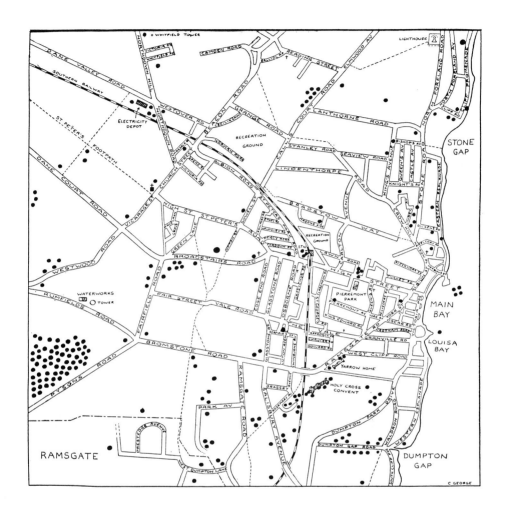

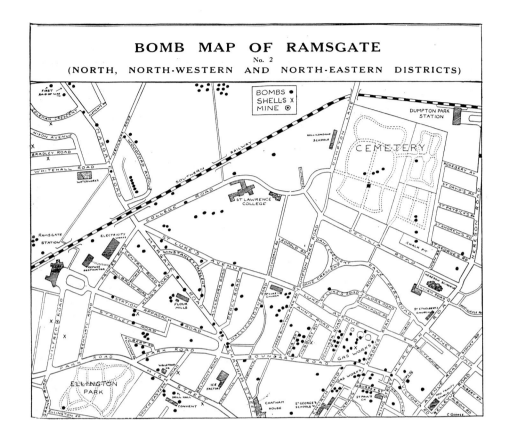

BOMB MAP OF RAMSGATE
No. 2
(NORTH, NORTH-WESTERN AND NORTH-EASTERN DISTRICTS)

THANET ADVERTISER AND ECHO
BOMB MAP OF CENTRAL RAMSGATE

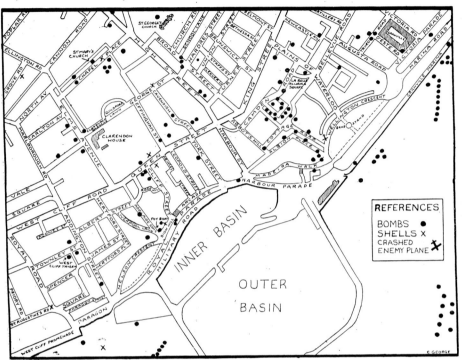

Bibliography

The purpose of this book is to provide a chronology of reference to events which affected the Isle of Thanet during the Second World War. Further reference to the bibliography will provide a more detailed selection of books of a specialist nature, and will offer the reader any amount of statistical data.

Divine, David, *The Nine Days of Dunkirk*, Faber & Faber, London.

Fraser, Flt. Lt. W., *The History of RAF Manston*, Ramsgate.

Hillary, Richard, *The Last Enemy*, Macmillan & Co Ltd, London.

Kempe, A.B.C., *Midst Bands and Bombs*, Kent Messenger, Maidstone.

Lund, Paul and Ludlam, Harry, *Trawlers Go To War*, W. Foulsham & Co. Ltd, London.

Mason, Francis K., *Battle over Britain*, McWhirter Twins Ltd, London.

Ramsey, Winston G. (Ed.), *The Battle of Britain – Then and Now*, Plaistow Press, London.

Ramsey, Winston G. (Ed.), *The Blitz – Then and Now*, Vol. 1, 2, 3, Plaistow Press, London.

NEWSPAPERS

Isle of Thanet Gazette
East Kent Times
Advertiser & Echo
Broadstairs & St Peter's Mail
complete issues covering the Second World War.

Index